ABOLITIONISTS, DOCTORS,
RANCHERS, AND WRITERS

ABOLITIONISTS, DOCTORS, RANCHERS, & WRITERS

A FAMILY JOURNEY THROUGH AMERICAN HISTORY

LYNNE MARIE GETZ

UNIVERSITY PRESS OF KANSAS

Portions of chapters 1 and 2 were previously published as "Partners in Motion: Gender, Migration, and Reform in Antebellum Kansas and Ohio," *Frontiers: A Journal of Women's Studies* 27, no. 2 (2006): 102–135, and are used here by permission of the University of Nebraska Press. Photograph on pages ii–iii: Hilda Faunce Wetherill and Ruth Jocelyn Wattles on trip to Chaco Canyon, ca. 1921. Courtesy of Carol Ann Wetherill Getz.

Published by the University Press of Kansas (Lawrence, Kansas 66045), which was organized by the Kansas Board of Regents and is operated and funded by Emporia State University, Fort Hays State University, Kansas State University, Pittsburg State University, the University of Kansas, and Wichita State University.

Library of Congress Cataloging-in-Publication Data
Names: Getz, Lynne Marie, 1956– author.
Title: Abolitionists, doctors, ranchers, and writers : a family journey through American history / Lynne Marie Getz.
Description: Lawrence, Kansas : University Press of Kansas, 2017. | Includes bibliographical references and index.
Identifiers: LCCN 2017026683| ISBN 9780700624898 (cloth : alk. paper) | ISBN 9780700624904 (pbk. : alk. paper) | ISBN 9780700624911 (ebook)
Subjects: LCSH: Wattles, Augustus, 1807–1876—Family. | Wattles, Susan Elvira, 1810–1898—Family. | Brown, John, 1800–1859—Friends and associates. | Wattles family.
Classification: LCC CS71.W353 2017 | DDC 929.20973—dc23 LC record available at https://lccn.loc.gov/2017026683.

British Library Cataloguing-in-Publication Data is available.

Printed in the United States of America

10 9 8 7 6 5 4 3 2 1

The paper used in this publication is recycled and contains 30 percent postconsumer waste. It is acid free and meets the minimum requirements of the American National Standard for Permanence of Paper for Printed Library Materials Z39.48-1992.

To Carol Ann Wetherill Getz

CONTENTS

Acknowledgments *ix*

Wattles-Faunce-Wetherill Family Tree *xii*

Prologue: From Plymouth Rock to Creede, Colorado—
A Family of Long Memory *1*

1. Susan and Augustus: Partners for Reform *11*

2. For Freedom and Equality:
The Wattles Family in Kansas *51*

3. Sarah: The Making of a Feminist Consciousness *79*

4. The Wattles Family in the Civil War, Part I:
A Scattered Home Front *100*

5. The Wattles Family in the Civil War, Part II:
Fighting for Union and Memory *134*

6. "My Dear Doctor":
The Medical Careers of the Wattles Sisters *177*

7. A Westering Family:
The Wattles-Faunces as Settler Colonists *210*

8. A Western Identity: The Wetherill Women *239*

Epilogue *271*

Notes *283*

Bibliography *325*

Index *341*

A photo gallery follows page 168.

ACKNOWLEDGMENTS

Over the many years I have worked on this book, I have incurred many debts. It has been a long and mostly joyful ride made smoother and more enjoyable because of the help and encouragement of family, friends, and colleagues. The book would never have been written, or even envisioned, without the encouragement, the assistance, and the memories of Carol Ann Wetherill Getz. This is her family's story, and it is because of her it was written.

I was so fortunate to have met Patti Morse Curtis, who allowed me access to her collection of family letters. Patti was truly a force of nature, and she is greatly missed by her family. I will always be grateful to her husband, Charles Curtis, and her son, Perry Curtis, for their continuing support in bringing the story of Patti's family to light.

My family has been immensely supportive. My cousin Cathy Getz went with me to archives as my assistant, drove me around the Navajo Reservation looking for the site of Hilda Wetherill's old trading post, and offered a great critique of early drafts of the book. She loves the history of her family and is even now organizing a Wetherill family reunion. My stepmother, Camille Getz, proofread the rough draft and offered many suggestions. She and my father, Melvin Getz, were always supportive and enthusiastic. My sister Jackie White came up with the idea for the book's subtitle. Sandy Wagner scanned photographs, while, I am sure, her husband, my cousin Bill Getz, offered advice. My cousin Dr. John Tooker answered questions about nineteenth-century medicine. Many different family members offered me room and board as I traveled to do research. For these and a million other favors and kindnesses, I owe so much to all my loved ones but especially Steve and Terri Getz, Jackie and Brent White, Chris Getz, Amy Getz and Tom Broderick, Debbie and Brian Brownell, Bill Lorton, Floyd and Judie Getz, Glen and Sue Getz, and Anna Brownell.

Colleagues have been enormously supportive throughout this long project. While I was writing the book, I was very fortunate to belong to a writing group at Appalachian State University (ASU), Writing Women's Lives. Neva Specht, Sandra Ballard, Maggie McFadden, Patricia Beaver, and Martha McCaughey are all excellent scholars and editors who graciously offered most helpful feedback on early drafts of the book. I will always remember our conversations and potlucks with great fondness. Susan Gray graciously steered me through a tough revision of an article for *Frontiers* that eventually became chapter 1 of this book. She has remained a valued role model. For the brief time I was privileged to have Bonnie Laughlin-Schultz as my colleague in the ASU History Department, I enjoyed sharing tidbits about Wattleses and Browns as we worked on our related topics. She was incredibly generous in sharing her research. Other colleagues who offered helpful comments on papers and presentations include Maria Montoya, Mary Hartman, Ellen More, Wade Davis, and Betsy Jameson.

I was very fortunate to have had a number of wonderful student research assistants over these many years. I benefited from their fresh perspectives, their inquisitiveness, and their enthusiasm. Many, many thanks to Susan Boone, Lydia Whitford, Rachel Lovelace, Steven Higley, Lindsey Collins, Nathan Love, and Emily Driver.

Many archivists and librarians around the country cheerfully offered me invaluable assistance. I would like to express my deep appreciation to Roland Baumann, archivist at Oberlin College, for being such a wonderful host during my visit. Alan Chilton and Sandy Clark went well beyond the call of duty in making available scanned copies of the entire Wattles Family Collection at the Wilson's Creek National Battlefield. I am grateful to Fred Blackburn and Victoria Atkins for making my visits to the Anasazi Heritage Center so enlightening, and for their wonderful hospitality.

I received generous financial support that enabled the travel and time necessary to complete this project. ASU generously provided me several University Research Grants and two Foundation Fellowships. I am also grateful to my colleagues in the History Department for awarding me the Greer Distinguished Professorship, which allowed me to take a semester off for writing. The Charles Redd Center at Brigham Young University provided me two John Topham and Susan Redd Butler Faculty Research Awards, which enabled me to travel to sites in Arizona and New Mexico.

The Oberlin College Archives granted me a Frederick B. Artz Fellowship so that I could conduct research there.

I am grateful to my editor, Kim Hogeland of the University Press of Kansas, for her efficient shepherding of this project and for answering a multitude of questions along the way. Kelly Chrisman Jacques and Michael Kehoe have been immensely helpful in the production and marketing processes. I also appreciate the very useful feedback from two readers assigned by the press, one anonymous and the other Nicole Etcheson. Their suggestions helped me to clarify the themes of the book and bring some sense to three generations of family history.

Wattles-Faunce-Wetherill Family Tree

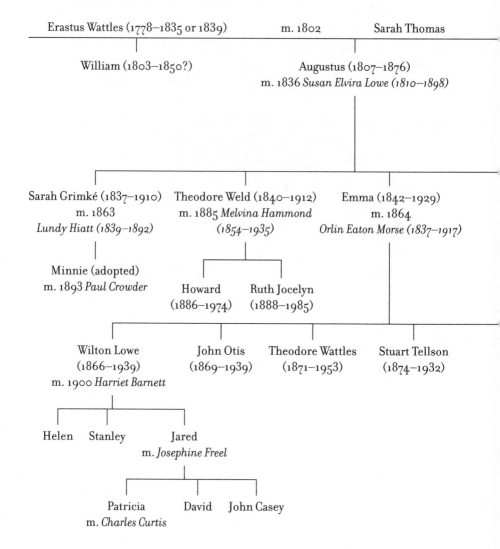

Erastus Wattles (1778–1835 or 1839)   m. 1802   Sarah Thomas

William (1803–1850?)   Augustus (1807–1876)
m. 1836 *Susan Elvira Lowe (1810–1898)*

Sarah Grimké (1837–1910)   Theodore Weld (1840–1912)   Emma (1842–1929)
m. 1863   m. 1885 *Melvina Hammond*   m. 1864
Lundy Hiatt (1839–1892)   *(1854–1935)*   *Orlin Eaton Morse (1837–1917)*

Minnie (adopted)
m. 1893 *Paul Crowder*   Howard   Ruth Jocelyn
(1886–1974)   (1888–1985)

Wilton Lowe   John Otis   Theodore Wattles   Stuart Tellson
(1866–1939)   (1869–1939)   (1871–1953)   (1874–1932)
m. 1900 *Harriet Barnett*

Helen   Stanley   Jared
m. *Josephine Freel*

Patricia   David   John Casey
m. *Charles Curtis*

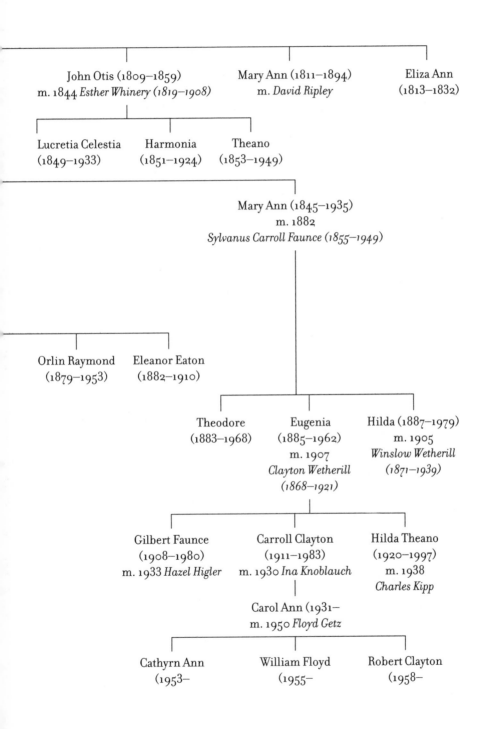

John Otis (1809–1859)
m. 1844 *Esther Whinery (1819–1908)*

Mary Ann (1811–1894)
m. *David Ripley*

Eliza Ann
(1813–1832)

Lucretia Celestia
(1849–1933)

Harmonia
(1851–1924)

Theano
(1853–1949)

Mary Ann (1845–1935)
m. 1882
Sylvanus Carroll Faunce (1855–1949)

Orlin Raymond
(1879–1953)

Eleanor Eaton
(1882–1910)

Theodore
(1883–1968)

Eugenia
(1885–1962)
m. 1907
*Clayton Wetherill
(1868–1921)*

Hilda (1887–1979)
m. 1905
*Winslow Wetherill
(1871–1939)*

Gilbert Faunce
(1908–1980)
m. 1933 *Hazel Higler*

Carroll Clayton
(1911–1983)
m. 1930 *Ina Knoblauch*

Hilda Theano
(1920–1997)
m. 1938
Charles Kipp

Carol Ann (1931–
m. 1950 *Floyd Getz*

Cathyrn Ann
(1953–

William Floyd
(1955–

Robert Clayton
(1958–

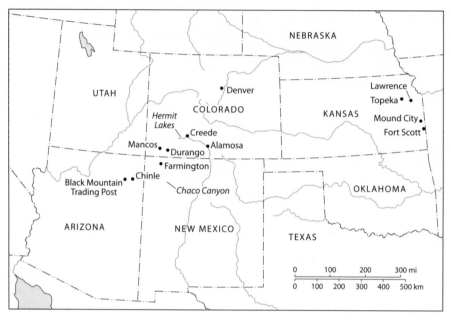

Kansas and the Four Corners Region. Map by Bill Nelson.

PROLOGUE:
FROM PLYMOUTH ROCK TO CREEDE,
COLORADO—A FAMILY OF LONG MEMORY

In 1741 the enterprising merchants of Plymouth, Massachusetts, decided to build a masonry wharf on top of a rock in the harbor. Hearing of the plan, ninety-five-year-old Elder Thomas Faunce demanded to be carried in his chair down to the harbor, where he proceeded to lecture the townsfolk on the significance of the rock. Onto this rock, he said, the first pilgrims stepped off the *Mayflower* in 1620, and he knew this because his father and other early settlers had told him this story when he was a young boy. Because Faunce's own father had arrived in Plymouth on the *Anne* in 1623, and therefore knew all the original settlers who had come on the *Mayflower,* and because Thomas himself had known these elders in his youth, Thomas Faunce's testimony was considered authentic, and Plymouth Rock was saved to play its part as an American foundational myth. The only problem with the myth was that there was no corroborating proof that Thomas Faunce's story was true. None of the original founders, nor anyone in Thomas's own generation, had ever before mentioned the rock. The basis for this foundational myth was the memory of a man in his dotage, recalling stories told to him in his youth by other very old men.[1]

On April 9, 1979, Thomas Faunce's great-great-great-great-great-granddaughter, Hilda Faunce Wetherill, died in Pacific Grove, California, and upon her wishes, her remains were taken to Creede, Colorado, to be buried next to her beloved sister, Eugenia Faunce Wetherill.[2] Hilda and Eugenia had also told stories, including the story of their ancestors settling in the Massachusetts Bay Colony. For generations Faunces had been telling the next generation that the family arrived with the first settlers to America. Sometimes the story relayed that the family arrived on the

Mayflower itself. The message was more important than the truth. The stories had new meaning for each generation, a new understanding that fit the circumstances of that generation.

Beyond storytelling, families also preserve their memories by choosing to keep the records and letters of previous generations. Such memory keeping obviously privileges the literate and wellborn, the people who wrote letters and produced documents. The records of families who played a significant role in public life found their way into archives more often than the records of poor and illiterate families. Ordinary, middle-class, literate families who valued their memories might not readily think their family records belonged in the archives, but they might preserve the family letters at home and pass them to the next generation. The interest, they might think, would be within only the family. They might think family was important enough that they would trace the family genealogy. That is what the descendants of Thomas Faunce did. Eugenia Faunce Wetherill saved family letters, records, and memorabilia; Hilda Faunce Wetherill compiled the family genealogy, going back to Plymouth. Like their venerated ancestor, they were memory keepers of the family lore. The stories were not necessarily true and could not always be proven by the methods of the professional historian, using corroborative evidence to establish veracity within reasonable doubt. However, the stories had meaning nonetheless. As William Cronon has suggested in writing about family memoirs, history proves what is true, but memory tells us what is important.[3]

This is a book about families, identity, and memory. I have taken a particular family and followed it through three generations, showing how the members of each generation acted in response to the historical developments they faced. The narrative is about the family identity and how that evolved from generation to generation. Circumstances competed with memory in determining the identity of each new generation and each different individual in each generation. To a great extent circumstances often won out, but the stories told, the character traits reinforced, and the family connections maintained all served as a check to keep the family identity from careening too far astray. Family stories, like all personal stories, are notoriously unreliable and serve the purpose of constructing meaning rather than truth. However, this is a book of history, not a compilation of family stories. I have documented every detail I could using the evidence left behind by members of this family, the people who knew them, and the institutions of their society. Where the family stories enter into the narrative, they primarily show how family members chose to remember the stories and what meaning those stories held for those who told them.

As with all history, the availability of sources determined the scope of the book. I was incredibly fortunate to have access to several large collections of family letters. My aunt Carol Ann Wetherill Getz, the granddaughter of Eugenia Faunce Wetherill, first introduced me to this family line when she shared with me the letters of her great-grandmother, Mary Ann Wattles Faunce. Mary Ann and other members of her family saved hundreds of letters and other family memorabilia across generations. Later I found another branch of the family through Patti Morse Curtis, who had inherited and saved the letters of her great-grandmother, Emma Wattles Morse, sister of Mary Ann Wattles Faunce. At the Kansas State Historical Society, along with archives in Ohio and elsewhere, I found many of this family's letters scattered among various collections. Finally, at the Wilson's Creek National Battlefield in Republic, Missouri, I found another large collection of family letters saved by another branch of the family before being sold to a private collector, then acquired by the National Park Service. These collections together contain many of the letters sent and received within the Wattles-Faunce-Wetherill family over three generations, ranging from the 1830s to the 1930s.

Few historians have such a wealth of untapped primary source material to explore and interpret, and I am very grateful for this opportunity. Especially remarkable, however, is that such stores of family letters exist at all. Few American families, outside of the extraordinary and famous, preserve even a fraction of the material kept by the several branches of this family. Members of this family, however, saw their history as something significant and passed on the material legacy to the next generation along with an identity that rested on a unique family history. Such devotion to maintaining a legacy as a family is a rarity in the United States, where many people have no idea about their family history before their grandparents' generation.

Recently, however, there have been signs of an awakening interest in our past generations, perhaps catering to a yearning for some sense of identity beyond the individual self in a highly individualistic age. Interest in genealogy has skyrocketed with easy access to online sites such as Ancestry .com. People can now easily have their DNA tested through services such as 23andMe and Family Tree DNA. Television programs have been created to respond to this spate of interest in family origins. Henry Louis Gates Jr.'s *Finding Your Roots* elicits a positive popular response by tracing the family lineage and even decoding the DNA of celebrities. Another television show, *Ancestry Roadshow,* invites ordinary participants to submit questions about their family history to professional genealogists and historians, who then track down the answers and share the results on the program.

Historians have also found a number of new ways to use the family as a framework for reimagining well-worn narratives of the past. A profusion of historical studies examining a wide variety of families has emerged, with attention given to the black descendants of Thomas Jefferson, the families of fur traders, seven generations of a midwestern working-class family, the African American families of New York City, a mixed white and Piegan family from Montana, and many others.[4] Such approaches promise new understanding by acknowledging the family as a crucial site for historical agency and decision-making. These new studies focus less on broad demographic life-course patterns and more on families as the places in which personal interaction occurs in response to social and economic developments and in which people negotiate the most important questions of their lives.[5] These "relational" histories reflect a yearning for identity rooted in time past and an awareness that connectedness across generations gives some meaning to people who might feel rootless and atomized in the incredibly mobile and fast-paced contemporary world.

Because I am using family history as a framework for understanding how Americans coped with the circumstances of social activism, migration, economic challenges, and war, I think it is important to contextualize family memory. French sociologist Maurice Halbwachs and other theorists on collective memory have suggested that personal memories survive and are shaped and reinforced only by the constant retelling and revisiting of them with persons who shared them. Anyone who has ever attended a family reunion will readily recognize the family as an ideal site for the reinforcement of constructed memories. Favorite stories are told, familiar photographs are passed around, and old memories are refreshed and refined. Family memories are socially framed, almost like groupthink. Whatever the group—be it society at large or the family—considers important, the individuals will remember as true.[6]

Families reinforce memories through rituals they create. Families who stay in one place from generation to generation have the luxury of developing rituals that thrive on proximity. Many American families, however, experienced great geographical mobility and thus had to develop other means of preserving collective identities. Susan E. Gray has shown how collective identities were restructured as groups of New England families moved to Michigan, where they reinforced Yankee identity through settlement patterns and institution building.[7]

Historians have drawn upon these insights to demonstrate how families use the past for recovering particular identities. For instance, Joan M. Jensen documented the history of Wisconsin farm families to understand for herself a rural identity her immediate family had left behind.[8] Looking at the context of the times in which ancestors lived can help us to understand our present responsibilities as we grapple with the consequences of past developments. Victoria Freeman explored how her European ancestors colonized North America so that she could fill in the gaps of family memory caused by what she calls the "amnesia of each generation." Freeman felt a need to capture this lost history in order to understand her own responsibility toward indigenous peoples. "The psychic history of each family," Freeman writes, "is embedded in both what is said and what is left unsaid; what is not talked about, repeated, or passed down can be as important, even more important, than what we are conscious of."[9] Family amnesia becomes social amnesia, enabling the shapers of national memory to forget or gloss over uncomfortable truths that live in the past. Tracing the truth embedded in family memory helps us to grasp the reality of the past while humanizing the behavior and decisions of the actors in that history.

Taking these frameworks as my starting point, I examine how an individual family demonstrates the process of maintaining certain aspects of an identity and creating new ones as this family moves geographically and occupationally across several generations. Within the Wattles-Faunce-Wetherill family, individuals altered personal identity in response to circumstances but maintained a family identity through letter writing, storytelling, autobiographical writing, and hagiographic writing about their ancestors. Memory keepers, mostly female family members who specialize in record keeping and storytelling, play a crucial role in families who successfully construct and maintain cohesive family identities. The Wattles-Faunce-Wetherills are a good example of a family that has relied on important memory keepers from one generation to the next. Because of the memory keepers who preserved the letters and other materials relating to this family, I was able to write this book.

Access to such rich collections of family letters has driven this work, but the lives of interesting people unfold here. Members of the family were not only fascinating in their own right but also because they knew other interesting people and participated in important historical events. The first generation consisted of the Wattles brothers, Augustus and John, and their wives, Susan and Esther. As abolitionists in Ohio and Kansas, they became close associates of Theodore Dwight Weld, Sarah Grimké, and John Brown, among others in the antislavery and early women's rights movements. In their lives we see at the personal level how the issue of women's rights emerged from within the abolitionist movement. These couples married relatively late in life by the standards of their time, thus displaying what historian Mary Hartman has called the late-marriage pattern, which led to more status within their households for these women. Under this pattern, Hartman argued, women in their early to mid-twenties who married men of the same age or slightly older brought with them more property and life experience and thus exercised more authority within the family.[10] I would argue that abolitionists also had an ideology of equality that contributed along with the late-marriage pattern to new thinking about gender roles. The antebellum reform movement in general and the women's rights movement in particular reflected the long process of men's and women's lives coming closer together and beginning to converge in common purpose. The recognition of the rights of women owes as much to their long-standing contributions to the household as it does to the rise of moral issues that propelled them into the "public" sphere.

Moving into the second generation, I examine how this family coped with the Civil War by looking closely at the family members on the home front as well as the men who fought as soldiers. The experience of this family reflected both the typical pattern of Northern families whose men left for military service and that of Southern families who experienced not only the absence of men but also the threat of violence in their own vicinity. The Wattles households lay on the Kansas-Missouri border, an arena of intense guerrilla warfare, and yet the families managed to go about their business with remarkable composure. The young men of the family, Eaton Morse and Theodore Wattles, enlisted in the Kansas Cavalry and participated in active campaigns in Missouri and Arkansas. Their letters home opened a window into the lives of soldiers that kept their loved ones not only informed but also actively engaged in the war.

I continue to follow this generation after the war, when Eaton and Emma Morse settled down to a conventional life but took an active role in shaping the family memory to emphasize the activist legacy of their parents. Emma's sisters, Sarah Grimké Wattles Hiatt and Mary Ann Wattles Faunce, attempted to live out that legacy by pursuing the nontraditional role of medical doctor. Mary Ann succeeded to a greater extent than Sarah in becoming a trained physician but faced the challenges of family life and child care with which professional women still grapple today. Mary Ann's colleagues, especially Emily Blackwell, Mary Putnam Jacobi, Sarah McNutt, and others created associations and networks to offer each other support as they dealt with the challenges of professional life. Finally, within the second generation, I focus upon Theodore Wattles, the only one of his generation to reject outright the family identity of progressive reformer. My analysis of Theodore places him squarely in the role of "settler colonist," not because he was the only member of the family who settled on western lands—he was not—but because he so clearly embraced the role. His case perhaps more than any other demonstrates how complicated family identity can become.

In looking at the third generation, I focus upon two women who started life on the East Coast but became the most quintessential of westerners. They also demonstrated one of the most complicated, and interesting, shifts in family identity formation by adopting the identity of their in-laws' family. Eugenia Faunce Wetherill and Hilda Faunce Wetherill married into a family whose members had been some of the first white people to explore and excavate the Ancestral Pueblo sites of Mesa Verde and other archaeological sites throughout the Four Corners region. The Wetherills helped to develop the western tourist industry by pioneering guiding and outfitting businesses, trading posts, and fish hatcheries. Choice and circumstances led Eugenia and Hilda to make identities for themselves that followed the Wetherill lead in catering to the public interest in western themes. Their sisters-in-law, Louisa Wade Wetherill and Marietta Palmer Wetherill, also followed the same pattern, each finding a means to survive in a tough environment through resourceful exploitation of the western mystique.

It is not my purpose, however, merely to chronicle this family just because it happened to be in the right place at the right time to observe and participate in some interesting historical developments. I believe that the history of this family helps us to see this historical period differently. A number of women's historians have challenged us to ask how our understanding of history might be different if we ask what the women were doing while the men were doing all the activities that normally earn the attention of historians. Gerda Lerner, Susan Armitage, Betsy Jameson, and others have urged historians not just to add women to the narrative but to see how the inclusion of women changes the questions and the analysis. I believe that if we examine women's lives, we cannot help but see families, and in doing so, we see history in a new light.

When men alone were considered the proper focus of narrative history, it too often appeared that they existed alone, achieving all their wonderful accomplishments with no supporting cast whatsoever, or if any supporting cast did merit a mention, it was the clichéd strong woman standing behind every strong man. However, honest engagements with family history reveal more nuanced relationships between men and women, changing both the questions we ask about them and the analyses of their lives in total. In families, individuals work and live in tandem with others. Even in times when patriarchal models prevail, women absolutely participate in decision-making if one looks closely enough. Women always contribute to getting the work done and keeping the family going. Women have always been a part of the mix in family life, and historians would document this if only they asked the right questions of the source material available.

Looking at families to tell the stories of the past does not lead to the exclusion of men, but it can lead to the decentering of men. Writing women's history, especially in an attempt to compensate for the lack of focus on women by past generations of historians, can sometimes place too much emphasis on what the women were doing and thus fail, as much historical writing does, to catch the interaction between people that is the norm of everyday life. When we learn to look at both men and women without any agenda or preconceived assumptions, then we can come closer to understanding human history as it really happened.

In her presidential address to the 2015 meeting of the Western History Association, Betsy Jameson spoke about women not included in the historical record even though they were interesting persons. She said, "They owe their absences, in part, to gendered assumptions about whose acts were important, whose stories worth saving, and to gendered historical categories."[11] When we look at families, it is hard to avoid asking questions about acts, stories, and historical categories perceived to be female and, in the past, considered uninteresting and unimportant. Jameson points to a number of categories devalued simply because they are associated primarily with women: domestic chores, household production, sexuality, and childrearing. Even when both men and women participated in some activities, such as labor organizing, the contributions of the women have been ignored, whereas the men's roles are highlighted. The categories in which men are grouped relate more often to big narratives such as nation building that occupy the attention of most historians and are deemed more important than the particular trajectories of families. However, I contend that the particular narratives of families will tell us quite a lot about how people interact with others and what they do within all these historical categories. Families are always part of the larger narrative because all the players belong to families. Even in the absence of traditional families, people form associations that act as families.[12] Nation building was not done by individuals acting alone but by persons who belonged to families and whose families helped to shape all their decisions.

Obviously, a single family's trajectory over time does not explain social change in itself. Great changes in society often come about because groups or individuals push for reforms or lead revolutions, often following the ideas of intellectuals or visionaries that defy their own family traditions. Social change occurs because of technological innovations, migrations, and natural events to which people must respond. However, over time people make decisions to follow certain ideas or practice different behaviors because it makes sense for their families. Thus, long-term social change could not occur without the involvement of families.

Family historians have focused on these broad changes, taking the demographic evidence of the conditions and behaviors of populations as the basis for examining how family life changes over time and what the circumstances of families might mean for society at any given time.

Often these analyses have implied that the family passively reacts to social forces, but family historian Tamara Hareven called upon historians to cast aside the stereotype of the family as a passive participant in historical events. Instead, she views the family as an active agent in social change.[13] This study answers Hareven's call by asking what the circumstances of a particular family did to shape that family's identity and then how that family contributed to social change. If we cannot look at the circumstances of every family, it makes sense to focus on certain families and then to ask how they compare with the wider population, which must be examined statistically in demographic studies.

Giving so much attention to a family of such modest significance requires some justification. As Joseph Amato said when writing about his own family, "Abstractions do not furnish good legs for human understanding. . . . Justification for writing of an individual family history lies . . . in the power of one family to represent another—and the value of presenting a single life from the past to the living present."[14] Thinking about the history of families should bring historical connections to life, enabling us to see a continuous past—if not from Plymouth Rock to Creede, Colorado, at least from some distant point of departure for our families to the present. Although technically not my own family, this is the family of my aunt and cousins, and as I grew up, we were all very close, living next door to each other on a large family ranch in Colorado. Like many extended families living in close proximity, our parents shared the responsibilities of childrearing. As a child, I spent time with my aunt's family at Wetherill Ranch, the guest ranch built by Eugenia Faunce Wetherill above Creede, Colorado. I knew my aunt's family legacy, I heard her family stories, and I benefited from having as a role model a strong female descended from Susan Lowe Wattles, Mary Ann Wattles Faunce, and Eugenia Faunce Wetherill. I sincerely believe, however, that any historian worth her salt would see the merit of taking never-before-used collections of family letters and through them seeking the larger historical meaning gleaned from close examination of this one family. Besides, who would want to miss out on a great story?

SUSAN AND AUGUSTUS: PARTNERS FOR REFORM

Sometime in 1834 Susan Elvira Lowe left Oneida County, New York, to travel to Ohio to begin work as a teacher in a school for free blacks in Cincinnati. With her friends Phebe Mathews, Emeline Bishop, and Lucy Wright, Lowe planned to join the cause of abolitionists Theodore Dwight Weld and Augustus Wattles, who were already hard at work helping blacks in Cincinnati. Gilbert Barnes, editor of the *Letters of Theodore Dwight Weld, Angelina Grimké Weld, and Sarah Grimké, 1822–1844*, wrote that the "Cincinnati Sisters," as they came to be known, had responded to a call in the *New York Evangelist* to go to Ohio for service in the free black community.[1] Wattles family tradition, however, told another story. Susan Lowe Wattles's children later related two different stories to explain their mother's motivation. Emma Wattles Morse claimed that Augustus Wattles himself had passed through Oneida County on a speaking tour in the spring of 1834, and that Susan, upon hearing his appeal for help in the Cincinnati work, picked up and moved to Ohio.[2] Emma's younger sister, Mary Ann Wattles Faunce, told the tale a little differently when she wrote the story for her grandchildren, saying:

> My mother, Susan Elvira Lowe, lived at Whitesboro near Utica, N.Y. She was at a Young Ladies Manual Labor boarding school, when a great lecturer on Antislavery came that way. His name was Theodore Dwight Weld, and his wonderful eloquence convinced almost everyone who heard him. Afterwards another lecturer came—Augustus Wattles—and

four of the young ladies in the school volunteered to go to Cincinnati, Ohio, and teach for the Antislavery society.[3]

Susan Lowe Wattles herself told a slightly different version of her own story in a brief autobiographical sketch, explaining that while she was at the Clinton Domestic Seminary, a "Mr. Wells came there to get teachers for the colored schools in Cincinnati."[4]

The differences between the versions of this story are slight and of little consequence in the overall narrative of these persons' lives. The Wattles children's versions hinted at a romantic encounter in which their father enticed their mother to embark on a marvelous adventure, but there is in fact no evidence to suggest that Augustus Wattles—or Theodore Weld— took the time away from their activities to travel east in the spring of 1834 to recruit teachers for the blacks of Cincinnati. For some reason the children embellished the story with more sentimentality than it actually deserved. Looking back on the history of this family, the historian is tempted to say that the likely true story is quite significant in and of itself. Susan and her compatriots' decision to travel to Cincinnati for the antislavery cause in 1834 challenged many prevailing notions about the behavior of women. It demonstrated the mettle of these independent and determined young women and shows why the involvement of women in the antislavery movement led inevitably to the campaign for women's rights. However, for some reason the true outline of the story did not seem enough for the family. The family was proud of Susan and continued to tell the story for several generations, but also inserted Augustus into the narrative for sentimental reasons, choosing to shape the memory to emphasize the connection between the two rather than highlight Susan's agency alone. Unwittingly, the Wattles children constructed a memory true enough in conveying the genuine partnership their parents formed but not entirely accurate in every detail.

Families tell stories for many reasons. Family stories are used to reinforce certain traits or values family members cherish, or to prevent children from wandering down forbidden paths, or simply to establish a common bond or sense of belonging. Some families seem to have a greater stake in presenting their stories to the outside world, perhaps because their ancestors had distinguished careers and the repetition of their stories sheds a positive light on the current generation. However, one thing is clear about family storytelling: like all constructed memories, adherence to fact is not necessarily a requirement. The purpose of the story matters most. As Elizabeth Stone has noted, "The facts of a family's past can be selectively fashioned into a story that can mean almost anything, whatever they most need it to mean."[5] The Wattles family had no distinguished ancestors who achieved fame and glory but nevertheless had an interesting, unusual, and often exciting family narrative showing that, as members of a family, their lives had moral purpose and they had contributed to significant changes in US history.

Augustus Wattles and Susan E. Lowe belonged to a generation that participated in some of the most profound events in the history of the United States. They stood on the far edge of the vanguard in these developments, urging, pushing, and prodding their contemporaries toward a radical future, one free of the scourge of slavery, offering greater equality for blacks and women, providing more dignity and opportunity for all. By the time of Augustus's death in 1876, some of this bold new future had been accomplished, such as suffrage for black men, yet even when Susan passed away in 1898, much still remained unrealized, such as suffrage for women. It is the nature of historical change to occur gradually. It is also the nature of historical change that it happens because individuals work to remake society, always in struggle against the overwhelming weight of the status quo. Augustus and Susan, along with John and Esther Wattles, became partners in this endeavor, forming an extended family unit devoted to changing the society in which they lived. Although such reformers always remained in the minority, the paths taken by the Wattles family typified those followed by many reformers of their generation. They came from New England backgrounds, having been steeped in the evangelical Protestantism of the Second Great Awakening. Motivated by the desire to make God's kingdom come alive in the United States, they developed an analysis of society that ultimately implicated not just slavery but also the oppression of women as great social sins. They embraced related reforms as well, particularly a dietary regimen they believed led to a more spiritually pure lifestyle, and spiritualism, which they thought opened the door to divine truth. They were, in a word, radicals in their time. If some human beings act as agents for change, surely we must count the Wattleses among them. Why they became activists, how effective their agency was, and what effect their activism had on the following generations are the questions explored here.

Susan and Augustus, along with other members of their families, joined a stream of migrants pouring out of New England into western New York, Ohio, Michigan, and Indiana in the 1820s and 1830s. This bustling hinterland had been transformed by the extension of the Erie Canal and the growth of small commercial towns and embryonic industrial centers surrounded by prosperous farmlands. Not surprisingly, such profound social and economic changes were accompanied by equally intense spiritual revolutions as waves of evangelical revivalism swept through the region between 1800 and 1840. The growth of this new, enthusiastic, and individualistic religious experience owed much to the desire of women to nourish piety in their husbands and children and to counter the influences of an acquisitive marketplace. These concerned women united in missionary societies and maternal associations to distribute Bibles and disseminate new ideas about Christian childrearing practices. By the time Susan Lowe arrived in Oneida County, New York, in the early 1820s, the role of women in organizing reform-oriented work in the name of evangelical Christianity appeared commonplace.[6]

Susan Elvira Lowe was born in 1810 in Fitchburg, Massachusetts, the first child of Jonathan and Susanna Perley Lowe. In 1821 the family moved to Vienna, New York, a small village in Oneida County. Like so many other early nineteenth-century Americans, Susan witnessed much grief in her family as she grew up. Of the ten children born to the Lowes, three died in infancy and three more died as young adults. Only Susan, two sisters, and a brother lived full lives. The family was deeply religious and followed the Congregational faith. Jonathan Lowe had worked as a mechanic in cotton factories in Massachusetts. After moving his family to western New York, he worked a small farm and in the winter made window sashes for sale. The Lowes believed in education for their daughters, unusual at the time. Susan attended common school until she was seventeen. Then she taught school until she was twenty-one, including a year at a missionary school in Detroit, after which she attended a female academy for a year and the Clinton Domestic Seminary for a year.[7]

The Lowes's commitment to female education reflected their drive to root their children in the middle class and an understanding that to accomplish this, women needed to master cultural literacy just as much as men did. Although few early nineteenth-century Americans attended school much beyond the elementary level, the emerging middle class was beginning to send both daughters and sons to academies and seminaries that offered the equivalent of advanced prep school instruction. Even fewer young men then went on to college, where most of them took theological training for the ministry. Access to these educational opportunities for women had far-reaching consequences, even though only a relatively small number of women benefited from them. Because the curricula of female academies and seminaries differed little from that offered males, women gained access to the same cultural legacy considered necessary for a young man to participate in a democratic society. Young women studied the arts and sciences, including moral philosophy, literature, geography, natural sciences, English grammar, algebra, geometry, and ethics. Except for deemphasizing Latin and Greek, schools for girls offered much the same curricula as those for boys. Above all, students were subjected to Enlightenment-based modes of thinking. They were expected to develop their reason.[8]

As Mary Kelley has pointed out, however, these schools for women also helped to enshrine constructions of gender that would remain in place through the Victorian era and beyond. In Kelley's words, "The purpose attached to the education of women was gender inflected."[9] Building on the notion that women should embody republican virtues so that they could raise solid citizens for the new nation, educators began to emphasize the moral superiority of women, suggesting that women excelled in piety and virtue and would influence their families in that direction.[10] Although this philosophy attributed to women an important role in civil society, it was not a public role. Thus began the commonly held assumption that women should predominate in the private sphere, where they would apply their natural attributes of piety and morality to the business of instructing and monitoring husband and children. Such an arrangement was considered the foundation of a stable republican society.

Conversely, adherents believed women should not enter the public sphere, where they ran the risk of having those delicate attributes sullied by the rough-and-tumble world of the market and political life. The separate spheres doctrine was reinforced by ministers, editors, and many women themselves, such as intrepid educator Catharine Beecher. As articulated in prescriptive literature and sermons, the ideology of spheres held that men and women occupied two separate arenas of life, both in terms of what they actually did and what their moral capacity encompassed. Though actual practice depended upon class, urban or rural setting, or other circumstances, the ideal held that men worked in the public sphere, where their aggression, acquisitiveness, and competitiveness ensured success. Women stayed in the private sphere to raise the children and keep the households, but more importantly, to exercise moral influence using their "natural" gifts of piety, purity, and submissiveness. Viewed in the context of the burgeoning market economy, this feminine domesticity was supposed to operate as a check upon the unrestrained self-interest and aggressive competitiveness of the masculine marketplace.[11]

Over the course of the nineteenth century, the full meaning of this "cult of domesticity" underwent great scrutiny as women contested the limits placed on them by the separate spheres doctrine. Ironically, the essentialist definition of women as morally superior beings came under far less challenge than the rights of women to act in the public sphere. In fact, nineteenth-century women more often than not embraced the view of their gender as naturally pious and virtuous and used it as a rationale for participating beyond the domestic sphere. As Carol Lasser, Stacey M. Robertson, Anne Boylan, Michael Pierson, and others have shown, many women used the doctrine of separate spheres to justify their reform efforts in the public sphere. This so-called domestic feminism allowed women to take a public role based on a belief in their moral superiority and natural understanding of social problems affecting women, children, and families. Especially in the 1830s, this view identified womanhood with religiosity and moral purpose, thus validating women who joined benevolent societies, temperance groups, and antislavery societies.[12]

The rise of a culture of voluntary association right along with new outlets for female education proved crucial in leading women to challenge the bounds of domesticity. Although women of all classes formed organizations for mutual aid, middle-class, white women predominated in groups dedicated to social reform, many motivated by religious impulse.[13] Within these organizations, so much more so than in their own family circles, women could use the language of civil society they had learned in their academies and seminaries. Their knowledge of the world around them came to bear on their strategies for moral reform and missionary work. These associations of like-minded women were for many of them the only activity outside of the home in which they could apply their advanced education. One of the great nurturing grounds for female benevolent societies was in western New York, where the Second Great Awakening took root and spread, spawning in its wake hundreds of organizations dedicated to individual and social betterment. Perhaps no other place would have been so heady in the 1820s and 1830s, so alive with the reverberations of revivals and reforms, as Oneida County. Here Susan and Augustus as well as Augustus's younger brother, John, spent some time, attended school, heard about and perhaps even attended meetings of societies and associations organized for reform. Many of those associations in Oneida County had been organized by women who implicitly or forthrightly argued for a greater role for women in public life. All around them were people who had attended revivals and experienced conversions that led them to believe society could be improved and even perfected by the efforts of pious, dedicated individuals.

The theology of the Second Great Awakening owed much to Oneida County resident Charles Grandison Finney. A gifted and charismatic speaker, Finney preached a modern, democratic doctrine rejecting the traditional belief in predestination and promising salvation to anyone who repented sins and embraced God's grace. Challenging not only dogma but also practice, Finney encouraged demonstrative conversion experiences and allowed women to pray in public. For Finney and other preachers of the "new measures," the conversion experience, as intense and emotional as it was, simply set in motion the true work of a Christian life: bringing about God's kingdom on earth.[14] Many of Finney's converts took seriously his directive to improve the society around them. They distributed Bibles, formed temperance societies, and tried to keep the Sabbath a holy day. Most opposed slavery, though few of them became outright abolitionists, choosing instead to champion gradualism and colonization as the eventual solution to the nation's most glaring sin. Colonizationists, fearing the presence of mixed-race communities within the United States, thought that freed slaves should leave the country and settle in colonies in Africa or elsewhere. Many believed slave owners should be compensated for their loss of property, and emancipation should occur gradually to ease the disruption it would cause. Only a small number of antislavery advocates became immediatists, devoted to the idea of emancipation without compensation for slave owners and the integration of freed blacks into US society.

While Susan Lowe attended and taught school in Oneida County, a young man from Connecticut arrived to attend Oneida Institute, a unique educational experiment for boys in Whitestown, New York. Although Susan would not meet Augustus Wattles until they had both moved to Cincinnati, their separate but comparable experience in Oneida County would give them a similar worldview. Augustus Wattles was born August 25, 1807, in Lebanon, Connecticut, the son of Erastus and Sarah Thomas Wattles. Both sides of the family could claim an impressive New England ancestry. Augustus's grandmother, Ann Otis Wattles, could trace several family lines back to *Mayflower* Pilgrims. The Wattleses arrived on American shores not long after, in 1652, and grandfather Daniel Wattles fought in the militia during the Revolutionary War. His son Erastus Wattles also served his country as a captain in the War of 1812. A "self-taught and ingenious" crafter of musical instruments, he once made a barrel organ "of uncommonly large size" for the local Congregational church.[15] A victim of alcoholism, however, he ended up on the county poor rolls and failed to make a positive impression in the lives of his children. None of them left a good word about him, and his death in 1839 occasioned little notice, not even the purchase of a tombstone. The stalwart parent was Sarah; her father, Peleg Thomas, also encouraged his grandchildren toward conventional, Congregational piety. There were five siblings in all. The oldest son was William, who moved to upstate New York and lived a conventional life until he left for California in 1850 and disappeared. Augustus was the second son, followed by John Otis, Mary Ann, and Eliza.[16] Both Augustus and John spent time in Oneida County, attending Oneida Institute.

Much as female schools contributed to greater efforts for social reform by women, Oneida Institute was a critical site in channeling the spirit of evangelical Christianity into efforts to eliminate slavery. The founder of Oneida Institute, George W. Gale, watched with approval as Finney's revivals whipped up religious fervor throughout Oneida County and western New York. Gale hoped to recruit many of Finney's recent converts to attend his school and train for the ministry. He proposed a school to "unite labor with the pursuit of study" so that poor students could afford to attend. This would keep them physically fit while training for the ministry. The first class of seven students took courses, worked in the fields, milked cows, and cut wood. At the conclusion of the term, some of the students found teaching jobs and several went on to become ministers. Gale proclaimed his manual training school a success.[17] Although Gale did not claim to have originated the idea, Oneida Institute became the premier model of the manual training school and an inspiration to a critical branch of US abolitionism.

Augustus and John Wattles both became ardent reformers of the "ultraist" bent, the most radical of progressive reformers in the antebellum period, who embraced abolition, women's rights, and a host of other unconventional movements that came to include spiritualism, utopianism, and dietary reform. Their path, like that of Susan Lowe, led through Oneida County, New York. We know little of the brothers' early schooling, but Augustus attended Oneida Institute beginning perhaps as early as 1827. There he became fast friends with Theodore Dwight Weld, a charismatic and talented young man converted by Charles Grandison Finney who had already made a name for himself as one of Finney's itinerant lecturers. Weld had entered Oneida Institute to train for the ministry and quickly became the natural leader of the student body.[18]

Their Oneida experiences made both Weld and Wattles lifelong adherents of the manual labor training ideal, which might have predisposed them to their eventual acceptance of immediatist abolitionism. According to Paul Goodman, the manual labor ideal led some antislavery advocates to go beyond colonizationism to embrace immediatism and racial egalitarianism. As Goodman notes, "In upholding the nobility of all forms of toil, manual laborism rejected both class hubris and caste prejudice, North and South."[19] By mixing manual labor with instruction, schools not only reduced costs for poor students but also encouraged respect for physical toil that cut across class and racial lines. It reflected a new trend in reform thinking that emphasized the integration of body and spirit and the necessity of tending to the health of both. Manual labor schools enjoyed some popularity in the 1820s and 1830s but achieved their greatest success in two schools known for their abolitionism. Oneida Institute and Oberlin College in Ohio were the longest-lasting of the manual labor training schools, and both became hotbeds of abolitionism.[20]

Oneida's transition to abolitionism paralleled that of Weld and Wattles. Weld had long opposed slavery, in part because he had traveled in the South and had seen the practice firsthand. He might have influenced Wattles and others at Oneida to share his views. Yet Weld remained a colonizationist until convinced to adopt the immediatist position while touring Ohio in 1833 and meeting with Beriah Green and other radical abolitionist professors at Western Reserve College. Back in Oneida in the meantime,

Wattles steadfastly clung to the colonization ideal, even organizing a handful of students into the Oneida Institute Colonization Society and getting himself elected president.[21] That fall, Beriah Green became the president of Oneida Institute, bringing to Whitestown a fiery brand of immediate abolitionism. Green went on to recruit black students and to transform Oneida into a "radical, interracial, abolitionist college dedicated to revolutionizing American society."[22] Augustus, however, was ready to move on, preparing to follow his friend Theodore Weld to Cincinnati, where he would enroll in Lane Seminary. Augustus's younger brother, John Otis Wattles, arrived at Oneida in time to be oriented by his brother and to be swept up in the excitement of Green's tenure.

Like a latter-day Pied Piper, when Weld decided to migrate to Ohio he took some two dozen Oneida boys with him. Weld believed the future of Christian missionary work lay in the West, in the vast Ohio and Mississippi River Valley. Efforts were under way to make Lane Seminary in Cincinnati the premier school in the West for training young men for the ministry. A wealthy New York philanthropist, Arthur Tappan, had given $20,000 to support the new educational venture and to hire one of the foremost religious figures of the day, Lyman Beecher, as its president. Beecher's status as an eminent, orthodox theologian who had accepted the doctrines of the new evangelism if not its more sensationalist methods brought immediate credibility to the new seminary in Cincinnati.[23] Beecher was not prepared, however, to deal with a passionate band of young religious zealots poised upon the brink of abolitionist epiphany, and that is just what Weld brought in his wake.

Enthused by the prospects of Lane Seminary and its new manual labor curriculum, Weld, Wattles, and several dozen fellow Oneidans joined students from across New England and the South to begin their training in 1833.[24] They felt a lofty calling to evangelize the West, as they declared to the "Christian public": the Ohio Valley was their "expected field," and they had "assembled here, that we might the more accurately learn its character, catch the spirit of its gigantic enterprise, grow up into its genius, appreciate its peculiar wants, and be thus qualified by practical skill, no less than by theological erudition, to wield the weapons of truth."[25] Devoted to their evangelical work, Lane students also wholeheartedly embraced the manual labor system. Although many students worked in the farming and mechanical departments, the print shop became the assignment of choice.

Staffing six presses, student workers turned out more than 150,000 copies of Webster's spelling books in 1833.[26]

For that first Lane class, however, the great extracurricular interest was slavery. Across the country opinions on slavery had flared in the wake of the violent slave rebellion led by Nat Turner in 1831 and the terrible retribution that followed. That year, in Boston, William Lloyd Garrison had published the first issue of his abolitionist paper, the *Liberator,* on January 1, 1831, calling for the immediate abolition of slavery. In a panic, Southern states tightened their control over slaves, and northern whites recoiled from any suggestion that blacks should be freed to come live among them. Undaunted, abolitionists came together in Philadelphia in December 1833 to form the American Anti-Slavery Society (AASS), dedicated to Garrisonian principles and managed by the generous Tappan brothers.[27] Antislavery agitation was gaining momentum but carried little credibility with the general public. In Cincinnati most citizens accepted slavery as an unpleasant fact, and those who actively opposed it joined the local Colonization Society. Among those was Lyman Beecher, president of Lane Seminary, and most of the students in his school.[28]

On the abolitionist side stood Weld, more convinced than ever that his destiny lay in leading a great crusade for immediate emancipation, beginning with his fellow Lane students. He had many opportunities in that first term at Lane to influence his peers through word and deed because a cholera epidemic raged through Cincinnati and the school came to resemble a hospital ward. Weld selflessly worked night and day to nurse fellow students, displaying the Christian charity that came so easily to his nature. Soon he was regarded as the natural leader of the class, a role he assumed without presumption. In the fashion of his mentor, Finney, he worked steadily to persuade fellow students to embrace the idea of immediate emancipation, talking with them individually, emphasizing the reality of slavery and the complications of colonization. Above all, the moral question loomed. Slavery was an obvious sin, but beyond that, the colonizationists' desire to remove blacks entirely from US society rested on an equally abhorrent sin of denying the essential humanity of all God's children. Weld urged his fellow students to take the difficult step of viewing blacks as equal human beings, worthy of their love and concern.[29]

Weld generated such interest in the conflict between colonizationism and immediatism that in February 1834 the students asked the faculty for permission to hold an open debate on the issue. Even though almost the entire student body professed to believe in colonization, and therefore to uphold the view of the faculty and school, the faculty declined to allow such a debate to occur. President Beecher feared the reaction of the public, and given the volatility of the Cincinnati community with regard to abolitionism, he had every right to be concerned. The students, however, proceeded without faculty approval, and for eighteen days Lane Seminary became the site of a remarkable dialogue. For two and a half hours each night the students of Lane took turns addressing two questions: "Ought the people of the Slave holding States to abolish Slavery immediately?" and "Are the doctrines, tendencies, and measures of the American Colonization Society, and the influence of its principal supporters, such as render it worthy of the patronage of the Christian public?"[30]

The Lane debates consumed Augustus Wattles and finally propelled him to abandon the idea of colonization and embrace immediatism. He attended every session and took careful notes that he later sent to antislavery newspapers in Boston and New York. His observations provided the most detailed and accurate accounts of the debates and revealed an abounding sense of pride in what he and his fellows had accomplished:

> We have just closed one of the most interesting debates that I have ever attended. For eighteen evenings we have discussed the subject of abolition and colonization; and what is very remarkable, not the least unkind or even unpleasant feeling has been excited. There has been no shuffling, no quibbling, no striving to evade the truth; but, on the other hand, candor, fairness and manhood, have characterized the whole debate. Every argument has been fairly weighed, every objection duly considered. Neither side finds any fault with the other. All are satisfied that justice has been done.[31]

Most of the speakers, according to Augustus's report, were students who hailed from slave-owning states, many of whom stood to inherit plantations and slaves themselves. They spoke of the realities of slavery, describing in lurid detail the frequent beatings and tortures perpetrated upon slaves. By the end of nine evenings, with only a few abstentions the assembly voted in favor of immediate abolition. On the second question, only one student voted in support of the American Colonization Society. Augustus had entered the debate intending to support colonization but emerged a partisan for abolition. As with a skeptic attending a religious revival only to undergo conversion, he bore witness to his change of heart:

> I have altered my opinion both in regard to the Abolition and Coloni- zation Societies. And as I have a large number of friends who take your paper, and in it have seen my endorsement to the colonization scheme, as President of the Colonization Society of Oneida Institute, and who know that I have talked upon the subject both in public and in private; and that I have written letters to promote its interests, and given and begged money to help forward its operations; I wish them to know that I disclaim all connection with it; that I believe its doctrines, tendencies and measures are calculated to subvert the best interests of the colored people, to strengthen prejudice, to quiet the conscience of the slave holder, and put far off the day of emancipation.[32]

For Augustus the Lane debates were life changing. He could no longer remain in the seminary, content with study for the ministry. He felt com- pelled to work for his newfound purpose of helping blacks to prove their worth as free and equal human beings. A fellow Lane student later recalled that "Augustus Wattles, . . . taking Mr. Weld with him, went to Dr. Beecher and opened his heart in substance as follows":

> "When I came here three months ago," he said, "from the State of New York, I had been for a year the President of a Colonization Society; I had discussed and lectured in its favor; I did unremittingly what I now see was a great wrong. I must do what I can to undo that wrong. Here in Cincinnati are three thousand colored people, most of them in great ignorance. Last night I could not sleep. My present duty is plain, which is to take a dismission from the seminary, throw myself among these three thousand outcasts, establish schools, and work in all practicable ways for their elevation." Dr. Beecher, as well as Mr. Wattles, was moved to tears. The Doctor gave him his dismission, adding "Go, my son, and may God be with you."[33]

Augustus left Lane Seminary to go live and work in the black com- munity of Cincinnati. On March 1, 1834, he started a school in one of the black churches and attracted so many recruits that he had to stagger the classes. "When this school was opened," he reported, "it was imme- diately crowded to overflowing with children and adults. The house not being large enough to contain them, sixty small children were admitted at 9 o'clock in the morning. After reading and spelling around, they were dismissed and the house was filled again by the larger and grown persons who went through the same exercises."[34] The demand for instruction was so great that Marius Robinson and other Lane students also volunteered to help Wattles. However, the growing school so angered many white Cincinnatians that mobs began to gather outside the church, and the instructors were forced to move their classes to the house of Baker Jones, a black man "of considerable wealth for that day; also a man of intelligence and advanced ideas."[35]

While working in the black neighborhood, Wattles took room and board from a black family and on several occasions escorted black women to sessions of school and church. These actions were viewed as transgressions of acceptable social practice by many citizens of Cincinnati and led to a greater public uproar than the debates themselves had. Newspapers in Cincinnati that had merely commented on the slavery debate taking place in the school now roundly denounced the apparent social mixing occurring in the city's black neighborhood. Students still at Lane received threatening letters, and citizens warned of mob violence.[36] Wattles's activities, real and exaggerated, caused the greatest consternation. In a spirited defense of their debate and its consequences, the Lane students felt compelled to answer these charges in legalistic detail. In a pamphlet signed by fifty-one former Lane students—though not by Augustus Wattles—the "Lane Rebels" addressed the charge that "one of the students of the Seminary boarded, for a time, with a colored family. The news of this outrage has caused so many ears to tingle, and excited such a fever heat in the community, that we yield to the entreaties of some of our friends in this vicinity, and state the *facts.*"[37] It was not true, protested the rebels, that this individual was a student at the time of the transgression but was "one who had previously taken a dismission from the Seminary for one year, [and] did engage in teaching a colored school in Cincinnati, and a part of the time while thus engaged, did board in a highly respectable and worthy colored family." Wattles, indeed, had left Lane to begin teaching in the black community. Furthermore, his seminary friends contended, lodging with blacks had been his own idea, and not only had he not consulted his former colleagues but when "informed of it we were divided in opinion as to its expediency; some of us thinking it unwise, and others decidedly approving it."[38] Those who did support Wattles's decision believed that he could acquaint himself with "the influences exerted upon his pupils at home, together with the internal relations, the family management, and all their domestic habits, tempers and manners; and thus, far more intelligently and effectually promote the elevation of the deeply injured class whose improvements he was earnestly seeking."[39]

The reaction against the activities of the Lane Rebels, and particularly the response to Wattles's close association with blacks in their own neighborhood, shows how steep were the social obstacles against the abolitionists and how important it was to challenge those obstacles. Even among the Lane students themselves, no consensus existed in favor of social equality for blacks and certainly not for social mingling. Although the threat of racial amalgamation most often raised the specter of black men seducing or outraging white women, in Cincinnati of 1834, even a white man did not freely mix with blacks and especially with black women. The Lane students felt compelled to answer this charge separately, admitting that the issue of most concern to the community was that a white Lane student had "promenaded the streets with colored girls." Again, without mentioning Augustus Wattles's name, they justified his actions even while reminding their audience that he was a *former* student:

> The brother spoken of above, who had previously discontinued his connection with the Seminary, did in two instances walk with colored women. Both of these women were married; were of middle age, and one of them, at least, the mother of full grown children. Further, these women were his own pupils; they had toiled out the prime of life in slavery, and were enjoying in his school the only opportunity they had ever had for learning to read. In one of these instances, he overtook the woman as she was going to obtain relief for a person in distress—she had never been at the place, and enquired the way of him. He went with her, and kindly pointed out the house. In the other case, he went with the mother of one of his scholars to a religious meeting, of a Sabbath evening.[40]

We do not know what Augustus himself thought about the furor surrounding his activities, but nothing seems to have diminished his enthusiasm for the work. It is clear that his Cincinnati activities marked the beginning of a career devoted to ending slavery and bringing about racial equality. This work put him at odds not only with the vast majority of Americans but also with fellow abolitionists, most of whom at best wavered on the question of racial equality and at worst displayed outright prejudice against blacks. Augustus might have been influenced by Weld in this direction because Weld had been known to counsel his abolitionist followers on the importance of the "elevation of the free Negro."[41] Even so, advocates of true social equality between blacks and whites were few in number, and Augustus Wattles gained a reputation as one of them. It was quite remarkable, then, that he found someone who supported and shared these views, and with whom he could establish a life partnership.

While Augustus immersed himself in the black community of Cincinnati, Susan Lowe learned of the Lane Rebels and their efforts to provide schools for blacks. Along with a few companions, Susan decided to go to Cincinnati to help. Unlike Augustus's migration to Ohio, Susan's decision to move challenged some common social expectations for women of the time. With her friends, Phebe Mathews, Emeline Bishop, and Lucy Wright, she went to Ohio without male escort, not even for the purpose of meeting a husband or fiancé or to attend to family business. Indeed, their business itself was suspect in that they intended to work and live among the free black population and teach in their schools. Although teaching by unmarried women was widely accepted by the 1830s, white women risked public disapproval by teaching blacks. Augustus acknowledged as much when he urged another young teacher, Mary Lukens, to ignore public opinion, saying, "One looking superficially would be apt to pity thee, and say poor fatherless child, she has no one to govern her. She has degraded herself by going to teach the blacks. I presume all this and much more like it, is said of thee. But it is idle wind."[42] Augustus might have given similar encouragement to Susan Lowe and her friends, who came to be known as the Cincinnati Sisters for their work in teaching the blacks of that city.

Female abolitionists not only challenged the etiquette of racial separation but also were among the first women to demand a participatory role in the public sphere. In 1836 Sarah and Angelina Grimké became agents for the AASS and began speaking to women's groups around New York City. Their public lecturing led the abolitionist movement to split over the question of the propriety of women speaking publicly on behalf of the cause.[43] Included in the criticism leveled against such "indecent" behavior was the charge that such women would become transitory and begin to move about freely on their own. Even women's rights advocates themselves were sensitive to such reproach. Henry Blackwell cautioned his wife-to-be, Lucy Stone, not to travel too far lest it provoke public censure:

> I do not think it would make any difference in the case of a lady unknown, but in you, to come a thousand miles to me might seem a violation of the customary etiquette of good taste, which might strengthen the many silly, or misinformed people (the last class a very large one) in the idea that you really are the migratory, unfeminine, ungraceful contemner of propriety which newspaper critics & common gossip pronounce woman's rights ladies to be.[44]

Independent movement by women thus was identified both as a problem in itself and as being linked to other presumptuous behaviors, such as demanding the right to speak in public. In the public mind female mobility could only lead to the complete undermining of the feminine domestic role. Such a fear was not unjustified. As historian Virginia Scharff puts it, "When women move around independently, they violate gender at a structural level, becoming actual forces of disruption and potential agents of historical transformation."[45] A woman traveling alone or in the company of other women is not obviously under the control of a man, nor is she obviously performing domestic duties, and so the act of mobility itself is a challenge to the prescribed roles for women.

Such charges do not seem to have dismayed the Cincinnati Sisters, who validated their work as a God-given mission. As Carolyn Heilbrun has observed, a spiritual call to service was the only sanctioned excuse nineteenth-century women could use to justify activities not ordinarily available to them.[46] As soon as they reached Cincinnati in 1834, the sisters plunged immediately into the work of teaching black residents, assisting Wattles in his Sabbath and adult night schools, visiting black homes, and forming self-improvement societies. In March 1835 Susan began to assist Phebe Mathews by introducing manual labor training in her school.[47] They earned high praise from their male associates:

> The Sisters are doing nobly. They are everywhere received with open arms. They visit, eat, and sleep with their people and are exerting a powerful influence in correcting their domestic habits. Their schools are well attended and prosperous. . . . They are pursuing their work

steadily and are the happiest circle I ever knew. They attend the meetings of the coloured people more or less every Sabbath which produces a very favorable impression upon them. On the whole they appear to be just the persons for the work in which they are engaged and with Br. Wattles seem to be carrying the work forward with a strong hand, strong in the strength of the Lord.[48]

This glimpse into the activities of the sisters hints at the latitude available to these young women, who were, after all, separated from their families and other familiar community influences that might have monitored and regulated their behavior. They worked with young men they scarcely knew, but with whom they shared an evangelical faith and a devotion to the antislavery cause. They lived in a boarding house with a landlady who seemed to approve heartily of their endeavors:

Our beloved Sisters have found a real friend in the Lady with whom they board as also good friends in Mr. and Mrs. Gridley who board in the same family. Three other boarders after doing what they could to oust the "Nigger" Teachers have themselves pulled up stakes and departed to the great joy of the whole family. Mrs. Cleaveland answered them in their innuendoes and threats that she should as soon turn her own children out of doors as those young Ladies. Thus the Lord has raised up friends for them.[49]

They might have found a warm circle of friends, but it was an embattled enclave in a city that detested abolitionism. They all suffered from acts of mob violence and had to endure public ridicule and vitriol. A friend later recalled, "Mr. Wattles and the lady teachers were daily hissed and cursed, loaded with vulgar and brutal epithets, oaths and threats; filth and offal were often thrown at them as they came and went; and the ladies especially were assailed by grossest obscenity, called by the vilest names, and subjected to every indignity of speech which bitterness and diabolism could frame."[50]

Incendiary responses to antislavery activity were not unusual in the 1830s, but abolitionists did not allow public disapproval to deter them. Instead, organizations such as the AASS and dozens of state antislavery associations sought more effective and visible means of persuading the public to change its views on slavery and free blacks. In April 1835, Ohio abolitionists came together in Putnam to establish the Ohio Anti-Slavery Society (OASS). Augustus Wattles attended, along with former Lane colleagues Weld, Henry B. Stanton, and many others. Wattles, already recognized as an advocate for the interests of free blacks, headed a committee to investigate the "condition of the People of Color, in this State" and authored the report. In it he admitted that most of the 7,500 black people in Ohio appeared "vicious and degraded, beyond remedy" and immersed in ignorance, "intemperance, gaming, and lewdness." It was a "gross injustice," however, to condemn them outright for their condition, given that they had been "systematically deprived of instruction in science . . . denied the protection of law, debarred the pursuit of lucrative employment . . . never [having] felt the magnet influence which a hope of elevation in society exerts in others." Yet despite this, "they are all anxious to have their children taught and to learn themselves."[51] Wattles cited his own experience as superintendent of the schools for blacks in Cincinnati as evidence for their enthusiastic desire for education.

Weld thought Wattles's report had "produced more effect than anything else that was done in the convention." Augustus found such praise embarrassing, writing to Susan, who had remained in Cincinnati, "Something was said of what I had done. It made me feel like a fool. When will men learn the true estimate of character?"[52] The courageous character of all the assembled abolitionists was on full display because they daily faced down the mobs that gathered to disrupt the meeting. One Putnam resident who hosted several delegates in her home awoke in the middle of the night to find a mob in her front yard "threatening tar and feathers" to her guests. When the drunken men outside opened a window, "Mrs. Howells immediately put it down, saying 'You rascal, how dare you open this window!' He then went to the other and opened it. Mrs. H. then put her head out and started parleying." She told them that "only a doctor, a minister, and a lawyer" were staying in her house, and the minister would preach the next day. She "invited them to hear him. They said . . . they would come to hear him preach, but if he did not suit them they would pay him another visit."[53] Augustus displayed similar courage in the face of the mobs, but he might have underestimated the dangers the abolitionist presence posed for the black residents of Putnam. He went to visit the neighborhood where the free blacks lived and found them "full of anxiety and love for the abolitionists. . . . They wake up in the night and pray God to protect the abolitionists." However, he also noted, "The colored people, by their discreet conduct, have avoided exciting any bad feeling toward themselves. They have kept away, entirely, from the abolition meetings."[54]

Wattles's work with and sympathy for blacks was noted by both blacks and whites. Blacks considered him a trustworthy and sincere ally as well as a practical organizer.[55] These qualities led Weld to recommend him to Lewis Tappan for appointment as an agent for the AASS. Weld said it would be difficult to persuade Wattles to leave his work in Cincinnati to go out into the field to organize antislavery activities, but Wattles "is one of our strongest young men and is in many respects better qualified to do good in the cause than any of the rest."[56] Weld believed the AASS should do more to promote the improvement of free blacks, and he thought Wattles would be well suited to this work.[57] Tappan agreed and notified Weld in August 1836 that the AASS had "appointed Wattles generalissimo of the colored people."[58]

In the meantime, Wattles had continued his work in the schools of Cincinnati while also serving as the corresponding secretary of the OASS. He and Susan Lowe were both on hand to witness some tumultuous events that reminded them they labored in an unsympathetic society. Augustus and Susan were among the two hundred delegates, some eighty of whom were women, at the second annual meeting of the OASS, held in Granville, Ohio. Although the town had a large number of antislavery residents, many of the community's leaders considered abolitionists too provocative in their calls for immediate emancipation and racial uplift. When no one in town would allow them a place to meet, they gathered in the barn of Ashley Bancroft, just outside of town. As the delegates heard speeches about the sin of slavery and the need for women to step up to work for the oppressed, local militia members gathered downtown, drinking whiskey and marching around to the tunes of a fiddle. When the meeting broke up and the delegates left Bancroft's barn, they were pelted with rotten eggs and beaten with clubs. Still, Augustus considered the event a wonderful success, reporting triumphantly to the *Liberator*, "A resolution passed to raise ten thousand dollars this year for Anti-Slavery purposes, five thousand five hundred of which were pledged on the spot."[59]

The Granville gathering reinforced a sense of solidarity among Ohio's abolitionists, but the response of the mob reminded them they were a tiny minority in a hostile and racist society. Back in Cincinnati Augustus and Susan again found themselves in the thick of conflict. Twice in the summer of 1836, mobs attacked the offices of the *Philanthropist,* the official newspaper of the OASS, edited by James Birney. The whites who participated in the attacks represented all levels of society, from hired Kentucky thugs to the children of prominent Cincinnati businesspeople accompanying their fathers in the melee. On the worst night of violence, the rioters broke up the presses and threw the pieces in the river before marching into the black neighborhood, where they ransacked stores, burned homes, and beat up anyone they could catch.[60] As corresponding secretary for the OASS, Augustus had been assisting Birney in putting out the paper, and he often visited the office and home of Birney and other members of the paper's staff. Augustus went with a delegation to meet with a group of Cincinnati businesspeople in an attempt to bring peace to the city but found that the city leaders were determined to shut down the abolitionist press.[61] With the newspaper temporarily silenced, the abolitionists continued to conduct schools for the black community.

All of this made for a rather exciting courtship. On June 24, 1836, Susan Lowe married Augustus Wattles in Cincinnati.[62] Theirs was not the only marital union forged in the ardent hothouse of the abolitionist movement. Other Cincinnati Sisters married Lane Rebels. Phebe Mathews married Edward Weed, and Emily Rakestraw married Marius Robinson.[63] Other Lane Rebels had gone back east and married women already devoted to the antislavery movement. The best known of these couples were Theodore Dwight Weld and Angelina Grimké and Henry Stanton and Elizabeth Cady.[64] In many ways these unions helped to redefine marriage and push the boundaries of gender roles. With their families a thousand miles away, the courtship and marriage Susan and Augustus enjoyed clearly took place without family supervision of any sort. All of these marriages seemed rooted in romantic interest as well as shared devotion to the abolitionist cause. The partners without exception all articulated some belief in greater latitude and independence for women. Most of them supported progressive views on childrearing practices as they raised their families. These abolitionist marriages easily fell within the definitions of companionate marriages that had become the norm in America by the 1830s. Marriages that occurred when both partners came to the altar as mature, experienced adults, each with ideas and perhaps some capital of his or her own, reflect the importance of the late-marriage pattern identified by Mary Hartman as so vital to social change in the Western world for centuries.[65]

Susan and Augustus made their marriage and family instruments to be used in their causes. Most of the big decisions Augustus and Susan made throughout their married lives—moving from place to place in Ohio, to Indiana, and finally to Kansas in the 1850s—they made in order to start a new school or community for blacks or to participate in antislavery activities. Unlike many pioneer brides who went only grudgingly with their husbands in the westward migration,[66] Susan Lowe Wattles embraced each new venture with the same enthusiasm Augustus did. Both participated actively in the public dialogue by working within organizations, writing letters, signing petitions, and giving public lectures. Their partnership might not have revolutionized the gendered roles of their time, but they pushed the boundaries of gender nevertheless by working together to get things done for their causes in a practical sense and by thinking consciously about the roles of men and women within marriage. Others in the antislavery movement also began to think seriously about the rights of women, and the Wattleses followed these developments closely.

Throughout their lives, Susan and Augustus demonstrated that their marriage was a partnership devoted to the improvement of society through abolitionism and women's rights. From what they said and did, it is clear that they loved and respected each other, relying on each other in their common endeavors. In many ways, their roles as husband and wife resembled those of evangelical ministers and their wives of the time. Ministers' wives such as Elizabeth Atkinson Finney, wife of Charles Grandison Finney, performed some of the most important organizational work of their husbands' ministries by recruiting women into auxiliary groups and preaching before female audiences. Ministers came to rely enormously upon their wives to keep up with the day-to-day duties of caring for the sick, running schools, and doing temperance work.[67] Although these women's spheres of activity expanded, however, they often did so within the bounds of the separate spheres ideology prevalent at the time. The wives of the clergy might have been able to push these boundaries more easily than other women did because they operated under the umbrella of their husbands' authority. As other women followed suit, they did so with the assumption that their ministers must approve. Such genies are hard to get back in the bottle.

Gender roles, however, do change slowly, and even these radical abolitionists divided labor by gender. Augustus plowed, harvested crops, and constructed buildings. Susan cooked meals, preserved food, and sewed clothing. As Susan's productive work, primarily in the manufacture and sale of butter, brought in more income in the new market economy, the family might have increasingly valued her contributions.[68] It is more likely, however, that the Wattleses' family values focused more on the esoteric than the material. Their spiritual values prevented them from seeing men and women as having dramatically different moral natures. Like other abolitionists, they viewed both men and women as moral beings, capable of exercising control over unruly passions. Women might have been more pious and nurturing, but men were quite capable of upright behavior.[69] In their words and in their actions, they said and showed that they believed both men and women had a duty to God as well as a God-given capability to work ceaselessly to perfect society. The Wattleses interpreted this constant struggle for perfection as an individual effort rather than an institutional campaign. As young adults, they rejected both the organized church and the political party as vehicles for reform, believing instead in the power of the individual to set an example as a form of moral suasion. They had become ultraists, the most radical of antebellum reformers. Robert Abzug argues that ultraism arose as a response to the growth of the commercial and increasingly industrial economy at the same time New England churches were losing their religious hegemony.[70] Such a concern with the moral ravages of materialism certainly animated the Wattles men and women. Susan and Augustus focused their efforts on the sin of slavery, but they also believed women should be empowered to help fight the evils of materialistic society and women were capable of doing so.

As a married couple, Susan and Augustus formed a partnership that in some respects typified that of an average farm family and in others resembled that of a minister and his wife. Although their marriage might not have been as equitable as either of them might have wished, they were not alone. Historian Chris Dixon has noted that abolitionist couples made much of their opposition to traditional marriage expectations, but in reality they had great difficulty overcoming those conventions. A number of antislavery feminists, notably Lucy Stone and Angelina Grimké, began their critique of traditional marriage by equating it with slavery. Male and female abolitionists alike rejected patriarchal authority and decried the vulnerability of abuse caused by female servility and dependence. They questioned the relegation of women to the private sphere and believed women had a unique contribution to make in reforming society. To achieve this, they tried to create domestic arrangements that allowed women the freedom to go out into public, but often this simply amounted to the woman *adding* public responsibilities to her domestic burden. Abolitionists did not want to be subjected to criticism that their women had become unfeminine or neglected their domestic duties. Lucretia Mott stood as the model for abolitionist wives: she managed a busy household, raised six children, and could never be accused of neglecting her domestic obligations. Yet she was also an active lecturer and indefatigable laborer for reform. This often kept her up into the wee hours of the morning completing domestic tasks or discussing reform strategies with an endless stream of houseguests. Her husband, James, approved and even encouraged her public work and gratefully acknowledged her domestic labors, but he did not help out with the chores.[71] To a great extent both male and female abolitionists still believed it was the special duty of women to attend to the needs of others.

Augustus Wattles might also have shared this view, even though Susan worked with him as a partner. He gave some suggestion of his ideal for a wife in a letter to Angelina Grimké upon her marriage to Theodore Weld. Congratulating Angelina, he also reminded her of her obligations to her husband:

> I rejoice with joy unspeakable that your hearts, your hopes, your aims are one, your comforts and your cares. I rejoice more on his account than thine I believe. He needs thy soothing care and sensible discretion; thy friendly counsel and intelligent advice. I have been so distressed for him that I have been well nigh tempted to go to N. York to look to him.
>
> I think thou hast sense enough to manage him and thy self too, in the particulars where I have the most concern, viz. his reckless disregard of his own health.
>
> I love him as I do my own body and willingly would lay down my life for his. But it is out of my power and he is out of my reach and the Lord could not manage this matter so he has deputized thee.

In all that thou hast written on the rights of woman, etc., my heart and my head approve it well. My wife also has a perfect sympathy with them and joins me in wishing you, blessed ones, happiness and peace on your pilgrimage.[72]

Clearly, even when both members of a couple had independently dedicated their lives to a cause and therefore had independent careers (and no one could say of the Grimké-Welds that *she* had become an abolitionist because of *him*), it was still the duty of the woman to care for and nurture the man.

Augustus Wattles's emphasis on "sensible discretion," "friendly counsel," and "intelligent advice" points to the moral role of the wife within the domestic sphere, but his endorsement of Angelina's views on women suggests that he agreed with Grimké rather than Catharine Beecher on the question of female moral authority. Beecher had idealized the private sphere as the focal point of feminine domesticity, warning that if women stepped out into the sordid world of business and politics, they would lose this power. Angelina Grimké had answered with her *Letters to Catharine E. Beecher in Reply to an Essay on Slavery and Abolitionism* in 1837. Grimké stressed the woman's responsibility to respond to the evils of society, especially slavery, and claimed the right of women to engage in public, political activities.[73] Agreeing with Angelina, neither Augustus nor Susan seemed to think that the very public activities of the Grimké sisters or of Susan herself would undermine their moral authority. On numerous occasions Susan publicly declared her belief in the obligation of women to exercise their moral authority in efforts to improve society. In 1840, she and Augustus each wrote a letter to the *Liberator* in support of Garrison's advocacy of the rights of women. Susan stated, "Women must know what their rights are, before they will realize the great responsibility which rests upon them, and perform the duties which they owe, as intellectual and moral beings to the human family and to God."[74]

The views of Susan and Augustus on gender roles place them squarely in the ultraist camp of antebellum reformers, but they were not even the most radical thinkers within their own family. That accolade belonged to John O. Wattles. Of all the Wattles family members, he had the most progressive views on social perfectibility; he was the one most restless who most needed to wander in the pursuit of those dreams. In all regards John was a more extreme idealist than his older brother, indeed, more than most reformers of his day. A fellow communitarian, Amos Gilbert, once said of John: "Colors are more vivid; odors more delicate, flowers more beautiful, and music more thrilling when tested by the senses of J. O. W. than by those of ordinary men;—he transcended transcendentalism."[75] John moved often throughout his life, always believing that the next utopian community, the next opportunity for spreading his views, the next sponsor he could persuade would bring about the great transformation of society. If his ideas had any chance for realization—a big *if*—he might have done better to stay put for a while and work harder at it. Mobility and the frenetic nature of his personality went hand-in-hand. His energy seemed uncontainable. Many people were drawn to this charismatic, dynamic, irrepressible dreamer.

His most dependable and indispensable convert was his wife, Esther Whinery Wattles. Together they formed a partnership based on fervent devotion to their causes and to each other. She came from a Quaker family already imbued with antislavery principles. When the two met in Ohio in the early 1840s, her mind had already been set in the direction of reform. After they married, they worked together, tilting at the windmills of communitarian life, but she was the one who kept the household on the ground. Although she indulged his passion for communal life, she also made wise investments in real estate that allowed the family to move to follow his whims. After his untimely death from an illness most likely made worse by incessant travel to spread his word, she not only kept her family together without marrying again but also made sure her daughters enjoyed an opportunity for education available to few females of their generation.

Having followed his brother to Cincinnati in 1836, John spent his first years in Ohio working as a tutor in Augustus's schools for blacks. He was not satisfied, as Augustus was, with the unremitting labor of teaching and community building. Beginning in 1839 and almost every year thereafter he returned to the East to travel the lecture circuit and attend antislavery conferences. During this period, he began to find others who shared his ideas about the road to perfection. By 1842 he had fallen in with a group of like-minded souls in Ohio who established the Society for Universal Inquiry and Reform, dedicated to eradicating human government, capitalism, and coercive relationships. The group opposed slavery, advocated dietary reform, and founded utopian communities as a way of hastening the establishment of a radical kingdom of God on earth.

Moving in these circles, John Wattles met his future wife, Esther Whinery. The Whinerys of Columbiana County, Ohio, were a staunch Quaker family with thirteen children, one of whom was Esther, born in 1819. When she was twenty, Esther committed herself to the antislavery cause and with other members of her family became ever more involved in reform activities, where she ran across John. Later she remembered:

> When I met John O. Wattles, heard him on dietetic reform, on woman's rights and temperance as well as slavery I thought him a great as well as a good man. Then came this terrible fever in our family, & he was so good & so helpful we felt we could & did love each other, but were in no haste to be married. In May 1844 the time seemed ripe for the fulfillment of our dream.[76]

John considered Esther his soulmate for eternity, and his romantic feelings for her he interpreted as the ideal basis for marriage, which he called "*a union of two spirits of the two sexes.*" In his wedding day remarks, which he immediately had printed in pamphlet form for distribution, he described marriage as a mystical union, easier to say what it was not than what it was. It was not "*strong affection* for each other," or a feeling of ecstasy at being in each other's presence, or even feeling pleasure at doing kindnesses to each other, but much more. "True marriage," he declared, "is a union of pure minds . . . for mental existence—during the continuation of the soul's immortality." True marriage was difficult to recognize, but the "feminine mind is more pure than the other—hence to *their* perception is the real union first manifested. And in a right state of society they would be as free to say it as to feel it." According to John it was to the detriment of society that governments legislated marriage and prevented sincere minds from finding their companions, for only when "one after another shall have found their fellow spirits, each joined to each and all joined to Divinity" would God's society on earth be realized.[77]

Linked in spiritual union, John and Esther moved on to assist in the work of constructing the perfect earthly community. In 1844 the members of the Society for Universal Inquiry and Reform purchased a tract of land in Champaign County, Ohio, and set about building the Prairie Home community. Both John and Esther nominally lived in the community, but only Esther seems to have resided there on a continual basis. While she settled in to teach the younger children of the school, John went on the road once again to lecture and recruit new community members. Unfortunately for the prospects of Prairie Home, however, he painted such an appealing picture of an idyllic paradise where everyone shared the fruits of God's blessings that soon the little utopia was overrun with a ragtag lot of lazy blabbermouths and free-loaders.[78] Esther observed, "Over one hundred gathered who thought they were ready for community life, but were, in reality, far from it. The selfish element was predominant in most of them. Husband could not see it as I did. In six months that farm was taken back for want of an honest and true business-like bargain."[79]

After the failure of Prairie Home, John and Esther moved to Cincinnati, where she taught school and he published a reform newspaper, the *Herald of Progression*. During most of their life together she was the one to pursue a practical livelihood and ensure the family finances. She proved a sharp businessperson and investor. He had good cause to trust her judgment, and he seems to have thought all husbands should accord their wives similar regard. In November 1845 he printed an excerpt from a letter received from his brother-in-law, David Ripley of New Jersey, who wrote: "Wife says write, thy letters and papers are very acceptable." Perhaps reading into it more than intended, John took the occasion to praise his brother-in-law on the grounds that his "'wife' is duly consulted, as she should be, on all important occasions, and her opinions properly respected—showing that she is an *equal,* and not a menial—a companion, and not an appendage—an intelligent being, and not a mere reticule to hang on a man's arm."[80] At least in this regard John practiced what he preached. Either out of principle or because he trusted Esther, or both, John never owned property in his own name but placed it instead under his wife's name. They believed, with good reason, that if she died, he would have a much easier time acquiring full title to her property than she would have if he predeceased her and left property in his name to her.[81] This proved a wise decision because the couple went on to live in three more utopian communities in Ohio, Indiana, and Illinois between 1846 and 1857. A flood wiped out the little Fourierist community of Excelsior on the Ohio River, and other experiments in Lake Zurich, Illinois, and West Point, Indiana, failed as well. Esther humored John each time he wanted to make a fresh start at a utopian community. When he went to Kansas in 1857 to check on brother Augustus's antislavery activities, Esther did not think he would want to stay. However, he wrote her with his customary enthusiasm for the beautiful prairie and the marvelous prospects for building a perfect community and asked her to come. He was also sick with the ague and unable to care for himself. Esther packed up her household and three children, made a few land transactions so they could afford the venture, and headed west.[82]

Both Esther and Susan had wandering husbands and might have honed their considerable independence out of necessity more than desire. During the first two years of their marriage Augustus and Susan spent a great deal of time away from each other. Consider the whirlwind of activity that was Augustus's schedule: following their marriage in June 1836, Augustus traveled around Ohio visiting black communities and collecting information about black schools in particular. In September he began his agency for the AASS and had racked up $37 in expenses by December 1. In November he attended the AASS Agents Convention in New York City and might have visited his family in Connecticut. Back in Ohio by March at the latest, he bought land in Mercer County and probably began building a home there, although it is not clear when Susan joined him. From March through June 1 he visited fourteen black communities and forty-four schools, covering 575 miles, helped to organize at least three black schools, and gave perhaps forty lectures. Among the places he visited were Mercer County, Dayton, Brown County, Springfield, Columbia, Putnam, Zanesville, Lancaster, Smithfield, Mount Pleasant, Steubenville, Wellsville, Lisbon, Salem, New Garden, and Cincinnati. He also attended the annual meeting of the OASS in Mount Pleasant in April 1837. Needing money, he spent a few months in Cincinnati during the fall of 1837 teaching in the black schools but was back in Mercer County in early December when Susan gave birth to their first child. He continued to travel through June 1, 1838, expanding his range into Indiana. His services to the AASS ended on June 1, more a result of lack of funds on the organization's part than his own wishes, and for a couple of months that summer he worked for the OASS as its financial agent.[83]

Despite long separations during the first few years of their marriage, Augustus and Susan did establish a home and start a family. However, even these markers of domesticity coincided with developments for the cause. As early as 1835 Augustus had dreamed of settling a colony of free blacks somewhere away from any white settlements where blacks could live in peace without suffering prejudice and violence. He believed if they had their own land, they could show skeptical whites they were capable of living and prospering as decent, upright citizens. If given a chance, Augustus believed, blacks "would rise to industry, intelligence, virtue and consequent respectability."[84] While still living in Cincinnati in 1835, Augustus had assisted recently freed blacks in purchasing land in Mercer County. In 1836, as he traveled around Ohio in his work as an antislavery agent, he scouted out potential locations for a settlement where he would live as a neighbor to blacks. In May 1836 he even traveled to Canada, Michigan, and Indiana to investigate possibilities there. Finally, he decided to settle among his friends in Mercer County, Ohio, and began to buy land there in March 1837.[85]

The shared commitment of Augustus and Susan was most evident in the Mercer County community. When they moved to Mercer County, probably in the spring of 1837, there might have been as many as two dozen black families in the vicinity and very few whites. Susan's family from Oneida County, New York, soon joined them. By October 1837, her father and stepmother, Jonathan and Susannah Lowe, her siblings Julia Ann and David, and a cousin, Perkins Lowe, had settled nearby in St. Mary's.[86] The Lowe family shared the Wattleses' commitment to the antislavery movement and the advancement of blacks. Within a few years, Jonathan Lowe moved his family just across the state line into Indiana. There, he helped to establish a town called Liber and donated land for the construction of a Congregational church and a school, Liber College, that admitted black students. Lowe taught at the school at least through the Civil War.[87] Susan's brother, David P. Lowe, only fourteen when the family moved to Ohio, might have stayed with Susan and Augustus after his parents went to Indiana. He became a lawyer, established a law practice in Cincinnati, and served as a police court judge from 1859 to 1861.[88] He helped the Wattleses with legal business as well as practical matters. When the Wattleses moved to Clermont County in the late 1840s, David Lowe helped to transport their goods and children in his wagon. After Augustus and Susan moved to Kansas in 1855, they wrote back to David, imploring him to join them. He finally did in 1861 and became a Kansas state judge and US representative to Congress after the Civil War.[89]

As with so many other American families who moved often, Wattles and Lowe family ties both encouraged and facilitated mobility. Their ties also reinforced ideological beliefs. David Lowe and other members of the Lowe family shared many of the idealistic views of social reform with Augustus and Susan. David Lowe assisted the work of Augustus and Susan in Mercer County, attended women's rights conventions in Cincinnati, and supported the free-state cause when he went to Kansas. Another sister, Elizabeth Lowe Byrd, married John Byrd, an antislavery Presbyterian minister. They lived in Albany, Ohio, a village in the southeastern part of the state, before moving to Kansas in 1855.[90] Family members not only helped each other as they moved across the country but also reinforced their family identity by marrying like-minded people, encouraging certain types of behavior, and imbuing the next generation with the same ideals.

In addition to giving freed blacks a chance to prosper as farmers, Augustus and Susan wanted to build a manual training school for blacks on the model of Oneida and their schools for blacks in Cincinnati. With Augustus away from home so often, Susan was in charge of this school, which at first met in their home, a primitive log cabin standing on some 190 acres near the village of St. Mary's. As time went on, they improved the buildings and acquired more land. Each year Susan set aside donations of money and materials so they could build a schoolhouse, but it was a slow business. In October 1839 she reported:

> Our school varies from sixteen to thirty, as they can be spared from the work on the farm. There are over fifty who attend at different times. I have received not quite $300 in money and some building materials. In the whole about one-fifth of what will be necessary to put up such a building as I propose. Several of our friends have contributed toward the erection of a school house and we did hope we should make out enough to build a small house this fall, but we could not do it: and deeply as we regret, we must still go on saying no to many applicants. The twenty-one emancipated slaves who came here last June are very industrious and steady in all their habits.[91]

Relying upon the goodwill of family and friends, the Wattleses built up their little community but amassed no material wealth themselves. Augustus found himself continually in debt, in part a result of repeatedly lending money to people who failed to pay him back.[92] Although he fretted about his perpetual lack of funds, he declared, "There is a nobleness, which the worldling cannot attain to, in the character of one who sacrifices worldly goods for spiritual gain—who sacrifices her own ease for the welfare of others, whose sympathetic heart listens with tenderness to the cries of suffering humanity, and in whose estimation our immortal spirit is of more countless value than worlds of wealth."[93]

No one in the small community grew wealthy, certainly not the Wattleses, but in terms of showing that freed blacks could live as self-supporting citizens, the experiment succeeded. Gradually word spread of the good work being done in Mercer County. In early 1841 an account from the *Xenia Free Press* made the rounds in the antislavery newspapers across the country. The author, identifying himself only as J. S. H., reported that about 24,000 acres had been taken up by the settlers, "some of the most wealthy and respectable colored persons from our populous cities. . . . Others are manumitted and self-ransomed slaves, who have purchased their freedom." Not only were they well regarded for their "honesty and industry" but "the truly creditable fact that ardent spirits are prohibited among them, speaks well for their habits of sobriety." Mulberry trees were cultivated with the intention of producing silk, and black mechanics, masons, and carpenters were kept busy in the nearby towns. "The history of this people," concluded the author, "has put to rest the lie so often repeated by people opposed to emancipating the slaves, viz: 'Set them free among us and they will starve to death, or steal, or get drunk, or in some way become a public nuisance.'"[94] The Wattleses' manual training school also impressed this Ohio observer. Although J. S. H. had never before heard of such a school, he thought it was the "best I ever saw, for it is truly democratic. It not only makes no distinction on account of age, color, sex, or clime, but it puts the rich and the poor on the same level." Every student "had to work out his board with his own hands, thus putting it in the power of every person of enterprise to become a good scholar."[95] This was the manual training school ideal in action, and many abolitionists were gratified to learn of its progress. Lucretia Mott, who a few years earlier had sent books to Augustus for use in his schools, called attention to his "manual labor school in Mercer County Ohio which is doing much more to elevate the colored man" than the abolitionists at Oberlin were.[96]

John Wattles also helped to spread the impression that the Mercer County experiment had exceeded all expectations. Writing in the *Herald of Progression* in 1845, John claimed it was

> one of the grandest arguments for Emancipation that has ever been made. . . . It will tell more for the ability of the colored people than a score of set speeches. When they began it was all wilderness, forty miles from market, not a tree had been cut. . . . Now they have large farms under fence and cultivation, bountiful crops are waving in ripeness, or are gathered and stored for winter. Nearly every settler is a member of the "Teetotal" pledge, and lawing is almost unknown among them.[97]

By this time, however, Augustus had lost his enthusiasm as well as his health. The hard physical work of farming, coupled with the demands of teaching and the rigors of the lecture circuit, had gradually taken their toll. The signs of decline had become apparent as early as the end of 1841, when he wrote to the *Pennsylvania Freeman* complaining of a nervous affliction that was nearly "unbearable." "The least friction of any kind," he lamented, "sets my teeth on edge and [sends] the cold chills all over me. My left foot and knee have sometimes [been] so swollen, that I could not get a boot on. So I go halting along, so lame and crippled up that I can sometimes scarce stir in my bed."[98] Despite these afflictions Augustus still managed to help his black neighbors by writing letters for them, helping them improve their farms and livestock, and assisting them with legal matters. Not to mention, hinted the editor who had printed Augustus's correspondence, "rescuing from the kidnapper such colored people as may have fallen into their clutches," a not-so-veiled reference to the Wattleses' participation in the Underground Railroad.[99]

In November 1841 Augustus traveled to Philadelphia for the annual meeting of the AASS. While there, he met the trustees of the estate of Samuel Emlen, a Philadelphia Quaker who had left $20,000 in his will for the support of a school for black boys. The Emlen trustees agreed to purchase the Wattleses' farm and school and appointed him superintendent of the school, now to be called the Emlen Institute.[100] This experience proved disappointing and rocked Augustus's faith in his kindred reformers. In 1845, when his brother John asked him to join a utopian community, Augustus answered despondently:

I do not expect to join a community soon; but Susan does. I intend to give what money I have got, and also to pay for the board of my children. If it suits me—I don't mean the plan, but the people, the spirit, the practice, the arrangement, &c., &c.,—may be I shall join. I am afraid of men. I used to be as big a fool as you are, and trust and believe them. But experience has anointed mine eyes. The scales have fall off, and now I see man as he is—a selfish, revengeful animal. Nothing but the practice of a man will convince me that he is to be trusted. "O for a lodge in some vast wilderness." I would much sooner go where I could not see the face of a human being for a year than to stay here or go into any community that I know of, or even heard of.

I don't hate man. I pity him. I fear him, not for myself, but on his own account. "My heart is pained—my soul is sick at every days account of wrong and outrage with which the earth is filled."

I love God and nature—the pure and the beautiful. I enjoy peace and holiness. I would give anything to live in a world of love. I thought I would make one of my own. I married a wife without fault. I bought land in the wilderness, far away from any human being. None came but what were greatly indebted to me for favors. I looked for friendship and love in return. But instead, anger and ill will came, because there was a limit to those favors. In an unguarded moment I gave others the power over my home. Now I must wander in sheep skins and goat skins again, and seek the caverns and dens of the earth. A Community I have never contemplated with pleasure. I like elbow room. The further men are off the better I like them—unless they are of the right sort—and the right sort are scarce.[101]

With limited evidence at hand we can only speculate about what drove Augustus to such despair in 1845. By selling his land to the Emlen trustees, he had relinquished his rights as a landowner and proprietor of the school. His lament that he had given "others the power over my home" reflected regret at this loss of control as well as a feeling of betrayal. Weary with the common run of human nature, he longed once again to move on to find a better place where he might realize his dreams. He also revealed fear that such a place might not exist, at least not one containing any other human beings. Augustus's words recalled other restless American pioneers who kept pushing farther and farther into the wilderness as one place after another became too crowded. However, Augustus did not seek space just for the sake of elbow room, or fresh land, or new economic opportunities; he sought peace, holiness, and love. Augustus's words in 1845 also suggested that he was exhausted. Within a few years, poor health forced him to withdraw entirely from community activities and move with his family to a small farm in Clermont County, near Cincinnati.

Giving up the Emlen school did not signal the end of the Wattleses' work for abolitionism and women's rights. They continued to participate in organizational work and dabbled in some of John Wattles's causes, including spiritualism and communitarian life. Augustus's health issues led him to acquire some formal medical training in Cincinnati. They also had a growing family. Susan seems to have enjoyed a blessing that few women of the time shared: there is no evidence to suggest that she ever lost a child. Her first child, Sarah Grimké Wattles, born December 7, 1837, was named for the feminist and abolitionist leader with whom the Wattleses were developing a strong comradeship through their friend Weld.[102] The Wattleses' only son, Theodore Weld Wattles, was born in 1840 and named for Augustus's old friend. Another daughter, Emma, was born in 1842, followed by Mary Ann in 1845.

We have some insight into the parenting methods practiced by Susan Lowe Wattles because she left a journal she kept while her children were young. Susan was quite a remarkable woman for her time, having received a better-than-average education for a girl in the early nineteenth century, traveled widely for missionary and antislavery causes, and taught in schools for free blacks. She somehow managed to avoid much of the typical gender conditioning that led so many of her contemporaries to embrace the cult of true womanhood, with its assumption of the superior emotional nature of women. She once offered a circumspect appraisal of her character that might help us to understand what sort of person—and parent—she might have been. Writing to her husband, she explained a lack of effusiveness by saying, "My youth was spent in learning to control my feelings not to express them. I early imbibed the perverted idea that *intellect* was the only truly noble part of the mind—and that to express strong emotion of joy or grief or love or hate was weak-minded and contemptible. To avoid expressing emotion I suppressed it as far as possible until I do not suppose I even *feel* as intensely as many persons do. Now I see and deplore the error but the effect of such a course of discipline can never be removed."[103] This quality certainly accounts for Susan's steadfastness in the face of danger and crisis, and it also helps to explain some of her approaches to childrearing.

Susan's practical philosophy of childrearing stressed obedience, self-control, and compassion. She taught her children to believe that their moral character lay in their ability to control impulses and to be kind to others. When Sarah was five months old, Susan began a baby journal of sorts, in which she recorded occasional observations about Sarah and later about her other children as well. As she said, "I think it best to make a little memorandum of the treatment and development of her physical intellectual and moral powers."[104] Susan's notes on Sarah's development reflect her most cherished values, especially independence, self-control, and a love of learning. When Sarah was two years old, Susan recorded that the child could "now talk whatever she wishes, uses all parts of speech. Her mind is very active & she is very fond of books. She has a very large imagination."[105] Susan was not afraid to travel with Sarah, taking her for her first journey when Sarah was six months old. Nor did she hesitate to leave Sarah behind with her father for three weeks while she was away from home. As Sarah grew older and acquired a little brother in 1840, a sister in 1842, and yet another sister in 1845, Susan tried to instill in her a sense of responsibility for the younger children. She found Sarah a willful child but susceptible to firm parenting. When Sarah was four, Susan lamented that she had "great difficulty in securing obedience and in governing her temper at times." Resorting to the method modern parents would call a "timeout," an exasperated Susan reported,

> When she persisted in disobedience I shut her in a room alone telling her she must not stay with me when she was not a good girl. I have no trouble with her now. She is uniformly pleasant and obedient. I think I have subdued her by calling into active and constant exercise her love for me—by expressing my great love for her and by being as kind to her and as thankful for the little favors she can do and wish her to be.[106]

Susan used many persuasive techniques with her children. She seemed particularly concerned with dishonesty and often caught little Sarah telling lies. To counteract this, she told Sarah "many anecdotes and read to her several stories showing the bad consequences which follow deceit and lies. And I have tried to impress her mind with the thought that God would not love her unless she spoke the truth." For all of Susan's dismay with five-year-old Sarah's fibbing, Sarah seemed to have been a quite normal child. "Another wrong habit," her mother wrote, "I think we have succeeded in correcting was saying and doing things purposely to vex her brother. This has been done by forbidding it and at the same time trying to excite her kind feelings."[107] Susan's journal does not tell us whether little Theodore ever vexed his sisters in return.

Never in her journal did Susan indicate that she or Augustus practiced corporal punishment with their children, and it seems unlikely that they would have given that Susan criticized use of the whip in other families. However, Susan was not above the age-old parenting practice of scaring the wits out of her children to protect them from potential danger. When Sarah was four, she took off to visit the neighbors without permission. "To dissuade her from doing so again," Susan wrote,

> I told her of a little girl who strayed away from home and got lost and died in the woods. She cried and sobbed a long time and said "I am sorry for that poor girl." I asked her what she thought about going out so again without leave. "Oh, I will not go again. I should feel very bad if I was in the woods and could not find the way home and had no father or Mother."[108]

Susan might also have mentioned the wolves that still roamed the woods in that part of Ohio.[109] Living in the wilderness, parents had good reason to strike fear in the hearts of their children.

Because they were living under isolated conditions, Susan and Augustus had little access to medical expertise and so had to treat their own children's illnesses themselves. They tried first and foremost to keep their children and themselves healthy through diet. They often practiced vegetarianism, although not as faithfully as John and Esther did. Sarah, after being exclusively breastfed for four months, was gradually introduced to a solid, vegetarian diet. Once, however, Augustus thought the toddler might benefit from eating a "little meat," but when they "perceived no good result from it she again returned to her vegetable diet."[110] Many of Susan's comments detailed the home remedies she used to treat common ailments. Sarah received catnip tea and peppermint oil for colds and "spice syrup of rhubarb and tea made of raspberry leaves, saffron & the bark of black berry root" for diarrhea. Susan also thought "bathing the bowels in peregoric is beneficial to her," although "twelve drops" given in "three injections made of peregoric & starch" seemed to have "affected her head."[111] Administering paregoric, an opium-based tonic, was not an uncommon practice at the time, but one wonders how often Susan used it. For ague Susan administered "cathartic pills, spiced Lobelia and pepper tea."[112] When Sarah developed severe rashes, Susan mixed sulfur with lard and rubbed it on her at night.[113]

Sarah spent her childhood years in an isolated, rural community of mostly free black families in Mercer County. Only a few white families in addition to the Wattleses lived there, but among those were Sarah's maternal grandparents, uncle, and aunts, who had all moved there from Oneida County, New York, to assist the Wattleses. Until Sarah was three or four, her father's work as an antislavery agent took him away from home for months at a time. All of the white adults were fervently antislavery, and her parents believed in racial equality. Although Sarah's parents were strong believers in God, they rejected the organized church, in contrast to her grandfather, Jonathan Lowe, a fiercely religious man who prayed several times a day and continually reminded his children of what they needed to do to earn eternal salvation. Black and white children attended school together, taught by Susan Wattles, and the children played together and became friends. Occasionally blacks lived in the Wattles home, although we do not know the exact circumstances. Some might have been there waiting to move into their own homes in the community, or they might have worked for the Wattleses. Some might have been fugitives or orphans. On one occasion, Sarah had the "company of two little colored girls about her size for three months past" who lived with the Wattleses. Susan commented that Sarah "will have to unlearn much that she has learned from them," but she does not elaborate on what those undesirable traits might have been.[114] She might have had in mind certain characteristics she had observed in former slave families that she believed education would alleviate. Writing to Betsy Mix Cowles, another abolitionist, Susan deplored that

> the domestic circle and all social relations are poisoned by the exercise of those unholy feeling which have grown out of the slaveholding relation. The husband tyrannizes over the wife and both, over the children, and they over each other. Retaliation is common among neighbors and

is taught not only by example, but by precept to the children. A little girl said to me "Mother says I shant take a strike and not strike back." Parents depend on the fear of the whip and deceit for the government and management of their children.[115]

Clearly, Susan thought former slave families made poor examples for her own children, but perhaps she thought the greater good was the example her family would set for these newly freed people. In any case she encouraged them to live, play, and attend school together.

Augustus Wattles might have been an ultraist reformer, but he was still a typical antebellum American when it came to economic development. Even the most progressive of reformers had to keep a roof overhead, and though they abhorred greed and the exploitation of workers, many had a surprisingly positive view of technological progress and marketplace access. Both Augustus and John Wattles considered proximity to railroads when choosing settlement sites and thought labor-saving machines would relieve workers of drudgery.[116] Augustus never went as far as his brother John in endorsing communal property, but he gave away a lot of his own money and was constantly in debt. Financial difficulties failed to deter him, and like most Americans of his generation, he kept an eye out for better prospects. In 1853, despite owing on some outstanding loans, Augustus and Susan moved again, leaving Clermont County, Ohio, for a farmstead in Jasper County, in central Indiana.[117] Augustus seems to have recovered from the afflictions that had bothered him in Mercer County, although at forty-six he was feeling the approach of age. Writing to his brother-in-law about packing their belongings, he urged David Lowe, "Don't forget my old arm chair. I am getting old you know."[118] Perhaps Augustus and Susan thought their activist days were behind them, little knowing that national events were about to pull them westward and into an even greater maelstrom than anything they had previously experienced. In 1854 Congress passed the Kansas-Nebraska Act, opening the territory to settlement and popular sovereignty. Antislavery and proslavery forces prepared to battle for control of the new government. Augustus seemed reinvigorated by the new challenge, and by the spring of 1855, the family was on its way to Kansas.

In Kansas the family members would solidify their identities as morally driven activists in the cause of abolition and women's rights. However, they had forged this character in Ohio, where Augustus and Susan had met, fell in love, married, and started a family. In the course of that commonplace trajectory of family formation they had also made decisions that marked them as unusual for their times. All families must respond to forces beyond their control. Augustus and Susan came of age at a time when a market economy and geographical mobility were becoming more pronounced in American life. The issue of slavery placed increasing strains on the political system, and new ideas about religion, gender, race, and community challenged old complacency. The Wattleses chose not only to welcome these changes but also to goad them on and to teach their children the righteousness of action on behalf of progress. They associated with individuals who held similar beliefs, thus exposing their children to potent influences and mentors who could reinforce the parents' activist instruction. These were conscious decisions made in response to sometimes overwhelming circumstances, not the stolid perseverance of folk just trying to get by the best they could. This particular identity began with them, and it would influence generations of the family to come.

FOR FREEDOM AND EQUALITY:
THE WATTLES FAMILY IN KANSAS

In one of the most dramatic events to occur in "Bleeding Kansas" in the 1850s, abolitionist John Brown led a band of raiders across the border into Missouri, killed a slave owner, and liberated his slaves. Fleeing with the freed slaves back into Kansas, Brown sought refuge at the home of Augustus Wattles. When Brown fell ill, he stayed at the Wattles home, and the Wattles daughters nursed him to health.[1] The three Wattles girls made different uses of the story when they were much older. Mary Ann Wattles Faunce told this story to explain to her grandchildren why she had chosen to become a doctor. Emma Wattles Morse recounted the story for the Kansas State Historical Society (KSHS) so that her children and the citizens of Kansas would remember the contributions of the early settlers. Sarah Wattles Hiatt looked back upon these events and felt her life had been a great letdown in comparison to those exciting days of Bleeding Kansas. The construction and use of such stories helped to establish an identity for the Wattles family that gave their lives meaning and structure even as the different members of the family branched out to live separate lives in far-flung places.

In moving to Kansas the Wattleses joined thousands of other Americans in a huge westward migration. For most Americans mobility offered the hope of material improvement for themselves and their children. For the Wattles families, migration served as a means of improving a sinful society. For them the perfection of society through the elimination of slavery and the elevation of women loomed over all other considerations. In some ways their migration to Kansas reflected the experience of other

Americans migrating to new frontiers: they moved in tandem with other members of their families, and they formed cooperative relationships with other like-minded settlers. Extended families helped and encouraged each other and at the same time created new bonds of community. This pioneer experience was a foundational factor in shaping the Wattles family identity. However, they created other circumstances for themselves because their ideology drove them, making their motivations more complex than those of typical pioneers. They had an entire movement of like-minded people behind them. Their kindred abolitionists were vitally interested in what happened in Kansas and closely monitored developments there. When assistance was needed for the free-state Kansas settlers, eastern friends raised money, gathered clothing, and sent food. The Wattleses received letters and inspirational literature from their friends in the East, all intended to keep their spirits high and their work proceeding. When Kansas became a free state and the nation was purged of slavery through the Civil War, the Wattleses could feel vindication for the work and sacrifice they had endured.

On January 4, 1854, Senator Stephen A. Douglas of Illinois proposed a bill that would organize the territories of Kansas and Nebraska based on popular sovereignty. Northern Free-Soilers and abolitionists denounced this attempt to repeal the Missouri Compromise of 1820. By the time the bill passed in May, proslavery and free-state advocates had already begun to implement strategies for capturing Kansas for their cause. Immediately Missourians and other southerners began to cross the border to lay their claims to the choicest lands, while a trickle of northerners from Maine to Illinois began to move to Kansas as early as the spring of 1854. Events moved more quickly than government agents could clear Native American land titles or surveyors could lay out townships. Even before the territory was opened to settlement, eager squatters and speculators staked out parcels and began raising rudimentary tents and shelters. Raging disputes over land claims became barely distinguishable from ideological differences on slavery. By March 1855 Kansas had 8,525 settlers, about 60 percent of whom hailed from slave-owning states. Defending their right to take their "property" into the territory, they had brought with them 193 slaves.[2]

In Indiana, the family of Augustus and Susan Wattles monitored events closely and made a fateful decision: they would move to Kansas to help to make the territory a free state. Having only recently arrived in Indiana, perhaps the Wattleses were better able to pick up and move than others more established. In the fall of 1853 Augustus had apparently seen the move to Indiana as a long-term strategy to get out of debt. Fearing creditors, he had arranged to buy a farm under the name of another man so that the property could not be taken away from him. Under this arrangement, he would begin paying on a three-year loan for the property beginning March 1, 1854, and after three years he could sell the land for a profit. He predicted that by then he would have collected money owed to him by others, an amount he estimated was four times what he owed. With that money and the proceeds of the sale of the Indiana property, he could pay off all his own debts and move his family back to Cincinnati.[3] Developments in Kansas disrupted these plans. In April 1855 the family left Indiana and went overland to Kansas, arriving on May 7, 1855.[4] Surviving records do not exist to determine their financial maneuvers precisely, so we do not know how Augustus disposed of his property or even how the family managed to afford the journey, but it seems clear Augustus and Susan decided to put the cause of a free Kansas ahead of the family's need for a more solid financial future.

The Wattleses traveled to Kansas in wagons, taking the overland route through Iowa, less expensive than taking a water route. It was also safer for free-state advocates to avoid going through Missouri, where proslavery zealots might harass or molest them. A few years later Edward Daniels, a booster for the Kansas Aid Society, tried to encourage other free-state settlers by describing the ease with which the Wattleses got out to Kansas. According to Daniels, the Wattleses traveled with their own four children and two other persons, one of whom might have been a boy named George, possibly African American. They took with them eight horses and several wagons, on which they had piled ploughs, furniture, and many other household goods. The Wattleses slept in their wagons at night and cooked their meals on open campfires. Their journey took twenty days, covering 700 miles, and cost them only $40, some $210 less than they would have incurred had they taken the water route.[5]

After arriving in Kansas the Wattles family established a claim about seven miles south of Lawrence in Douglas County, in a valley between the

Kansas and Wakarusa Rivers. Lawrence had been established the previous summer by settlers in the New England Emigrant Aid Company, an organization devoted to making Kansas a free state. Beginning in February 1854, Eli Thayer, a schoolteacher in Worcester, Massachusetts, had worked to organize the company to assist antislavery emigrants willing to move to Kansas. By July the first train of settlers was on the way, arriving on the Kansas River on August 1, 1854. There they established the new town of Lawrence, naming it after Amos Lawrence, one of the officers and benefactors of the company.[6] At first, however, Lawrence was an embattled island of free-state sentiment in the midst of a proslavery sea. In the first territorial election held in early December 1854, the proslavery candidate for territorial delegate received 2,258 votes to 553 combined for the free-soil candidates. Even if the 1,700 or so fraudulent votes cast by Missouri Border Ruffians had not been counted, the proponents of slavery had prevailed over their free-state opponents. The willingness of Missourians to cross over the border to participate in or simply disrupt Kansas elections injected a threat of violence that made moving to Kansas a fearful prospect. Free-state settlers undertook the risks out of a deep-seated belief that the Kansas Territory should be open for settlement by free white men seeking land where their families would prosper. Only a minority of free-state settlers ever claimed to be true abolitionists, and many believed blacks should be prohibited from settling in the territory.[7] The Wattleses, as devoted abolitionists who held even more radical views about the desirability of racial equality, found very few like-minded settlers in Kansas. Almost immediately upon arriving in Kansas, however, they began to cooperate with a wide variety of free-state settlers.

The residents of Lawrence and its vicinity witnessed their share of conflict over land claims and other issues having nothing to do with the slavery question, but after the contest for control of the territorial government began, every argument seemed to revolve around slavery. The territorial legislature would write the new Kansas Constitution, so the election of delegates to the legislature was of vital importance. The territorial elections held on March 30, 1855, were marred by hundreds of Missourians coming into Kansas to cast ballots for the territorial legislature and to intimidate free-state voters and election officials. Not surprisingly, the election results showed a lopsided victory for proslavery candidates, but the margin of victory itself attracted scrutiny. Twice the number of ballots had been cast than registered voters who resided in the territory. The actions of the Border Ruffians had been so egregious that the free-state settlers and the national press would not let the matter rest without protest. So many complaints came in that Territorial Governor Andrew Reeder called special elections for May 22 for six districts where poll violations had been particularly blatant. In the Douglas district surrounding Lawrence, Augustus Wattles was chosen as a delegate to the territorial legislature.[8] The proslavery legislature's committee on credentials, however, refused to seat the delegates elected in the May 22 referendum, leading the free-state citizens of Lawrence on a path to rejecting the proslavery legislature altogether. Mass meetings were held in Lawrence throughout the summer of 1855, culminating in a great Free-State Convention at Big Springs on September 5 and a subsequent convention in Topeka in late October, where a free-state constitution was written. By the end of 1855 the territory of Kansas had two opposing legislatures.[9]

In many ways the immediate involvement of Augustus Wattles in these political developments came as no surprise. The family had moved to Kansas to promote a free state, and part of this battle was waged in the political arena. Yet in other ways this approach was a significant departure for Wattles. The Wattleses were true abolitionists who had proven themselves not only in opposing slavery but also in promoting social equality for blacks. This placed them in a minority within the Kansas free-state movement, not to mention within the national abolitionist movement itself. The Wattleses had never involved themselves in electoral politics, preferring to use moral suasion through writing and lecturing to change people's minds about slavery. In this sense they were "ultraists" who believed that a corrupt society could only be corrected by radically reforming all social institutions, including the political process, and that to participate in those institutions was to risk corruption.[10] When the antislavery movement underwent its great schism, most ultraists, including the Wattleses, had sided with the Garrisonians, who eschewed political action, against the more conservative and political-minded Tappans and James Birney, even though the Tappans and Birney had been their old friends.

The urgency of the Kansas situation probably explains this brief foray into electoral politics, but pressure from other free-state settlers might have been a factor as well. Augustus was well regarded by his new neighbors in Kansas, many of whom saw him as "one of the noblest, most generous and devoted of the Free State men,"[11] and they might have persuaded him to run for the legislative seat in May 1855. His enthusiasm for politics did not last long, however. Although Augustus did participate in several of the free-state meetings that occurred during the summer of 1855 and protested his ejection from the proslavery-dominated legislature, he did not attend the Big Springs or Topeka conventions that autumn.[12] In fact, from August to October he was not even in the Lawrence area but was scouting for a new farm for his family near Fort Riley.[13] Augustus's brief foray into electoral politics in the 1855 elections appears to be an aberration, an act perhaps taken in the enthusiasm of just having arrived in the volatile territory or at the behest of others. After 1855 his activities on behalf of freedom went in other directions, but one of those paths was even more out of character than participating in politics.

Augustus Wattles had always espoused peaceful means in the fight against slavery. Even though he had faced mob violence, there is no evidence to suggest he ever advocated violence in return. In Kansas, however, he had to contemplate violence. Violence dogged the Wattleses' experience in Kansas from the moment they arrived through the Civil War. In February 1855, a free-state militia called the Kansas Legion was formed in response to predation by proslavery settlers and Missourians. The New England Emigrant Aid Society (NEEAS), with which Augustus would soon be associated, was secretly buying up Sharps rifles and sending them out to Kansas in boxes labeled as books. George Washington Brown, editor of the Lawrence newspaper *Herald of Freedom,* which Augustus later helped to edit, openly advocated taking up arms and secretly assisted the efforts of the NEEAS to bring arms into Kansas.[14] Charles Robinson, one of the leaders of the free-state side, claimed in the wake of the March 30, 1855, election, "Our people have now formed themselves into four military companies & will meet to drill till they have perfected themselves in the art. Also companies are being formed in other places & we want arms. Give us the weapons & every man from the north will be a soldier & die in his tracks if necessary to protect and defend our rights."[15] Augustus might well have joined one of these militia groups and indeed was photographed with one group and a howitzer cannon in 1856. Augustus stands in the middle of the group, his hand resting on the cannon.[16] In Bleeding Kansas it was difficult to avoid exposure to violence, and Augustus engaged in it. However, he and Susan undoubtedly went through much soul-searching to reach the conclusion that violence in Kansas was unavoidable. We have no direct evidence from the Wattleses themselves, but a letter from Sarah Grimké answering one from Augustus delves deeply into the issue. On April 2, 1856, Grimké wrote the Wattleses about their "present perilous & difficult position." She understood why Augustus might choose to participate in violence and gave an inkling of how wrenching the decision would be for him:

> If desiring, as I have no doubt you do, to promote the best interests of the people of Kansas you religiously believe that the best means is to settle it by the sword, to become yourself a bearer of the sword & with your own hand perhaps transfer a brother man to another sphere of existence Do it dear Augustus and God speed your efforts for the race—If on the other hand you feel in the depths of your spirit that you are called to endure rather than to resist Stand by the conviction come what may—It is impossible for one to decide positively what is the right course for another to pursue under given circumstances, and as you remark. "Kansas produces a rapid development of the lower faculties— No government, no religion, no women to restrain—men are not only left without their usual checks to vice, but they are aggravated by privations & wrongs"—Yes my brother accumulated incentives to revenge, to struggling to maintain the rights appertaining to every human being, rights grievously outraged & trampled upon—for the purpose of establishing slavery surround & bear hard upon you—What I should do myself I dare not say God help you & yours so to act in this crisis that you may keep a conscience void of offences.[17]

As Augustus and Susan struggled with their consciences, they became involved with another family of Kansas settlers who would define violence as a divinely sanctioned means, bringing not just the Wattles family within the web of hostilities but catalyzing the entire nation to war. That Augustus would become one of the closest friends of John Brown in Kansas speaks to the parallel trajectory of their lives and their hatred of slavery. That Augustus could not condone John Brown's plans to invade Harpers Ferry attests to Augustus's essentially pacifist nature. Members of the Wattles family opened their hearts and home to John Brown, but in the end they could not go to the extremes Brown did.

The Wattleses met members of John Brown's family very soon after arriving in Kansas. The first of the five Brown brothers and their families arrived in Kansas in late April 1855. John Jr. and Jason, who arrived at the family's camp near Osawatomie on May 7, joined them the same day the Wattleses put down stakes near Lawrence. The Brown claim lay some twenty-five miles south of the Wattleses' homestead.[18] The first recorded meeting of Browns and Wattleses occurred on June 8, when both Augustus and John Brown Jr. attended the Free-State Convention in Lawrence and served together on the Committee on Resolutions.[19] The senior John Brown arrived in Kansas on October 7,[20] and the friendship with Augustus Wattles began soon after. Brown and Wattles knew of each other and might even have met some years earlier through antislavery circles in Ohio. Testifying before a congressional hearing on the Harpers Ferry incident, Wattles said of Brown, "I had a knowledge of him in Ohio, several years ago, but I was not intimate with him until 1855, in Kansas. I saw him first in Kansas in the fall of 1855."[21] In any event, their life experiences and devotion to abolition formed the basis of a natural alliance.

The family histories of John Brown and the Wattleses followed parallel lines. John Brown, like Augustus and John Wattles, hailed from New England Puritan stock. Brown was slightly older, born in 1800, in Torrington, Connecticut. Like the Wattleses, Brown's family line went back to the pilgrims of Plymouth and Duxbury and counted among them Indian fighters, Revolutionary War heroes, and soldiers of the War of 1812. John Brown's father, Owen, migrated to Ohio with his family, though much earlier than the Wattleses, arriving in the Western Reserve in 1805.[22] The antislavery views of both Brown and Wattles grew out of a deeply religious belief that all men were equal in the sight of God. Brown, like Wattles, defied social convention and abolitionist peer pressure in living and working among black people. Wattles's work in Cincinnati might have inspired John Brown and his brother Frederick to organize "a circulating library, a regular evening school, and a select female school" for the blacks of Randolph, Ohio, in 1834. Augustus Wattles learned of these developments while conducting his survey of black education in Ohio, noting that these schools had about 200 students.[23] Brown might have known about the Wattles's Mercer County community in Ohio before he attempted a similar experiment in New York. In 1849 Brown settled his family in a community of free blacks in North Elba, New York, where he regarded his neighbors much as Augustus had his in the Mercer County settlement.[24] Both Brown and Wattles placed their devotion to abolition above material gain and spent most of their adult lives in near poverty.

However, Kansas in the 1850s was a frontier community, not just an arena to play out the slavery question, and settlers had to attend to the practical necessities of frontier life. The Wattleses were certainly accustomed to starting over on a new homestead and eking out a living from the land, and in Kansas they planted wheat and corn for their own use, kept milk cows and chickens, and grew vegetable gardens. Like American emigrants have always done, the Wattleses encouraged other family members to move west so they would have kinfolk to share the work and help meet the challenges of frontier life. For this American family antislavery agitation became the shared work. The first family to join the Wattleses in the Kansas venture was Susan's sister Elizabeth Lowe Byrd and her husband, John, who left Ohio for Kansas in May and arrived by June 1855. The Byrds had been living in Albany, Ohio, a small village in the southeastern part of the state known as a way station on the Underground Railroad. John Byrd was a Presbyterian minister with antislavery views, so he and Elizabeth might have been inclined to move to Kansas without encouragement from Augustus and Susan. No surviving correspondence between the two couples has been found, but it is likely that the Byrds followed the Wattleses' move with great interest. Whether they got any encouragement from the Wattleses, the Byrds' decision to go to Kansas was made quickly. Writing to her brother, David Lowe of Cincinnati, Elizabeth said that they had "quite recently concluded to move west" and would tell him more about it when they passed through Cincinnati in a few weeks on their way to Kansas.[25] The Byrds settled first on a farm near Leavenworth, later moving to Lawrence. John Byrd established a church and the Union Sabbath School and was taken prisoner by proslavery ruffians during the conflict in the tumultuous summer of 1856. Word about his imprisonment reached family back in Indiana in bits and pieces, leading Elizabeth's sister, Julia Ann Weber, to speculate that he might have been "among those whom Geary released."[26]

Both Susan and Elizabeth worked on their brother David, trying to get the successful Cincinnati attorney to relocate to the new territory. Although he and his family did move to Kansas during the Civil War, he did not jump at the opportunity as quickly as his sisters had done. In February 1856, the Wattleses were considering a move to a farm near Fort Riley, about 100 miles west of Lawrence, and Augustus wrote to David trying to persuade him Kansas was destined to be a free state, and the violent disruptions caused by Border Ruffians only affected the Lawrence area:

> I regret you have concluded not to come to Kansas. You are just the man to come both for your own and your children's good. Do not let the disturbances here deter you. There is no pro slavery party in Kansas Territory. The pro slavery party is in Missouri. The voters nearly all came from there & returned again. So did many members of the Legislature. All the important offices were filled by men living in Missouri when they were appointed. They moved to Kansas to fill the appointment, and as the people would not recognize them or employ them they moved back again. Mr. Jones who was appointed Sheriff of Douglas Co. was, at the time, Post Master of Westport Mo. I was told yesterday by a man who is well acquainted with him, that he still retains that office and that his family resides there, and at this time he is with them. He is a fine looking resolute man, and was selected for the office of Sheriff, because of his courage & firmness. The great object seems to be to annoy Lawrence, or break it up as a rival of trade. Lawrence is also the center of resistance to pro slavery aggression.
>
> You will notice the disturbances never go any further west than Lawrence. Lawrence has wealth, and strength, & intelligence and courage. Consequently Lawrence must be conquered. They keep military guards there night and day. The Missourians have collected stores on the border and will make a descent whenever they think they can be successful. As the Gov. of Mo. and the President of the U.S. both connive at their aggressions we are obliged to defend ourselves. And this is called treason by the Missourians. But it is none of their business.
>
> You will say "all this is a very poor argument for my coming to Kansas." I want you to understand, first, Kansas will never be a slave state. The settlement all over the Territory are opposed to slavery. Of the real bona fida settlers of the Territory not more than one fourth or one eighth are pro slavery. If things were ever so quiet here I should not recommend you to settle in or around Lawrence or any other frontier town. You can now get a good farm joining mine, for $200, when it comes in market. I intend this to be at least 100 miles west of here,

near Ft. Riley. I intend to move there in the spring. You come on and go with me. Bring your family & all, come without fail.[27]

While Augustus put forth his best boosterism, Susan gave her younger brother sound, practical advice as if she knew he would change his mind and head west. She told David and his wife,

> If some power does not bring the Missourians into subjection, you must be sure to come on a boat commanded by a free state man, else you may be put off in some Missouri wood yard. Now I am going to take it for granted that you are coming and, take the liberty of making a few suggestions. Augustus says "bring all the furniture you want." But I want to specify. The first thing, (that I have wanted more than any thing else) is a tin safe.—Pack it full of bed clothes and then nail some half inch boards over the tin and it will pass for a box. Cover the front of your bureau with an old bed-quilt and bind it on well with a bed-cord and sew the cord to the quilt in several places. And I would bring the table in the same way. Fill it with the bed clothes that you want to use on the way, that is if you take a deck passage as I suppose you will if it is comfortable weather, thus saving money enough to buy a good cow, or two. Butter sold at Ft. Riley last summer for 50 cents a pound and they were not half supplied. Milk crocks and jars sell for 15 cts a gallon, perhaps you had better bring tin pans. I have six and wish I had brought more.
>
> Please get for me a butter mold that will hold a *pound.* They are turned out of wood. Summer pasture costs nothing and hay only the carting and sod corn can be raised at 20 ct per bu.
>
> I would get milk pans of a size you can put in the *safe* then you will be sure of a place secure from flies and dust.[28]

Susan's advice to David revealed her for the practical frontierswoman she was. However, in some ways she was also a lonely frontierswoman, not an uncommon experience for women who had left comfortable homes in established communities. Susan missed most the companionship of other women, even though her own family of four children and several boarders gave her much company. She told her brother life in Lawrence had been somewhat disappointing in terms of friendships, even though her own family life sustained her:

For our sakes I do hope you will come this spring if we are to move an hundred miles further west. I have all along rather hoped that circumstances would combine to keep us nearer Lawrence—Not because I have personal acquaintances there, to whom I am strongly attracted, but I have all the time been hoping that I should find some women there to love. And the post office advantages are better there than further west. But somebody must go on to the frontier and we will not be backward in doing our part of that work and if that part of the country progresses as fast as this we shall very soon begin to imagine that we are "right in the middle of the world." If we could only induce a few families to come there who had children about the ages of ours so that we could have a school, we should feel at home immediately. If you come we shall all be very glad, and if you do not come, I have no fears but what I shall be happy there. My own family circle furnishes me enjoyment, and also plenty of employment.[29]

The Wattleses had four children of their own and the young boy George with them as well. The oldest, Sarah, was just eighteen, old enough to have taken out a land claim in her own name in Kansas. The only son, Theodore, was nearly sixteen and likely helped Augustus with much of the farm work and constructing their homes in Kansas. Much was expected of the two youngest children as well—Emma, who was thirteen, and Mary Ann, who was ten in 1855.

By the end of 1855 it was clear the conflict in Kansas was only beginning. In early December a ruckus ignited along the Wakarusa River, south of Lawrence and right in the Wattleses' neighborhood. A proslavery man killed a free-state man over a disputed land claim. In retaliation a gang of free-state men began burning proslavery cabins. The proslavery sheriff arrested a free-state man for torching cabins only to have another batch of free-staters "liberate" the prisoner from the sheriff's custody. The Wakarusa War was on. Even though only one other person was killed, both sides mustered hundreds of heavily armed men and stood at the ready until the situation was diffused by the territorial governor. The proslavery faction camped out near the small settlement of Franklin, just a few miles from the Wattles cabin. The free-state militia gathered in Lawrence.[30] Although the Wakarusa War might have been more bluster than mortal combat, it caused tremendous disruption and concern for all living in the Lawrence area.

Winter snow and ice blew in, and Kansans hunkered down for a few months to try to keep their hastily constructed cabins warm despite the chronic lack of firewood. However, that spring hostilities erupted again, resulting in the Sack of Lawrence on May 21, 1856. Proslavery forces, determined to wipe out what they considered a "hotbed of abolitionism," rode into Lawrence and destroyed the Free-State Hotel; dumped the presses of the free-state newspapers, the *Herald of Freedom* and the *Kansas Free State,* into the river; plundered homes; and arrested free-state leaders, including G. W. Brown. The men of Lawrence offered little resistance.[31] The proslavery offensive and the seemingly cowardly free-state response propelled John Brown to commit one of the worst atrocities of Bleeding Kansas, the cold-blooded murder of five proslavery settlers along Pottawatomie Creek on the night of May 24–25. Brown managed to elude arrest for the attacks, but his sons John Jr. and Jason were captured—even though they had not participated in the killings—and John Jr. lapsed into temporary insanity as a result of the treatment he received.[32] For months following the Pottawatomie Massacre hostilities flared between proslavery and free-state factions. Brown and his company participated in battles at Black Jack and Osawatomie that sealed his reputation as a skilled and courageous military leader in Northern abolitionist opinion and as a dangerous and fanatical murderer in Southern proslavery eyes. Again escaping capture and benefiting from a truce established by the newly arrived Governor John Geary, "Captain" John Brown, his sons, and their families left Kansas in late September.[33]

Members of the Wattles family remained on their homestead during the clashes of 1855–1856, but they were neither passive nor neutral in the conflict. They gave assistance in every way they could, by lending horses and sheltering combatants and newly arrived emigrants in their home. Susan and the children cooked meals and nursed the sick, knowing they could be subjected to violence at any moment. Emma Wattles Morse recalled an episode in August 1856, when Augustus invited a company of men to stay at the Wattles home, telling them to "feed their horses from his field, also themselves; and Mrs. Wattles served as many meals as she could; in the house the table could only seat six at a time, but was filled and cleared and refilled as fast as biscuit and corn bread could be baked and bacon fried, until after midnight."[34]

Such generosity eroded the family's resources. In October 1856 Augustus wrote to G. W. Brown to ask if the Kansas Central Committee of the NEEAS might have funds to compensate free-staters who had suffered property losses. He had not wanted to ask for assistance, he explained, but he was sick and had no money to support his family. His account of costs incurred over the previous year gives us an idea of what he and his family had experienced:

My first loss was a pair of horses worth $300. When the disturbances first commenced last fall, one of my horses was lent & rode further & faster than he ever was before & tied out in the prairie over night in the rain, took sick & died very soon.

I had a man working for me whom I hired to go to Lawrence & stay through the war. I let him have the other horse to ride. He said he rode it into a hole or ravine when the horse fell & injured itself so that it died.

I then let Mr. Lowry & Warren & others have a mule to ride while organizing the state during the winter. It was very hard riding—very cold weather & very difficult to get food & shelter for the mule. And if she had not been a mule she would have died from hardship. As it was the mule got sick & has not got over it yet. I lost her work during the spring. And to say nothing of her services, I lost by her sickness I think $30. I gave for the mule in Mo. $170. I kept several free state men who were sick & some refugees & some emigrants, from one to ten at a time without compensation. Mr. Haskell who went up north for men to defend Lawrence in Nov, was taken sick immediately on his return to staid with me from that time till the middle of April about twenty weeks. He was poor, sold some of his clothing & other things, got money enough to go home and returned to Maine. His board was worth $50, & during some of the time he worked a little, say $10, worth. Our house has not been free from sick persons since. Some times as many as four & five at a time. I have kept no account. For the last six months I should estimate our visitors at an average of six per week 26 weeks & 2'p per week would make $390. Some of these have paid a little, say in the whole, $90. So many people using our quilts & blankets lying on the floor & in the tents has used them nearly all up. So we are minus this item. A new tent which is valued at $20 & which I procured at Ft. Riley last fall went into the service by request of Col. Lane & has not been returned. It is worth $15.00. One of my best oxen which I paid $100 a yoke for last spring was killed in Lawrence about the last of August. The ox was worth $50.00.[35]

The Wattleses were not the only Kansans to suffer financially during this period. The hostilities of 1856 nearly spelled economic disaster for the young territory. The vital river trade that carried people and goods up the Missouri from St. Louis came to a virtual standstill, and overland trade was hampered by attacks and theft carried out by guerrillas on both sides. Immigration tapered off, thus diminishing the flow of new money and capital in circulation.[36] Facing another bleak Kansas winter, Augustus sought to hire himself out for some kind of work to support his family. Naturally he looked to his friends in the antislavery community. Although he received no compensation from the Kansas Central Committee, his appeal to G. W. Brown resulted in a collaboration between the two antislavery men. Brown, whose *Herald of Freedom* office had been destroyed along with his presses during the Sack of Lawrence, had endured a four-month imprisonment at the hands of the proslavery government. While he languished in jail, his wife went east to campaign for funds to ransom her husband and restore the press. Brown was able to resume publication of the *Herald of Freedom* on November 1, 1856.[37] He did so with the assistance of Augustus Wattles. Brown had located an available press and type in Manhattan, Kansas, and sent Augustus to retrieve them. Brown reported, "We paid A. Wattles $104 for hauling the press and type from Manhattan, he having made two trips—the first an unsuccessful one—and the second, compelled to journey a long distance, out of the direct course, consuming three entire days, to escape a guerrilla party of Border Ruffians, who were reconnoitering in the vicinity where he was teaming."[38] Not only did Brown use Wattles's services as a teamster but also he recognized Augustus's talents and experiences as an antislavery propagandist and hired him on as the assistant editor, at the salary of $100 per month.[39]

While working on the *Herald of Freedom,* Augustus's primary assignment was to write a history of Kansas. On November 22 Brown announced, "As soon as the health of our assistant will permit, he will commence, and publish through successive number of the *Herald of Freedom,* a connected series of articles on the leading events of the history of Kansas."[40] A month later Brown informed readers that the promised history of Kansas would begin in January with a new chapter appearing each week. At the conclusion the entire manuscript would be bound into a book. It would not be possible to produce a definitive history of Kansas, Brown warned, but he assured readers Wattles was capable of doing the job as objectively as anyone could. Brown boasted,

> The author of ours is not connected with any of the various factions in Kansas, is not ambitious, nor seeking for position; but is a humble worker in the great Free State cause, and has shown his interest in the country by coming here at an early day, with his family, and has gone to improving the soil and country independent of the petty cabals which have distracted neighborhoods and communities.[41]

Chapter 1 of the "History of Kansas" appeared on January 17, 1857, beginning the historical narrative with an account of French settlement and the 1803 acquisition of the Louisiana Territory by the United States. Through January 16, 1858, installments of the history appeared every few weeks, outlining the organization of the territory under the Kansas-Nebraska Act, the disruption of early elections by Border Ruffians, the establishment of competing legislatures and territorial constitutions, and the violence leading up to the Sack of Lawrence. By that time, however, Augustus Wattles was no longer working as assistant editor, having had a disagreement with Editor Brown. In November 1857, Brown reported that Wattles had taken leave to visit his family in Moneka, where the Wattleses had recently relocated. Then on January 16 Brown explained to readers that he had removed Wattles because of a misunderstanding.[42] He never explained the basis of their falling out, nor did he mention Wattles again in the pages of the *Herald of Freedom.*

While working at the *Herald of Freedom,* Augustus became even more closely involved with the Kansas Emigrant Aid Company, which had reorganized its activities under the National Kansas Committee in June 1856. Wattles was appointed to the Second District Committee on July 4, 1856.[43] Relations between the national and local committees became strained. In late 1856 Thaddeus Hyatt and W. F. M. Arny, representing the National Kansas Committee, arrived in Kansas to investigate complaints about the local committee.[44] Given the chaotic nature of Kansas and the inflated expectations undoubtedly shared by many emigrants, there were bound to be many complaints from settlers who arrived in Kansas only to find conditions less hospitable than desired. The problems with the National Kansas Committee, however, stemmed less from unsettled circumstances on the ground than from the grandiosity of the scheme. The organization had hoped to take funds raised in the East, use that money to recruit and outfit settlers, shepherd those emigrants out to Kansas, and assist them in getting established so that the settlers would support the free-state cause. Even after moving its headquarters to Chicago, the National Kansas Committee had difficulty overseeing agents in the field, leading to charges of widespread graft. It was almost impossible to please everyone through the distribution of loads of goods, mostly clothing and food donated for the relief of Kansas settlers. It was no secret that the Kansas Emigrant Aid Company also sent guns and ammunition into Kansas, especially the feared Sharps rifle, the most up-to-date technology in lethal weaponry available at the time, thus justifying reprisals against the company from many proslavery people.[45]

Arny, the transportation agent for the National Kansas Committee, was appalled to find Kansans "living on Pumpkin and Green Corn Grated and nothing else" and the "state of things existing with regard to the Central Committee which rendered it necessary in my estimation to have the people of Kansas reorganize the Committee."[46] If Arny thought some of the Kansans were inept, some Kansans thought he was imperious. One local committee member who had charge of the Lawrence storehouse complained, "I got along with Arney for a few days without any serious difficulty till he continued to regard the store as his property & treated me as a subordinate."[47] But Arny apparently trusted Augustus Wattles and was able to work with him. Arny arranged for boxes of donated materials to be delivered to Augustus for distribution and appointed him to a committee to investigate and oversee disbursing agents in the territory.[48] Augustus reported some of his observations to Thaddeus Hyatt of the Kansas National Committee, pointing out that one of the captains leading an emigrant train had abused and swindled settlers under his care, causing a large group of them to return to Illinois. He told Hyatt that the treasurer of the local committee was so unreliable that no one would sign a bond for him. He also accused the members of the Kansas Central Committee of such great failing of character that "in order to screen themselves from public censure for mismanagement, turn round and make charges themselves against the National Committee, thinking it was by raining suspicions on others to draw off attention from themselves."[49] Augustus had little to do with the Kansas Central Committee after that, although he continued to disperse donated goods sent from the east and delivered to the *Herald of Freedom* office. The Emigrant Aid Company itself withered and came to a halting end by that spring.[50]

During this period the relationship between Augustus Wattles and John Brown deepened and became more complicated. Wattles claimed not to have known about Brown's complicity in the Pottawatomie Massacre, even though speculation and suspicions about Brown's guilt ran rampant in the territory, making it difficult for Brown to move about openly. Late in the summer of 1856 the Wattles family harbored Brown and his sons and their families for more than a week. As Wattles later told the US Senate committee investigating Harpers Ferry, "The troops were attempting to arrest him, and he came to stop with me on his way from Ossawatomie to Nebraska. He was attempting to collect his cattle together, and what property he had in Ossawatomie, and sell it; and he had the women there to take them down the river; and he had his sons there, and their wagons, to go back to Ohio."[51] After Brown left the territory in the autumn of 1856, Wattles became a point man for him in Kansas, filtering information to and from Brown, who spent most of his time campaigning for support in the East. One of Brown's biographers, F. B. Sanborn, observed, "Through one of these friends, Augustus Wattles, then living at Lawrence, [Brown] sent messages to others."[52] In his correspondence with Wattles, Brown demonstrates that though he may have left Kansas, he did not consider his interest there concluded. Writing under the pseudonym Nelson Hawkins in April 1857, Brown thanked Wattles for letters he had received:

> They give me just that kind of news I was most of all things anxious to hear. I bless God that he has not left the Free-State men of Kansas to pollute themselves by the foul and loathsome embrace of the old rotten whore. I have been trembling all along lest they might "back down" from the high and holy ground they have taken. I say, in view of the wisdom, firmness, and patience of my friends and fellow-sufferers in the cause of humanity, let God's name be eternally praised! I would most gladly give my hand to all whose "garments are not defiled"; and I humbly trust that I shall soon again have opportunity to rejoice (or suffer

further if need be) with you in the strife between heaven and hell. I wish to send my most cordial and earnest salutation to every one of the chosen.[53]

Wattles continued through the summer to feed information and advice to Brown. After Brown wrote to Wattles in June announcing his plans to return to Kansas, Wattles advised Brown, "We talked over matters here, and concluded to say, come as quietly as possible, or not come at present, as you may choose."[54] Wattles seemed worried that Brown might stir things up just at a time when the violence in Kansas had abated and the struggles now centered in the political arena. Under a new territorial governor, Robert J. Walker, the great question for the free-state faction was whether to boycott the June vote for a new constitutional convention. With the free-state advocates sitting out the election, a proslavery convention resulted and the so-called Lecompton Constitution endorsed slavery. Even though Territorial Governor Walker urged free-staters to accept the results of the Lecompton convention, he won little support from the proslavery advocates. Trying desperately to be fair and firm with both sides, he only aroused the suspicions of both.[55] Free-staters began to divide among themselves, with those supporting Walker arguing that the boycott against elections should be abandoned. G. W. Brown of the *Herald of Freedom* supported Walker. So did Augustus Wattles, for a time. He took part in meetings to organize the free-state response to the Lecompton Constitution, he entered petitions to protest voting irregularities, and he joined a delegation to the governor to negotiate free-state participation in the next territorial election.[56] As G. W. Brown fell increasingly out of favor with more militant free-staters, Augustus was presumed in thrall to the *Herald of Freedom* editor. A supporter of John Brown, James H. Holmes, wrote later that summer to John Brown, suggesting that through Wattles, G. W. Brown might learn too much. Holmes said:

> I have a word of caution to say in regard to Mr. Wattles. He is a friend whom I most highly esteem; yet he is so connected in politics that I think it unsafe for you to communicate to him any plans you would not like to communicate directly to Governor Walker. For this reason: Mr. Wattles is under George W. Brown; and both believe in submitting in good faith, under Governor Walker, to the Territorial authorities.

Governor Walker comes to town frequently, and stops at the "Herald of Freedom" office, in secret conclave with G. W. Brown.[57]

Holmes need not have worried about Wattles's loyalties, however. By the end of 1857 Wattles had broken with the editor of the *Herald of Freedom* and was preparing to leave Lawrence for Moneka. He remained at the *Herald of Freedom* office long enough to finish his "History of Kansas," and then he relocated to Linn County.

While Augustus had been embroiled in Lawrence politics through 1857, his brother John Wattles had been traveling around Kansas, looking for another ideal spot on which to start the perfect community. He chose a site in Linn County for the new town he called Moneka. He might have first seen Linn County when he passed through the area on his first visit to Kansas in 1853, before the territory was organized for white settlement under the Kansas-Nebraska Act. He had visited missions operated by the Methodists and Quakers and reported his observations about slaveholding by Native Americans in eastern newspapers.[58] In February 1857 he was again in Kansas, forming a company consisting of his brother, Augustus, and five others who laid out the town of Moneka. By that summer John had built a frame house of local lumber, and Augustus followed with construction of a stone house completed by 1859. By 1858 the town consisted of a two-story hotel, a schoolhouse, John Wattles's lumber frame house, and Augustus Wattles's stone house as well as a few other farm buildings.[59] John envisioned a great future for Moneka and lobbied widely to bring a railroad through the town. He worked with a group of settlers who sought to have the Topeka & St. Joseph Railroad extended through Butler, Missouri, to Moneka and on to Emporia, Kansas.[60] Although the railroad never arrived, the presence of the two Wattles families made the new village a lively place. Significantly, the Wattleses were now an extended family, where adults could work cooperatively with each other and cousins could get to know each other. Augustus and Susan's children now ranged in age from Sarah, twenty-one in 1858; Theodore at eighteen; Emma at sixteen; to Mary Ann at thirteen. John and Esther's daughters were Celestia, nine in 1858; Harmonia at seven; and Theano at five. Sarah joined John, Esther, and her mother in organizing and teaching in a school for the younger children.

Several observers wandered through Moneka in 1858 and wrote interesting descriptions. Charles Goodlander visited the place and thought it somewhat strange: "We . . . reached Moneka for dinner, a point some few miles north of the present Mound City. The dinner was not much of an improvement over that of Squireville, as it consisted mostly of vegetables. By the way, the people who settled this town were vegetarians and the women wore bloomer costumes. About all the inhabitants were named Wattles."[61] British journalist James Redpath had come to Kansas out of an intense sympathy with the antislavery cause. He was enchanted with the little township of Moneka and its inhabitants:

> Moneka, in Linn County, on the Little Sugar Creek, is situated on one of the loveliest valleys in Kansas. The scenery is very beautiful, and the soil fertile. It was located in the winter of '56–57. There are now about 20 buildings on the town-site, including one of the best-kept hotels in Southern Kansas: several stores, a blacksmith and wagon shop, and a large two-storied building for school, church, and lecture hall. The best school outside of Leavenworth or Lawrence is located here; not only the primary branches, but all studies necessary for a finished education, are taught. A large literary society is also organized, and holds regular meetings. Lectures are delivered during the winter by John O. Wattles, Esq., and others. From a knowledge of the people of this settlement, the writer knows of no more refined and intelligent community in Kansas.[62]

Life in Moneka might have been as idyllic as John Wattles had ever hoped a utopian community could be, had it not been situated in the middle of Bleeding Kansas. The violence that had plagued Lawrence and its vicinity the previous two years now followed the Wattleses to Linn County. Since 1856, the southern counties of Linn and Bourbon had been in "a state of seething turbulence," as Richard Hinton observed.[63] Several Blue Lodges, as the proslavery secret groups were called, routinely sent men to intimidate and drive out free-state settlers. Free-state settlers gathered to retaliate in like manner. The usual disputes over land claims complicated these struggles. By the winter of 1857–1858 both sides had marshaled fierce militias that swept the countryside, devastating homesteads and chasing whole families out of the territory. The governor sent federal troops to try to quiet the situation, but instead some became partisans in the fight, attacking free-state settlers.[64] The chaos reminded Augustus Wattles of "old times in Lawrence." In April he wrote to a friend describing an execution-style killing of a free-state man carrying messages from Captain James Montgomery to the men in Moneka. The proslavery guerrillas came armed to the Moneka Hotel and threatened to shoot a judge who tried to settle them down. Before moving on, they threatened to burn the entire town. All the mayhem was causing an exodus of free-state settlers. "Nearly all of the settlers have left the Little Osage," according to Augustus:

> There is not an inhabitant of Sprattsville left. I met at Moneka freight wagons of movers with 30 yoke of oxen going north who left the vicinity of Mapleton. They were free State men. They tell the most distressing tales. Today I have seen several pro slavery families moving from the Marmaton & Little Osage. They tell tales equally harrowing—property stolen or destroyed—families violently removed—men shot down in cold blood—and the whole county in anarchy & blood. No man obeys the laws & but few appeal to them.[65]

The Wattles families had no assurance they would be spared a violent attempt to eject them from the territory, but unlike many other families, they remained determined to stay in Moneka.

The pinnacle of violence in the disturbances of 1858 came in May, when a proslavery party led by Charles A. Hamilton captured eleven free-state men, lined them up in a ravine on the Marais des Cygnes River, and shot them. Five of the victims lay dead, while the others, wounded, lived to tell the story and identify the perpetrators. Very little justice was to be found in Bleeding Kansas, however, and Hamilton was never arrested for the crime. He later became a colonel in the Confederate Army. The Marais des Cygnes Massacre outraged the free-state people of Kansas and shocked newspaper readers across the North. Naturally, John Brown was as outraged as anyone. Since leaving Kansas in September 1856, Brown had spent most of his time drumming up support among sympathetic donors in the Northeast. But support for what? It is not clear when Brown first devised his plan to attack Harpers Ferry and to incite a slave insurrection, nor is it certain who knew of this plan. It is quite possible anyone who gave financial support to John Brown in the period of 1857–1858 thought he or she was supporting the free-state cause in Kansas because Brown was using his Kansas exploits as the basis of appeal for funds. Some have even suggested Brown only returned to Kansas in 1858 to convince observers that his only objective was a free Kansas and not the more grandiose and inflammatory Southern plan.[66]

Brown arrived back in Kansas in June 1858 and found Lawrence and Topeka had settled down considerably from two years before. Farther south, however, passions were inflamed following the massacre on the Marais des Cygnes River. Homesteaders fled their farms, and raiders swept the countryside looting the easy pickings. Augustus Wattles apparently thought John Brown might do them some good in this hour of tension, and he invited the captain to come to Linn County.[67] Augustus later explained to the Senate committee that investigated Harpers Ferry what Brown's role had meant to the free-state citizenry. In a panic following the massacre and fearing further attack from proslavery marauders crossing the Missouri-Kansas line, they had organized to guard the border:

> We all assembled; some 200 men more or less, I think, assembled on the line and detailed a company to stand guard all the time; to ride up and down the line and keep watch of this body of men and see that they did not break in. It happened in May, just at the time people should be plowing and planting, and it took citizens away from their work. Brown came in at this time and wanted to know if he could be of any service in guarding the line. I told him that he could, and we should be very glad to have him. We had sent to Governor Denver for arms, and to come down there; and the governor had promised to assist us. At my suggestion, a paper was drawn up, which Brown signed, and all the men who went into his company to guard the line signed, stipulating that he should not go into Missouri on any provocation whatever, and that no man in Kansas should be disturbed for his political opinions. I signed that also, and all the citizens to whom it was presented, who lived along the border, signed it.[68]

Brown assured Wattles he had come to Linn County for defensive purposes only and to demonstrate that the free-staters would not be intimidated. To make a further symbolic point, Brown chose to locate on the very spot where the Marais des Cygnes Massacre had occurred just weeks before. Constructing a fortified building, he gathered his loyal followers around him and took in four of the survivors of Hamilton's atrocity. Brown drew up a contract to organize the group into a military corps called Shubel

Morgan's Company. The fifteen men who signed the Articles of Agreement, including Augustus Wattles, agreed to abide by strict rules of conduct. They would maintain "a gentlemanly and respectful deportment" and avoid "all profane or indecent language." No one would drink intoxicating beverages or "leave camp without leave of the Commander." They would distribute all property equally among the members, "promptly and properly" punish "acts of petty and other thefts," and contribute equally to the labor needed in camp. "All prisoners who shall properly demean themselves shall be treated with kindness and respect, and shall be punished for crime only after trial and conviction being allowed a hearing in defense."[69] The Articles of Agreement reflected Brown's sense of discipline and righteous comportment but suggest little as to the purpose of the company. Company members were bound to give "implicit obedience" to the commander, but there is nothing to indicate whether defensive or offensive measures were to be pursued. In fact, very little came of Shubel Morgan's Company because Brown fell ill with one of his recurring bouts of ague, which kept him inactive through much of August and September. For two weeks of this period Brown stayed with the Wattles family in Moneka, nursed by Augustus, Susan, Sarah, Emma, and Mary Ann.[70]

That fall and early winter John Brown linked up with James Montgomery, a passionate antislavery man with a penchant for bold military ventures. Montgomery had ruthlessly defended the interests of free-state settlers in southern Kansas and could muster an imposing militia force when necessary. Brown respected him as a man of action, and the two collaborated in building a fort on the Little Sugar Creek from which they sallied forth to attack Fort Scott and other proslavery enclaves.[71] Though these actions angered some in the free-state camp, Montgomery remained a close ally of Augustus Wattles. Like Brown, Montgomery valued Augustus's counsel even when the latter advocated more peaceable measures.

Throughout this sojourn in Kansas, Brown continued to plan and recruit for his raid on Harpers Ferry. He remained secretive about the plan, however, informing only select associates about the proposal. While visiting Brown at this time, abolitionist reporter Richard Hinton was told of the scheme by John Henri Kagi, one of Brown's most loyal companions. Both Hinton and Kagi frequently visited the Wattleses, but they, apparently, never told the family about the Harpers Ferry plan. Or so Augustus claimed when called before the Senate committee that investigated the Harpers Ferry attack. Yet all observers attest to the great regard John Brown and Augustus Wattles held for each other. In his memoirs Hinton writes that of all Brown's Kansas friends, the Wattleses occupied a special place.

> There were no doubters, cowards, or trimmers among John Brown's Kansas friends when the war issues finally came. But the personal regard and friendship of the two Wattles families, at Moneka, Levin [sic] County, with the unbending Puritan leader, was an incident almost idyllic in character. Their homes were always open to him and his men, while the Captain was loved by the charming group of girls who made them so attractive.[72]

Trusting Augustus to keep his secret, John Brown probably did tell him about the Harpers Ferry raid and might even have asked him to go along on the venture. Wattles kept the secret, and even when asked by congressional investigators, he did not admit to prior knowledge of it. Wattles did explain that he had philosophical differences with Brown on the question of using violence to eradicate slavery. He told the Senate committee he and Brown had discussed "the principles of abolition":

> I have heard him give sentiments like these . . . "I have been at your abolition meetings, mentioning in Massachusetts and Ohio, and your scheme is perfectly futile; you would not release five slaves in a century; peaceful emancipation is impossible; the thing has gone beyond that point." I recollect this distinctly from the ridicule which he attached to a remark I made. I said that a forcible emancipation was worse than slavery. He said that his plan was to put arms in the hands of the slaves; give them their choice, stand behind them so as to protect them in a free choice . . . and if they chose to go into slavery, let them stay in it. I said it was an impossibility to give them arms, referring to the expense and difficulty of furnishing them. He said he had a plan for an arm for them better than a musket—a long pike. What he said as to emancipation in that way, I supposed was a matter of opinion, which I had no idea had anything practical connected with it.[73]

Brown had tested Augustus's loyalty on many occasions, from the aftermath of the Pottawatomie Massacre, when he expected Wattles to believe in his innocence, to entrusting his life and health to the care of the Wattles family. One last time in Kansas, John Brown called upon the Wattleses for assistance, putting the entire family at risk. In December, Brown staged a dramatic raid into Missouri in which he and his men "liberated" eleven slaves and murdered a slave owner. Fleeing with the freed slaves and assorted contraband taken from the raided plantations, Brown sought refuge with the Wattleses in Linn County, where as a matter of course they were accommodated. James Montgomery, staying with the Wattleses that night, was awakened by the noise of the freed slaves "as they warmed around the stove while Mrs. Wattles was getting supper." Montgomery "put his head down the stairway and said, 'How is this, Captain Brown? Whom have you here?' Brown exultantly waved his hat around in a circle, 'Allow me to introduce to you a *part* of my family. Observe, I have carried the war into Africa.'"[74]

The Wattleses, no strangers to the peril of hiding runaway slaves, helped Brown send the fugitives along to other stations on the Underground Railroad, and then over the next month continued to harbor Brown from time to time, even though there was a $3,000 reward for his arrest. The Wattleses refused to hand him over to authorities, even though some in the free-state faction wanted to do so. Augustus called the parties together and remonstrated with Brown, urging him to see that his actions had imperiled the tentative peace that prevailed in the region. He drew up a written agreement calling for "all criminal proceedings for any action connected with politics to be quashed" and pledging that "all parties shall in good faith discontinue acts of robbery, theft, or violence of any kind—on account of 'political differences.'" The document was signed by Augustus Wattles, John Brown, James Montgomery, and others. Its principles were confirmed a month later in a law signed by the governor.[75] In the meantime Brown promised Wattles he "would remove the seat of the trouble elsewhere."[76]

Brown did leave Kansas for good soon afterward but not before he sat down at a desk in the Wattles home and wrote out a letter to the New York *Tribune*. In his "Parallels" John Brown drew a comparison between the Marais des Cygnes Massacre and his raid into Missouri to free eleven slaves. He pointed out that eleven men were murdered simply for the crime of being free-state men, and yet "what action has ever, since the occurrence in May last, been taken by either the President of the United States, the Governor of Missouri, the Governor of Kansas, or any of their tools, or by any pro-slavery or administration man, to ferret out and punish the perpetrators of this crime?" Yet when "eleven persons are forcibly restored to their natural and inalienable rights, with but one man killed and all 'hell is stirred from beneath.'"[77] Brown had made his point, but he then exited Kansas, leaving chaos in his wake. While Brown escorted the freed Missouri slaves to safety in Canada, the Wattles family braced for more violence. Augustus was warned he had been targeted for assassination or expulsion by a posse organized to drive free-state men from Linn County. He recalled,

> This man had come in there to take charge of the posse which was raised to arrest certain men in the county, or to kill them or drive them out, and that my name was on the list, perhaps the first on the list; and other prominent men, old settlers there were on the same list; and this man who told me advised me to leave the county, as they were every day threatening to come over and kill me. . . . I took no measures against them but to go up and see Governor Medary. He said this posse was got without his consent, . . . and he would put a stop to it.[78]

Augustus faced these dangers with equanimity and resolve and demanded the same of his family. He justified defense of John Brown as part of the great struggle to end slavery, even if the two disagreed on the appropriate means to do so. Even when Brown's full plan to free the slaves was revealed in the fated attack on Harpers Ferry, Augustus Wattles stood by the man and the cause. In the aftermath of Brown's October 1859 raid on Harpers Ferry, Augustus joined a group of would-be rescuers in November 1859 and traveled as far as Hagerstown, Maryland, in an attempt to rescue John Brown from jail in Virginia. The expedition returned to Kansas after learning Brown did not want to be rescued.[79] In February 1860, Augustus was called to Washington, DC, to appear before the Senate committee investigating the Harpers Ferry raid. He had been summoned because a letter from him had been found in John Brown's possession after the latter's arrest. Wattles acknowledged his relationship with Brown and disavowed any prior knowledge of the Harpers Ferry raid but refused to condemn his old ally.[80] A little more than a year later the nation would plunge into war, spurred along by Brown's precipitous action.

The Kansas experience had a profound effect on the Wattles family. The family identity was molded by the prelude of their midwestern lives but forged in the fires of the Kansas conflict. The second generation never forgot they were Kansas pioneers who had fought for free-state status and enabled John Brown to march forward in his daring campaign to end the scourge of slavery. These memories shaped the family's sense of itself for generations to come. The Wattles family offers us a narrative of a family shaped by extraordinary circumstances. Wattles women became strong, independent, and engaged citizens, and Wattles men, although never abandoning some traditional ideas about what women should do to nurture the family, nevertheless stood by their strong women. Migration into new frontier areas helped them to appreciate these changes. By its members' conscious choices, this family both responded to circumstances and helped to change those circumstances. The identity its members forged as a family emerged as a result of these unique experiences.

SARAH:
THE MAKING OF A FEMINIST CONSCIOUSNESS

Awaiting execution in a Charleston, Virginia, jail in 1859, abolitionist John Brown reflected on the road he had taken to arrive at the federal arsenal at Harpers Ferry. Acutely aware of his own historical legacy, he presumptuously but correctly assumed that many of those who had helped him along the way would come to see their association with him as a great event in their lives. Brown wanted to acknowledge some of the debts he had incurred and repay them by enveloping those privileged individuals with a bit of his limelight. Writing to his wife, Mary, he recalled the care bestowed upon him by the Wattles family in Kansas, singling out the Wattleses' eldest daughter, Sarah. Brown wrote to Mary,

> I am most glad to have you meet with one of a family most beloved and never to be forgotten by me. I mean dear gentle Sarah Wattles. Many; & many a time has she, her Father, Brother, Sister, Uncle & Aunt; (like Angels of mercy) ministered to the wants of myself; & of my poor sons; both in sickness & in health. Only last year; I lay sick for a quite a number of Weeks with them, & was cared for by all; as though I had been a most affectionate Brother, or Father. Tell her, that I ask God to bless, & reward them all forever. . . . It may possibly be that Sarah would like to copy this letter, & send it to her home: if so, by all means let her do so.[1]

Mary Brown had met Sarah Wattles while making her way to Virginia to visit her husband in jail following his conviction for the raid on Harpers Ferry. Along the way she had been invited by an abolitionist friend, Rebecca Spring, to visit Raritan Bay, New Jersey, where the Springs had established a community of reformers, including Theodore Dwight Weld; his wife, Angelina Grimké Weld; and her sister Sarah Grimké, who ran Eagleswood School, the community's coeducational boarding school.[2] Among the Eagleswood students allowed to meet Mary Brown was young Sarah Wattles.

Sarah's association with John Brown as well as the Welds and Angelina's sister Sarah Grimké was a serendipitous and life-changing circumstance that reflected the importance of family networks in constructing identity. The Wattleses' network of abolitionist friends exposed Sarah to role models and opened her to horizons the average girl in the antebellum United States did not enjoy. Although it is a truism that family networks provide economic and social opportunities to children, the legacy given to Sarah Grimké Wattles by her parents and her parents' friends tilted her toward a feminist view of social justice and women's place in the world. Every family tries to transmit its values and worldview to the next generation through parenting practices and storytelling. To a certain extent, every family has a measure of control over these processes, and attempts to ward off the negative effects of circumstances beyond its control. Whom a family associates with professionally and socially is both a matter of choice and chance. The people who become role models in a young person's life often have close ties to the family and might even have been selected to take a special responsibility for a child through godparenthood. Parents' decisions about who will influence their children are certainly one of the most important means of transmitting ideas and values to the next generation.

Sarah Wattles had wonderful female role models as she grew up in Ohio and Kansas. First and foremost, of course, was her mother. Susan Lowe Wattles was an independent-minded and highly practical woman who taught school, campaigned against slavery and for women's rights, and ably shouldered the burdens of pioneer life. Sarah's aunt, Esther Whinery Wattles, was equally independent, capable, and intelligent. However, Sarah Wattles also had as a mentor and role model one of the leading feminists of the time, Sarah Grimké. This unique relationship reinforced in Sarah the values of spiritual integrity, social justice, and gender equity that she learned from her own family and from the progressive circle of friends her parents cultivated within the antislavery movement.

Sarah Wattles, the first child of Augustus and Susan Wattles, was born on December 7, 1837, in Mercer County, Ohio. One of the first decisions parents make in shaping the identity of a child is in naming her. For the first seven months of Sarah's life, she apparently had no middle name. Then on July 8, 1838, Susan announced in her journal, "We have this day added the name of Augusta to our dear baby, Sarah Augusta Wattles, dear, precious name; may she live to honor it by her usefulness."[3] She gave no further explanation for their decision to name their daughter after her father, nor can we surmise whose idea it was. However, it did not last, for on Sarah's first birthday her mother inserted in her journal, with no explanation, "We have concluded to call her Sarah Grimké Wattles."[4] Young Sarah might have lived a life worthy of her father's name, but now she was named after one of the leading feminists of the day.

Growing up in the isolated community in Mercer County, Sarah went to school and played with the children of the Wattleses' black neighbors. On a few occasions a black family came to live with the Wattleses for a time, and Sarah played with those children.[5] There was hardly a time in her childhood when she was not exposed to an integrated community. Her parents wanted her to have other diverse experiences as well. In the summer of 1847 Susan sent Sarah to live for ten weeks with the family of a German minister in New Bremen, Ohio, so that she could learn to speak German. Their residence was nine miles from the Wattles home, and because Augustus was traveling back East all that summer, Susan transported Sarah over to the minister's home and retrieved her once a week for a visit at home. Susan reported that Sarah "had many sad cries about being away from her home but on the whole she bore the separation heroically and learned very well."[6] For Sarah it was an opportunity to become fully immersed in speaking the German language, though it could not have been a pleasant experience. The minister and his wife would not allow her to play with other children because they would speak English with her. They forbade her from reading her own books in English, making her read exclusively in German, even before she could understand enough German to follow a children's story. However, she learned quickly to understand her teachers' spoken words, and soon she could recite the Lord's Prayer in German.[7] The experience gave her enough of a foundation in the language that she studied it further in later years and taught it. Perhaps the greatest lesson she might have learned, especially for a little girl not yet ten years old, was how to live independently away from her family. That seemed to be one of Susan Wattles's most important parental objectives, even though she found it excruciating to say good-bye to her children when they left home.

Susan and Augustus never had much economic capital to pass on to their children, but their social capital in the form of a circle of friends and associates was quite substantial. Both Susan and Augustus had traveled widely working for the antislavery cause, and both had been deeply involved in the personal networking intrinsic to the operation of antislavery organizations. They met people at meetings, stayed in people's homes as they traveled around, and corresponded widely with comrades across the North. As one of Theodore Weld's trusted agents, Augustus came to know Angelina Grimké, whom Weld married in 1838, and her sister Sarah Grimké. Susan and Augustus were plugged in to the network of evangelical, reform-minded activists in the North, and these associations opened doors for their children, though not by any deliberate planning. Simply naming their oldest child after Sarah Grimké did not ensure the younger Sarah would turn out like her namesake and certainly did not guarantee the elder Sarah would take an interest in the child or have an opportunity to act as an influence in her life. However, somehow it turned out Sarah Grimké did take an interest and had an opportunity to exert a lasting impact on Sarah Grimké Wattles.

Sarah Grimké had been born in Charleston, South Carolina, in 1792 to a distinguished slaveholding family. As a young girl she yearned for education and secretly read her father's law books but found her ambitions thwarted by a society that allowed only the option of marriage for women of her class. She and her youngest sister, Angelina, detested slavery and moved to Philadelphia to escape life in a society that perpetuated it. By the mid-1830s the sisters felt called to speak out against slavery in ways that astonished and dismayed some of their kindred abolitionists, not to mention the anger it provoked in South Carolina. Angelina published her forceful *Appeal to the Christian Women of the Southern States* in 1836 and soon thereafter began speaking to audiences of both men and women, causing a scandal that rocked the abolitionist movement and brought down upon them the scorn and condemnation of many influential clergy. Sarah lacked the self-confidence to be an effective public speaker but nevertheless wrote many significant essays on abolition and women's rights. After Angelina's marriage to Theodore Dwight Weld, the two sisters mostly retired from public life but with Theodore operated several boarding schools in New Jersey.[8]

It is not clear on what occasion either Augustus or Susan Wattles first met Sarah Grimké in person. If Augustus attended the Agents' Convention of the American Anti-Slavery Society (AASS) in New York in November 1836, then he would have become acquainted with both Sarah and Angelina Grimké, the only women attending this training session for agents. Although there is much circumstantial evidence to suggest Augustus made it to this meeting, there is no positive proof he did.[9] Augustus was invited to the wedding of Angelina Grimké and Theodore Dwight Weld in 1838, and although he was unable to attend, he wrote to Angelina, assuring her, "In all that thou hast written on the rights of woman, etc., my heart and my head approve it well. My wife also has a perfect sympathy with them and joins me in wishing you, blessed ones, happiness and peace on your pilgrimage."[10] The Wattleses were thus aware of both the activities and the published ideas of the Grimké sisters, among the most radical feminist statements of the day. Apparently this is why, on their daughter's first birthday in December 1838, they added Grimké as her middle name.

The surviving correspondence between Sarah Grimké and the Wattleses dates only from 1850, so we have no way of knowing what contact, if any, they had with each other before that date. From 1850 on, however, numerous letters exist to reveal a deep friendship between Sarah Grimké and Augustus, a great regard for Susan on Sarah's part, and a close relationship between Grimké and young Sarah Grimké Wattles. This bond seems to have begun when Sarah Wattles was visiting her uncle and aunt in Newark, New Jersey, in 1850. David Ripley, a prosperous businessperson in Newark, New Jersey, had married Augustus Wattles's sister, Mary Ann. In 1850 Sarah Thomas Wattles, the mother of Augustus and Mary Ann, also lived with the Ripleys. Sarah Grimké Wattles, twelve at the time, spent several months with the Ripleys in the spring and summer of 1850. It is unlikely the family allowed a twelve-year-old to travel unaccompanied from Ohio to New Jersey, so probably one or both of her parents had come east with her to visit the relatives in Newark. The Grimké-Welds had just moved to a farm near Belleville, New Jersey, less than ten miles away from Newark, where they started a boarding school. Surely Augustus would have gone to nearby Belleville to visit his old comrade, Theodore Dwight Weld, where he would also have met Angelina and Sarah Grimké, or perhaps the Grimké-Welds came over to Newark. In any case Sarah Wattles stayed on for a protracted visit, during which time she fell ill for more than a month, and Sarah Grimké came to visit her during that illness. Both Sarahs wrote to the Wattleses back in Ohio about these visits. The elder Sarah tried to persuade the Wattleses to allow their daughter to come to live with the Grimké-Welds and to attend their school, telling Augustus and Susan, "If Sarah comes to us we shall have a loadstone to attract you all."[11] Although Sarah Wattles returned to her family soon after this, Grimké did not abandon her efforts to bring the younger Sarah to be with her in New Jersey. Eventually Sarah Wattles did go east again to live with the Grimké-Welds and study with them at their school, but in the intervening years Sarah Grimké corresponded frequently with Sarah Wattles and her parents.

Although only Grimké's side of the correspondence has survived, we can still sense the influence she had on the Wattleses and their children, especially young Sarah. Augustus and Susan eagerly read everything the Grimké sisters wrote, including Sarah's *Letters on the Equality of the Sexes*, published in 1838, which Gerda Lerner has called "the first comprehensive feminist argument presented by an American woman."[12] In the book Grimké forcibly argued for the right of women to enjoy the same educational and vocational outlets men did. Reflecting her own resentment at being denied these opportunities, Grimké attacked the biblical basis for the belief in male superiority, maintaining instead that the Bible offered ample support for the equality of the sexes.[13] Women should be able to pursue any vocation they chose, she thought, although she did believe in the cult of domesticity, which viewed the home as the particular province of women. Because of their natural moral superiority, women should raise children and keep the home as a refuge for their husbands. Their influence should not stop there, however, and indeed, because the moral character of women superseded that of men, Grimké believed, they should operate in the public sphere as well. In these beliefs Grimké reflected the dominant attitude of most nineteenth-century feminists. She never rejected marriage as the most desirable state for women, but she believed women should be free to choose their partners and should enjoy equality and dignity within marriage. She especially deplored the sexual abuse of women within marriage, including the physical toll on women's health incurred from too many pregnancies, and condemned coverture laws, which gave husbands control over their wives' property.[14]

Sarah Grimké's feminism derived in large measure from her own anger and frustration at being denied the same opportunities her brothers enjoyed. She valued a sympathetic male ally, however, as she showed in her correspondence with Augustus Wattles. Sarah often expressed deeply heartfelt sentiments about her own life and aspirations, as she did in 1852 when she wrote to him lamenting that she had not accomplished more in her life but ascribing it to the limitations placed on women, especially the lack of educational opportunities. "In early youth I was a worldling," she told him,

> but I enjoyed not its frivolities [for] there was a sting in them which poisoned them—I was naturally independent, longed for an education that would elevate me above the low pursuits of sense, but I was a girl & altho' well educated as such, yet the powers of my mind were not called into exercise—I looked with longing eyes on my brother's superior advantages & wondered why the sinful fact of being a girl, should shut me up to the necessity of being a doll a coquette a fashionable fool.[15]

Throughout her correspondence with the Wattleses, Grimké emphasized the importance of education for girls and advocated in particular for young Sarah. When the Wattleses moved to Indiana in the summer of 1853, they again had to make their own schools with Susan as headmistress. Sarah probably did her first teaching during this brief period in which the family lived in Indiana. Susan not only provided most of the education for her children but also she taught them to teach. Sarah, Emma, and Mary Ann all taught school, helping younger siblings and other children. Their example had been their own parents, who largely educated their children at home; started schools in Mercer County, Ohio; and had met while teaching at black schools in Cincinnati. Wherever they went, the Wattleses taught their own children and any other nearby children needing instruction. They also tried to provide ample reading materials for the entire family by subscribing to magazines and newspapers. It was, indeed, a family tradition to send reading materials and subscriptions to family members and friends, wherever they were. Sarah's correspondence with Sarah Grimké added another element of mentorship to the younger woman's development. Grimké offered a uniquely feminist perspective on everything from marriage to spirituality.

Sarah Grimké steered her young protégé toward a teaching vocation. With the "tenderest love and interest for thee," the elder Sarah wrote young Wattles in November 1853, "I rejoice to find that you are keeping your eye steadily on the important work of teaching." Grimké, worried about Wattles's health as she attacked a heavy reading program, warned her to be "careful not to overtask your self body or mind."[16] As the Wattleses settled in to their new circumstances in Indiana, Sarah became the primary instructor for her younger sisters, Emma and Mary Ann, and might even have taught a neighborhood school of some sort. In May 1854, Grimké expressed concern that Sarah might try to teach a school term just to earn some money, despite having recently recovered from the measles. "I feel however very doubtful about your keeping school this summer," she counseled,

> unless you feel strong & quite up to the undertaking. You need time to regain your strength, time to go on with your own improvement. Do not undertake it merely to make money enough to bring you to me— our Father will provide for that—School keeping, to be well done, to yield satisfaction to the teacher & improvement to the pupils, must be a spontaneity of the soul, I believe that desire to do this blessed work is a spontaneity of your soul, the only question is one of time & fitness—I only drop these hints dear Sarah. Your parents & yourself must judge.[17]

In the spring of 1855 the Wattleses moved to Kansas to work for the free-state cause. Sarah Grimké became a source of encouragement and inspiration, writing often to Augustus as he wrestled with the challenges of responding to the violence of the Kansas situation. She also collected and sent supplies such as clothing for the family and other free-state settlers. She continued a practice she had begun while the Wattleses were still in Indiana of sending reading material for the family. When *Aurora Leigh*, the epic novel by Elizabeth Barrett Browning, was published in 1856, Grimké wanted Sarah to read it because it was the "first epic written by a woman, . . . a grand effort of intellect & heart. Such portraitures of woman as she may be, as she will be, as some few of us now are, cannot fail to stir up within us the elements of progress & carry us forever on the tide of improvement."[18] She also paid for subscriptions for the *Una* and the *Lily*, and the companion version for girls, the *Little Pilgrim,* to be sent to the Wattleses. The *Una,* founded in 1853 by Paulina Kellogg Wright, was the first feminist periodical published by women in the United States.[19] The *Lily* was a temperance and women's rights periodical founded by Amelia Bloomer and later sold to Mary Birdsall, an old friend of Susan Wattles's from Richmond, Indiana.[20] These periodicals, in which they could read articles and letters from Elizabeth Cady Stanton, Susan B. Anthony, Lucy Stone, and others, kept the Wattles women informed on the latest developments in the small but important network of women's rights advocates. One other noteworthy gift Sarah Grimké bestowed might have been a factor in Sarah Wattles's ultimate choice of vocation. In 1856 Grimké's good friend Harriot Kezia Hunt published her autobiography, *Glances and Glimpses; Or Fifty Years' Social, Including Twenty Years' Professional Life,* which discussed her career as a physician. Grimké sent a copy to the Wattleses and was highly gratified that both Sarah and her mother read and appreciated the book. "You would love my friend Dr. Hunt if you knew her," she wrote to Sarah, continuing, "She is a true, noble, loving spirit." Grimké was pleased to have introduced Susan and Sarah to Hunt's book, saying she hoped "it may awaken in mothers more of the maternal feeling and lead them as well as fathers to see what homes ought to be and how they must labor to make them the dwellings of love & peace." She thought Susan especially could "appreciate its high moral & love tone."[21]

Reading Hunt's autobiography would have reinforced the feminist messages the Wattles women had already read in the Grimké sisters' own writing. Hunt used her sharp wit to play with sacred notions, as when she declared,

> I say nothing of the public condition of women in relation to government. Faneuil Hall was not our Cradle of Liberty. We had no hand in the rocking. If we had had, perhaps the child would have turned out better. But men rocked that cradle! There as everywhere, we have no civil rights, but those which are dependent on the will of our legislators doled out to us by ignorance, caprice, or whim.[22]

Hunt's autobiography made a strong case for educating girls and allowing women to pursue occupations beyond the household. Some of her most forceful language was reserved for denouncing the evils that resulted from the limitations facing married women. Too often, she said, she had seen families fall into ruin when the husband was disabled or disinclined to meet his responsibilities and the wife unable to provide because she had not been educated for anything but domestic duties. "How many widows have lost their home,—" she asked, "how many fatherless children have been thrown upon the world,—when all this distress might have been avoided had the wife and mother known, as every woman should know, the business relations of her husband, and been prepared for action!"[23]

The Wattles family was predisposed to act upon this advice. In territorial Kansas women as well as men filed for land claims. This was a topic the family had probably mulled over before because Esther and John Wattles had placed land in Esther's name and publicly discussed their rationale for doing so. When Augustus's family decided to move to Linn County in the spring of 1857, Sarah Wattles filed for a land claim. By 1862 she proved up on the land, even though other family members lived on the land while Sarah went east for school.[24] Sarah adored her Uncle John and enthusiastically followed his lead as he inspired family and neighbors to form a women's rights organization. On February 2, 1858, John gave an address in Moneka on women's rights. The women and men in his audience decided on the spot to form the Moneka Woman's Rights Association, the object of which was "to secure to woman her natural rights and to advance her educational interests." Esther Wattles was elected vice president, and Sarah was chosen secretary. Also signing the organizational charter were Susan E. Wattles and her daughter Emma as well as Emma's future husband, O. E. Morse.[25]

Hearkening back to her work as corresponding secretary for antislavery societies in Ohio, Susan Wattles took up her pen and began to write letters. One of the first people she contacted on behalf of the new society was Clarina I. H. Nichols. Nichols had already established herself as a forceful advocate of women's rights before she migrated to Kansas in 1854. She had published a newspaper in Brattleboro, Vermont, in which she promoted women's rights, abolitionism, prohibition, and Fourierism.[26] Having divorced an abusive husband and experienced the struggles of single motherhood, Nichols focused on issues relating to the legal and property rights of married women. She had endorsed women's suffrage in 1849, defending it in the language of domestic feminism.[27] For Nichols as it was for the Wattleses, the opening of Kansas to settlers came as an opportunity to construct a more perfect society, one without slavery but with expanded rights for women. Nichols moved to Kansas in October 1854, settling first in Lawrence, where she corresponded with eastern newspapers, touting the prospects of the new territory and the perseverance of its free-state settlers, especially the women. In early 1857 Nichols and her family settled in Wyandotte County, where she edited a free-state newspaper, the Quindaro *Chindowan*.[28]

Nichols provided experienced counsel to the Moneka group, but she found in Susan Wattles a collaborator who displayed the expertise gained through years of laboring in antislavery organizations. Susan kept Clarina informed of the group's continuing discussions but also wrote letters to Wendell Phillips, Susan B. Anthony, and other eastern sources for funds to aid Nichols's campaign to include women's suffrage in the new Kansas Constitution.[29] Like the Wattleses, Nichols saw the creation of a new state in Kansas as an opportunity to realize the goal of women's rights. She believed

> that I could accomplish more for woman, even the women of the old States, and with less effort, in the new state of Kansas, than I could in conservative old Vermont, whose prejudices were so much stronger than its convictions, that justice to women must stand a criminal trial in every Court of the State to win, and then pay the costs. . . . I went to work for a Government of "equality, liberty, and fraternity," in the State to be.[30]

By establishing a women's rights organization and working for inclusion of women's rights in the new state constitution, the Wattleses and Nichols proclaimed their belief that women as well as men had the right to participate in American life. By this action, they declared women citizens, and in doing so, they joined a very small but growing number of Americans who had begun to believe women should enjoy full citizenship. Challenging the assumption that women could not be citizens was no small accomplishment. Lori Ginzberg has argued that the actions of a very ordinary group of women in upstate New York issued a similar challenge. In 1846 these women signed a petition demanding full and equal rights for women, and by doing so they questioned the dominant message that women's citizenship was *unthinkable*.[31] The activities of the Wattles families suggest that other ordinary people, having absorbed the messages of evangelical Christianity, abolitionism, and perfectionism, felt it was possible to challenge quite a number of established assumptions. Furthermore, and quite significantly, they believed that by passing the new assumptions to the next generation, they would bring about real and permanent change.

Sarah received much positive reinforcement for feminist views from her own family and from Sarah Grimké, and territorial Kansas provided many opportunities for practical training in meeting dire emergencies. No woman in Kansas could expect to tend only to her own domestic circle and ignore the turbulent conflict swirling all around her. The Wattles women had no intention of remaining aloof from this fight. Through the tumultuous years of Bleeding Kansas, the Wattles house served as a shelter and medic station for the free-state side. For months at a time the wounded or homeless could be found in the Wattles homestead, ministered to by Susan, Augustus, or the other two girls. One visitor in particular always signaled a particular danger, though it did not prevent the Wattles from welcoming and sheltering him. John Brown showed up at the Wattleses' place near Lawrence during the troubled aftermath of the Battle of Osawatomie in 1856, and the Wattleses helped some Brown family members to get out of the territory. In 1858 Brown spent many weeks recovering from illness at the Wattles home in Linn County with Sarah and the other girls nursing him. In December of 1858, John Brown sought refuge at the Wattles house for the eleven slaves he had just liberated in a bold raid into Missouri. After sending the freed fugitives on to another safe house, Brown stayed, sick and nursed again by the Wattles family, writing his "Parallels" at Augustus's desk. It is a measure of the Wattleses' devotion to abolition that they stayed in Kansas even as their children were exposed to such dangers. They well knew the risks of this choice as well as the costs of living on the frontier. They worried most of all about depriving their children of educational opportunities. They had provided as much schooling as they could themselves and had joined with other families to form schools and hire teachers. However, they were committed to providing their daughters higher education, if at all possible. Although it was beyond their own economic means to send Sarah east to attend school, they were able to do so with the help of their friends.

From the start of their relationship Sarah Grimké had urged Sarah Wattles to come to New Jersey to join the Grimké-Weld household and attend their school. Grimké hoped she would be able to help young Sarah with the costs of her education, and many times she expressed confidence that when the time came, God would somehow provide her the means to do so. That time finally came in early 1859, when Susan Wattles sent Grimké word that Sarah would be able to come east to attend Eagleswood School. In her reply to "My dear Susan and precious Sarah," Grimké "rejoiced at the prospect of having you here" and was pleased to be able to offer some financial assistance. "It has," she said "been one of my dearest wishes to give you as good an education as money could purchase."[32] Grimké's efforts on behalf of Sarah Wattles remind us that young women simply could not take education for granted in the mid-nineteenth century. Someone had to make a deliberate commitment—a conscious decision—to follow through on educating girls. In Sarah Wattles's case she benefited not just from her parents' commitment but also from that of a significant friend of the family.

It was also a sign of her family's commitment to female independence and capability that Sarah Wattles traveled alone across the country to attend Eagleswood School. Her account of her journey reveals the rigors of travel before the Civil War, when railroad gauges had not yet been standardized, ferries carried railcars one-by-one across rivers, and steamboat travel still intermittently supplemented rail service.[33] To get from Kansas to New Jersey, Sarah first went by boat and rail to Cincinnati, where she stayed with family for a few weeks. From Cincinnati she "came through Columbus & Steubenville, changed cars at Newark, O., and again at Pittsburg at eight and a half P.M., breakfasted at Harrisburg at five minutes past six, left the cars at Philadelphia at ten [and] went up the river about eight miles on a boat to take the Camden & Amboy R. R. and arrived at N.Y. at three o'clock." Although Sarah had wanted to get off at Newark, New Jersey, the conductor would not release her baggage until the train arrived in New York, so she had to go into New York, collect her luggage, and take the same train back to Newark. Along the way the other passengers refused to open the train windows despite overwhelming stuffiness, so she could barely keep any food down. Still, she was pleased with her trip, saying "I have had no trouble at all coming here alone—everyone with whom I have had contact was very kind to me. We came thro' from Cincinnati to N.Y. in thirty hours, the fare is $20. This included the omnibus and boat at Philadelphia, and ferry at N.Y. in fact everything except meals."[34] Finally upon arrival in New Jersey, Sarah was warmly embraced by her uncle and aunt,

David and Mary Ann Ripley, and her grandmother, Sarah Wattles, who lived with the Ripleys in Newark. This would be her home-away-from-home while she attended Eagleswood School in nearby Perth Amboy.

The Grimké-Welds had been operating Eagleswood School since 1854, when Theodore had been invited to become headmaster of the school at the Raritan Bay Union, one of the numerous utopian experiments that sprang up in the antebellum United States. Unfortunately, this one met the same fate as those John and Esther Wattles had joined. The Raritan Bay Union had been founded by Marcus and Rebecca Spring, veterans of another failed Fourierist phalanx, and about thirty kindred association-ists who had purchased 270 acres on Raritan Bay near Perth Amboy, New Jersey.[35] Some of the residents failed to hold up their share of the respon-sibility, and as Carol Berkin points out, the association "was not radi-cal enough to challenge traditional divisions of labor between men and women," so the domestic burden on Angelina and Sarah only increased.[36] The school itself, under Theodore Weld's guidance, might have been more radical than the utopian community that spawned it. The boarding school was housed in one wing of a large, three-story stone building; here the Grimké-Welds settled into a six-room apartment and began to shape their innovative school, which they promised would "combine the advantages of home nurture, in physical, mental, and moral training, with instruction in Literature, Science, and Art." Theodore implemented some of the most radical educational theories of his time, starting with the idea of teaching girls and boys together, a principle prominently explained in the school's brochure: "Well assured that, under a wise and careful supervision, the education of the sexes *together,* is most favorable to purity and simplicity of character, propriety of demeanor, attention to personal habits, refine-ment of feeling and manners, and the symmetrical development of the whole mind; we propose to receive as pupils, children and youth of both sexes: thus instituting our educational processes upon the basis of God's model school—the family."[37]

Theodore governed the school as principal, with Angelina teaching history and Sarah French, but all three took on many more tasks than just instruction. Seeing to the students' moral development required constant vigilance and gentle persuasion. Bad habits were simply not to be toler-ated—and were enumerated in the school rules: "Profaneness, impure language, indecent actions, reckless violence, impracticable temper, the use of tobacco, opium, or hasheesh, in any form or of intoxicating drinks as a beverage" could lead to expulsion.[38] The Eagleswood schoolteachers were largely fortunate in their students, mostly recruited from abolitionist and other reformer families. Misbehavior was kept to a minimum, and the most noteworthy rebellion was a student protest against the vegetarian Grahamite diet the Grimké-Welds initially offered. A typical meal might consist of "rice and asparagus, potatoes, mush and Indian bread."[39] According to Sarah Grimké, the uproar had begun with just a few students so "seized with home-sickness—and the savory smells of broiled chickens, roast beef &c did so marvellously stir the animal appetites that they came near deserting in a body."[40] Even the Grimké-Welds eventually gave up vegetarianism and took to eating meat once a day, sparing any further student unrest.

Sarah Wattles could not have found Eagleswood more to her liking. As a mature young woman of twenty-one, she had waited too long and had come too close to missing out entirely on such an opportunity to quibble about rules of behavior. She relished the experience. She arrived at Perth Amboy in time to attend the spring term of 1859, which began May 12 and lasted through July 22.[41] Her arrival caused somewhat of a stir among the other students, as the only classmate to hail from Kansas and an eyewitness to the great, bloody struggle being fought there. Teachers and students at Eagleswood had been following events in Kansas, even taking up donations so they could send boxes of clothing to the suffering free-state pioneers during the darkest days of the conflict.[42] When her father, Augustus, visited her at Eagleswood in July 1860, he was told by Cornelia Weld, Theodore's sister, that when the students learned a girl from Kansas was coming, "there was quite a buzz in the school." They all supposed that she would be "coarse & rude & ignorant etc. etc. etc." Sarah soon proved them wrong, however, becoming "a general favorite of all teachers, pupils, & parents." The students had voted to make Sarah the reader of all the young women's papers at the commencement ceremony, making her father very proud.[43]

Sarah's days at Eagleswood were busy and varied. "My days are divided thus," she wrote her mother:

First bell rings at six, when we get up. 2nd or breakfast bell rings at seven. If we are not at table within five minutes after the bell, we are marked tardy. At eight o'clock the 2nd school bell rings. We have one minute to go to our seats in. At ten the girls have recess & boys drill, from half past ten to eleven I recite geology or physical geography. From quarter past eleven to twelve Shakespeare. From twelve to ½ past girls drill. Then dinner. At two school begins. Two to quarter of three practice surveying. Quarter of three to quarter past, German, then till four drawing. An hour and a half study hour in the evening.[44]

Sarah hastened to assure her mother that such a busy schedule was not too taxing for her. "Now I expect you are aghast at the studies I have mentioned as mine, but you really need not be for they sound a great deal bigger than they are. I feel very well indeed, and at home & happy, consequently in good working condition."[45] Sarah, in fact, was having the time of her life. She took part in school plays, including the 1860 production of *The Rival Queens*.[46] She reveled in the new friends she made at Eagleswood, including Weld's own family. The atmosphere at Eagleswood encouraged communal activity and friendly interaction. It seemed as if every noteworthy reformer of the day came to visit Eagleswood at some time or another. Guest lectures were given by Ralph Waldo Emerson, Horace Greeley, Henry David Thoreau, Bronson Alcott, William Cullen Bryant, and William Henry Channing, among others. James Birney, the erstwhile Cincinnati editor and Liberty Party presidential candidate, came to live out his days at Raritan Bay. An old Lane Seminary comrade, Henry Stanton, and his wife, Elizabeth Cady Stanton, brought a son to attend the school.[47]

Although many of Eagleswood students came from antislavery families, none would have had the experience Sarah Wattles brought with her. She was, quite amazingly, a landowner in her own right. Her land claim in Kansas became the family homestead, but it was entered in Sarah's name, and she might well have been the only woman in all of New Jersey who could honestly say she owned a piece of land in Kansas. Sarah had "loved the freedom & wildness" of Kansas prairies and forests,[48] and she had known Indians still living a mostly traditional lifestyle on the western frontier. The most harrowing tales Sarah might have told, however, would have been about the conflicts of Bleeding Kansas. For nearly five years the Wattleses had lived in neighborhoods where armed gangs roamed, threatening to kill all the abolitionists and once even placing a bounty on her father's head. During the chaotic months following the Sack of Lawrence the Wattleses had harbored dozens of wounded or sick neighbors, while Sarah, her mother, and her sisters nursed them and fed them. Sarah had known John Brown and his sons. Sarah might have shared these stories in October 1859, when news of John Brown's Harper Ferry raid reached Perth Amboy, and everyone learned Brown had been captured while trying to start a slave insurrection.

The small community of abolitionists at Perth Amboy was hit hard by the Harpers Ferry incident. Rebecca Spring, one of the founders of the Raritan Bay Union, had corresponded with Brown, gone to visit him in jail, and helped arrange for Mary Brown to travel to Virginia to visit her husband in prison. After the execution of two of Brown's coconspirators, Aaron Stevens and Albert Hazlett, Spring arranged for their bodies to be brought to Eagleswood for burial.[49] Sarah Wattles had been one of the Eagleswood students who met with Mary Brown on her way to Virginia, and she would have attended the ceremonies for Hazlett and Stevens. She might even have met them in Kansas when they rode in to the Wattles home with John Brown's band and eleven newly freed slaves in December 1858.[50]

Sarah stayed in New Jersey until the fall of 1861, when the nation mobilized for war. Her aunt and uncle in Newark, who anxiously watched over her during her eastern sojourn, would not allow her to travel alone with the country in such unsettled conditions, and she had to wait to travel in the company of family friends. Biding her time in Perth Amboy while waiting for a suitable escort, Sarah met another Harpers Ferry coconspirator, Charles P. Tidd. Tidd had joined John Brown in late 1856 in Kansas and stuck with him through the raid in 1859. During the actual raid Tidd had cut telegraph lines and helped to liberate a number of local slaves, including those of Colonel Lewis Washington, great-nephew of George Washington and the most prominent planter in the area. Tidd then was left to supervise the just-freed blacks in guarding the schoolhouse that was to be the rendezvous point when the raiders extracted themselves from Harpers Ferry. When word came that Brown and his men were caught inside Harpers Ferry, Tidd and several others managed to escape through the mountains and eventually made their way north to safety, despite a $2,000 bounty on each of their heads.[51] Tidd sought refuge in Canada until the Civil War broke out, then, returned to the United States to join the military. At some point he visited Rebecca Spring at Perth Amboy and attended a reception where he met and flirted with Sarah Wattles. Rebecca Spring, writing to Mary Brown, said Sarah had "encouraged him, and he went away perfectly happy." Unfortunately, according to Rebecca Spring, Sarah's father had objected to the young man because he was not educated.[52]

Augustus might well have had other objections to Tidd, whom he had known in Kansas. Tidd accompanied Brown to southern Kansas following the Marais des Cygnes Massacre in May 1858. When Brown, using the alias Shubel Morgan, formed a militia company in the hopes of avenging the deaths of the Marais des Cygnes martyrs, Augustus and Tidd were both in camp and signed up for Shubel Morgan's Company on the same day. Augustus quickly lost interest in these martial activities and went home. Tidd, on the contrary, went on to ride with James Montgomery as he led his free-state gang in sacking Fort Scott, rescuing a free-state prisoner, killing a proslavery leader, and generally causing mayhem throughout the southern counties over the next few months. Montgomery's activities, aided and abetted by John Brown, caused Augustus to encourage Brown to leave the territory with his freed slaves in December. He would have considered Brown's men, Tidd among them, as part of the rabble stirring up trouble. No doubt Tidd would have looked and acted like quite a rough character under these circumstances. In the best of times Tidd was described by Richard Hinton, an admirer, as a "man of sturdy frame, about five feet nine inches in height, with a large, well-shaped head, set well forward on broad shoulders. . . . His perceptives were active and dominant. Of bilious, nervous temperament, his complexion was dark, eyes, beard, and head also, features strongly marked, expression grave, even stern. In temper, he was somewhat saturnine and dominant. A little overbearing, and fond of practical jokes and sharp teasing. This led to quarreling at times."[53] Tidd was not the sort of character Augustus wanted for his eldest daughter's suitor.

Sarah attempted a lofty defense of Tidd's character, writing her father to say

> I am not surprised by what you write, except that I thought, in this instance, the changed manner of life, the leaving of the dark and unclean for the pure and light indicated a character strong and upright in itself, one which had nobleness enough to strive with all its strength to escape from modes of life and associations, which from his youth up he had

been associated with—and so did not recognize till late that they were soul-killing and base.[54]

Still, she assured her worried father that "C. has no longer power to affect my happiness, nor to mar the harmony or wholeness of our home circle," but she did think she would maintain "a friendly occasional correspondence with him if he should return from the Burnside Expedition." She persisted, saying, "He is human you know, and he has loved me really, and has tried to be good.—but as he is not I can be only a friendly acquaintance to him, there can be no harm in that."[55] Less than a month later, Sarah learned that Tidd had died of typhus fever onboard ship at Roanoke Island. Rebecca Spring, who had transmitted the news, commented that Sarah's response "seemed very sad."[56]

When she learned of Tidd's fate in March 1862, Sarah had been home in Kansas for several months and was teaching school, but it was clear she had reached the turning point that many nineteenth-century women came to after having completed some advanced education. The loss of an exciting romantic prospect just reinforced for her the limited options she faced. An educated woman of Sarah's age living in rural Kansas could teach school, but beyond that she had little hope of other opportunities. Her old mentor, Sarah Grimké, longer accustomed to the frustration of limited options and the consolation of fate and duty, wrote to bolster Sarah's spirits, saying,

> I know thou wouldst keenly feel thy separation from the many at Ea-
> gleswood who love & cherish thee, but thou hast a brave heart & the
> ministering angels will help thee to bear that, and to fulfil thy duties
> in the new sphere to which thou has been called, . . . it seems to me a
> beautiful place for mental & moral development, for refinement & un-
> selfishness—with perhaps a little too much ministration to the animal
> nature.[57]

If Grimké thought Kansas a little wild and too conducive to the "animal nature," perhaps she hoped her protégé would act as a civilizing force. This was an optimal time in Sarah's life to take on the role of activist, as her own mother had done in the 1830s. Indeed, Sarah did instigate an episode that prefigured a lifelong devotion to temperance. In December 1861, Sarah led five other young women, armed with hatchets and axes, into a saloon in Mound City, where they proceeded to smash all the bottles and kegs they could find. While Sarah's younger sisters Emma and Mary Ann and their collaborators, the Botkin sisters, kept the bartender busy, Sarah walked out onto the street where a whisky drummer had stopped his wagon and was standing among the crowd watching the spectacle. Sarah calmly strolled around the wagon and opened all the spigots on the barrels, letting the whiskey run out onto the street. The drummer accosted Sarah, threatening to strike her down, but Amelia Botkin stepped between them and promised to split his head open with her hatchet if he did not back off. Townspeople intervened and nearly lynched him for even suggesting that he might hit a woman. Sarah, Emma, and Mary Ann, "almost drunk from the whisky fumes," returned home as conquering heroines.[58]

In the Wattles family, saloon-busting was a noble act, and the family would undoubtedly have supported further efforts for a cause if Sarah had chosen such a path. Her mother, in fact, expected it of her and considered apathy a youthful phase her children would outgrow. Writing to her mother at Christmas in 1859, Sarah recalled an occasion when she had told Susan

> tho' I admired exceedingly the life of sacrifice & self devotion you & my Father have lived, and was glad you lived so, I meant to live for myself & those nearest me, striving to surround them and myself with the comforts and elegances of life, instead of working for the elevation of the degraded and the relief of the oppressed. I remember perfectly your look and love when you replied, "I hope you will see better before long." I think I see better, now, & hope I shall never feel so again.[59]

Susan Wattles expected her daughter to take an active role in social reform, and Sarah internalized the obligation. It was no surprise Sarah showed interest in the temperance crusade. Combating the evils of drink had been a major focus of many a female voluntary society, and most antebellum reformers had advocated temperance along with other causes such as abolition. In many ways temperance was the quintessential reform issue that could justify women emerging from the domestic realm to exert their moral leadership in public. The social costs of alcoholism fell disproportionately on the family, whose vulnerable women and children suffered from loss of income, domestic abuse, and neglect. This was more clearly the concern of women than even the evils of slavery. In the postemancipation era temperance emerged as the most visible issue that brought women out to work together to make society a better place. The leaders of the temperance movement, especially Woman's Christian Temperance Union (WCTU) president Frances Willard, appealed to the tenets of the cult of domesticity in asserting the right of women not only to work in the public sphere for prohibition but to be granted the franchise as well. No cause, not even woman suffrage itself, enlisted as many women as temperance did in the decades following the Civil War.[60]

Sarah Wattles abhorred the evils of drink and believed women had the right to step into public to fight it. Few had been so well prepared to lead a life of activism in support of a cause. Yet although Sarah Wattles would be a responsible, decent citizen who championed the causes of woman's suffrage, education, temperance, the single tax, and populism in whatever ways she could, she never became the kind of activist her parents had been. Up to the age of twenty-four, everything that had occurred in her life prepared her to become an active agent for social change, but the circumstances she met as an adult, not the least of which were very limited opportunities for women, resulted in a much less influential agency than even she might have expected for herself. Her life was certainly not ordinary, but the change she effected was found on the local and personal level. Born in time to be influenced by her mother's generation, she was just a bit too old to benefit from the new opportunities that would open for women in the post–Civil War era. Birth order played an ironic role in her life—as the oldest Wattles daughter, Sarah benefited most from the mentorship of her parents' associates and a mature understanding of the events of a momentous time in history, but she just missed out on a sea change that occurred for women just after the Civil War. Sarah would be able to study medicine as an apprentice to her husband and to practice medicine with him, but unlike her younger sister Mary Ann, she was unable to attend medical school. Like her mentor and namesake before her, Sarah Grimké Wattles acquired a feminist consciousness but found few outlets through which to apply it.

THE WATTLES FAMILY IN THE CIVIL WAR, PART I: A SCATTERED HOME FRONT

For fourteen-year-old Mary Ann Wattles the summer of 1860 began in disappointment. "Our bathing place is all dried up," she wrote her older sister Sarah; "not a single drop of water left in it." It was still May, but already it was a "*rawful* hot day" and she felt "like a 'sack.'"[1] By early July she reported "some of the hottest weather" she had ever seen, with the thermometer reading 112 degrees Fahrenheit. The day before "the wind came from the south as if it had passed over a bed of live coals." They had shut the windows to keep out the hot air. "It realy seemed as though a body *would burn up* to [go] out doors." The roses, verbenas, and most other flowers had withered away, few vegetables had even sprouted in her garden, and "what are up are dying."[2] The worst drought in the short history of white settlement in Kansas was well under way. No snow had fallen the winter before, and no rain would fall in Kansas until April 1861. Throughout the state crops failed and starvation threatened. While Mary Ann lamented the loss of her swimming hole and peas, philanthropists in the East raised money and provisions to send, once again, to beleaguered Kansans.[3]

For the nation as a whole the year 1860 was one of the most pivotal in all its history. In the presidential election Republican Abraham Lincoln tried to reassure nervous slave owners that he would do nothing to interfere with slavery in the southern states, even though he professed a personal hatred of the institution and would do whatever he had to in order to prevent its spread to free territories. Southerners did not trust him and threatened secession if the standard-bearer of the sectional party of the North was elected. Lincoln got the needed electoral votes, and South Carolina led the South in seceding from the United States of America. By year's end an anxious nation waited to see how the crisis would unfold.

In the meantime, families went on with their lives even as the politicians bickered and blustered their way to civil war. As the nation hurtled toward the beginning of its most tragic episode, families across the country continued to pursue livelihoods, indulge in romances, recite pledges of matrimony, bear and raise children, and bury loved ones. Each family faced its own peculiar and unique circumstances, which exposed them to greater or lesser degrees of disruption as a result of the war to come. The Wattles families became female-headed households during the war, a family model that has intrigued historians of women's history because of the disruptions to traditional gender roles that emerged from such experiences. These families sent men to war, leaving women on their own to keep the family together and run farms or businesses. Wartime experiences have often been critical turning points for changes in women's occupational opportunities, civil rights, and gender roles because women demonstrate their capabilities and earn respect in the absence of their menfolk. Although the Wattleses fit within a well-known model of a wartime family, their unique circumstances did not conform exactly to what we might expect to see in such a family, and so they alert us to the importance of looking at the particular to understand why people make the choices they do. Not a typical family during the decades leading up to the Civil War, the Wattleses would not have a typical experience in most ways during the war. The Wattles women had already established their role within the family as one having considerably more authority and agency than in a typical antebellum family, and their wartime experience greatly reinforced their beliefs that women could, should, and would step into roles of great responsibility and influence.

Nevertheless, Susan Wattles probably did not expect that she would be the head of the household throughout the entire war. She could not have been surprised that her son, Theodore, would enlist and go off to war, nor that her daughter's fiancé, Orlin Eaton Morse, would join the Union Army. However, she could not have anticipated that her beloved husband, Augustus, would spend the war years living in and around New York City. Only one member of her immediate family remained with Susan in Moneka, Kansas, throughout the war: her teenaged daughter, Mary

Ann. Eldest daughter Sarah was still in New Jersey when the war broke out, came home in late 1861, married in June 1863, and left Kansas the following year. Daughter Emma left Kansas in the summer of 1862 to go to a water cure spa in western New York, where Eaton joined her in the fall of 1864 so the two could marry. Theodore Wattles enlisted in the 5th Kansas Cavalry in the summer of 1861 and returned home only for very brief visits during the war. Susan relied upon a network of friends and neighbors, including her recently widowed sister-in-law, Esther, living nearby, to help her negotiate the circumstances of the Civil War.

In many ways the Wattleses' experience of the war resembled that of Southerners more than that of their fellow Northerners. Although few Northerners would go through the war without some disruption, qualm, or fear disturbing an otherwise normal routine, hardly a Southerner alive could confidently say his or her family was safe from invaders, marauders, privation, or the breakdown of law and order. Those people living along the Kansas-Missouri border, however, had experienced conflict for some time by 1860, and the years 1861 to 1865 only quickened the chaos, mayhem, and terror they already knew well. Missouri became the scene of "the most widespread, longest-lived, and most destructive guerrilla war in the Civil War."[4] Because this random violence could and did spill over into Kansas, anyone living along the border became subject to the terrors of "an endless cycle of robbery, arson, torture, murder, mutilation, an endless cycle of revenge and revenge and revenge . . . using the most brutal and physical means," as historian Michael Fellman tells us.[5] Bushwhackers—gangs of marauders from Missouri—and Jayhawkers—bands of roving men with identical intent but originating in Kansas—preyed upon vulnerable homesteads and defenseless towns in both states. Although bushwhackers generally terrorized pro-Union folk in Missouri, and Jayhawkers mainly rode into Missouri to attack and plunder "secesh" sympathizers, both groups were known to assault like-minded people, and Jayhawkers occasionally attacked pro-Union Kansans in Kansas. The most feared bushwhacker, William C. Quantrill, aided the Confederate Army when it suited him, particularly during General Sterling Price's last-ditch invasion into Missouri in August 1864. However, primarily, Quantrill was a guerrilla fighter and a brutal one at that. Quantrill orchestrated the single-most significant event of the Civil War in Kansas, the raid of Lawrence on August 21, 1863, when he and his men swept into town burning, looting, and killing 150 citizens. After the "massacre" at Lawrence, the mere rumor of Quantrill could send men, women, and children running for the woods all along the Kansas border.[6]

The war did not spare Linn County, situated on the Missouri border some sixty miles southeast of Lawrence and twenty miles north of Fort Scott, the major federal installation in southeastern Kansas. In 1860 Linn County had 6,335 residents, most of whom lived in small hamlets and farms scattered around the county. The county seat, Mound City, had a population of 1,165.[7] The two Wattles families lived in Moneka, a village of less than a hundred souls, about six miles north of Mound City. As the national secessionist crisis unfolded in early 1861, the Wattleses watched with great anticipation as Kansans rushed to form militia groups. Across the border agitated Missourians, remembering that the slave-liberating incursions of John Brown and James Montgomery came out of Linn County, gathered in gangs of armed men to make a few initial forays into Kansas. In mid-February 1861, Emma Wattles wrote to sister Sarah, "Last week the Missourians were in here twice." They killed "Mr. McGrew, a Minister who lives five or six miles south of here, took a free colored man who was driven from Arkansas by the law excluding free blacks from the state." Although McGrew's wife and children were also at home, the Missourians spared them. McGrew, Emma continued, "had two or three guns in the house but was out of caps so the villains met no resistance as there was over twenty of them. It would have been more than useless to resist without ammunition." Emma went on to comment on the politics behind the raids.

These parties are "Missouri State Militia" organized to protect their border against "Montgomery and his Jayhawkers." The fact of the matter is they are extremely anxious to have Kansas invade Missouri. Their convention you know meets tomorrow to consider the secession question. The 28th they vote on it. Now there is a strong Union sentiment in Mo. and the secessionists think that if Kansas would do something do anything that would be construed into an aggression the Union party would out of State Pride if nothing else vote themselves out of the Union so they would defend themselves against Kansas, who being a state now they deem worth of more respect than the Territory was. Kansas people, however, don't make it their aim to do first as the Missourians want them to so they take a good many things greatly that they would not if they were not going to accommodate their friends across the line even than themselves by doing as they want them to.[8]

Militants in Kansas restrained themselves from invading Missouri in the spring of 1861 but wasted no time in organizing militia groups. By the time the governor officially called for Kansans to form militia groups on June 17, many men had already joined the militia and were getting ready to defend the state. Several regiments came together at Fort Scott under the leadership of "Doc" Charles Jennison and James Montgomery, both veteran fighters from the Bleeding Kansas years. Montgomery, a solid friend to both John Brown and Augustus Wattles, stood firmly in the abolitionist camp, whereas Jennison more likely paid lip service to the antislavery cause and seemed to be one of those men who lived for brutality and banditry, whatever the cause. His followers had the dubious honor of being the first to be called "Jayhawkers," but the term was soon applied to Montgomery's men and then to all pro-Union Kansas guerrilla fighters as the war continued.[9] Among the citizens of the southern counties who knew both men well, Montgomery remained a respected figure, but few had any illusions about the sordid character of Jennison. As the men of Linn County considered their options in the spring and early summer of 1861, Jennison's presence as a prospective leader of troops acted as a damper on some of the enthusiasm for mustering. Eaton Morse fully intended to join the US Army to fight for Kansas and the Union but hesitated only because Jennison was in charge of the first regiment forming at Fort Scott. Keeping her sister posted on developments, Emma reported on June 9 that a cavalry company from Mound City had gone to Fort Scott to join the new regiment and that "Eaton Morse went from here, he was the only one." However, Eaton had not yet committed to join the company. Instead, Emma said,

> he went to see what was to be done and let the rest of the boys down here know how things were coming on up there. Dr Jennison was Captain from here but they were to have another selection and it was thought that Seaman would get the office, he is now first Lieutenant. Jennison is a brave man but he has no discretion and another very serious objection is he drinks. If Seaman had been Captain when they started instead of Jennison they would have had a much better & more numerous

company although there will be a good many who will go from here if they are needed provided the Captain is changed, if not in an independent company.[10]

By the end of the summer the recruits were sorted into three official units, the 3rd, 4th, and 5th Kansas Regiments, with James Montgomery, William Weer, and Hamilton P. Johnson in command, respectively. Together they made up the "Kansas Brigade." Jennison's Jayhawkers retained an ad hoc status, free to pursue guerrilla activity or to aid the formal US Army troops on their own whim.[11] Eaton Morse and Theodore Wattles both joined the 5th Kansas Cavalry.

With Theodore going off to war, Susan Wattles found herself in charge of a mostly all-female household. Her widowed sister-in-law, Esther, lived nearby in a similar household with her three daughters. Both households had no male authority figures, although the families took in male boarders at times and had male hired hands. Many women during wartime found themselves in similar circumstances, with Southern women experiencing the same threat of random violence the Wattles women faced. Families in Kansas also feared Indian attack, which remained a possibility during the Civil War but did not occur except in the western regions of the state. Under these circumstances it might have been considered strange that Susan's husband, Augustus Wattles, did not make every possible effort to stay home with his family. That he did not, and in fact seemed positively cavalier about his extended absence, is perplexing and invites some scrutiny.

Augustus resided on the East Coast for most of the war years. Subpoenaed to testify before Congress on the Harpers Ferry investigation, Augustus spent several months in Washington, DC, in the spring of 1860. While in the capital, Augustus lobbied for an appointment as an Indian agent. Many individuals in the antislavery movement had cared deeply about the welfare of Native Americans, especially in opposing Andrew Jackson's removal policy in the 1830s.[12] Augustus, however, had shown no particular interest in them until moving to Kansas, home to numerous tribes in the 1850s. From 1820 to 1850 a number of tribes from the Ohio River Valley and upper Midwest had voluntarily relocated there or had been removed to Kansas by the federal government. The Shawnee, Delaware, Pottawatomi, and others had been granted lands in territorial Kansas but still faced pressure from settlers who coveted that land and often harassed these nations. When it came to Indians, many free-state and proslavery whites agreed that they wanted them to go. Kristen Tegtmeier Oertel, a historian who has examined Native Americans in territorial Kansas, noted that most whites in Kansas, including abolitionists, placed Native Americans in a racial hierarchy, believing them inferior in intelligence to blacks and thinking Christianized Indians superior to those who preferred to maintain their own spiritual practices.[13] The unusual mix of indigenous peoples in Kansas lent itself to such invidious comparisons. The more acculturated groups were placed on lands made available by pushing aside other tribes native to Kansas. Missionaries arrived to serve various nations, and by the time white settlers were allowed in under the Kansas-Nebraska Act, Native Americans of varying degrees of acculturation could be encountered throughout eastern Kansas. White settlers increased the pressure on traditional Indian-held lands, and those indigenous to Kansas, such as the Kaw and Osage, tended to resist encroachment more forcefully than the newcomers who had more knowledge of Christianity, the white legal system, and entrepreneurial capitalism.[14]

Both Augustus and John Wattles became interested in the Native Americans they observed in Kansas even though their views reflected the ethnocentrism common to other abolitionists in Kansas in the 1850s. The Wattles brothers tended to see Native Americans through the lens of their primary concern of slavery. John Wattles had taken note of Native Americans on his exploratory trip to Kansas in 1854, but his observations focused on these Indians' slaveholding. While visiting the Shawnee Methodist Missionary Station, located southwest of the village of Kansas (the future Kansas City), he found that a chief owned slaves, whereas most of the other Indians condemned slavery and called themselves the Freedom Party. At the Quaker mission several miles to the west, the missionaries elicited John's sympathy because they had prohibited slavery and as a consequence were "suffering much from the opprobrium of *Abolitionism.*" The Quakers were doing wonderful work, however, and "seem to have the confidence of the Indians," according to John.[15] His observations reflect the tendency of whites to evaluate Native Americans through their own perspectives. John Wattles was primarily concerned with slavery, not with understanding native cultures. If some Native Americans owned slaves, they were not as commendable as the ones who adopted the "anti-slavery principle" and might be associated with abolitionists. Nor did it occur to him to look more deeply into these Native Americans' practice of slavery to see how it might have fit within native cultural traditions of slavery or whether the slavery he witnessed was practiced as chattel slavery, might have been a status symbol for a chief, or might blend elements of both cultural contexts.

Augustus Wattles also interpreted the Native American experience through the lens of his concern about slavery. In his series "The History of Kansas," written for the *Herald of Freedom* in 1856–1857, he explained federal removal as a colonization scheme masterminded by John C. Calhoun to place obstacles in the way of northern "free labor" pioneers intent upon settling Kansas. The presence of Native Americans would prevent the territory from becoming a free state. However, he implied, missionaries had come to Kansas and thwarted this plan by instilling the "right" values in the Native Americans through acculturation. Identifying progress with the adoption of white culture and abolitionism, Wattles stated, "The Shawnees, who were free roaming savages, have become under the peaceful influence of the Friends, tillers of the soil and citizens of the United States. Their dwellings, fields and orchards can be seen by the traveler as he passes through their settlements, and marks the progress of their race."[16]

Richard Hinton provided another small hint about the evolution of Augustus's views on Indians. Hinton accompanied John Brown on several occasions when staying at the Wattles home in Moneka, and during one such visit, Hinton claimed that Brown depicted Kansas Indian policy as a creation of the Southern slaveocracy. According to Hinton, Brown "called Mr. Wattles's attention to the policy which covered Kansas more than any other part of the trans-Missouri region with Indians removed from Ohio, Michigan, Illinois, Indiana, and other States, and stated that for over twenty-five years but one man of Northern birth had been appointed Indian agent to any one of the dozen tribes living within the section then organized as the Territories of Kansas and Nebraska; a large portion of Colorado and Wyoming being then included."[17] Although this idea sounds suspiciously like Augustus's own explanation of Kansas history in the *Herald of Freedom*, we will take Hinton at his word and ascribe the thoughts to his hero, John Brown, rather than jump to the conclusion that Hinton altered the conversation. In any case this talk with Brown could have reinforced Augustus's views that more Northerners with antislavery leanings ought to become Indian agents. Whatever the origin of the motivation, in the spring of 1860 Augustus decided he wanted to become an Indian agent and spent several months in Washington, rubbing shoulders with the crowds of office-seekers who hung about the Capitol seeking federal appointments.

During these months Augustus incongruously experienced a case of gold-bug fever. Two years earlier, gold had been discovered in Colorado, setting off one of the biggest gold rushes in US history. In 1859, more than a hundred thousand people streamed to Colorado, then called Jefferson Territory, and another twenty thousand were on their way in 1860 when Augustus apparently thought about going himself.[18] In the surviving Wattles family papers there is an odd letter of introduction written for Augustus by one S. W. Cone of Sumnor, Kansas. Writing on May 12, 1860, while in Washington, DC, Cone addressed the envelope to F. R. Ford, Esq., Park City, Jefferson Territory. "I introduce to you my very worthy and esteemed friend Augustus Wattles of Moneka, Kansas, an early friend and pioneer of our Territory," writes Cone. "Mr. Wattles is one of the best men of Kansas and any facillities you may afford him in furtherance of his interests I shall regard as a personal favor."[19] Two other documents suggest that Augustus somehow acquired a couple of mining claims in the Union Mining District, located in Clear Creek County above Denver. The Union district was the heart of the Colorado gold rush and the site of mining camps that would develop into the towns of Georgetown, Idaho Springs, and Empire.[20] One claim certified that "Augustus Wattles has this Day claimed and Recorded Claim No. Thirty Five above Discovery in Union District Lower Gulch and that he is the owner of the same according to the Records in my Office. Union District, September 15th AD 1860. W. F. Shedd/Recorder."[21] A separate claim made on September 16 stated that Augustus had recorded a claim "Sixty Eight on the Carter Silver Lode East from the Discovery Claim."[22] Neither of these handwritten documents had any official printing on it, and there is no indication they were genuinely issued in Colorado.

No evidence exists to confirm that Augustus actually went to Colorado in the late summer and fall of 1860, and much circumstantial evidence suggests he did not. He would have had to make the trip between late July, when he was in Newark, and December, when he was back in New York. Such a journey would have taken a considerable sum of money, one item

Augustus Wattles never had in abundance, and he would have had to be healthy to do it, again a complication. It is unlikely he would have gone west without going to see his family in Kansas, but there is no evidence of such a visit. No one in the family ever referred to Augustus making a trip to Colorado to do some prospecting. However, these documents—a letter of introduction and two mining claims from 1860—exist. Augustus and family members held on to these documents, passed them down, and kept them with a treasured trove of letters. These claims obviously meant something to Augustus and his family. Perhaps Augustus acquired the letter of introduction and was then hoodwinked into thinking he was purchasing valid mining claims from someone in Washington or New York. Perhaps he and other family members kept these claims because they thought they were authentic and might someday be used. Perhaps he actually made the trip.

Although it would be interesting to know if in fact Augustus made the trip to Colorado and back, that is not the most important issue here. Rather, we should ask what it meant that Augustus was even thinking about going to the goldfields. Throughout his life Augustus had often decried materialism and greed, and he had never amassed any personal wealth. Despite this embrace of poverty and an ethic of generosity toward others, Augustus briefly succumbed to the allure of gold and the prospect of striking it rich, reminding us that contrary motives can exist simultaneously. Paradoxically, Augustus was able to contemplate some sort of participation in the gold rush at the same time he was preparing for a humanitarian mission to the Native Americans of Kansas. Like so many others of his time, he could repeatedly move farther west hoping to improve his family's situation and extending the reach of white settlement without thinking such settlement was wrong because of the prior claim of Native Americans to the land. He condemned the cruelty shown to these nations and argued they should be treated humanely, but he never questioned the morality of Euro-American conquest of the continent. He was apparently unable to correlate the advance of gold rushes and settlement with the resulting impact upon the Indians. The gold rush he thought about joining proved an utter catastrophe for the high plains tribes living in western Kansas and eastern Colorado, in addition to the Ute people in the mountains. Augustus had no way of knowing the Colorado gold rush was setting in motion developments that would forever transform the homeland of the Ute,

Cheyenne, Kiowa, Arapaho, and Lakota peoples, destroying the resources of grass, trees, sheltered river valleys, and bison herds upon which they depended.[23] Ironically, at the very same time the gold rush was shattering the livelihood of the high plains tribes, Augustus Wattles began his own personal crusade as a friend of the Indian.

Appointed a "special agent" in May 1861, Augustus was sent to visit the Sac and Fox, Kaw, Chippewa, Ottawa, Delaware, and Osage nations living under the Central Superintendency in Kansas. Commissioner of Indian Affairs William P. Dole wanted to know if these tribes would remain loyal to the Union or if they would be lured away to ally with the Confederacy, as some Cherokee had done. Emma Wattles announced the arrival of Augustus in Moneka with a bit of her dry wit, saying, "Father got home Tuesday the 14th of May and Wednesday the 22nd left for the Indians taking Theodore with him, leaving our family in a deplorably *headless* condition."[24] Augustus launched into his new job with enthusiasm, writing frequently to Dole about the conditions the Native Americans faced. The Osages, located only forty miles from Moneka, were "loyal to the U.S. Government and will fight for their Great Father, at Washington, but must be protected from bad white men at home." Even as he wrote, whites were gathering to go attack the Osage Reservation, he warned.[25] At the Sac and Fox Agency he noted that the indigenous people lived under "rude and destitute" conditions, cheated by the traders and agents who were supposed to be administering annuities. One trader owned the wholesale business that furnished the goods for annuities and "made out orders for Indians in the precise amounts of annuity payments and then told each Native that he had already received his goods."[26] Everywhere Augustus found starving Native Americans living under desperate conditions.

In September, Augustus reported again to Dole on the Osages, this time that violence had indeed been committed on their lands and surrounding territory. John Matthews, "formerly an Indian Trader amongst the Osages, has been committing depredations at the head of a band of half breed Cherokee all summer," he wrote. Matthews's gang had attacked and burned Humboldt, Kansas, before moving back into Indian Territory. Lieutenant Colonel James G. Blunt was dispatched with two hundred men to follow and apprehend Matthews, and Augustus went with them. Blunt came across Matthews and sixty men at the Quapaw Agency, where Matthews was killed. Blunt found on Matthews a commission from Benjamin

McCulloch, the Confederate commander in Indian Territory, "authorizing him to enlist the Quapaw and other Indians on the Kansas frontier" in order to clear southern Kansas of pro-Union settlers. Augustus urged Dole to send new US agents to maintain the loyalty of the Osage or risk seeing them succumb to McCulloch's entreaties.[27]

By November, Augustus had submitted his reports and was back in New York, where he met with "the leading politicians & philanthropists" on behalf of the native peoples.[28] He delivered at least one lecture as the featured speaker at a meeting on Indian reform, organized by the "friends of the Indian in N.Y."[29] A reporter for the *Sunday Mercury* identified him as "Mr. Wattles, of Kansas, late Special Indian Agent of the Government" and declared that "if his statements stand uncontradicted, we have another evidence of the baseness of many of the leading brigands in the rebel army." Augustus argued that corrupt Indian agents, many of whom were now Confederate generals and "warm Secessionists," had been swindling the Native Americans of Kansas since the administration of Andrew Jackson. He claimed, "All the Indian agents, so far as I can learn, were ultra Pro Slavery men, and looked upon the Indians as they do upon the negroes— fair subjects for speculation and fraud." Warning that the tribes of Kansas had "become nearly extinct by disease and starvation, in consequence of their privations," Wattles declared, "The American nation cannot afford to lose the Indian race. The earth sees no other like it. So much of calm courage, so much of native eloquence, so much of true nobility, so much of unselfish friendship, is not found in any other race or people."[30] In Augustus's speech we can hear the notes of many of the standard shibboleths of the Indian reform movement: the belief that the Indians were headed for extinction, the romanticizing of the noble savage, and the indictment of a politicized spoils system.

Augustus and Susan indicated that his work on behalf of Native Americans continued through the war years, but it was probably sporadic because of his poor health. He traveled to Washington, DC, several times in an attempt to be paid for his survey work, eventually receiving $469.50 for his efforts as a "special agent," and he applied for but apparently never received an appointment as an agent to native tribes in Oregon in 1863.[31] Augustus spent the rest of the war in the New York area, pursuing treatments for vaguely defined afflictions. It is difficult to say what caused his suffering, but he had often been sick previously. His early work as a traveling antislavery agent, coupled with the rigors of forging new home-steads, had taken their toll and left him complaining of poor health as early as the mid-1840s. He and his wife and daughters referred to his health problems several times in 1860 and 1861. It is quite unlikely that he ever fully recovered from whatever ailed him during the war, and he probably spent the years up to his death in 1876 with severe disabilities. What is clear, however, is that from 1861 to the end of his stay in the East in mid-1865, he sought out and received medical care from a series of spiritualist healers. Augustus believed his illnesses were caused by bad spirits, and the only hope for a cure was to talk to the dead.

Spiritualism was an immensely popular religious movement in the 1850s and 1860s, drawing in millions of followers across the United States and Europe. As odd as it sounds to observers today, spiritualism appealed to people who demanded a "scientific" religion, meaning something that could be seen and observed with one's own eyes. Seeing was believing, and a thing was real if it could be perceived through the senses. This was empiricism in its most literal meaning, and this was what many people understood as science at the time. Many respectable citizens, including judges, senators, businesspeople, and editors, professed their belief in spirits because they had witnessed these apparitions in person and could find no other explanation for them except that they had been called forth by mediums in séances. Spiritualism attracted a wide range of people, some of whom had become exhausted by the emotional demands of evangelical revivalism and some who simply wanted the reassurance of life after death. The movement appealed to Universalists, followers of a frontier religion that emphasized salvation for all, and to free thinkers, ultraists, and atheists.[32] Spiritualism became the religion of social reformers who had "come out" of established churches and of utopianists who dreamed of living harmoniously in communal life. It also appealed to people who had lost loved ones, especially children, at a time when regular medicine offered little remedy for so many common diseases. The yearning to see a departed loved one, even if just a faint and barely recognizable specter, explains why spiritualism retained its robust following through the Civil War, when so many men died on faraway battlefields, leaving families without even a body to bury at home. Because spiritualism gave women a voice and a role as mediums and professed the equality of the sexes, women felt welcome there, and the advocates of gender equality, who often adopted other reform causes, flocked to spiritualism as a religion that brought all of their concerns into one focus.[33] John O. Wattles had been an early recruit to spiritualism and had extolled its virtues on the lecture circuit. Angelina and Sarah Grimké were also early adherents, as were Elizabeth Cady Stanton, Lucretia Mott, and Martha Coffin Wright.[34]

Augustus Wattles also became interested in spiritualism early in the life of the movement. Augustus sat in on the first séance in Cincinnati on September 26, 1850, when an itinerant clairvoyant, Mrs. G. B. Bushnell, convened a spirit circle at the home of Dr. Joseph R. Buchanan, a professor at the Eclectic Medical Institute of Cincinnati and a pioneer investigator in psychometry, a form of phrenology. In that first experience Augustus wanted to know if the medium knew anything of the fate of his brother, William Wattles, who had gone to California and had not been heard from since.[35] Over the next few years Augustus consulted healing mediums for an illness that had rendered him unable to "walk, work, or read," according to Sarah Grimké.[36] Healing mediums were said to cure illness by consulting the spirits, who might "prescribe proper homeopathic, Botanical and Electro-magnetic remedies" or by the laying on of hands to draw out disease. Medical mediums, mostly women, would examine the patient while in the clairvoyant state.[37] Augustus seemed to believe these trance healers drew out the bad spirit from the afflicted person and absorbed the spirit themselves, and for a time the noxious spirit might reside within the medium, seeming to cause great harm to the healer. It was a common observation that mediums often suffered from frail health and chronic syndromes.[38] Augustus must have expressed doubt about the ethics of the practice because Grimké counseled him to remain open to the healing powers of the spirits, telling him,

Your physical weakness must be one of great trial & suffering. Dear brother I trust you will be relieved. Why not let it pass on to the Medium if he suffers but a short time and you would find permanent relief. Why not? What a question. Because you cannot feel it right well try it again & again the time may come. Does the Medium really endure or only appear to endure pain? Does he feel the effects of it in his waking state? Does it appear or advance his spiritual progress? I know deeply the sentiment "I had rather die in want than not feel for torments of others." It is Christ-like, it is worthy of you. I have no doubt you have striven hard to do right that you have done what seemed to be the dictates of your highest nature. I love you for all. I blame you for nothing. Accept my tenderest sympathies.[39]

Perhaps the spirits did help to put Augustus's mind at ease because he seems to have recovered enough by 1854 to move his family first to Indiana and then to Kansas, where he led an active life with only periodic bouts of recurring illnesses. However, in his debilitated condition in New York City in 1861, he again sought out the assistance of healing mediums. He stayed for a while at the home of one Mrs. Schriber, a healing medium who led him through a very stimulating séance on December 4, 1861. He described the spirit circle in detail to Emma, whom the family believed to have clairvoyant powers. "How delighted you would be to see & hear what I see and hear from our dear spirit friends," Augustus wrote his daughter. Mrs. Schriber first called up the spirit of a Southern, slaveholding clergyman who showed no remorse for holding humans in bondage. The attendees of the circle carried on a lively debate with the clergyman, who claimed that "he held property when he lived on the earth & he held it yet and he would not sell all he had & give to the poor. He held slaves also & he held them yet. He needed them & he would keep them. . . . The slaveholder said he had never been talked to so before & he considered it an insult." After this stubborn apparition left in a huff, "a negro woman who got possession of the medium expressed herself in the mildest joy at the discomfiture of the slave master & the freedom of his slaves." Then, much to Augustus's wonder and amazement,

The table commenced to move and finally it stood up on two legs at an angle of 45° for two or three minutes. Mrs. S. said, this is a new influence, the spirit wants to be known, call the alphabet. The table without coming down would nod at the right letter as the alphabet was called, until the name of Emma Morrison was spelt. I expressed my pleasure at this recognition, when a feeling like a shower bath came down on me, making [me] jump nearly out of my chair. She says she has kept a watch on me all summer & she will continue it till I die. After she had left Harriet Howell took the medium and said she was called the soldiers heroine that Emma had joined her in rendering such aid as she could to the soldiers who were killed in battle. A lady medium who was a stranger to me was entranced and came and stood by me. She said I see a flower growing near you about as high as your head. Its blossoms are of the most beautiful hue representing your deeds of charity and the rich fragrance which perfumes the air are the emotions of your soul. Sarah will remember the spirit of Birdie the Indian girl. She then wove a wreath of flowers and put it around my head. And much more, very much which to be appreciated must be seen.[40]

Augustus's enthusiasm for spirit circles might have been the reason he stayed on in New York rather than try to return to Kansas during the war. He genuinely believed healing mediums had the capability to treat illnesses such as his, whatever his illness was. He probably hoped to assuage the grief he felt as a result of the death of his brother John in September 1859. However, he also might have convinced himself to stay in New York because he found a comfortable place to dwell, complete with a sympathetic caretaker and warm family environment. Sometime in 1862 he moved in with a young woman with children, a believer in spiritualism, whose husband was away in the Union Army. Jenny Gould took care of Augustus and treated him as a father figure, even writing to Susan and Emma as if she were a member of the family. These circumstances seemed to suit Augustus quite well, and he made no effort to make the arduous trip home to Kansas. In the meantime, back in Kansas, exciting and dangerous developments continued to take place in Linn County, each episode duly reported by Susan or one of the girls to Augustus. He did not seem excessively worried about them. He expressed utmost confidence in Susan's ability to keep the family safe and sound with the threat of hostilities all around them. "I see by the papers that the Indians and Missourians both are threatening you," he wrote to her in late November 1861. "You may suffer, but you are prepared for it, consequently it will not be as hard for you as it will be for those who dread it." Clearly unconcerned that he might sound somewhat patronizing, he offered counsel and advice to her:

The means and end of the war are in the hands of God, therefore I fear nothing, either for myself or for you. Did I not know your faith I should suffer for you, but as it is, I know your heart rests in faith, and God preserves you. Teach the children to look from Nature up to Nature's God. Teach them how you derive courage & strength from the unseen world. Talk over the evidences of immortality & spirit influence. Teach them to walk boldly up to duty, even if by so doing they bring upon themselves hardship & toil & poverty. Do right & fear not. Fear hath torment. Death is better than fear, & duty is better than death. As you are, so I wish the children to be; above the world, above fear, above death: in the discharge of duties always faithful, esteeming & loving each other—lightening the burdens of life by cheerful and happy hearts.[41]

If Susan felt any resentment at being left alone to face bushwhackers and Indians, she showed not a trace in her reply. Assuring him, "I believe the good spirits will cure you and assist you to complete the benevolent and humane work you have begun," Susan responded with her typical unflappable confidence. "Our children are not in the least disturbed by the threatening dangers of the war," she said. "They feel as I do determined to stay here as long as the soldiers are fighting for Kansas—unless our house is burnt down. Esther has the same determination."[42] True to her word, neither Susan nor her daughters seemed much alarmed by the conflict that occasionally disturbed their otherwise ordinary farm life. In fact, Emma appeared to relish relating gory details of raids and murders to her father. In a confused but lively ramble, she described an exchange of raids that occurred in November 1861:

A week ago last Tuesday Morning . . . 47 Missourians lead by the sherif of Bates County came in to Potosi. They went to the house of Mr. Manning called him out of bed and shot him killing him instantly he was an unmarried man. They then went [to] Mr. Upton who was living in the same house, woke him out of bed and shot him right before his wife. They got 22 horses two wagons and harness with the wagons beside several smaller things. As soon as they had finished their work they started back. Two men heard the offray and took their guns and went to the ford of a creek that they would have to cross and when they came along fired at them killing two or three men. Mr. Speaks one of two, steped a little from behind a tree in loading and was shot. They had no farther interruption. Mrs. Upton is almost crazy it is said from the shock. Her husband was so near the bed when they shot him that his brains spattered the sheet!! and his wife in the head. Such demons are not cannot be men. The next Friday . . . a company of Jayhawkers & a company of Home Guards went into Bates County went to the houses of a good many of the men but could find nobody, not a sign of the sheriff nor his company . . . & so left it. But the Home Guards (Capt. Dobbins) went there after they were gone and burned the house & stable. Our men went into Butler Friday night. The Company they were after left Butler Friday morning. There is a small company going tomorrow in to the State probably as far as Clinton.[43]

The Wattles women also grew accustomed to hearing rumors of troop movements and imminent attacks. In December 1862, Susan told Augustus about the frenzied preparations that followed a dire warning. "Last Sunday a messenger galloped to the door with news from . . . the commander at Ft Lincoln saying that the Missourians were approaching in large numbers near Barnesville and called on every man who could bear arms to come to Ft Lincoln." Most of the men of Moneka had gone off hunting, and the "only man on our hill was James Way and he ran some bullets and started." The more exposed families gathered in their neighbors' houses, according to Susan:

About 8 O' Clock that evening Mr. Hiatt & his wife moved over to the Way's and David's children came here. Then Eli took our wagon and went for his Mother and she came about midnight with bed bedding and wearing apparel; saying that there were 600 secessionists at Barnesville—4,000 at Ball's Mill and three thousand at Ft. Scott—that a spy had been arrested who said that the eastern borders of Kansas was to be attacked at all large places on Sunday & Monday.

By Monday morning, Susan said, "the stories were no worse and by noon they were much better," and by that evening "the Kansas Brigade— (minus 2 regiments) arrived and camped between here and Mound City." Later she learned that the reports had been greatly exaggerated: there had been only "80 men east of Barnesville and they were the other side of the line there was no enemy at Ft Scott but they heard there were some at Dry Wood." Things had calmed down enough that she could casually tell Augustus, "The children have gone to the Big Sugar to gather Hickory nuts."[44] Life went on.

The ordinary business of life included educating the children, which the Wattles women would never forego no matter what tumultuous strife went on around them. Susan, Sarah, and Emma all taught school in their home in Moneka or in a neighbor's home. Susan's youngest daughter,

Mary Ann, plus the three "girls," Esther's daughters Celestia "Cettie," Harmonia "Monie," and Theano as well as children and young adults from among their neighbors attended day school, and those who lived far away boarded either at Esther's or Susan's house. Their school regularly had between a dozen and two dozen scholars a term. Mary Ann described a typical school day to her father, saying, "When I go to school, I study my Physiology lesson, till recess, then I recite it. Then I set the copies, and hear a class in Colbarn's Arithmetic. Afternoons I study my Chemistry lesson till recess after recess I recite my lesson and then go over to Aunt Esther's and practice my music lesson till school is out."[45] When Augustus wrote insisting that the girls could study agriculture in the evenings, Susan responded by telling him, "We read Macouly's History evenings when the girls are not occupied with their lessons. Mary Ann and Cettie recite German evenings and sometimes physiology."[46] The girls were not slacking off in his absence.

There was always work to be done in the fields or garden, or in putting up food, or washing or mending, or milking or churning, or any other number of tasks involved in farm life. The girls had their assigned chores and their designated livestock. They kept about 150 chickens, but Mary Ann claimed some of them and supervised them all, also helping with the milking. When Sarah married and began her own household, their father wanted Mary Ann to give some of the livestock to her older sister. Mary Ann demurred, writing him, "I have about fifty little chickens. There are none of them large enough to eat yet though. We milk four cows, two old cows and two heifers that don't kick at all. The cows are Pied, and Bloss, and the heifers are Rosz, and March. Bloss is yours; the rest are Theodore's." Surely her characteristic deadpan wit applied when she continued, "Of all those animals you mentioned that I was to give Sarah for a setting out, I possess nothing but the chicken, and I am afraid to give her that for fear she'll eat it: that is what she does with chickens, and I don't like to have my chickens eaten."[47]

Susan and Esther each managed their farms, renting out fields as they could or planting and harvesting with the help of hired men.[48] Labor was plentiful, even if their hard cash to pay for it was scarce. They took in boarders and hired day laborers. Recently freed slaves, called contraband by all when brought in by the hundreds by the army, willingly became wage-earning farmhands or went to work for blacksmiths and other tradesmen in the war-stimulated economy around Fort Scott. In November 1861, Susan reported, "Two hundred contrabands came with Lane's Brigade. 100 were in Mound City Friday evening."[49] Susan employed one young black man named Tom, although it is not clear from the correspondence whether he was freed before or during the war. He did, however, look out for his best chance and sometimes for excitement. Tom went with a company of Jayhawkers on a raid into Missouri and had a hair-raising time. Susan described the outing to Augustus:

> Mr. Sterns & Tom went with a company into Missouri. They had for guide a union man who had been plundered & driven out of Missouri. They went to the east side of Bates County. They took a great many horses & oxen & wagons loaded—got back nearly to Butler, ten or twelve miles then ran into a company of secessionists of about two hundred. They took all their ox wagons and the horse wagons by throwing out some of their loading escaped the rear guard fought five times their running a few miles. The enemy would overtake them and they would stop and fight again—this until they reached Butler. At one time Mr. Stern's horse gave out and Tom saw five secessionists running to cut him off. He ran his horse to shooting distance and killed the leader's horse, he then raised a shotgun which was lying before him and a ball from the enemy skewered the breech to pieces while in his hand, he then loaded and fired his Sharps Rifle as fast as possible (while they were firing at him), until Mr. Stearns got out of danger. They expected the enemy were following them and they ran their horses all they could from Butler to the Trading Post. Tom got home at midnight Wednesday night and has been nearly sick ever since. [50]

It was difficult to keep laborers with so many armies nearby, not so much because adventure beckoned but because the military paid higher wages. A year later Susan reported, "Tom has gone to work for the officers in the fifth regiment. He cooks for a mess of five and is promised fifteen dollars a month and has his horse kept."[51] She still had Stearns to help with the chores and soon hired another black man and a black girl.[52]

Susan needed the help by this time, for in the summer of 1862 Emma left Kansas, leaving only Mary Ann at home. Emma had often suffered from various ailments, including migraine headaches. The affliction that probably sapped her energy the most, however, were swellings on her neck that her family were at a loss to diagnose. She would later learn that this was scrofula, the inflammation of lymph glands in the neck, also known as tuberculosis of the neck. In children scrofula is usually associated with atypical mycobacterium, or nontuberculous mycobacterium (NTM), but in adults it is almost always caused by the tuberculosis bacteria, or *Mycobacterium tuberculosis.*[53] Emma probably began to experience scrofulous swellings as an older teenager and was diagnosed in her early twenties, so there is a good likelihood that she had tuberculous scrofula. This would not have been understood at the time, and there was no cure for tuberculosis in the nineteenth century; only in the twentieth century were antibiotics developed that could bring the dreaded disease under control. Emma's options for care were severely limited in rural Kansas, but even if she had been living in an urban area, the state of American medicine would not have offered her good alternatives. It was not the availability of medical care that determined Emma's choice of treatment but rather her family's ideological beliefs. Ultraist reformers such as Augustus and Susan tended to be drawn to alternative medicine.

In the antebellum era US doctors did not enjoy the same professional status physicians did in Europe. There was nothing regular in the training of "regular" doctors, as allopathic physicians were called. Beginning in the 1830s every state that had previously passed laws requiring licenses to practice medicine rescinded those regulations. Even though there were numerous medical schools for regular medicine, no one was required to attend one in order to practice medicine. Individuals could simply opt to study under an experienced physician to gain the necessary knowledge to claim themselves qualified to practice medicine, or they could attend any number of sectarian medical schools that proliferated in the nineteenth-century United States. The Civil War demonstrated the downside of this haphazard pattern of medical education and certification, when it was discovered many doctors lacked the skill for competent practice under duress. Nevertheless, from the 1830s until the 1870s no state required medical licenses to practice medicine, and regular doctors practiced alongside a wide range of sectarian medical practitioners. The general public could be excused for its lack of confidence in regular physicians during this period because most of them still practiced a form of "heroic" medicine, which involved extreme treatments such as excessive bleeding and purging.[54] Added to this, however, was another factor that demystified doctors in the United States from the 1830s through the Civil War. The generation that came of age in the 1830s—Augustus's and Susan's generation—simply had little respect for any privileged authorities, including trained physicians. Jacksonian-era Americans had faith in common sense and native intelligence, believing that each individual could make up his or her own mind about most things, including which medical practice to follow. The loosening of laws governing medical practice reflected the faith in the common person's ability to comprehend medicine with a minimum of training. Sectarian or "irregular" medical competitors seemed to the layperson just as effective, or more so, than allopathic doctors.

As with so many other movements of the first half of the nineteenth century, medicine came to be seen as an arena for republican reform, and many of the individuals who pursued other reforms also participated in sectarian medical movements. The Wattles families and other reformers felt naturally drawn to irregular medical practices, which reflected their interests in restructuring society along less hierarchical lines. Augustus Wattles received some medical training while in the Cincinnati area in the 1840s. In 1852 Sarah Grimké asked Augustus if he was "still" practicing medicine, and his daughter Mary Ann, who studied medicine at the Blackwell sisters' Woman's Medical College in the early 1870s, learned from Theodore Weld, her father's old friend, that Augustus had once attended medical lectures.[55] Most likely, Augustus sat in on lectures at the Eclectic Medical College of Cincinnati, a Thomsonian school established in the late 1840s. Augustus knew several faculty members from this school, including Drs. Joseph R. Buchanan and J. S. Garretson, who, like Augustus, were all spiritualists and participated in séances together.[56] Thomsonianism, a movement started by a New Hampshire farmer named Samuel Thomson, held that all disease resulted from imbalances of heat and cold in the body. Natural remedies came in the form of two botanicals, lobelia (Indian tobacco) and cayenne pepper, which would be applied to remove the digestive tract of obstructions or to cause perspiration.[57] Other popular health reforms, such as dietary reform, had close ties with Thomsonianism. The John Wattles family practiced vegetarianism, although the Augustus Wattles family did not seem to have adopted that dietary reform. John Wattles included many articles about dietary and medical reform in the *Herald of Progression*, and even in Kansas the Wattleses were able to keep up with the latest dietary or medical fad happening across the country by subscribing to publications such as the *Water-Cure Journal,* which purposefully cost only $1 a year so that the general public could afford it. Augustus became interested in water cure and did his first "plunging in cold water" in 1847.[58] So when Emma Wattles kept falling ill in 1861 and 1862, Susan Wattles was as supportive as a mother could be when Emma announced she wanted to travel east in the middle of the Civil War to check into a water-cure spa in western New York.

Water cure, or hydropathy, had its roots in Europe and made its way to the United States in the 1840s. The theory of hydropathy depended primarily on the belief that water constituted a universal remedy for dissolving and expelling disease from the body. Adherents thought applying water externally, either cold or hot depending on the circumstances, drew diseased matter through the pores of the skin. Water could be applied through wrapping the body, spraying the naked body, sitting in steam, or immersing the body in hot or cold water. Water could also be consumed in large quantities to dissolve various obstructions in the system. Water cure, like all irregular medical practices, took a gradual, noninterventionist approach in contrast to the extreme drugging and bleeding procedures of regular medicine. Hydropathic centers also combined treatments with training in healthy living patterns that could lead to lifelong wholesome habits. Water-cure practitioners urged their clients to get regular exercise and lots of sunshine, to wear loose-fitting and light clothing, to avoid alcohol and caffeine, to eat wholesome food, and to avoid excessive stress and too much sexual stimulation. The water-cure movement also had the effect of giving women a positive self-image that naturalized female physiology and afforded them a sense of control over their own health. As Susan Cayleff, a historian of the water-cure movement, points out, regular doctors viewed the normal functions of the female reproductive system as medical problems that rendered women unfit for intellectual work or any other activities beyond the domestic sphere. Hydropaths, on the other hand, treated the female system as natural and woman's reproductive functions as normal processes unrelated to their mental capacities. Water-cure physicians urged their patients to adopt hygienic life practices, thus giving women the confidence they needed to make decisions about their own health and their family's well-being.[59]

Emma chose to go to the water-cure center in Dansville, New York, operated by Dr. James Caleb Jackson. The Wattleses were already familiar with Jackson's work through his reputation as the first physician at Glen Haven Water Cure and his articles in the *Water-Cure Journal*. As early as 1847, Jackson had argued against the use of purgative drugs such as mercury or calomel, used in regular medical practice, and promoted water therapeutics. His advocacy of healthy living habits, such as simple food, fresh air, and exercise, influenced the water-cure movement and became the standard in water-cure treatment. Jackson fit right in with the democratically minded reform movements of the time with his attitudes on class and wealth. He directed his message to the working people of the United States, castigating the rich for their exploitation of labor and their excessive leisure activities. He was an abolitionist and an advocate of temperance and women's rights. In 1858 Jackson and his partners purchased a house near the village of Dansville, New York, and called it "Our Home on the Hillside," otherwise known as the Dansville Water Cure. Here several female physicians joined him, including his adopted daughter Dr. Harriet Austin, his daughter-in-law Dr. Kate Jackson, and Dr. Fanny Hurd Brown, daughter of co-owner F. Wilson Hurd. The fee for treatment at the Dansville center was set on a sliding scale, "applied at the discretion of the Jackson family."[60] The program at Dansville involved water therapeutics and a hygienic lifestyle that included dress reform. Although all Dansville personnel advocated women's rights, Harriet Austin was especially enthusiastic about dress reform, becoming a leading advocate of the movement and a founder of the National Dress Reform Association. She designed a bloomer-like outfit of short skirts and trousers that became known as the "American costume" and encouraged residents at Dansville to wear it.[61] Another aspect of the healthy regimen was a vegetarian diet consisting of whole grains and fresh vegetables. Dr. Jackson invented a breakfast cereal he called "Granula," a "breadcrumb mixture made of graham flour and water, the first cold cereal breakfast food and precursor to John Harvey Kellogg's Grape Nuts."[62]

Upon her arrival in September 1862, Emma Wattles would have gotten off the train at the Wayland Station, just outside of the small village of Dansville, New York.[63] She would have been met by someone from "Our Home" and taken in a wagon or buggy to the roomy four-story house on the hillside. The Jackson family and partners had completely refurbished the place in the four years since acquiring it, adding on separate buildings for men's and women's bath houses and landscaping the previously unkempt ten acres of surrounding grounds. The bracingly cold water required for treatments came from four "never failing springs" that gushed from the hillside above the house. The quiet, idyllic surroundings matched the soothing calm of the day-to-day routine of the family-like atmosphere inside the house. Jackson set the tone as physician in chief; his wife, Lucretia, served as matron; and son Giles worked as cashier and bookkeeper. F. Wilson Hurd, the co-owner, had the position of steward, and Jackson's adopted daughter Harriet Austin was the first, though by no means the only "lady physician." By the time Emma arrived, Our Home had hired seven more physicians to serve an increasing clientele.[64]

Father Jackson, as he was known at Our Home, benevolently dominated the institution. Several times a week he held "lecture hour" at half past six in the morning, and everyone—staff and patients—had to be there on time, even if they were "brought in wheel chairs and deposited on cots on the dais," as Dr. Kate Jackson remembered. Years later she recalled "the wet 'headcaps' of white linen worn by nearly everybody, sick or well," as they listened to these early morning talks. Father Jackson

> was an original thinker, with strong convictions and the courage of his convictions. . . . He was a leader and pioneer in proclaiming a new gospel of health and of living—a gospel that comprehended the needs of the soul as well as of the body and that summoned his hearers to a life of spiritual control over bodily and mental conditions, habits and tendencies, as well as over material things and circumstances prejudicial to human health and welfare.

Although "he sometimes aroused anger by his criticisms of modern life-destroying ways of living, . . . he never failed to send his audience out to breakfast in high good humor, with new ideas, new courage, new purpose and hope."[65]

For someone like Emma who had endured debilitating physical problems, even the promise of renewed health must have been invigorating. For years Emma had suffered headaches that lasted for weeks and prevented her from studying too much or doing any strenuous work. She was also affected by gout, which left her legs stiff and painful, and from hard swellings on her neck and throat. The doctors at Our Home diagnosed these swellings as scrofula and told her this condition caused all the other troubles. Jackson explained to Emma that her brain had been overly cultivated and "used up vital power faster than [her] body could manu-facture it." He advised her "to keep quiet & stop thinking & studying" and simply to "vegetate." Emma protested that she "never had been to school & never had studied but very little," which the doctor doubted since she appeared highly cultivated. The doctor then asked her how she had lived, and Emma described to him her life in Kansas. She said,

> When I ran over to him the outline of Kansas life, he said the living out doors & the simple diet had been the very best thing for me. If I had been treated as girls usuly are I would have been a confirmed consump-tive before this. That I owed my life to my mothers knowledge & care. Then in speaking of our excitement [of the] Border Ruffains, he said that was bad for me. That I could use up in an hour or two of excitement more power than would be restored in a month and in that way I was constantly using my force that was capital for future use and as pre-scription the most important article was to keep quiet, not think, smile just as little as I could get along with, be happy & contented & keep up good courage.[66]

In addition, Emma's therapy was to take "3 half baths & three sitz baths a week all at temperature 85° reduced to 80°. And beside that wear abdomi-nal bandages wet all the time" for about six weeks. After that her prescrip-tion was

> 3 packs a week followed by half bath 85°, 80° for two weeks. I had three 30 minutes and after that I took them 45 min for three to five weeks. . . . The next prescription I had was every day a hip pack with fomentations on kidneys & stomach & bowels & also on my neck on these swellings. This was followed by a sitz bath at 85° for 5 minutes & foot bath 100°. Then be washed, & rubed thoroughly in the bath, after which, wiped dry rubed & go to bed then every night, have sitz baths at half past 7 fifteen minutes, at 88° foot bath 110°.[67]

Although Emma was advised to remain mentally quiet, she still was en-couraged to exercise moderately and follow a healthy diet. She reported to her father, "I walk from one to two miles before breakfast, then a half or a quarter just before bath and often dinner at five o'clock or thereabouts. I walk again from one to two miles and a half." Like many of the patrons of water-cure establishments, she embraced the new diet and wanted to continue it after returning to her normal life. "I have not seen a bit of fine flour or meat since I came here," she wrote.

> I don't eat salt at all nor pepper nor spice of any kind. I breakfast at 8 and dine at 3 and we don't have any supper. I don't use either milk, cream or butter. We have graham flour made in to mush & crackers or biscuit with out yeast, or soda, or any thing except water and unbolted flour. Then we have apples raw & stewed & baked & made into pies. Baked beans & boiled, rice & rice puddings, cabbage & cracked wheat & pumpkin pies, etc, etc, etc. I think I have improved a great deal since I came here. I have not been able to see my gain much until the last two or three weeks, but I feel uncommonly well. Last week I gained four pounds and a half. I weigh now 123 and that is 6 pounds more than I weighed when I left home. Dr. Hurd told me to night that I hardly looked like the same woman I did when I came here.[68]

Emma seemed to thrive in the atmosphere of Our Home. Augustus, however, wanted his daughter to join him in New York City and to seek treatment from healing mediums, as he was doing. Emma seemed torn between wanting to stay at the water cure and pleasing her father. She urged her father to consult with a Mr. Bemis who "believes that Healing mediums are very effective" and who had been at the Dansville water cure "so long he can very well compare the relative merits of the two places."[69] However, Augustus replied, "I do not wish to consult [Mr. Bemis] nor anyone about your coming here. I know you will be better off here for the same money than you are there. And I believe you will get well as fast."[70] Augustus assured Emma that Jenny Gould would welcome her into her home and take care of her as well as she was taking care of him. Her father's request left Emma with a dilemma because she preferred to stay in Dansville but could not afford to remain much longer. She wrote to tell Augustus she would come to New York but on the condition that

> when I come there I want to continue to live just as I do here as regards diet. I shall not be willing to come there unless I can have unbolted flour and I don't want wine nor beef steak. If I go from here before I am cured I go to live out the health principles taught here for I think them the most reasonable, the most sensible teachings I ever heard—or heard of.[71]

With a heavy heart, Emma went to Jackson to explain that she had to leave because she could not afford to stay. His answer astonished her. Emma related the conversation to Sarah, telling her Jackson asked

"if there was no difficulty about procuring the means you would like to stay! would you? There is no other reason for your going?" I told him I should like above all things to stay but that I could not so it was useless to want to stay. "I will make you this offer—you shall stay until spring or longer if necessary and the debt shall be strictly a debt of honor between you and us. Neither your Father nor friends shall be responsible or held accountable for it and you shall pay us when you can conveniently." He said I should wait to pay the money until I could earn it if I wanted to, that if they did not make me well enough to study and teach then I should not pay any thing, and if I was cured I could easily pay. . . . I represented to him that he did not know me—but he said "tut tut. Now darling if you want to stay stay and don't trouble yourself about it any more. I know I am safe and you are too. Now dear Good Morning" and he kissed me and sent me away with my heart so high in my throat that I could not speak. He is a such a Good Man. The family have been very very kind to me. I don't know why, or why he should make me the offer he has. He says though that he can read any body through & through and knows more about us than we do about our selves.

What ever the reason may be I am satisfied with the result. I am going to try to write shorter letters home & fewer. But Glory to God I am going to *stay* & *get Well*. *Halleluja* I will come home so well that I can study a blue streak and not have the head ache at all. Hooray. "It must be now the Kingdom coming And the land of jubilee."[72]

Jackson showed Emma Wattles the compassion and generosity for which the entire Jackson family and Dansville staff were known. Emma not only stayed at Dansville and continued to receive water-cure therapy but also remained beyond her treatments and took over the position of bookkeeper after the death of Giles Jackson in late 1863. For Emma it was a serendipitous opportunity to remain with her new circle of friends and earn her own living in an environment that valued independence for women. Even her father could not complain, writing, "I am very glad you have got your machinery cleaned & that it runs without friction." Still, Augustus wanted Emma to come and live with him and Jenny Gould, promising that Jenny "lives very plain—no pies or cakes. Graham bread as much as you please & good plane beef & mutton, with such vegetables as you like. She says tell Emma I will get for her whatever she wishes."[73] However, Emma had no desire to leave Dansville and resolved to stay there until her fiancé, Eaton Morse, came there to marry her. Eaton, whose wartime experiences will be examined in the next chapter, arrived in Dansville in October 1864, and the two were married on October 18 at Our Home. Eaton then returned to Kansas to begin the process of settling into civilian life. Emma remained on at Our Home until March, working as the center's bookkeeper and caring for Augustus, who had come to the water cure to take treatments.[74]

With her brother at war and her sisters beginning their married lives, Mary Ann Wattles was the only child of Susan's to stay at home through the war years. Although Mary Ann's responsibilities naturally increased, she also enjoyed some of the ordinary experiences of youth. She went swimming in creeks with her younger cousins, raised cats "quite largely," picked wild berries and nuts, and even went to the occasional dance party. Her mother and aunt were her schoolteachers, and she was an attentive student. Another teenager might not have absorbed the gravity of the war that encroached upon their lives, but Mary Ann did. If anything, she took it as a matter of course that life was always as serious as these years demonstrated and that it was her duty to respond appropriately.

On October 25, 1864, two weeks after Mary Ann's nineteenth birthday, a battle occurred in Linn County, Kansas. The Confederate general Sterling Price, after wreaking havoc throughout Missouri in a last-ditch effort to reclaim the state for the Confederacy, led his army into southeastern Kansas. The Confederates had pillaged with such desperate enthusiasm that they now labored to haul along behind them scores of wagons heavily laden with plunder. Struggling to get the wagons across Mine Creek, just south of Mound City, Price's army was overtaken by Union troops. The Union victory at the Battle of Mine Creek was the last gasp for Rebel forces in Missouri and Kansas. The dead were buried and the wounded were taken to several makeshift hospitals in the area, including the schoolhouse in Mound City, where Mary Ann Wattles went to help nurse the wounded men. In unsanitary, improvised conditions Mary Ann helped stanch bleeding wounds, emptied bedpans, and watched men suffer in agony. When she returned to the Wattles home in Moneka, she fell sick for several weeks with "brain fever." Susan wrote to Augustus that Mary Ann's "sickness is caused by having spent two weeks in the dreadful atmosphere of the hospital."[75] Her brief experience as a wartime nurse could have repulsed her, but instead it had just the opposite effect. Mary Ann decided to become a doctor. Although the chances that a young girl raised in rural Kansas during the troubled years of Bleeding Kansas and the Civil War could succeed in becoming a doctor might seem rather slim, Mary Ann Wattles accomplished it.

Augustus Wattles eventually came home in June 1865, riding in an ambulance from Leavenworth to Moneka, his health never to recover entirely.[76] In the end he had gone to Our Home on the Hillside in October 1864 with Jennie Gould, and stayed there under Emma's care until she left for Kansas, and then for a few months longer, receiving water-cure treatments. Perhaps he had stayed in New York so long because he truly believed he would find the cure to his physical ailments, first through spiritualism and then water cure. As an ultraist reformer of his generation, he came naturally to these beliefs. Spiritualism and irregular medical practices of all sorts went hand-in-hand with the compulsion to improve this world by ridding it of sins and perfecting the individual. Augustus's beloved brother John had enthusiastically embraced these movements as well, and it is hard from a distance to know which brother led the other to any particular idea. It is not hard to imagine, however, that after John's death in 1859, Augustus would have wanted to connect again with his brother's spirit and that the loss of John might have unsettled Augustus enough to intensify his interest in the spiritualist movement. He was predisposed to believe that spiritualist healing mediums or water cure would restore his health. As with other reformers, such as his comrades Theodore Weld and Marius Robinson, the activist life took a terrible toll on Augustus's health, and he suffered recurrent breakdowns from an early age. His prolonged sojourn in New York, which began in a zealous whirlwind of activity devoted to reform of conditions for Native Americans, ended with a visit to Jackson's water cure in an attempt to find relief for a persistent physical malaise.

Whether he had done so intentionally, Augustus was not present for his family during the war. As it turned out, Susan and Esther and their daughters were more than equal to the task of staying on alone. They managed quite well as far as we can tell. Although it is doubtful that either woman welcomed these circumstances, we are hard pressed to find a word of complaint. The only indication we have in the surviving correspondence that Susan ever came close to chastising Augustus was in remarkable letter in which Susan refutes a claim from Augustus that she was unhappy with their circumstances. To the contrary, she objected, he had misjudged her. She was neither unhappy nor depressed "by want and poverty and toil and care," as he had put it. It did make her sad to think he would have "such an opinion" of her, but still she went through her days "with cheerful thankful heart." Augustus had apparently believed Susan resented the role of Jennie Gould in his caretaking and accused Susan of being ungrateful. Susan begged to differ, saying, "I am truly sorry that I neglected to speak of the gratitude to Mrs. G[ould] in that letter. I am *very thankful indeed.* I presume that on this she has received my hearty thanks that is, if some of my letters have not been miscarried or you could not have formed such an opinion of my state of mind." Susan was even willing to have Gould come to Kansas to stay with them. "I think I should like her company," she said, "and if knowing how retired and how rough we live she still wants to come I said I shall be very happy to see her here and give her all possible assistance in her studies." Susan's outlook on her war experience was reflected in her statement, "When I have had work to do that was hard such as carrying fodder across a muddy field in the rain, I have not felt impatient but thought this is my part of the war and I am thankful that the rebels have not burnt the fodder or drove off the cattle."[77]

The Wattles family persevered through the Civil War. Scattered to the four winds, beset by hostilities all around, faced with a household and a farm to maintain, still they emerged at the end of the war having eluded death and destitution. Many families were not so fortunate. Susan and Esther both demonstrated they were capable of managing households and farms on their own, and their daughters were all prepared to set out in life as strong, confident, and interesting individuals. Whether they embarked on nontraditional careers or adopted more conventional lifestyles, each of the six Wattles girls became a living embodiment of their parents' belief in a "new womanhood."

For the Wattles women and countless other American women, the Civil War was an unforgettable experience in their lives. Susan and Esther's experience of maintaining a school and operating the family farm in the absence of menfolk was replicated across the North. Thousands of women crossed gender boundaries in going out into the fields to plant and harvest crops, taking over the running of businesses and schools and managing the family finances while the men were away. After the war many of these women took from these experiences new confidence and aspirations for further education, public work, and political rights. Elizabeth Cady Stanton sensed a wider enthusiasm for women's rights as a result of all the nontraditional work women had done during the war.[78] Yet, not all historians agree that the war was a clear and definite turning point in breaking down conventional gender expectations. Many women were happy to return to their familiar roles after the men returned. Many men insisted they should. In postwar debates about suffrage some men linked the right to vote with service in the military, thus excluding women from eligibility for full citizenship.[79] Stanton might have been trying to rouse women for a struggle that was lagging and would take many more decades to bring to fruition. What seems clear is that some opportunities for women opened up after the war, especially in education, which resulted in a phalanx of college-educated women who then pursued reform efforts and social work in the Progressive Era. The women's rights movement continued its work, with very modest gains made by the generation who had lived through the war. Some of these developments were stimulated by women's wartime experiences, but perhaps much of this would have happened with or without the war.

For the Wattles women the Civil War was not so much a turning point as a stimulus to continue the patterns they had already set for themselves. For Susan the war brought tremendous responsibilities and required hours of strenuous labor that she might not have endured had the war not come. However, Susan had always taken on challenging work that pushed her to the limits of her energies in the absence of her husband. The wife of an antislavery agent already knew what it was to stretch the boundaries of gender expectations, and she simply continued to cross those borders during the war. Susan was intrepid, but she also knew her limits. She remained on the Moneka farm; she did not venture out to follow armies or to nurse soldiers in military hospitals. She considered the work she did in educating the neighborhood children and harvesting the crops sufficient to fulfill her wartime duty. Certainly it was more than enough. When the war came to a close and Augustus came home, she became his full-time caretaker, a role that occupied her until his death in 1876. She was happy to see him upon his return, grateful that someone had cared for him during the war, and content to support him through his waning years. She also continued to do what she could for the cause of women's rights, writing letters and spreading suffrage literature during the 1867 campaign to give women the vote in Kansas.[80] She then turned her full focus and energy to assisting her daughters as they raised their families and pursued their careers.

Neither was the war much of a pivotal experience for Susan's daughters or nieces, if we expect to see a significant shift in the direction of their lives. Esther Wattles might have taken her girls back East sooner if the war had not intervened, but after she was widowed, her intent was clear. After John's death in 1859, Esther was determined to leave Kansas and see to it that her daughters got the best education available to women at the time, and for her that meant enrolling them in the preparatory program at Oberlin College and the undergraduate course after that. The war did not make Esther Wattles the capable, independent, and financially astute woman she was. Life with John Wattles had done that. Sarah Wattles also had been largely shaped by her experiences before the war, and her courtship, marriage, and early married life with Lundy Hiatt showed hardly any impact from the ongoing national conflict. In later years Sarah became active in the Woman's Relief Corps, the auxiliary of the Grand Army of the Republic, but even that can be seen as a logical outcome for activist women who believed in the power of networking and organizing to accomplish good, a lesson Sarah learned from her mother. Emma Wattles spent the war as a soldier's fiancée, which carried its own burdens of excitement and worry, but otherwise she pursued her own interests in traveling across the country to seek relief for her health problems from an alternative medical establishment. It was hardly the conventional choice, but it was exactly what she would have done if there had not been a war. At the end of the war she made the conventional choice to marry, start a family, and become a homemaker, but both she and her husband were lifelong advocates for women's rights and temperance as well as faithful keepers of the family memory of reform.

Because of her age, Mary Ann Wattles might have been shaped to a greater degree by the wartime experience than her sisters. Sixteen when the war broke out, Mary Ann witnessed the war as an alert and intelligent teenager who keenly felt the absence of her father, who saw her beloved brother ride off to fight, and who stood with her mother through reports of real violence and rumors of marauding bands of lawless men in the neighborhood. In the last year of the conflict she volunteered to nurse wounded soldiers in a makeshift field hospital. She emerged from these experiences knowing how to remain calm and collected in a crisis and determined to become a doctor so that she could do important work. Had the war never happened, she undoubtedly would have gotten an education and pursued a career anyway, but the war gave her a temperament, character, and calling that she might not have had otherwise.

While the war was going on, of course, the Wattles women could never forget that two members of the family served on the front lines of the war. Theodore Wattles and Eaton Morse both enlisted in the Union Army and were assigned to the 5th Kansas Cavalry. Though they saw action in the nearby states of Missouri and Arkansas, their experiences seemed a world away from their homes in Linn County, Kansas. They returned from the war having undergone many of the same events while serving in the same unit, but each was affected in different ways. As with the women of the family, we need to see their experiences from each individual perspective to fully comprehend the impact of the Civil War on the soldiers of the family.

THE WATTLES FAMILY IN THE CIVIL WAR, PART II: FIGHTING FOR UNION AND MEMORY

Eaton Morse could not bring himself to burden his fiancée, Emma Wattles, with all the gory details of life in the US Army, so when he was wounded, he wrote to her sister Sarah instead. "I am suffering severely from a hurt I got in my left side in the skirmish at Salem," Eaton told her. Eaton's unit, the 5th Kansas Cavalry, had marched with General Samuel Curtis into Arkansas in April 1862 and had met fierce Confederate resistance at Batesville, on the White River. For the next few months Union raiding parties fanned out across northern Arkansas, engaging scattered Confederate forces wherever they found them. Eaton rode with these roving Union troops, and on July 6 he and "Lt. Herington . . . with 60 men attacted and drove back nearly 3 miles 300 Texas Rangers & Arkansas troops," he recounted to Sarah.

> I led the charge or rather the chase for after firing a few shots they did not stop to fight. In the midst of the fray my horse jumped into a deep hole that had been washed with heavy rains but so overgrown with bushes that I did not notice it. The horse fell partly upon me, lameing himself badly and I owe to that fall for more suffering than I have ever known in the same time before. Nearly six weeks have passed and I have not been fully clear of pain in the whole time. I got hurt on the 6th July and on the 16th 8 days after we reached this place during this whole time we were in constant danger, enemies in every direction by thousands when we had but hundreds.[1]

Although Eaton wrote candidly to Sarah about his escapades, he admitted that he was not as forthcoming in his letters to Emma Wattles. "I tell her the facts so that she will not be deceived," he told Sarah, "but I write not at all what I see or think for her imagination would color my thoughts with privations and dangers that the picture would haunt her night—& day. It is bad enough looking on the bright side."[2] The full extent of soldiers' experiences was never reflected in their letters home, but families still tried to follow their movements by piecing together information from their correspondence and newspapers. For the soldiers as well as the families at home, this connection was vital for sustaining their courage throughout the war. Family bonds mattered during the war and would continue to shape the memory of the war long after it ended.

Emma's sweetheart became a part of the Wattles family while the two were courting before the war. Born in 1837 in Huron County, Ohio, Orlin Eaton Morse had gone to Kansas with his brother in 1857 to seek his fortune. The Morse brothers settled in Moneka and opened a store. As an ardent abolitionist, a teetotaler, and a supporter of women's rights, Eaton could not help but draw the attention of his neighbors, the Wattleses. Eaton was on hand to become a member of the Moneka Women's Rights Association, founded by Emma's Uncle John and Aunt Esther in 1858. In March 1860, Eaton might have thought he would impress Emma Wattles if he nominated her to the editorial committee of the Moneka Literary Society. He was right.[3] Emma was very taken with the solid young man, and so was her entire family. Theodore Wattles, Eaton's best friend, thought Eaton was one of only three young men "of incorruptible moral principle to be found in this immediate neighborhood."[4] It is not clear when Eaton and Emma became engaged, but they had pledged themselves to each other by the time he left Kansas with the 5th Kansas Cavalry in early 1862.

Theodore Wattles and Eaton Morse both enlisted in the 5th Kansas Cavalry in the summer of 1861, Theodore as a sergeant and Eaton as a lieutenant. By 1864, when Eaton mustered out, he was a captain and Theodore was a first sergeant, but they remained together in the same company throughout the war. An intricate network of communication kept the Wattles family informed of their soldiers' whereabouts and well-being. Many letters passed between Eaton and Emma, and Theodore, Susan, Sarah, Mary Ann, and Augustus all wrote numerous letters, with enough surviving that we can know how the soldiers fared and what their loved ones thought about them as they served. Eaton wrote long, verbose letters, whereas Theodore wrote terse and ungrammatical ones, and everyone else relayed whatever they heard to each other about the men, even if it was just rumor. Emma probably saved every letter she received from Eaton, most likely passing them on to her children and grandchildren. Many of his letters to her but none of hers to him seem to have survived. A handful of Theodore's war letters to his parents survived. From these extant records, something of the life of the 5th Kansas Cavalry can be reconstructed, and we can know a bit of what the family of these two soldiers knew about their activities during the war.

No matter what the individual members of the family were doing, the safety and welfare of their soldiers in uniform were never far from mind. Worry about family members serving in the military is obviously a universal factor in all wars, and as the previous chapter and multiple other works demonstrate, the absence of men during wartime places extra burdens on women and children, causing them to go beyond traditional gender roles and responsibilities. Sometimes these circumstances lead to permanent changes in the life of a particular family, not merely because the women and their roles have changed. War changes the men who participate in it.[5] No soldier going off to war, and no family who remains behind, knows what will happen to him in that war or how it will affect him. The possibilities are endless. If he survives, he might be maimed. If left intact physically, he might be scarred emotionally. If he left home a generous and loving soul, he might return cynical and mean. The effects might even be more positive than negative. He might have gone off to war as a shy and meek person and return brimming with confidence and positive self-esteem. A soldier might discover leadership skills he never knew he had or return with greater compassion for all human beings. However, one factor is likely to hold true for all families and their loved ones who go to war: circumstances will be changed as a result, and the family dynamic will shift.

The Wattles family sent a son and a future son-in-law to war in 1861. Both had been raised in staunch reform-minded, God-fearing if not churchgoing, abolitionist families who valued sobriety and goodwill toward all humanity. As ultraist reformers their philosophic bent leaned toward pacifism, but having gone to Kansas in the 1850s, they understood the role of violence in the conflict over slavery. Eaton, the shopkeeper, knew his letters and figures better than Theodore, the farm boy did, but

Theodore had an advantage over Eaton in handling animals and guns. Although they had similarities and differences, their mutual service in the 5th Kansas Cavalry would result in a unique outcome for each man and his family. After the war, the differences between them grew sharply. For all the Wattles family but Theodore, the Civil War reinforced an identity based on their parents' participation in the abolitionist movement. Theodore, in contrast, wanted nothing to do with his family's idealism after the war. The family's memories of the war were constructed not only around the wartime experiences of Eaton and Theodore but also about the abolitionist cause that preceded it. The war was a noble cause, and they honored the memory of the soldiers who fought it, but its meaning was shaped by what had precipitated it.

When Theodore Wattles joined the Union Army, his parents worried not just about his physical safety but also about his moral condition. Susan and Augustus apparently accepted that he had chosen to enlist, even though they had good friends in the reform community who remained pacifists and expressed shock that the Wattleses' son had joined the US Army.[6] Many abolitionists had followed William Lloyd Garrison's example of maintaining strict pacifism even through the years of Bleeding Kansas and John Brown's Raid on Harpers Ferry. The war posed a difficult challenge that became all the more poignant because the children of many of the abolitionist activists of the 1830s were now in their early twenties and in their prime for military service. Many sons raised by abolitionist parents, such as young George Garrison, the eldest son of William Lloyd Garrison, chose to enlist only after the war took a decided turn toward the elimination of slavery following the issuance of the Emancipation Proclamation. Garrison respected his son's decision and endorsed the war as an antislavery war as well as God's punishment of the United States for slaveholding but still tried to talk his son out of enlisting. Many other Quaker and pacifist friends felt greatly disturbed when their sons joined the military.[7] Augustus Wattles seemed more ambivalent about the war than Susan; he was deeply troubled by the heavy losses the war exacted in the early years and feared Lincoln was not sufficiently antislavery to bring about emancipation. The entire Wattles family was distressed when Lincoln countermanded General John C. Frémont's order to free the slaves of secessionists in Missouri.[8] However, other than Augustus's qualms about the tremendous loss of life, none of the Wattleses questioned the need to go to war to free the slaves. Susan even expressed a little pride in her son, writing to Augustus: "Does this date remind you of Theodore? He is 22 years old today. . . . How many long years of toil and care since he was a babe. *Then* you was laboring unceasingly for the abolition of slavery by moral means: *now* our boy is enlisted in a war of blood to destroy it."[9]

During the first year of the war Theodore and Eaton were stationed near enough to Moneka that they could easily return to the Wattles home on twenty-four-hour furloughs. Their company spent many months at Fort Lincoln, little more than an encampment on Mine Creek, east of Mound City in Linn County. Writing to Augustus about one visit from the boys, Susan professed, "A very great satisfaction it is to me that Theodore keeps so near us that I can wash and mend for him. He comes gladly and stays as long as he can."[10] Not only could Susan care for Theodore by doing these small tasks for him but also she could watch out for the changes she feared military service would cause him. After the troops moved out of Kansas, however, she could only wonder. Although friends thought army life would be good for Theodore, Augustus and Susan worried about their son's moral development. Augustus wrote asking what Susan thought about military life for Theodore. "My opinion is that it is a very poor place to make a great and noble soul," she answered, "and I earnestly hope that he will be satisfied when the volunteer service is disbanded to return to the quiet labors of peace; but I fear that he will not at least if they are disbanded soon. I know he likes it now. I think he feels that steady hard work would be almost unbearable. I have not any hope that he will improve while in the war. If he does not become worse I shall be exceedingly grateful."[11] Theodore must have heard enough about this from his parents, for he wrote Augustus, "You and Mother seem to bee very uneasy about my morals I don't see but what a man can bee just as good in the army as any where at least it hase not made any diferance with me."[12] That was in late 1862. By the end of the war Theodore was a much-changed man.

The 5th Kansas Cavalry spent most of the war in Missouri and Arkansas, where they fought in both pitched battles and guerrilla warfare. The brutality of much of this action was sufficient to desensitize any decent man. The ruthless barbarity of the antebellum border conflicts continued into the war. When the 5th Kansas Cavalry, under its commander, Colonel Powell Clayton, rode out of Kansas in March 1862, its first engagement was a retaliatory strike against the Confederate sympathizers of the village of Rock Prairie, Missouri. Some Union men had been killed there, so the men of the 5th Kansas burned twenty homes and killed twelve guerrillas before moving on to Carthage and Springfield.[13] We do not know how they knew which twelve guerrillas to kill, but perhaps it did not matter.

By April the 5th Kansas had crossed into Arkansas under the command of General Samuel Curtis, who hoped to take Little Rock and then follow the Arkansas River down to the Mississippi. Confederate guerrilla units frustrated that plan, and it was late summer before the Union Army occupied Helena, the largest port on the river between Memphis and Vicksburg and a vital staging point for the Union campaign to gain control of the entire Mississippi. Theodore and Eaton went on several missions from Helena into Mississippi as Union forces gradually surrounded Vicksburg during the winter and spring of 1862–1863. On November 25, 1862, the Union Army, with 10,000 infantry and 1,800 cavalry including the 5th Kansas, left Helena and crossed the Mississippi River on a search-and-destroy mission to Grenada, Mississippi. This action was intended to support Ulysses Grant's advance against Vicksburg from the north and then to prevent any Confederate force from moving against General William Sherman's army as he attempted to take Chickasaw Bluffs, just a few miles north of Vicksburg. Although Sherman failed to oust the Confederate's well-entrenched defenders on the bluff, the men from Helena had some success in destroying railroads and railroad bridges around Grenada.[14] Theodore succinctly described his part in the expedition in a letter to his mother: "We went down the river ten miles on a boat landed in Mississippi marched out 10 miles to Hardy station 8 miles from Granada burned a bridge on the Memphis and Granada R.R. then ten miles further to the sentral Miss R.R. burned one bridge then marched back 30 miles and laid over one day to let it rain."[15]

Theodore's letters often must have left his family wanting more information, whereas Eaton usually wrote in great detail and as regularly as he could. When he did not write Emma at least once a week, she noticed and worried. In March Theodore and Eaton were again sent into Mississippi to guard the Yazoo Pass, between the Mississippi River and Tallahatchie, leaving Emma without a letter from Eaton for two weeks.[16] When she finally heard from him, she passed the news on to other family members. Theodore and Eaton had left Helena on February 17, she reported. They took with them only two days rations. They were taken by steamer to Moon Lake Miss. 25 miles from Helena by water, . . . then marched some 8 or 10 miles through mud and water and when they reached Yazoo pass camped on the plantation of a rebel who had left for Secessiondom and after they had reached there found they were to stay until the pass was cleared and the fleet intended for the attack on the rear of Vicksburg had passed into the Cold Water. . . . He said they were supposed to be guarding the pass but there was no enemy near and all they had to do was their own camp duty and amuse themselves with reading, rowing, hunting & fishing and from all accounts I guess they enjoyed it pretty well.[17]

Soldiers in war usually face long periods of boredom interspersed with moments of frenzied chaos when they encounter combat. It appears from their letters, however, that Theodore and Eaton kept quite busy while stationed in Helena. Both were well suited for their positions and seem to have been conscientious soldiers, and as a result they were given many responsibilities. As a first sergeant Theodore excelled at drilling men, supervising the care of equipment and horses, and maintaining discipline. Eaton was promoted to captain early in the war and proved as adept at writing reports as leading men in battle. Eaton had clearly earned the trust of his superior officers, as evidenced by an assignment in May 1863 in which he led a contingent of six soldiers on a mission to Little Rock under a white flag. Theodore went along and described the outing to his mother without telling her its purpose. "The next day [May 25] we started to Little Rock with a flage of truce Cpt Morse and six men a distance of 125 miles when we came to the rail road thirty miles from Little Rock Morse, Engean, Baird and I got on the cars and went in to town it is quite a pretty place. I saw no troops except the guard at the bridge and one Co on Provost guard in town they said the army was camped two miles back."[18]

The biggest event of their year spent in Helena, however, came on the Fourth of July of 1863, when the Confederate Army, with 7,600 men under General Theophilus Holmes, attacked Helena hoping to take advantage of the recent departure of the bulk of Union soldiers for the imminent attack upon Vicksburg. The 4,000 remaining Union troops, including Theodore and Eaton, dug in on four hills on three sides of the town, with gunboats patrolling the Mississippi River to the east. The well-positioned fortifications stood firm against a poorly coordinated Confederate assault, and the federal forces won the day.[19] Theodore's report of the battle to his father was striking for its overall brevity and exaggerated account of the enemy's losses as well as his typically creative spelling. "We have had a battle here at last after so many fals allarms," he wrote. "The enemy attacted us on the morning of the fourth We repulsed them in fine stil. Their loss was three thousand killed wounded and prisoners. Ours was one hundread and fifty. I suppose you have seen account of the [battle] ere this. The loss of our regt was three killed one prisoner and ten wounded."[20] The actual casualties for the Confederates were 173 dead, 687 wounded, and 776 missing or taken prisoner, while the Union side had 57 dead, 146 wounded, and 36 missing.[21] However, neither soldier nor family cared much for accurate statistics.

Following the battle of Helena, the Union forces under Major General Frederick Steele pushed up the White River to Clarendon, met up with another Union force coming south from Missouri under Brigadier General John Davidson, and headed toward Little Rock. The capital of Arkansas, much of its population having fled south, fell to Union forces on September 9. A week later Gen. Steele sent the 5th Kansas Cavalry, under command of Col. Clayton, to occupy Pine Bluff, some fifty miles southeast of Little Rock on the Arkansas River. Located at the point where the Arkansas Delta meets the timberlands, the town of Pine Bluff, with 1,396 residents in 1860, sat on a high headland overlooking the Arkansas River and Lake Langhofer, which served as the town's harbor. Steamboats traveling from the Mississippi up the Arkansas River to Little Rock stopped in Pine Bluff to pick up cargoes of cotton grown on the many plantations filling the vast flatlands that fanned out to the east of the town. Deep pine forests stretched westward and southward. Streams, creeks, and bayous permeated the entire area. Because of this geography it was critical, yet challenging, to hold Pine Bluff and to attempt to pacify the population of its surrounding territory. The forests and rough terrain to the west provided cover for guerrilla activity, whereas the numerous plantations presented several complications an occupying force would have to manage. The plantation owners demanded protection of their property, in particular their cotton. If carefully reconciled, the planter families could be a stabilizing presence especially in influencing the local yeomanry. Their slaves, however, began to run away as soon as the Union Army occupied Pine Bluff, and these "contrabands" became the responsibility of the US

Army. So many blacks sought refuge in Pine Bluff that Col. Clayton ordered several camps constructed especially for their use right outside of town, where they resided under army protection. These blacks performed manual labor for the army throughout the occupation, and when Pine Bluff was attacked by Confederate forces, they played an important role in the defense of the town.[22]

Six weeks after the 5th Kansas moved into Pine Bluff, a Confederate force numbering 2,500 men under General John Marmaduke attempted to recapture the town. On the morning of Sunday, October 24, troops assembled in the town square in preparation for weekly inspection by Col. Clayton. Suddenly a scout rode in with news that pickets had stumbled across a unit of Rebels sneaking up on the town. Quickly Clayton ordered dozens of "contrabands," freed slaves who had congregated in Pine Bluff, to make a barricade of cotton bales across all the streets leading to the town square. Soldiers positioned cannon in the square. Small contingents of cavalry rode out to harass the oncoming Confederates, while the remainder of the 550 federals took up positions in the town. From 9:00 in the morning until 2:00 that afternoon Confederate guns battered the Union barricades without managing to drive the defenders from the square. They did manage to destroy half the buildings in downtown Pine Bluff and set fire to 600 bales of cotton. Finally, the Confederates withdrew, but only after seizing 300 former slaves and driving off hundreds of horses and mules.[23]

Eaton Morse and Theodore Wattles both participated in the "Action at Pine Bluff," the news of which Emma proudly relayed to the family. She reported hearing from them both following the battle, but those letters have not survived, so we do not know which one of them sent to her a copy of Gen. Steele's Order 41, which she in turn passed on to her father. In this document Gen. Steele praised the 5th Kansas for its defense of Pine Bluff and claimed that Marmaduke had attacked the town with 4,000 soldiers, about twice the number of actual Rebels. Emma contended, "The order was written after receiving Col. Clayton's first dispatches and by prisoners they had taken they found that Genl Cabel with 1500 men was there—so they were still more brave and deserve so much more glory."[24] It probably would not have mattered to Emma that Brigadier General William Cabell and his dashing cavalry were nowhere near the Battle of Pine Bluff. The true facts of the battle would have been enough for her to believe that her fiancé and brother were gallant heroes, but still she enjoyed bathing them in "so much more glory."

The Battle of Pine Bluff solidified Col. Clayton's reputation as the Union's most talented cavalry commander west of the Mississippi, but he was not universally popular with his soldiers. Neither Theodore nor Eaton thought highly of him. Originally from Pennsylvania, Clayton had settled in Leavenworth, Kansas, in 1855, where he engaged in surveying and land speculation. When the Civil War broke out, he joined the Union Army as a captain and participated in the Battle of Wilson's Creek in southwestern Missouri in August 1861, earning notice as a cavalry officer. Promoted to lieutenant colonel and then colonel, he was placed in command of the 5th Kansas Cavalry in early 1862.[25] At that time Theodore and Eaton both complained to Emma that Clayton was "a proslavery man" who did not "lack much of being a secessionist. At least he believes more in Slavery than he does in the Union." The comment was not entirely fair to Clayton, but still Emma was "sorry the boys have to serve under such an officer, it is hard enough that they must be away without being under such a man."[26] Susan also seemed aghast at what she heard about Col. Clayton. Eaton had written to her that several officers allegedly resigned because of Clayton's views on slavery, and another was "under arrest because he refused to let some of his men go and guard a slaveholder and his slave (which he had found in camp) to their home, and guard his house that night." Even worse, Susan reported, "A slave woman whom Clayton had given up to a union man, was rescued the night following by some soldier and colored men and brought into camp; she had been severely whipped and was chained. The master came again for her, but she could not be found."[27] Some months later a delegation of Confederate officers came into camp at Helena to return some prisoners. The behavior of Col. Clayton and other officers outraged the soldiers, who

> thought the officers paid altogether too much respect to them. Col Vandiver commanding the Brigade paid every attention to them, even went security for them at the sutlers for $300 worth of goods. The soldiers were very angry—in one of the Iowa Regts. they hung Vandiver in efige and some one in the 5th Kansas put up a finger board pointing to Col. Clayton's tent and on it "*Southern Aid Society*" They say that if the Cols.

& Majors don't quit helping the secessionists so much they are afraid there will be some trouble in the camp.[28]

Although Eaton passed on less-than-flattering stories about his colonel, he was also fair-minded enough to recognize Clayton's strengths and to give Clayton credit for his leadership in battle. He valued Clayton's influence enough never to cross him, winning himself an exemplary recommendation at the end of his service.[29] However, on moral issues Eaton Morse could never be Clayton's man. Eaton was a steadfast teetotaler and despised what he considered the excessive drinking of his fellow officers. He was also as honest as a soldier could be and as true and faithful as any sweetheart could want. On all these counts, Eaton was a much different man than Clayton. The colonel drank heavily and enjoyed indulging in the habit with his officers. Even the puritanical Eaton could not help being drawn into some of the revelry, as he reported to Emma. One night Eaton accompanied fellow officers to "serenade" Col. Clayton:

> The usual routine was gone through music outside, an invitation in and something to drink and cigars inside. I would like such a thing if it was not for this practice of always drinking. We came back down to lead group quarters, went in with the charitable object of keeping the Col. awake until after midnight when he had to go the rounds of the guards. There was a piano in his room and we made "Old Hundred" "Lenox" "Coronation" and many others of the good old pieces suffer besides some of the old songs. We succeeded admirably in keeping the Col. awake and saw him mounted and off on his rounds and then found our own homes.[30]

Not all of the colonel's antics were equally appreciated by his men. After returning to Helena from an especially strenuous mission, Clayton contrived to pull off a "sham" battle between the Union cavalry and artillery, just for "fun." Many of his officers thought the stunt was foolish. "Inspired, according to one of his company commanders, by 'the intoxicating bowl,'" Clayton goaded an artillery officer into staging a fake battle against his cavalry. As told by Clayton's biographer William Burnside, "Clayton and the commander of an artillery battery argued over the number of times the artillery could fire before the Fifth Kansas could sweep across two hundred yards and overwhelm it in a cavalry charge. Despite protestations by nearly all the regimental officers, six artillery guns were loaded with blank cartridges and the Kansas cavalry charged and vanquished the artillery. However, in the dense clouds of smoke fifteen men were thrown from their horses and several were severely injured."[31]

Eaton's greatest scorn for Clayton rested on what Eaton saw as fraternization with other officers' wives and local Southern women. Eaton assumed the worst when he witnessed Col. Clayton with women of dubious reputation, and he was not hesitant about criticizing the women as well as the colonel. According to Eaton, Clayton cavorted with the wife of an Indiana cavalry officer who "has long forgotten what virtue ment. Besides her there are two or three women connected with the Theater, and some few that have come in from the country. With women like these Col. Clayton, Col. Grey, and others of their rank associate, ride and walk in public and do worse in private."[32] Both Eaton and Clayton's biographer obliquely suggested that Clayton's relationship with his future wife might have started with a dalliance connected with his duties as an officer in Helena. After the war Clayton married Adaline McGraw of Helena, whose father was a steamboat captain and hotelier and served as a major in the Confederate Army. Union officers took over McGraw's hotel during the US Army occupation, leading to Clayton's initial acquaintance with Adaline. According to William Burnside, "A persistent tale is that Colonel Clayton once arrested Adaline for her defiant behavior, for she was a spirited Southern lass."[33]

Eaton also believed Clayton had profited from speculation or graft during the war, reporting to Emma, "Those that have the best opportunity of knowing say that Col Clayton has made $40000.00 . . . on hay and corn which have been taken from rebels."[34] Clayton undoubtedly found some scheme for making money during the war because he came out wealthier than when he joined. At war's end he and his brothers were able to purchase a large plantation near Pine Bluff, where Clayton made his home after the war. The lax moral standards of Clayton and other officers left Eaton deeply demoralized, as he revealed to Emma:

> I am really disgusted with the army and were it not for the cause I would not stay another day. To be forced to associate every day on friendly and equal terms with gamblers and drunkards and men that are using their official possessions to swindle the good men that would be sent to the

penitentiary could their transactions be brought to light are among the trials of a respectable man in the army. I want to get out of it or at least get away from here. I see and know too many things without the power of changing them that I wish to get away.[35]

Given Eaton's personal disapproval of his commanding officer, it is ironic that Col. Clayton thought very highly of Captain Morse. Clayton chose Eaton for special duty on several occasions while the 5th Kansas was stationed in Helena, and in Pine Bluff the colonel appointed Eaton to the position of provost marshal, arguably the most important office in an occupied town after that of the commanding officer himself. Although Col. Clayton directed all aspects of the occupation of Pine Bluff, including the use of the town as a springboard for military missions into the countryside, Provost Marshal Morse oversaw the daily administration of the town and all its dealings with the civilian population. The provost marshal and his staff issued passes, trade permits, and rations; received taxes and fees; repaired the streets and put out fires; heard and settled complaints; and administered the oaths of allegiance. Acting as the local police, jury, and judge, the provost marshal had the difficult duty of watching out for spies among the local population and ascertaining who was loyal and who was merely pretending.[36] Provost Marshal Morse directed and carried out the occupation strategy of the US Army in the garrisoned town of Pine Bluff, Arkansas.

That occupation strategy had evolved as the Union Army moved into the South and encountered Confederate-sympathizing Southerners. During the first year of the war most US Army officials believed only a small, elite portion of the Southern population supported secession and rebellion. Convincing themselves that most Southerners really favored the Union, US Army officials at first implemented a policy of tolerance and reconciliation that came to be known as the "rosewater policy." Experience with actual occupied Southerners, however, revealed the hollowness of these assumptions. Southerners did not welcome federal troops as saviors come to liberate them from evil, elite slaveocracy. Instead, most Southerners remained resolutely loyalist to the Confederate cause and defiant toward the Yankee invaders, pouring out venom and hatred toward federal soldiers, calling them names, flaunting Confederate flags, and cursing them roundly. By the end of 1862 US Army officials abandoned the rosewater policy in favor of a "hard" policy of subjugating the South and impressing upon Southerners the error of their ways.[37] Southern women in particular seemed especially vitriolic in their speech and behavior, indulging in what Drew Gilpin Faust has called their "legendary hostility toward invading Yankee soldiers."[38]

Both Northern and Southern men adhered to standards of gender propriety that required men to protect ladies as long as those women performed the expectations of their gender by deferring and submitting to men. Union military leaders acted in contradictory ways in dealing with Southern women in occupied territory as they tried to figure out whether to treat women as ladies or as the enemy. Federal officers often restrained enlisted men from harming upper-class white women, although no such protection was given black women.[39] Some Southern women even acknowledged that Union soldiers acted more gentlemanly than they had expected they would.[40] There were a few places in the South such as Natchez, Mississippi, where the predominating planter elite tilted toward Unionism, making the local population more welcoming to the occupying general Thomas Ransom's policy "to pacify the local citizens and convert more of them to Unionism through a combination of economic restraints and a relative leniency."[41] Elsewhere friendly cooperation was more often than not eclipsed by poorly veiled or outright hostility as Union soldiers learned what Southern women would do to support the Confederate cause. Many women took the example of the ladies of New Orleans, who viciously harassed occupying troops, haranguing them verbally, spitting on them, and emptying chamber pots on their heads from verandas. The occupying general Benjamin Butler outraged Southerners everywhere by issuing Order No. 28, declaring that any woman who demeaned a federal soldier would be treated as a prostitute and imprisoned.[42]

As the Union Army moved into the South, military authorities struggled to deal with the women who carried letters across the lines or smuggled gray cloth to Confederate soldiers, without insulting them or denying them the respect due genteel women. Frustrated with the pro-Confederate activities of the women of Missouri, Commanding General Henry Halleck ordered women to take a loyalty oath in order to enter hospitals housing prisoners of war.[43] Guerrilla warfare brought with it a unique role for women that frustrated occupiers even more, especially those whose gender expectations constrained ungentlemanly behavior. Jurist and philosopher Francis Lieber, who advised President Abraham Lincoln on a military code of law for the Union Army, had emphasized the importance of civilians in enabling guerrillas to operate. Put simply, there could be no guerrilla warfare without the vital supply lines provided by civilians, and those civilians were mostly women. Women who provided guerrilla fighters food, clothing, shelter, and information were therefore combatants, and the Lieber Code allowed military authorities to take measures to curb their activities.[44] The guerrilla warfare so prevalent in Missouri and Arkansas involved an intricate network of sympathetic civilians, Confederate soldiers, and civilian guerrilla fighters. The Union Army managed to garrison and pacify many towns but never completely controlled the countryside, which remained a wide-open no-man's land where ruthless encounters occurred on a regular basis.[45] The treatment received by a Southern woman thus depended on where she lived, not necessarily what activities she might have pursued. Any woman living on an isolated country homestead could be assumed to be helping the guerrillas, and harsh treatment against her and her family might follow without any due process. However, a woman living in a garrisoned town, even if she was carrying information to Confederate military personnel, had a much better chance of being treated with the respect thought due a lady of the time. In occupied towns the interaction of Union officers and Southern-sympathizing women often became a delicate dance of subterfuge, flirtation, and suspicion in which the men could never be quite sure about the women's true thoughts or actions. On this shaky ground Eaton Morse was intensely uncomfortable.

The troops occupying Pine Bluff under the command of Col. Clayton had two somewhat incongruous assignments. They had to hold and pacify the townspeople of Pine Bluff and its immediate environs, and they were to use Pine Bluff as a center of operations to launch missions to suppress Confederate resistance in south-central Arkansas. Regular Confederate soldiers as well as Southern-sympathizing civilian bushwhackers roamed throughout the region surrounding Pine Bluff, and Col. Clayton ordered near-constant raids of varying sizes and duration in which his troops usually engaged armed combatants. Within the town itself and among the neighboring plantations Clayton mandated a different sort of strategy, one more akin to the "rosewater policy" of Grant than to the Lieber Code of treating women as combatants. Clayton encouraged his officers to fraternize liberally with the upper-class women of Pine Bluff, and many of his officers took this duty quite seriously. Captain Morse, if we are to believe the letters written to his fiancée, Emma Wattles, carried out this duty as conscientiously as any other orders but with little enjoyment.

While provost marshal in Pine Bluff, Eaton's position brought him into daily contact with the local citizenry. He kept order in town, heard complaints from civilians, and settled their disputes. Beyond his official position, however, he and other officers were expected to monitor influential women in town and surrounding plantations, many of whom had husbands or brothers serving with Confederate forces. Regular visiting on Saturday evenings and Sundays seemed part of the routine as were frequent dances and balls. Officers dressed in their best uniforms for these occasions, and apparently the women donned fetching apparel as well. Eaton duly reported all of these doings to Emma at the water-cure Our Home on the Hillside in Dansville, New York, the entire time he was in Pine Bluff. Perhaps the two betrothed sweethearts enjoyed telling each other of their encounters with members of the opposite sex. We know from extant letters that Eaton went into great detail about his activities, but we do not have Emma's letters to Eaton to know how she responded. Only her letters to the rest of the family confirm that she also had young male friends in Dansville. Eaton's letters suggest that Emma might have been jealous on occasion because he rushed to reassure her she was first and foremost in his heart, even as he danced the night away with "secesh" women. After one such dance, he wrote her:

I am glad that you are so willing that I should dance the fancy dances. I knew that you would not think me wrong but I like to have you tell me as they are danced more than anything else here while Contra dances reels &c are known nothing of so one would [be] lost in a ballroom if he did not dance some of the fancy dances. It is not that I find so much real enjoyment in these dances, but in doing so I can contribute to the enjoyment of others which is always enjoyment to me. And always darling when I dance with another and my arm partialy encircles their waist as we swing in the giddy whirl of the dance my spirit is dancing with [you]. Few of them are as tall as you are so I look over them into the eyes that always looked directly into mine as we passed in the dance. I always have you with me in all pastimes we have enjoyed together. Some of the ladies have laughed at me for the dignified abstract way in which I go through the figures. They would not have wondered if they had have known who my thoughts were dancing with, the knowledge would not be very flattering to them had they it in their possession.[46]

The occupation of Pine Bluff afforded the Union troops regular excitement because scouting parties went out into the countryside to seek out rebels and engage guerrilla factions, but as in any war, soldiers had many idle hours to fill between missions. Visiting local women was not an unpleasant duty for many of the officers, and no matter what protests Eaton made to the contrary, occasionally his remarks revealed a certain amount of enjoyment in the activity. In late January he reported several outings to Emma. He had

> found time day before yesterday with Lt. Stone to ride out two miles to Dr. Womacks and spend an hour or two with the young ladies. Yesterday Dell, Lt. Goff 28 Wis Inft & I rode out to Mr Keelies but found but one of the ladies at home and she poor girl was sorely afflicted with a felon on her hand. The others were out horse back riding. Today Lt Lefler Lt Murphy & Lt Jenkins are out there. These country ladies get many more calls than those in town for nearly every one enjoys the ride quite as well as the visit.[47]

Despite occasionally enjoying himself, however, Eaton earned a reputation as "the Puritan" during his stay in Pine Bluff. Writing to Emma, he scoffed at her suggestion that his vanity had been puffed up by so much feminine attention and told her Col. Clayton had once introduced him to two ladies by saying, "This is Capt. Morse, the Provost Marshall better known at Pine Bluff as the 'Crabbed Man.'" One of the women knew him well and "thinks it a good joke and makes a most unmercifull use of it. My being an abolitionist and strictly temperate wins me more unpopularity than anything else. I am a constant thorn in the sides of the drinking public and that realy means everybody here."[48] His attempts at regulating public consumption of alcohol won neither him nor the Union occupiers in general any favor from the local population. In January 1864, the Union sutler got hold of several barrels of wine and ale and claimed that Col. Clayton had given him a permit to sell it. No one had bothered to tell Captain Morse about it, and the first Eaton knew of it, the streets were filling with drunken reeling men. I had not heard that there was a drop in town before. I soon found out the cause and in spite of Col Claytons permit I stopped the sale and placed a guard over the liquors. Officer & citizens remonstrated but I was firm. and told them that for once Col Claytons permit availed them not. The Col came along soon after. I told him what I had done. He said "That's right" and to those that went to him afterwards for orders for some of the liquor he said "I leave those things entirely with Capt Morse." If he keeps his word the liquor trade will not be worth much in this town. I forbid the Capt of the last steamer selling a drop while here. and by so doing kept many a poor topic dry. I afterwards gave the man in charge of [the sutler's] liquor permission to sell it by the quantity to citizens and the officers each one becoming responsible for its use—I care most to keep the show of its use off the streets though if any more come and the Col does not interfere I shall forbid its sale entirely.[49]

Eaton faced a lost cause in trying to keep the town dry, but other aspects of pacification could not be abandoned so easily. Pro-Confederate sentiment ran high in Pine Bluff, and all the Union officers knew it. Their efforts to win the cooperation of the town's women only partially succeeded, if that, and if Union military authorities had any illusions they had won over the Southern ladies, Eaton did not. He told Emma about a group of resolute Confederate women who declined all invitations to dances given by Union officers and refused to invite any federal soldiers to their own dances or homes. He doubted the sincerity of those who came to the dances and fraternized with Union men, suspecting them of hiding their true feelings beneath a façade of civility. The women of Pine Bluff would hardly have been the only Southern women to use such subterfuge to survive an occupation by Union troops, but Eaton did not appreciate the ruse. "I can hardly call it enjoyment," he wrote Emma, "this seeming friendliness with people that would see you hung with little feeling for you if it is enjoyment at all. It is of a negative kind and worth but little though I do laugh in my sleep at their ill concealed hatred of us."[50] Eaton reserved special scorn for women he himself had misjudged. Early in the occupation he had become acquainted with Miss Ruth Stephens and told Emma she was the only woman in Pine Bluff whose company and conversation he enjoyed. He believed her inclined to Unionism despite having a brother in the Confederate Army. Eaton had made it possible for her and some friends to cross the lines to visit their kin serving in the Confederate forces. However, "her visit south has spoiled her," he complained to Emma;

> she comes back most abusively secesh. A lady friend of hers came up with her and wishing to take some goods back she had to take the oath and by request of Miss Stephens I went to their house to fill out the papers and administer the oath. Miss Stephens made use of the occasion to make light of the oath and the ceremony to such an extent that I became thoroughly roused and told the young lady about what at least one federal thought of her. Then took my hat and left the house. She is the lady that thought I did not care a straw for any lady. She can safely make an application of that remark to herself.[51]

Eaton had little confidence in the sincerity of quite a number of Pine Bluff citizens when it came to taking the oath of allegiance. He had good reason to doubt the goodwill of Southern women when it came to the loyalty oath. Across the Confederacy, the oath incited seething outrage among women, who chafed not merely at the idea of swearing loyalty to a despised government but also to the notion that the hated government had such power to interfere in their private affairs.[52] Under orders from Col. Clayton, citizens could not be employed or cross the lines unless they took the oath. Eaton reported that by mid-March "nearly all the citizens have taken the Oath," but he doubted they had truly disavowed their disloyalty. "Some of the bitterest secessionists took the oath and in less than two days had their names placarded all over the town for some office in the re-organization of the state. One of these candidates is now carrying a black eye which one of our soldiers gave him for shouting for Jef Davis. I expect the thrashing converted him."[53]

Although Eaton excoriated unrepentant secessionists, he had the highest praise for one young man who had fought for the Rebel side. "I think I wrote you of Lt. Hall CSA comeing in and taking the oath," he told Emma:

> He belonged in Sandusky Co, Ohio, was in Texas when the war broke out and so got into the southern army. He was stationed here for a long time and became enamored and finaly engaged to Miss Sue Harding a Young Lady of this town. She is a violent secessionist and his coming in

and taking the oath so exasperated the lady that she broked the engagement and the young gent has gone on to his home in Ohio. I am of the opinion that he did one of the best acts of his life when he renewed his allegiance to the govt. and one of its richest fruits was his freedom from this southern miss.[54]

During the year Eaton and Theodore spent at Pine Bluff, Eaton very seldom accompanied the cavalry on the various forays into the field to find and engage the enemy. Theodore, on the other hand, frequently went on missions in pursuit of Confederate troops or civilian guerrillas. Consequently, Theodore experienced a much different war than his friend and future brother-in-law. Although we cannot say their different experiences made them different men throughout the rest of their lives, it is true Theodore witnessed and participated in a much more prolonged period of ruthless warfare than Eaton did. Although Eaton had taken part in pitched battles and counterguerrilla operations during the first two years of his service, his tenure as provost marshal was mundane compared with the outings undertaken by soldiers who rode through the Arkansas timberlands searching for enemy soldiers and dealing with Confederate-sympathizing citizens. Theodore's greater restiveness at war's end might have resulted from extended exposure to this brutal form of warfare.

By mid-1863 the war in Arkansas offered little hope to the Southern cause, yet Confederate forces and sympathizers continued to resist federal takeover and on several occasions posed a significant threat to Union control. The Union occupied the garrisoned towns of Fort Smith, Little Rock, DuVall's Bluff, Helena, and others; controlled the Mississippi, Arkansas, and White Rivers; and held the countryside of the northern and eastern portions of the state at least in name. The Confederates held southwestern Arkansas and operated sporadically throughout much of the state's rural areas. Soldiers and bushwhackers of both sides foraged widely, making life frightening and miserable for civilians. Economic activity nearly ceased, and many families faced destitution and starvation. Beyond the occupied towns, near anarchy reigned.[55] After the war many Arkansas women recalled the horrors of living under the threat of visiting Yankees, whom they blamed for their troubles more than Southern marauders. Mrs. M. M. Hendrix of Big Fork remembered how anxious she felt for her four children's welfare after her Confederate husband died in battle. She might have managed, she said, because she "could work in the field and chop wood and I had some provisions laid by and the house was comfortably furnished, but federal soldiers came and robbed me of everything, not leaving a mouthful at times for myself and little ones."[56] Of all the federal soldiers in Arkansas, however, soldiers from Kansas earned the worst reputation when it came to "looting, wanton destruction, and brutality," in the words of Arkansas historian Thomas A. DeBlack.[57] The 5th Kansas contributed to this unfortunate characterization. Mrs. S. D. Dickson of Lockesburg was left at home with two children when her husband went to serve with the Confederate Army. She could barely write of "all I did suffer when Col. Clayton, the Northern man, was at Pine Bluff." As she remembered,

> He sent his men to make raids on the Southerners and destroy all they could, besides taking everything of value for themselves. The first thing they started out to do was to take everything they could find. Twenty bales of cotton were taken out of the smokehouse at one time, five horses were also taken. They searched the house and got every article of any value they could find. Sometimes it would take one and a half days for us to get any food.[58]

According to her reminiscences, Mrs. Dickson's slaves remained with her, doing "all they could on the farm with hoes for we had no horses. One time the Federals overtook the slaves hauling cotton from the gin, and it was taken from them." Another time Col. Clayton sent twenty wagons to her farm to take "three large barns of corn" and 2,000 pounds of meat from her. "Clayton's men went down in our pasture, and all the beeves were killed and taken away."[59]

Memories that remained so vivid forty years after the end of the war might have been embellished or perhaps displaced from one federal regiment to another or even from civilian guerrillas to Yankees, but it hardly mattered. The 5th Kansas came out of the war with a dark reputation for its actions in Arkansas, and it is very possible Theodore Wattles participated in some of that soul-rending work. No explicit confessions of brutality emerged in his brusque letters, but we would not expect to see any such references. When Eaton wrote of Theodore, he put the best face on everything his friend did and described few personal details. "Theodore started this morning with twenty men under Lt. McCarthy on a scout for four days in the direction of Monticello," Eaton told Emma in a typical report about her brother's activities. Theodore's unit had gone out in response to

vague rumors that the enemy were advancing from the South, in large force and the citizens generally believed that the town would be attacked, but Scouts have been out and report no advance, but that the Saline river for miles up and down was picketed by the rebels. But there was not the least evidence that they were crossing except in small squads yesterday and today two Lieutenants and eight men were captured. Most of these are Texans belonging to Parson's famous Brigade.[60]

The closest Theodore himself came to telling anyone what his experience might have been like were in letters to his father, who, ironically, was the most ambivalent about the war of any in the family. Yet Theodore described the weapons the soldiers of the 5th Kansas carried, boasting that in addition to the Sharps rifle and Colt navy revolver all the men in his company had, he also carried "a six inch Aleno revolver such as the one you gave me & a light saber there is but one other as good in the Regt." On a recent expedition they had

marched thirty five miles and bridged a creek. The second thirty miles, within five miles of Cotton Plant where we heard there was no forse there and that the bridge across a bayou had been distroyed so that we could not get to it, the third day we started back & on the night of the fourth arrived in camp. What the object of the scout was I don't know. We killed one man and took several prisoners, perhaps that's all that was intended.

While out on expeditions, Theodore continued,

we live well at night when [in] camp we expect to have set potatoes chickens fresh, ham, eggs, butter, milk and corn bread, sit up half the night cooking & eating. When we go in to camp evry fellow takes something. chickens, goose, bucket of butter a canteen filled with honey whiskey or milk. some times an enterpriseing chap brings in a mule which he sells to the sutler before morning for ten or fifteen dollars. That's the way the war goes down here.[61]

Theodore offers no explanation of the origins of the food, the whiskey, or the mules, but many pillaging soldiers experienced guilt and remorse during and after the war for their part in depriving civilians of their livelihood.[62]

Unfortunately, Augustus's correspondence to Theodore has not survived, although Theodore acknowledged receiving letters from his father. Early in the war Augustus despaired that "thousands are killed & thousands die" in the conflict,[63] and certainly he worried for Theodore's life, as any parent would. However, we have to wonder what he thought about the prospect that *Theodore* might have killed someone, even if it was in a great conflict to end slavery. Theodore did not brag about his exploits to his father, but there was no mistaking the confidence in his ability to do his part in the war. In January 1864, Theodore participated in a significant fight that included four days of hard riding and skirmishing with a large force of Confederates. Eaton, who stayed behind in Pine Bluff, described the battle in two full pages to Emma, whereas Theodore laconically outlined the action in a few lines. According to Eaton,

> Col. Clayton had taken off with all the available force in the direction of Monticello 12 miles from here at a bridge. They encountered the rebs drove them from their posision and there waited until daylight. They then pushed on and soon came upon them and for ten miles a running fight was kept up through swamp and wood and field, our men steadily pushing them back not once stopping but forcing them from tree and log. Our force was not more than 550 men. The force of the enemy was from 1000 to 1500. It was Shelby's old Missouri force. The men represent it as being one of the most exciting affairs that they had ever taken part in.[64]

Theodore reported the same battle by telling Augustus,

> We have had considerable scouting lately and some fighting. We started from here at twelve oclock on the night of the 18th of Jan. Met the enemy twenty-five miles from here next morning at ten oclock had a runing fight for six miles then came back here that night. We lost one man killed and one wounded since died and killed eight. Gen Shelby is said to bee one of them.

Then, after passing on some news about friends, Theodore said he could not describe the battle and closed the letter to his father, saying, "Don't know that I killed any one, am a pretty good shot."[65]

Both Theodore and Eaton avoided the worst debacle suffered by Union forces in Arkansas, though Eaton helped to manage the flow of wounded and captured soldiers that came through Pine Bluff from the battlefield. The Red River Expedition of March–April 1864 was supposed to eradicate the Confederate presence in northern Louisiana and southern Arkansas and pave the way for a Union invasion of Texas. Gen. Steele would march his army south from Little Rock to meet up with Major General Nathaniel P. Banks, who would come up the Red River to take Shreveport, Louisiana. Steele never made it to Shreveport. General Sterling Price sent the only Confederate troops he had—two cavalry divisions—out under Generals John Marmaduke and Jo Shelby to harass Steele's advancing troops. The Union forces, low on supplies and fighting off cavalry attacks, managed to reach the town of Camden by mid-April. Badly in need of food for his army, Steele sent nearly 200 wagons with an armed escort out to a small town reported to have a large store of corn. After seizing the supply of corn, the Union troops were set upon by a large Confederate force at Poison Spring, fourteen miles west of Camden. The Confederates, which included brigades of Texans and Choctaws from the Indian Territory, killed or wounded more than 300 Union soldiers, captured 170 wagons full of corn and other supplies, and drove off with 1,200 mules. The 1st Kansas Colored Infantry Regiment sustained the worst losses of all and suffered the greatest brutality. The Choctaw troops gave no mercy to wounded or surrendering black troops but shot them dead and scalped them. Out of 400 soldiers in the unit, the 1st Kansas Colored had 117 men killed and 65 wounded at the Battle of Poison Spring. Three days later Steele attempted to send another supply train to Pine Bluff, and Confederate forces ambushed it at Mark's Mill. The result was the same. The Union force suffered great casualties, and every black person in the company was killed. A federal soldier reported, "There was not an armed negro with us & they shot down our Colored servents & teamsters & others that were following to get from bondage as they would shoot sheep dogs."[66]

Within days Steele's army stole back to Little Rock but did manage to repulse a Confederate follow-up attack. In Pine Bluff Eaton helped with the wounded and counted the dead. He sent Emma a breathless description of the aftermath of the calamitous campaign. It was a "lamentable sight this long line of Ambulances with the maimed and mutilated braves," he wrote. "I talked with many of the wounded as they were waiting to be transferred from the ambulance to the church which we have turned into a hospital. They hardly seemed to think of their wounds but on their faces was the flush of pride and on their tongues were words of cheer and exultation." Eaton admitted that he "almost envied them this situation as they related to the incidents of the desperate fight." Although the fight lasted only a few hours, the result was 500 killed and wounded men. However, Eaton most wanted to relate to Emma the fate of the black soldiers of Kansas, some of whom had been acquaintances from Moneka:

> Both the Kansas colored regiments were engaged and behaved most gallantly, both regiments took canon and what is better did not take a prisoner, every man was bayoneted. They have taken retaliation in their own hands. . . . Col. Williams of the 1st Kans. Colored was out from Camden with a train and 1200 colored troops and was attacked by at least 6000 rebels and every soldier or officer that was taken or wounded was murdered and the officers scalped among these was Lt Chas Coleman who I believe you used to know. Huddleson was wounded slightly but got away. Yesterday these negros had an opportunity of paying them back in their own coin. It is reported that Gen. Kirby Smith was wounded yesterday and that one of his generals was killed. Gen. Rice of our army was wounded. They have quite a force now so to make us realy safe ever should the enemy come. There are no particulars about our fight a few days ago we don't know who is dead and who are prisoners. After the rebs had picked up their dead and the wounded the woods got on fire and nearly all our dead were burned so as not to be recognized. There were nearly 100 of our dead found on the field but we can have no idea who they are until the prisoners got back there was nearly 200 wounded. Over 50 defenseless negroes were killed. Two of our 60 one of them Henry Carbon of Moneka are among the missing, probably prisoners from all we can learn all our officers that are missing were taken prisoners. Most of them wounded.[67]

For several weeks the Pine Bluff garrison remained on alert, but no Confederate attacks came. The war for Eaton and Theodore settled into a monotonous routine of responsibilities associated with the provost marshal's office. Eaton seems to have attached Theodore to his own office somehow, and although scouting parties continued to engage guerrilla fighters in the countryside, neither Eaton nor Theodore reported the latter being involved. The 5th Kansas Cavalry was due to muster out in late July, and Eaton expressed his impatience in long letters to Emma. Before leaving Pine Bluff, Eaton looked back on his time in the Union Army and felt most proud about having gone through the war without succumbing to corruption. Witnessing the behavior of fellow officers had been the most eye-opening and disillusioning aspect of the war for him. "The temptations to be dishonest have been great here," he wrote to Emma.

> Those that are temperate and economical just make both ends meet, and those that drink gamble & do worse must speculate & steal. So that there is not one officer in five that has not done something in this line that he would prefer his friends at home would know nothing of. Those that have the best opportunity of knowing say that Col Clayton has made $40000.00 and Lt Hillyer the Quarter Master is reported to have made considerable amounts on hay and corn which have been taken from rebels.

He did not regret not following their example of self-indulgence or self-aggrandizement, although he acknowledged that he could have emerged from the war a much richer man.

> I have not wanted in opportunities to make money in this way. I was offered at one time $6000.00 worth of cotton to decide a cotton case that came before me in favor of one of the claimants. I would have been safe to have made the decision in favor of the person offering the bribe for the evidence was nicely balanced and my decision was final. I was however satisfied that the cotton should be confiscated and turned the whole lot 72 bales worth $20,000 over to the government. I could have made 13,000 dollars since I have been here, had I been a little dishonest, and have been thought just as much of by most people, but I should hardly have tolerated myself.[68]

By mid-August 1864, Eaton and Theodore were on their way via steamboat and railcar to Leavenworth, Kansas, where they would muster out of the US Army.[69] Eaton and Emma were both impatient to be married as soon as his military service ended, which posed a logistical problem because she had committed to remain at Our Home on the Hillside in New York through the end of the year. They decided that after his mustering out, he would make a brief visit to Moneka, Kansas, where Theodore would stay.

Then Eaton planned to travel east, stopping to see his own family in Ohio before going on to New York and Emma. They would be married at Our Home. Theodore and Eaton were joyously welcomed home by the Wattles family in Moneka. Eaton visited old friends and caught up with his brother, Orlando, who had failed miserably to meet up to the standards of his older brother while Eaton was away. One senses that Orlando had let their joint business ventures slide and perhaps had married a woman not quite to Eaton's liking, but such disappointments did not deter an otherwise loving reunion. The real business at hand, however, was getting back East to marry Emma, and by October, that had also been accomplished. No other family members except Augustus were close enough to attend the wedding, and even Augustus might not have made it, writing to Emma that he would come if his brother-in-law David Ripley could lend him money but to go ahead with the ceremony.[70] By March 1865, Eaton and Emma Morse were back in Kansas, settling into their new life together. Eaton apparently experienced very little restlessness at war's end and made a smooth transition into civilian life. He and Emma started a family and eventually had five sons and a daughter. All the Morse children attended college, including their daughter, Eleanor. They lived on a farm where Eaton and his boys raised prized purebred hogs. Eaton also sold furniture, delved into Kansas state politics as a staunch Republican, and became a trusted bank auditor. In the 1890s and 1900s he became the primary organizer of annual reunions of the 5th Kansas Cavalry chapter of the Grand Army of the Republic (GAR). He was a lifelong teetotaler.

Theodore Wattles emerged from the Union Army a more troubled man than his friend and brother-in-law. When he first reached home, he told his father he had no intention of going back into the US Army, but neither did he want to "stay home and studdy I have not time or inclination. I do not thirst for glory & knowledge Money is the mane thing in this world."[71] In six months' time he had changed his mind, telling Augustus he "couldant stand it out of the army," and he reenlisted for a $630 bounty and the promise of another $100 bonus after a year of service.[72] Theodore's emphasis on making money would have been a deep blow to Augustus, who despised greed and who lived nearly hand to mouth all his life. Theodore might have harbored some resentment of Augustus's values, and although he did not sharply rebuke his father, he declared his independence from the older generation's idealism. Writing to Augustus from Camp Stoneman outside of Washington, DC, Theodore told him, "God humanity and the ignorant negroes can look out for themselves. I will not consider any proposition which does not have for its exclusive object the benefit of myself and those near and dear to me."[73]

After his military service was done in early 1866, we lose track of Theodore through the family letters. We do not know how his relationship with his father evolved in the years between the end of the war and Augustus's death in 1876. There are hints that he attended a bookkeeping course, perhaps in Chicago, and he might have gone back to Kansas for a while. No definite sign of him appears until 1875. Theodore had gone west, as so many Civil War veterans did, to seek his fortune and adventure. He wandered around the Navajo Reservation of northern Arizona and New Mexico before heading to the mining district of the upper Animas River in the San Juan Mountains of Colorado. There he found a niche for himself that seemed to please him. With a friend he started a freighting business, hauling supplies and logs to the mines around Rico. He homesteaded some land near Mancos, built himself a small cabin, and began to farm even as he continued to hire out his team and wagon. He married, had two children, and struggled to support them on a farm with poor soil during times of volatile markets. The work ground him down and ruined his health, and he might have compensated for a rough life by drinking too heavily. In many ways he was a typical western settler.

The Wattles family survived the Civil War without casualties, unlike so many other families. The two family members who fought actively in the war experienced it differently in part because one was an officer and the other a sergeant, even though they spent the war in the same unit. Eaton Morse entered the war a solid, morally upright, and conscientious man, and nothing that happened to him in the conflict appeared to have shaken that steadfast character. He intensely disliked what he saw in other men, but he did not give in himself to the lure of drink, wantonness, or corruption. He continued to believe long after the war was over that the twin causes of Union and emancipation were well worth the effort and sacrifice. Theodore Wattles, on the other hand, came out of the war with a restless spirit and profound disillusionment with his parents' high idealism. Theodore had never been a studious child, and as the only boy in the family probably did a lot of manual labor and animal husbandry as he grew up, but he did receive the same moral instruction as his sisters did. He had experienced wartime conditions as a teenager in Bleeding Kansas, but it was never violence just for the sake of violence, even in the harshest conflict. Yet somewhere along the way Theodore abandoned his faith in his parents' utopian dreams and their dedication to the cause of improving the lives of black people.

The nature of war is that it breaks apart the lives of many, even those who survive. Even for families that survive the war physically intact, the experience is a watershed, a profound event families do not choose but that is thrust upon them. War is a time when the family loses control of its own destiny and must respond to events rather than shape them. The war affects all the members of the family, not just the person who goes into the military and leaves home to participate. For the Wattles family the Civil War was the culmination of a generation's struggle to bring about the end of slavery. Every member of this abolitionist family knew what this war was all about, why it had to be fought, and why its outcome was significant in the life of the nation. The war and emancipation might well have served as the crowning achievement in the narrative of this family and in its members' own sense of identity. In constructing their family memories about the war, however, the heroics of their fighting men played a distinctively secondary role to the part performed by their abolitionist parents and especially to their father's association with John Brown. The war had meaning to the Wattles family because it was the culmination of the much more significant crusade of freeing the slaves, and the great hero of that struggle was John Brown. To the Wattles children, their father deserved the greatest honor of any in the family because he had supported John Brown. They maintained this as the favored family narrative even as Americans at large contested the positive memory of Brown and the abolitionists and came to embrace a culture of reconciliation that downplayed the cause of emancipation.

John Brown's reputation did not fare well in the aftermath of the Civil War, and the Wattleses' defense of their father's association with Brown reflected awareness that Brown's fall from grace meant Augustus's glory would be tarnished as well. Almost as soon as the war was over, Southern writers began the "Lost Cause" defense of the Confederacy, arguing that the North, led by rabid abolitionists, had forced the South into secession and war unnecessarily, and the South responded only to defend the states' rights doctrine of the Constitution. In this view slavery had not been the cause of the war and would not have been a sore point between the sections if the abolitionists had not created such a fuss about it. For defenders of the Lost Cause, John Brown was a villain of the most heinous sort.[74] As long as Reconstruction was ongoing, Northerners interpreted the Civil War as a just cause to end slavery and viewed John Brown as a heroic soldier in that crusade. In the late 1870s, however, Northerners began to contest the meaning of the Civil War and the role of slavery in the conflict. Motivated by a desire for national reconciliation, some Northern writers and politicians adopted the Southern view of abolitionists as troublemakers and John Brown as a fanatic and a madman. Slavery was conveniently forgotten as a cause of the war, and emancipation, as well as racial justice in the aftermath of Reconstruction, disappeared from Memorial Day speeches now dedicated to the heroism and sacrifice of both Union and Confederate soldiers.[75]

Survivors of the old days of Bleeding Kansas entered this war of words, with much of their argument focused on John Brown and his actions' significance in Kansas history. This pot had been stirred by the revelations of James Townsley, published in 1879, attesting to Brown's complicity in the Pottawatomie Massacre of May 1856.[76] Brown himself had denied responsibility for the murders of five proslavery settlers carried out under his orders by his sons, son-in-law, and Townsley, and many of his followers, including Augustus Wattles, had chosen to believe Brown's assertion at the time. Townsley's revelations were soon followed by a denunciation of John Brown by the former editor of the *Herald of Freedom,* George Washington Brown, who in 1880 published *The Truth at Last: History Corrected. Reminiscences of Old John Brown*. G. W. Brown argued that John Brown had received far too much adulation for his exploits in Kansas, which had done nothing to advance the free-state cause and had served only to stir up chaos and mayhem in the territory. G. W. Brown had been inspired to write "corrections" of the historical record after attending a celebration of the Old Settlers of Kansas held near Lawrence in September 1879, celebrating the twenty-fifth anniversary of the founding of Kansas. There, he said, he was surrounded by "the *real* heroes in the strife; those who a year earlier than old John Brown, had settled in Kansas; who had taken their families with them; who had sacrificed everything but honor for the triumph of a principle."[77] G. W. Brown intensified his attack on John Brown in *False Claims of Kansas Historians Truthfully Corrected,* published in 1902. Arguing that

John Brown "went to fight, not to settle" in Kansas, the former editor called the old abolitionist "a parasite, working, not for the freedom of Kansas, but to embroil the Union in sectional strife, hoping thereby to hasten the extinction of American slavery."[78]

The battle for John Brown's reputation in Kansas had a tenacious champion in Franklin Adams, another old settler and secretary of the Kansas State Historical Society, who believed not only in John Brown's heroism but in the importance of preserving a positive view of Brown for the cause of Kansas history. Adams doggedly collected all the documents and memorabilia pertaining to John Brown he could find, including items he solicited from the Brown family. In 1882 he invited Mary Brown, widow of John Brown, to visit Kansas, and he arranged a grand reception for her at the Kansas statehouse.[79] Adams also sought testimony from old settlers about their experiences in Bleeding Kansas, often asking for specific information that might cast a positive light on John Brown and his Kansas friends. In 1887 Adams contacted Eaton Morse and others to confirm an old story that a group of Kansas men had attempted a rescue of John Brown while he was in a Charlestown, Virginia, jail awaiting trial. Adams urged Morse to write an account of the rescue attempt.[80] Eaton promised Adams he would write something about the attempted rescue but did not complete the project until 1903, when he gave an address to the Kansas State Historical Society, "An Attempted Rescue of John Brown from Charlestown, VA., Jail," subsequently published in the *Kansas State Historical Society Collections*.[81] According to this account, Augustus Wattles, James Montgomery, and other Kansas men traveled east to Hagerstown, Maryland, in late October 1859 with the intent of rescuing John Brown from the jail in Charlestown. One member of their party gained access to the jail and was able to speak with John Brown, who told him he did not wish to be rescued because he believed his execution would have a greater impact on public opinion than if he survived. Thus rebuffed, the would-be rescuers returned to Kansas. To Eaton Morse, the rescue attempt constituted great heroism. "By their devotion to the cause of freedom in the early Kansas days," Eaton wrote, "by their patriotic service in the army and good citizenship afterward, these men made a record that might well be emulated by any group of American citizens."[82]

To Eaton and the other members of the Wattles family, it mattered that Augustus would be remembered as John Brown's strong and loyal friend who would risk his life in a daring rescue attempt. The stories that they passed on, however, did not skew the truth, as they remembered it, simply to reinforce the importance of the relationship with Brown. It was also important to them to be accurate and to agree among themselves on what was truthful. Some people in Kansas believed John Brown had told Augustus Wattles and James Montgomery about his plans to attack Harpers Ferry when Brown was last in Kansas, in December 1858. If true, this would imply the two Kansans had faithfully guarded Brown's secret rather than alert authorities. It would also mean Augustus Wattles was lying when he testified before a Senate committee investigating the Harpers Ferry incident that he had had no prior knowledge of the plan.[83] In 1887, in response to Franklin Adams's letters of inquiry about Brown's activities in Kansas, a former Moneka resident, Theodore Botkin, claimed he had seen maps and documents proving that Brown had tried to recruit both Augustus Wattles and James Montgomery, that they both refused to support the raid, and that Montgomery's widow had preserved the evidence in an old trunk.[84] Adams sent Botkin's letter to Eaton, who knew nothing about it and asked Emma to contact other family members to see if they remembered the events. Susan Wattles, then living with Mary Ann in New York, wrote back indignantly, wondering

> what could induce Botkin to write such an article of lies. The last time John Brown was with us, was before we moved into the stone house. My husband was sick, in bed. Capt. Brown did not speak definitely about his plans when he found my husband objected to his idea Capt Brown said "Kansas has suffered enough, I think it is my duty to draw this excitement away from here."

Susan claimed Mrs. Montgomery brought a trunk to the Wattles home after her husband's death and asked Augustus to examine the contents, but "there were no such maps or plans in it." Susan urged Emma to write to Mrs. Montgomery and ask her to write to Secretary Adams. "I should like to have her statement corroborate ours," Susan concluded.[85]

Sarah Grimké Wattles Hiatt also recalled the evening Brown spent at the Wattles home in December 1858, in which she heard the conversation between Brown, Montgomery, and her father. Sarah remembered, "My work made it necessary for me to go in and out of the room where they sat, & once when I went in Capt. Brown stopped in something he was saying,

Father said 'you need not stop, my children never repeat anything they hear said,' so the conversation went on." She continued, saying,

> The only thing I distinctly remember was the Capt's (Brown) saying that he felt impelled and bound to do anything for the freeing of the slaves, that he would do if his own brother were a slave, and justified in any means that he would resort to free a brother; and he quoted the text about "remembering those in bonds as bound with them," implying that he considered it a direct command to himself. Again he made some remarks about "carrying the war into Africa." I do not know just what he said but father replied quite at length setting forth the futility and folly of any conflict with the U.S. government, and Montgomery emphatically endorsed what he, father, said.[86]

Although Sarah's comments leave the reader wondering just what "conflict with the U.S. government" was discussed, she left no doubt about what she thought of Botkin's version of things, declaring, "Theo. Botkin must have been drunk when he wrote that letter."[87]

Emma Wattles Morse solidified the family story in 1928, when she published a highly adulatory biographical sketch of Augustus in the *Collections of the Kansas State Historical Society*. In her "Sketch of the Life and Work of Augustus Wattles," Emma offered a flattering version of her father's life, glossing over many details of stories that would have shown Augustus as an admirable figure had they been told truthfully but that depicted him as positively saint-like in her telling. Here she referred to the conversation Sarah had witnessed but said of it that "Brown gave no hint of the plan he was forming" and that "no one thought of his plan to go to Virginia." She related, "When in October the papers told of Brown's fiasco at Harper's Ferry no one was more surprised than were his friends and associates in Kansas."[88]

On the whole it makes little difference whether Augustus knew beforehand that John Brown was going to attack Harpers Ferry, but it mattered a great deal to the family to get this point right in their telling of the story. By 1928, when Emma wrote the biographical sketch of Augustus, there was no one left alive to corroborate her version, yet she adhered to what she, Susan, and Sarah had decided was the truth. It mattered to the family that Augustus Wattles should be remembered for his work as an abolitionist, including his support of John Brown, but not for refusing to help John

Brown attack Harpers Ferry. The stories of the abolitionists become the favored family memory, even eclipsing stories about the Civil War itself. The Wattles children did not write about or publish stories about the Civil War experiences of the veterans in the family. Eaton's wartime service could easily have been considered exemplary, but he chose not to write about it. Emma wrote no paeans to her husband. The important memory was that of their abolitionist parents, not their soldiers who fought in the war.

This is not to say that the family discounted the importance of Eaton's Civil War experience but rather that the memory did not reflect his own glory alone. For Eaton himself, the comradeship with his fellow soldiers ultimately seemed to matter more. In the 1880s Eaton became the secretary of the 5th Kansas Cavalry Association of the GAR. Until 1900 he organized almost annual reunions of the association, usually held in Kansas City, Missouri, or St. Louis so that attendees would have good railroad connections. He corresponded with former members of the unit, wrote to their families, and updated the roster every year to indicate who had died. He contacted his old company commander, Col. Clayton, who had gone on to become a Reconstruction governor of Arkansas and make a nice fortune for himself. Clayton wrote back, grateful to Eaton for organizing the reunion:

> It is my intention to attend the encampment at St. Louis, and I trust that yourself and as many of the old 5th boys as can, will be present. The roster of officers and men of the 5th Kansas is, I think very complete, and must have cost you a good bit of labor to get it up, and will be a valuable list for the survivors of the old regiment.[89]

For Eaton and for Theodore, who never attended a reunion of the 5th Kansas but did join a GAR association in Colorado, the meaning of the Civil War was found in being together with fellow veterans.

Across the nation, North and South, Americans tried to find meaning in the Civil War by honoring soldiers. Veterans' organizations such as the GAR and Confederate Veterans of America remembered their old comrades at their meetings and reunions, but the women's auxiliary organizations led the way in constructing the most lasting rituals of remembrance.[90] Sarah helped to construct her family's memory of the Civil War by participating in the memorialization of the soldiers, choosing to do so as a member of the Woman's Relief Corps (WRC), the women's auxiliary of the GAR. As president of the Mound City WRC in 1906, Sarah gave a

Memorial Day address at the Mound City Cemetery. It was typical of hundreds of addresses presented that day across the country. She stated:

> Sisters of the Woman's Relief Corps—Brothers of the Grand Army of the Republic!—It is our privilege—our part of this day's sacred duties to offer tribute to the memory of the unknown dead—to those whose graves—if they have graves are marked with the word "unknown." They passed from life unnoted. They are martyrs whose halos are seen only by angelic vision—heroes the note of whose fame is heard only on the celestial shore.
>
> > "Somewhere the long grass
> > Over lonely graves
> > Sobs in the rain.
> > Somewhere the wild wind
> > Vainly o'er them raves
> > Who rest from pain
> > Somewhere through weary years
> > They weep whose salt slow tears
> > Fall for refrain."
>
> To those darkened lives this is our tribute. To those stricken bleeding hearts this our offering of sisterly sympathy. The Woman's Relief Corps comes to the graves of the nameless heroes with reverence, honor and deepest gratitude.[91]

Like her countrywomen, Sarah saw it as her sacred duty to memorialize the Civil War dead, especially the unknown fallen soldier. It was a recognition of individuals who had unreservedly given of themselves and who had acted out of a sense of duty for the greater good. This was something Sarah instinctively understood because her parents had instilled it in her from childhood. What she did not say in this brief address, that her family had sent two men to fight in this war, surely crossed her mind that day. Just as likely, she had paused at the grave of her father and mother in that same cemetery and considered that the cause of the war was the great crusade of their lives, and the least that she could do was to remember it.

Susan E. Lowe as a young woman, ca. 1835.
Courtesy of Carol Ann Wetherill Getz.

Augustus Wattles.
Courtesy of Kansas State Historical Society.

Sarah Grimké Wattles Hiatt (*left*) and Susan E. Lowe Wattles. Courtesy of Carol Ann Wetherill Getz.

Theodore Wattles.
Courtesy of Carol Ann Wetherill Getz.

Mary Ann Wattles Faunce.
Courtesy of Carol Ann Wetherill Getz.

Emma Wattles Morse.
Courtesy of Carol Ann Wetherill Getz.

Orlin Eaton Morse.
Courtesy of Carol Ann Wetherill Getz.

Woman's Medical College of New York class of 1870. Front row (*left to right*):
Emma Ward, Ellen E. Mitchell, Dr. Emily Blackwell, Celestia A. Loring, Laura
Morgan. Back row (*left to right*): Charlotte Ford, Mercy N. Baker, Nancie Nouella,
Ellen Hammond, Mary J. Studley, Mary Ann Wattles, Dr. Fulton. Courtesy of
Carol Ann Wetherill Getz.

Susan Lowe Wattles and her
granddaughter Hilda Faunce,
ca. 1890. Courtesy of Carol Ann
Wetherill Getz.

Win and Hilda Wetherill. On the back of the photo, Hilda wrote: "We've just nailed up the well to save water for the dance crowd. (last summer) 'Covered Water' trading post, Black Mt. Arizona, 1915." Courtesy of Carol Ann Wetherill Getz.

Clayton Wetherill. Courtesy of Carol Ann Wetherill Getz.

Gate and sign of Wetherill Ranch, Creede, Colorado. Frank Wills, head wrangler for Eugenia Faunce Wetherill, ca. 1940. Courtesy of Carol Ann Wetherill Getz.

Eugenia Faunce Wetherill (*center*) and unknown guests at fishing cabin on Ruby Lake, Colorado, ca. 1930. Courtesy of Carol Ann Wetherill Getz.

Sylvanus Carroll Faunce and Mary Ann Wattles Faunce in the early 1930s at Wetherill Ranch. Courtesy of Carol Ann Wetherill Getz.

Eugenia Faunce Wetherill and Hilda Faunce Wetherill with Eugenia's 1955 Chevy.
Courtesy of Carol Ann Wetherill Getz.

"MY DEAR DOCTOR": THE MEDICAL CAREERS OF THE WATTLES SISTERS

In 1878 Dr. Emily Blackwell wrote to her sister Dr. Elizabeth Blackwell about the prospects of the Woman's Medical College of the New York Infirmary, which they had founded ten years earlier. Emily, who was prone to pessimism and periodic despair, predicted the financial ruin of the school and lamented that she no longer possessed the enthusiasm needed to direct it. The only bright spot she saw was the group of dedicated young women doctors working at the women's infirmary and teaching at the college. "There have grown up around the Infirmary," she wrote to Elizabeth, "a group of active, able, well educated young workers who are really my successors rather than my contemporaries. Putnam will make a more scientific reputation in the profession. Cushier will be a more brilliant & popular practitioner—Baker, Wattles, McNutt & White will all bring in certain practical qualities, and as Americans seem to fit in to New York life more than we ever did."[1]

Despite Emily's dire predictions, the Woman's Medical College remained in operation, with Emily as dean, until its merger with Cornell University Medical School in 1899. Of the "active, able, well educated young workers" touted by Emily, we know a great deal about Mary Putnam Jacobi, who did stake out a reputation as an advocate of scientific investigations in medicine.[2] Elizabeth Cushier, Mercy Baker, Mary Ann Wattles, Sarah McNutt, and Victoria White were all early graduates of the medical college who remained with the school and infirmary at least through the first years of their careers. As Emily Blackwell's domestic partner, Elizabeth Cushier lived with Blackwell until the latter's death in 1910 and helped manage the college and infirmary until its closure.[3] Sarah McNutt worked as an attending physician in the infirmary and instructor at the college for twenty years, specializing in obstetrics. In 1884 she became the first woman admitted to the American Neurological Association.[4] Mercy Baker graduated with her MD in 1872, a year after Wattles and five years before McNutt and White.[5] As members of the first generation of professionally trained female physicians in the United States, they faced challenges that still confront women who wish to pursue a career while raising a family. Their pioneering work, however, opened many doors previously closed to women.

The generation of women who came of age right after the Civil War, who had witnessed the conflict as children and teenagers, grew up with anxiety, sickness, injury, and death all around them. As nineteenth-century women almost all of them would have been called to nurse a sick family member at home. Some of this generation also nursed wounded soldiers during the war. Northern women grew up believing implicitly in the righteousness of the Union cause, and as adults this translated into a firm conviction in the correctness of their own causes. They became progressives, populists, and suffragists. After taking advantage of the new opportunities for education for women, they struggled to find something to do with their degrees and found that they had to define what it meant to be a woman in a profession. Many of their concerns, especially the challenges of the "double shift," combining profession and family, remain real issues for women to this day.

In her book *Restoring the Balance* Ellen More looks at the various ways nineteenth-century female physicians defined their roles as doctors, professionals, and private women. She suggests this generation of women doctors wanted to establish a professional identity that included scientific respectability, service to society, and a balance of work and home life. They particularly felt called to address the conditions of women and children.[6] This generation did explore the many ways a professional woman could balance public and private life, and indeed, because medicine was the first profession outside of teaching or nursing that large numbers of women entered, women doctors were the first cohort of professional women in a male-dominated field to face this daunting challenge. Many of these women remained single; certainly some of those believed a career was incompatible with a family life. Some abandoned their career to enter a marriage and have children. Very few attempted to do both at once.

Two of Susan Lowe Wattles's daughters became doctors and sought to combine career and family. Sarah Grimké Wattles Hiatt never received a professional medical degree but completed an apprenticeship with her physician husband and was considered a doctor in her own right with a practice of her own after his death. Sarah and her husband formed a partnership that allowed her to experience the satisfaction of a professional career while remaining within the bounds of an acceptable domestic life. Mary Ann Wattles Faunce received medical training from one of the premier medical schools for women and followed up with postdoctoral training in Europe. She became a member of the faculty of the Woman's Medical College of the New York Infirmary and carried on a practice for women and children. Their mother, Susan, facilitated Mary Ann's career by moving to New York to care for Mary Ann's small children while she continued to teach and practice. Without Susan's assistance, it is doubtful Mary Ann would have been able to balance her career and family.

In 1863 Sarah married Lundy B. Hiatt, a young man who had moved to Kansas with his own abolitionist parents from Indiana.[7] Lundy already had some medical training, perhaps during an apprenticeship, and had been practicing medicine in Kansas since 1861. In 1864 he and Sarah moved to Chicago so he could pursue further medical studies.[8] Lundy's training as an apprentice would not have been considered odd by their contemporaries. Medical education in the United States in the mid-nineteenth century was haphazard and inadequate. Many aspiring doctors still took an apprenticeship with a qualified preceptor to prepare for a final oral exam. If they passed, they received a diploma that qualified them to practice almost anywhere. Most of the medical schools at the time of the Civil War operated as proprietary ventures for profit, with few admission standards, short terms, and limited affiliations with hospitals for clinical practice. The inadequacy of US medical education became most apparent to American students who traveled to Europe to seek better instruction. In the French and German schools, Americans encountered medical training based on empirical and experimental science rather than merely theoretical knowledge. As these doctors returned to the United States, they demanded reforms in the US educational model. The Civil War, which revealed the deficiency of too many doctors, accelerated the movement to reform the nation's medical training.[9]

In Chicago Lundy attended Lind University, which had opened in 1859 and would be absorbed by Northwestern University in 1870. A homeopathic institution, Lind had adopted some of the more progressive features of medical training at the time. Lind required prerequisites for admission, longer terms of study, three graded annual courses, dissection, and clinical instruction for graduation. The school went to great lengths to recruit qualified professors.[10] Lundy's boast that "it is said we have the best faculty in the United States" suggests these reforms had already attracted attention for the young institution.[11] No matter that the curriculum reflected advanced thinking, however, Lind did not admit women to its classrooms. Yet Lundy and Sarah studied together. Whatever he learned, he came home and taught Sarah.

In early 1865 Sarah had written to Sarah Grimké about studying medicine with Lundy. Grimké, thrilled to hear from her young friend, wrote back immediately. "I hoped you were attending the lectures with the Dr.," she said, "but fear as you say 'Lundy says the professors are very attentive &c &c' that you get them second hand." Even if Sarah was not attending classes herself, Grimké hoped she would push ahead with her plans for a medical career addressing women's health issues. "Have you studied, or do you intend to practice obstetrics?" Grimké asked. "It is a branch that belongs so specially to woman that I long to see it monopolized by her for I cannot help believing that every delicate woman suffers intensely from having a man with her at a time when all the tenderness & refinement of woman's nature is needful to the sufferer." She feared, however, that obstetrics would tax Sarah's own physical capability for the work, saying, "The exposure, & loss of sleep involved in this practice will render it unsuitable for you as your health is not very strong."[12] No evidence has been found to suggest that Sarah ever took a formal exam or received a formal medical diploma, but Lundy's tutelage gave her the knowledge to practice medicine throughout her life, mostly in conjunction with him but also on her own.

After completing their medical studies Sarah and Lundy Hiatt lived and practiced in Indiana, Missouri, Texas, and Kansas. They spent the longest stretch of time in Wise and Denton Counties in Texas, where they moved in 1871 and lived off and on for three decades. In the time Sarah and Lundy lived in Denton County, conditions in north Texas changed immensely, along with those of the rest of the state. Outsiders poured in hoping to cash in on a new economy in the wide-open spaces now made safe for entrepreneurialism and land hunger alike. Urban centers grew, but the vastness of the countryside between them left most Texans living on the land, raising as much cotton and wheat as they possibly could to make themselves something more than subsistence farmers. Between the Texas weather and the banks, too many farmers failed to make a go of it, and tenancy for both blacks and whites continued to increase well into the next century. Post-Reconstruction Texans' antipathy to government made state and local governments alike small and ineffectual, evidenced by the poor quality of roads and schools.[13] Rural Texas was a tough place to live but even more difficult for a reform-minded, educated woman who craved the society of others like herself.

The Hiatts were typical country doctors in many ways. They had to establish a practice by gradually winning the confidence of the people in their community. They reached a lot of their patients by traveling by horseback or buggy to their homes. With inadequate supplies and insufficient hygiene, they had to deal with sudden outbreaks of typhoid and epidemics of measles. They patched up broken bones, fractures, and burns as well as they could without access to the latest medicines or techniques.[14] Sarah served as assistant doctor, nurse practitioner, nurse, receptionist, clerk, and bookkeeper in their practice. She also served as physician and nurse for Lundy, for he was often sick and they moved frequently because of his health. Like other rural doctors, Sarah felt isolated and out of touch with trends in medicine and society. As a Northern, middle-class woman with a Republican and abolitionist background, Sarah's relationship to her rural, Southern neighbors had the potential to be problematic. She avoided being shunned as a carpetbagger, but she found few kindred souls, and the isolation of her position often discouraged her.

Writing to Aunt Esther Wattles in 1887, Sarah thanked her for sending the *Woman's Journal* and other progressive literature and explained why she could not do more for "God & Humanity." "Of course I could not believe more thoroughly in temperance and woman suffrage than I do," she wrote, "but where I live I am entirely cut off from any cooperation with organized work. & the people neither think nor read in modern channels, so those papers are society to me." Sarah respected her Texan neighbors and remained on very friendly terms with them, but she offered her aunt a wry observation:

> Those who visit me generally come to talk about their ails & aches to the doctor's wife, & in that way I have opportunity to put in a good word of some kind very often for health is a subject that is widely related— dress—dirt—temperance, &c, &c, &c, but I fancy that much of what I say is set down to my "queer northern notions." A woman who does not dip snuff, abhors tobacco generally, objects to coffee & swine flesh, & corsets and will not taste even a Christmas egg nog is "queer" & can be accounted for only by the fact that she is a Yankee. . . . They are all friendly & neighborly but I feel sure would be quick to suspect & resent a new fangled northern innovation, such as a ladies literary club, a mother's meeting, a W.C.T.U., or even a sewing circle.[15]

Sarah understood the importance of belonging to an organized group of like-minded women if she was to pursue reform activities. Residing in the rural South during and immediately after Reconstruction not only meant she lived among people who disagreed politically with her but also it left her wanting the key element that had made female benevolent reform activity possible. Sarah desired to do more for the social causes she cherished, but she knew that as long as she lived in an isolated rural community, the means for such activity was beyond her. When she did live for a brief time in an urban setting, she jumped at the chance for more liberal company. In 1877–1878 Sarah and Lundy temporarily moved to Lawrence, Kansas, where Sarah immediately joined a women's reading club consisting of old friends and relatives. She reveled in the group's Bible study and reading of James Freeman Clarke's *Ten Great Religions,* the liberal Unitarian writer's popular study of world faiths. They read modern literature as well, and Sarah enjoyed hearing papers read aloud regarding Longfellow, Wordsworth, and Shelley. She even read one of her own on Coleridge.[16] These were not idle pursuits for women who had little else to do; Sarah's workload had not changed simply because they had moved to a town. Such homosocial organizations had been the bedrock of antebellum women's reform activity since before her mother's time, whether the women involved were discussing literature or intemperance. In these groups they had learned the arts of networking and organizing, which undergirded their participation in the public sphere.[17] Without such groups individual women such as Sarah faced overwhelming odds against their successful social activism and found themselves even more disfranchised as citizens. Sarah Wattles Hiatt's life illustrates for us the importance of these women's networks, as she moved back and forth from isolated rural communities with no room for women's organizations to places where women did participate in organized benevolent work.

During her time in Texas Sarah did little in the way of active reform work. While the Texas constitutional convention of 1875 was meeting, however, she did write a memorandum to the convention requesting that woman's suffrage be included in the new state constitution. It was referred to the Committee on Suffrage, where it was buried and forgotten, but Sarah got some encouragement from letters of support she received from a scattering of prominent male politicians in the state. At that time, she felt optimistic because the women of Texas at least had more control over their property than women in most other states. She also noticed that with illiteracy so widespread in Texas, often the women could read even though their husbands could not. This led her to believe Texas women would heartily support a public education system sooner than men would, if only they had the vote.[18] This dream of rising female political power did not take into account the predominance of paternalism in Texas culture, as Sarah would discover the longer she lived there.

While living in Denton County, Sarah apparently never found any like-minded women interested in sustaining a local affiliate of the Woman's Christian Temperance Union (WCTU), a suffrage organization, or even an organization devoted to the single tax, the three causes dearest to her. WCTU local chapters certainly existed in Texas, the first having been established by Frances Willard herself during a tour of the state in 1882. Willard had not found a very promising field in Texas, however. Willard, who visibly embraced evangelical Protestantism, found that Southern evangelicals did not share the propensity for social activism that had proved so important to Northern evangelical reform activity. Southerners also rejected the idea that women had a duty to become moral leaders. Paternalistic attitudes in Texas and other southern states stifled women's public activities. Nevertheless, by the time Willard had finished her tour, she had inspired a number of Texas women to form local WCTU chapters; by 1887 there were about 100 such groups in Texas.[19] The state's prohibition movement, however, largely marginalized these woman-led organizations because male Texans came to the forefront of efforts to prohibit alcohol through local option votes and a constitutional amendment. The WCTU and women's open participation in the movement were both linked to Northern interference and thus widely discredited.[20]

Sarah encountered many of these attitudes in rural Denton County. There was no WCTU local chapter in Bartonville, although Sarah did hear of some women in the town of Denton "speaking and preaching" on temperance, and she thought they might be WCTU workers. She told her sister Emma it was almost amusing to "hear some of the comments on that fact by people who have never heard a woman speak in public," but she doubted progress would be made very quickly in Texas. "I do not know whether anything less than the light of the millennium will be able to penetrate the dense darkness of the ignorance and prejudice that prevails here in the rural districts. It *may* be different in the towns, but I do not know."[21] Sarah often alluded to the poverty of her neighbors, but to her, the explanation for their profound ignorance lay in the lack of a print culture. After all, her own family had never been particularly well off in terms of material wealth but had always found the means to acquire ample reading materials. Sarah lamented the plight of the young people of the county, writing to Emma, "I do feel so sorry for the young people here. There is such utter dearth of all that should enrich and brighten the lives of the young. Such bare homes, without books or papers, almost, and entirely without such a thing as *Scribner's Monthly*, or *Harper's*, or *St. Nicholas*."[22]

Sarah offset some of the isolation she felt by corresponding with family, even though the demands on her time and energy often left her unable to write as frequently as she would have liked. Sarah and Lundy had no children of their own but adopted an orphan girl named Martha McGee, whom they called Minnie and who took the surname Hiatt. Although no mention is made in surviving letters about the circumstances of the adoption, census records indicate that Minnie was born around 1874 in Texas.[23] Sarah badly wanted to maintain relationships with her growing nieces and nephew, and to make it possible for Minnie to know her new cousins. Sarah could not afford to visit her siblings' families very often, but when she did, she stayed for months at a time. In the meantime she wrote letters to nieces and nephews in which she inquired after their schooling, sent them family keepsakes, and occasionally offered their parents advice. For instance, when sister Emma expressed some concern about how her daughter Eleanor was turning out, Sarah had a spirited response. Eleanor was six at the time, had five older brothers, and was growing up on a farm, apparently stretching the boundaries of appropriate feminine behavior. Sarah told Emma not to worry: "Tell Eleanor to be a 'Thomas boy' if she likes to. Its all right. Miss Alcott and Miss Willard and—Aunt Sarah!— were 'Thomas boys,' and did live & thrive and grow notwithstanding—or in consequence—and it is the most thoroughly enjoyable part of existence, in this world. May all life be as pleasant as that part of it."[24]

Sarah also countered some of her personal and professional isolation by corresponding with her youngest sister, Mary Ann. Sarah's circumstances could not have been more different from those of Mary Ann. Though separated in age by only eight years, Mary Ann had opportunities Sarah could not imagine. Ironically, although Sarah's birth order had positioned her in the right time to benefit from the mentorship of Sarah Grimké, she came of age a little too early to take advantage of new opportunities for women in medical education. Mary Ann, on the contrary, had the great fortune of coming of age right at the end of the Civil War when women's educational opportunities were about to multiply.[25]

With Sarah Grimké Wattles as a big sister, it is no wonder Mary Ann Wattles might have gotten a notion that she could do whatever she wanted to do when she grew up. They both had the benefit of having Susan Lowe Wattles for a mother, for few women of the time could have combined the qualities of practicality, compassion, spirituality, and perseverance with the desire for women's rights Susan possessed. However, as the younger sister of Sarah Wattles, Mary Ann was encouraged from childhood to think about what women could do to make the world a better place to live. Sarah was receiving just that message in letters from her namesake, Sarah Grimké. The older Sarah also sent radical reading materials for the Wattles girls, such as the new women's rights journals, the *Una* and the *Lily*, in which a curious young woman could read articles by Amelia Bloomer, Elizabeth Cady Stanton, and other feminists. Both Susan and Sarah read Harriot Kezia Hunt's autobiography, sent to them by Grimké, and either one might have suggested to Mary Ann that women could follow Dr. Hunt's example and become a physician if they were so inclined. Sarah Wattles likely served as Mary Ann's primary teacher for the equivalent of grammar school. Sarah was teaching the younger children from her mid-teens until she married in 1863, with a brief hiatus while she was in New Jersey attending the Grimké-Welds' boarding school. Even after Sarah married Lundy Hiatt, she continued to serve as a role model for her younger sister by studying with her husband as he attended a medical school in Chicago.

Mary Ann had the advantage of watching and following her big sister. She also had the advantage of timing. Although she was only eight years younger than Sarah, Mary Ann had an easier time getting into a medical school than Sarah did. Partly this was a result of family circumstances and the ending of the Civil War, but it was also a factor of the steady though gradual opening of opportunities for women to go to school. Sarah had very limited educational options and only got to attend the Eagleswood School because of the personal relationship between her family and the Grimké-Welds. Even so, she did not get to go to Eagleswood until she was twenty-one years old, and then she could stay for only a year and a half of schooling, which did not even result in a diploma of any sort. Mary Ann, on the contrary, got to go to Oberlin College when she was twenty years old and complete an undergraduate degree.

Mary Ann's upbringing did more than give her a predilection toward feminism. All her life she was characterized as steady in temperament, practical, down to earth, and calm in a crisis. Her character reflected the western experience. Mary Ann had been born in a frontier community in Ohio and had already moved twice with her family when they picked up and moved again to Kansas when she was not quite ten years old. Her earliest memories involved her family's responses to grave dangers and real catastrophes. In her later years she recalled moving with her family to Clermont County, Ohio, to help the survivors, including her aunt and uncle, of a flood that had wiped out the settlement of Utopia, a communal experiment on the Ohio River.[26] In Kansas the family lived with the threat of impending violence or dealt with the human consequences of violent action. These days of peril made quite an impression on young Mary Ann, as reflected in the stories she told her children and grandchildren. Several generations later her stories are still remembered and repeated. Carol Ann Wetherill Getz, Mary Ann's great-granddaughter, recalls a family story passed down from Mary Ann about Bleeding Kansas. When the family lived in Moneka, they feared roaming gangs of Missourians and proslavery Kansans, so Mary Ann's parents drilled their children to pile their clothing close to their beds in the order that they would put things on, then to run to a cave nearby the homestead and hide until it was safe to come out.[27] Another great-granddaughter, Mary Ann Kipp Hairgrove, recalls being told that when John Brown and his men came to the house, the girls were instructed to hide out in the attic so as not to attract the unwanted attentions of the young men. Mary Ann Wattles remembered looking out the cracks in the wall of the attic to see John Brown and his band of rugged men sitting on long tables in the yard, eating watermelon.[28]

Through all the dangers faced by the family through the years of Bleeding Kansas and the Civil War, Mary Ann learned to manage crisis and conflict with practical good sense, calm, and coherence. Her circumstances afforded her no other choice. Especially during the Civil War, Mary Ann was called upon to take great responsibility on behalf of her family. The few surviving letters we have from Mary Ann during the war reveal a teenager who did take on a great deal of family responsibility but who also reveled in the simple joys of country life. She milked the cows and rounded them up when they wandered off the farm. She helped her mother haul posts for fences, and because hired help proved unreliable, the two of them put up the fence. She helped gather grain harvests and kept an eye out for wild gooseberries. More than anything she loved to go swimming in the local creek with the "girls," as she called her younger cousins next door. She took pride in managing a large chicken flock and chided herself good-naturedly for having thirteen cats, asking her sister Sarah, "Don't you think we are going into the business of raising cats 'quite largely'?"[29]

Mary Ann, along with her cousins Celestia, Harmonia, and Theano, all attended the school Susan and Esther had organized in their little community of Moneka. Sarah Wattles, among other women, assisted Susan and Esther as instructors. Pupils from outlying areas came to stay with either Susan or Esther, and some local families sent children daily. Among the boarders at Susan's house was Jennie Montgomery, daughter of Captain James Montgomery, the leader of the Linn County free-state militia and a fast-rising officer in the Union Army. Throughout the war there were usually two and sometimes more student boarders staying with Susan and Mary Ann, so there might have been around a dozen total scholars in school at any given time.

With the end of the war Esther Wattles decided to move back to Ohio, where her daughters could have better educational opportunities.[30] She settled in Oberlin and enrolled the girls in Oberlin College, which offered a preparatory curriculum in addition to college courses. Mary Ann went with them and took the Literary Course at Oberlin, graduating with the bachelor's degree in 1868.[31] At Oberlin Mary Ann developed a close relationship with Professor John Morgan and became lifelong friends with his daughters, Eugenia and Elizabeth ("Lizzie"). Eugenia received a bachelor's degree from Oberlin in 1865 and a master's several years later, then went to Europe for further study. She returned to the United States to teach at Oberlin and Vassar before taking a position as professor of philosophy at Wellesley College from 1880 to 1900. Lizzie also graduated from Oberlin and spent most of her adult life living in Europe, where she studied modern languages, literature, and music and tutored pupils.[32] Another Oberlin friend was Helen Goodwin, who graduated with Mary Ann in 1868 and pursued a literary career until she married in 1879.[33] Mary Ann saved all her correspondence with these lifelong friends, along with the letters of her professional associates, reflecting her sense of the importance of a supportive group of well-educated, like-minded women in her life. Such networks were indispensable to professional women at a time when their numbers were so few and their very right to seek higher education and careers was not universally accepted.

After graduating from Oberlin, Mary Ann decided to pursue a medical degree. She had done enough nursing of the sick and wounded to have acquainted herself well with the demands and potential horrors of medical work. Her niece, Ruth Jocelyn Wattles, recalled Mary Ann telling her, "She decided to study medicine because all her life nothing had been considered important unless it was a matter of life and death. Medicine she thought would be a matter of life and death."[34] In 1869 Susan Wattles took Mary Ann to meet with Dr. Emily Blackwell at the new Woman's Medical College of the New York Infirmary.[35] We do not know why Mary Ann chose the New York school over other more-established women's medical colleges, but it might simply have been that the Wattleses knew of the Blackwells' reputation through abolitionist circles or women's rights literature. According to Emily Blackwell all the students of Mary Ann's class came as a result of "direct personal influence," three sent by other physicians and "the other four [including Wattles] all called on me last spring and entered as the result of a personal interview."[36] It is not likely Mary Ann ever met Elizabeth Blackwell, but according to Elizabeth's autobiography there was an old family connection. Elizabeth Blackwell remembered the Wattles brothers from Cincinnati in the 1830s, when the Blackwell family lived in the city and associated with the community of radical reformers that included Augustus and John Wattles.[37] Whether anyone remembered or noted this past association in 1869, or if this in any way influenced Mary Ann's decision to attend the Blackwells' school, we do not know from surviving records. It is intriguing, however, to contemplate once again how small the world of antebellum reformers was and to consider this close connection another example of the legacy of the family's reform identity.

Whatever her motivation, Mary Ann Wattles enrolled in the first class of the Woman's Medical College of the New York Infirmary. In doing so, she entered the small but growing troop of women just breaking into the male-dominated world of medicine. Mary Ann's improved chances for medical education owed much to the women who founded the Woman's Medical College of New York. A few women such as Harriot Hunt had practiced medicine even though denied access to medical schools, but finally Elizabeth Blackwell became the first woman to receive a diploma from a medical college in the United States in 1849. Blackwell attended Geneva Medical College in New York, even though the school then closed its doors to women after admitting her. A few state schools admitted women, but most women seeking medical training turned to a handful of women's medical colleges then being established, beginning with the Woman's Medical College of Pennsylvania, established in 1850. Based on the idea that women should have the best scientific training possible in order to deflect opposition to the idea of women doctors, the women's medical colleges were in the forefront of reforming medical school pedagogy.[38]

Elizabeth and Emily Blackwell recognized that if women were to be respected equally as physicians, they would need the most advanced training they could get, preferably at coeducational schools. The Blackwell sisters had founded the New York Infirmary in 1857 to provide medical care to poor women and children by qualified female physicians, but they discovered that too few women were being admitted to coeducational schools and the training for women doctors was uneven. They decided to establish their own medical college for women, and in 1868 they opened the Woman's Medical College of the New York Infirmary. Elizabeth helped sister Emily get the school off the ground, and then she retired to their native England in 1869, leaving Emily in charge. Elizabeth kept up with the business of the school through correspondence but never returned to teach. Their curriculum reflected the highest standards of the new medical pedagogy, including a three-year course progressively graded. During their first year students studied anatomy, chemistry, physiology, *materia medica*, and histology while learning to dissect human body parts and beginning their work in the laboratory, which they continued throughout the three years. During their second year they repeated anatomy, physiology, and chemistry and moved on to pathological anatomy, practice, surgery, obstetrics, therapeutics, and hygiene. In the third year they repeated the advanced classes and began to work in the clinic. According to the school catalog, "During this year each student enjoys the privilege of attending upon ten cases of obstetrics in the infirmary wards; of witnessing operations at the infirmary, as also at other hospitals in the city; and may listen to the clinical lectures given in the Bellevue amphitheatre."[39] The emphasis on laboratory work and experience in clinical settings made the curriculum of the Woman's College of New York one of the more progressive in the country, exceeding the standards of many medical schools for men. Mary Putnam Jacobi, who had trained in Europe and was accustomed to the more advanced medical education offered there, praised the New York college for its inclusion of laboratory work, especially in anatomy and pharmacology.[40]

Mary Ann Wattles graduated from the Woman's Medical College of the New York Infirmary in 1871 and gave the valedictory address at commencement. A notice in the *Medical Record* of April 1871 stated, "The Valedictory address was gracefully delivered by Dr. Wattles, who told why young women study medicine. It won frequent and just applause, now for its playful wit and now for its noble expression of earnest purpose."[41] In her speech Wattles spoke of the many reasons a woman would want to study medicine, suggesting women doctors were not a monolithic group but each woman might have her own reasons for doing so. "Some do it from natural industry," she explained. "They must do something—something that shall seem worthwhile—that shall satisfy in its demands a keen and well-trained intellect, a kind and sympathetic heart; and they see in the medical profession absorbing and useful activity." Other women studied medicine out of the ambitious "desire to be known for noble deeds." Still others acted from "a natural obstinacy, because someone else has said they can't do it, or that they shan't do it." Some women sought economic independence and the chance to earn their own money, Wattles continued, and others were motivated by the "fascinations of pure science" or were "actuated by pure pity for the anguish of physical pain." Then, tongue in cheek, she said some women become doctors because "they want to earn their living by an *easy* method" and went on to say that school teaching, the only other profession open to women outside of the domestic circle, was eminently more taxing than the practice of medicine. Wattles thanked the Board of Trustees and the faculty, noting, "The more gratefully we acknowledge our indebtedness to you, since we are not wholly ignorant of the criticisms to which your course has subjected you, among your professional associates." She challenged her classmates to go out into the world with new eyes and great expectations, saying, "We ask uncompromising, unprejudiced judgment. If our work is well, we claim the reward of well-doing. If it is ill, we claim the reward of ill-doing. We want no flattery—no undeserved praise. But we do want the praise we earn, and just encouragement."[42]

After graduation Mary Ann Wattles joined the faculty of the Woman's Medical College of the New York Infirmary as an assistant demonstrator and clinical assistant. In 1877 she was promoted to the rank of lecturer of anatomy and the following year to professor of anatomy, the position she held through 1889. As a demonstrator she performed dissections, and as a professor she lectured while a junior demonstrator dissected. While taking her class, students performed dissections, gaining a "practical acquaintance with the various tissues and organs" while "the hand is trained in the use of instruments necessary to the future surgeon," according to her course description. Each student was "expected to make two dissections of every part of the human body; and ample material is provided."[43] As a faculty member Mary Ann was known to uphold the standards expected of the college. In 1879 Mary Ann lobbied the Association for the Advancement of the Medical Education of Women for support for the creation of a chair of histology and pathological anatomy. The school instituted the courses and expanded facilities to provide the laboratories necessary for the work. Mary Ann also insisted on maintaining high admissions standards by requiring students who had attended less rigorous medical schools to take coursework in dissection, histology, and *materia medica* when transferring to New York.[44] Her commitment to the empirical and experimental approach to medical education came not only from her training in New York but also her further study in Europe.

American women, like their male counterparts, had to study medicine in Europe if they wanted to learn the latest scientific discoveries and technologies. For most women it was the only way to work in a clinical or hospital setting as a student. Officially, French, Austrian, and German schools prohibited women from attending medical school classes, but some professors let them sit in on their courses.[45] Mary Ann spent two years studying in Europe from 1875 to 1876.[46] She attended classes in Leipzig, Munich, and Vienna and might also have studied in Paris. All we know is what is revealed in a few letters she wrote home and others sent to her by friends while she was still in Europe and after her return to the United States. Some of Mary Ann's experience and that of many American women studying in Europe is reflected in several letters from Elizabeth Cushier and E. B. Ryder, who shared rooms with Mary Ann in Vienna.

In 1875, while Mary Ann Wattles studied in Leipzig, her fellow alumnae and colleagues Annie Angell and Elizabeth Cushier were studying in Vienna. Elizabeth, who was taking courses on nervous diseases and children's diseases, found most of the courses open to women. In addition, she worked in the children's clinic. Elizabeth tried to persuade Mary Ann to join her in Vienna:

> I have heard from you through your Angell and learn that you are distinguishing yourself in tying arteries. Are you almost ready to try Vienna? I expect to begin a course on Gynecological Operations immediately after the holidays and shall be very pleased to have you take one at the same time. Dr. Angell will have left Vienna by that time and her room will be ready for you. So if you can arrange your work in Leipzig so as not to have your time too much broken up, I wish you would come.[47]

Yet even in these happy circumstances the women ran into obstacles. As a member of the faculty at Zurich in the 1860s, Dr. Theodore Billroth had helped to pioneer the admission of women to European medical schools.[48] In 1875 he was teaching in Vienna. Elizabeth informed Mary Ann that there were "plenty of private courses here with which you can occupy the remainder of your time. Billroth's surgical clinic however and indeed none of the hospital clinics are open to us. I have asked and been refused."[49] Elizabeth seemed to take this setback in stride, although she worried about doing well in the eyes of her colleagues back home. After receiving a letter from home, she wrote Mary Ann,

> I believe ... that we are expected to be very wise when we go back. I think when the time comes I shall be afraid to go or else I shall have to reconcile

myself to the prospect of their disappointment. What I accomplish each day seems but such a drop in the great ocean of medical science that I am kept in a constant state of humiliation by my ignorance.[50]

In urging Mary Ann to come to Vienna to study, Elizabeth claimed, "When Dr. Angell leaves I shall be the only woman at any of the clinics and I believe the only woman student of medicine in Vienna."[51] This turned out to be an exaggeration, as Mary Ann discovered when she did go to Vienna in the spring of 1876 and found several other American women there. After Mary Ann's return to the United States that September, E. B. Ryder wrote to her from their old apartment, now occupied by other female medical students from the United States. "I am in the Hospital again this winter," she reported, "and am delighted with my advantages there." Their professors asked about Mary Ann and wished her well. In a surprising turnaround, "Bilroth is very pleasant to all the ladies and admits all without a remark."[52] Ryder thought she had "never worked so hard (and had so little to eat) as this winter. I go to Post Mortems every morning at eight and am on duty every hour until eight in the eve. I do not intend to work so hard after this month."[53]

The precarious footing on which women found themselves in European schools as well as the constant criticism they endured were reflected in Ryder's communication with Mary Ann the following winter. Despondently, but with her sense of humor intact, she wrote:

> You see: there has been eight ladies here this winter. Six Americans and two Russians and so some of these noble male Austrians became frightened for fear some dreadful thing would happen if this thing continues and therefore called a meeting of the faculty and decided after the close of the winter term no more ladies should be allowed to attend any of the university lectures or clinics and that they as individuals loose no time in letting the aforesaid ladies know that they were not wanted.
>
> So this has made it pleasant and then the weather has been just dreadful. One *male* American doctor has died here this winter and another is not expected to live. These facts prove beyond a doubt that men are not strong enough to *study medicine!*[54]

Determined to refute objections to the study of medicine by women, Mary Ann and her colleagues sought out the best professors willing to take female students and pursued the latest theories and practices. They seemed acutely aware of the obligation to return to the United States with new knowledge that would help to advance the practice of medicine not just by women but in general. While in Leipzig Mary Ann observed surgical operations using the new Lister method, not yet practiced in the United States or even fully accepted in Europe. Joseph Lister, a British physician, had explored new ways of combating infection in hospitals by treating wounds with carbolic acid and administering a spray of carbolic at the operating table during surgery. For a time after Lister first published his results in the *Lancet* in 1867, many physicians challenged or ridiculed his ideas.[55] In Leipzig, however, Mary Ann Wattles observed the Lister method and wrote approvingly of it to Emily Blackwell.

> The operation is performed under a cloud of carbolic acid spray, the part having first been thoroughly scrubbed with a solution of salicylic acid. The wound is then dressed with first a glazed & perforated protective to keep the cotton from sticking & let the pus out—then cotton, that has been soaked in a 20% solution of salicylic acid, and dried, then more cotton, not so strong, perhaps 2 or 3 per. cent. then bandaged. The dressings are usually not changed oftener than twice a week, in cases of old suppurating abscesses. And not removed for eight days, in cases of amputation. It appears to me that they use a great deal of material; but they say it is much cheaper than the old way, in that they change the dressings much less often, and the patients stay in hospital so much shorter time.[56]

After returning to New York in September 1876, Mary Ann settled into her work at the Woman's Medical College of the New York Infirmary. While she was away, the college building, located at 126 Second Avenue, had been renovated. She returned to a refurbished building where the top floor housed the Confinement Ward, the "airiest, lightest, brightest, and most desirable locality in the house," according to Adaline Kelsey, a friend and colleague at the college. Located on the fourth floor, the Confinement Ward was reached by a "beautiful broad stair case." A new furnace had been installed, and the operating room and another room "have the Linoleum."[57] The trustees had carried out a campaign to raise the money for the renovations, and Mary Ann had given a donation toward the project. When the fund-raising campaign fell short, Samuel Willetts stepped in and gave the entire amount—$10,000—needed to complete the project.[58] The college now had ample space for its classrooms, clinics, and living quarters for many of the students and staff.

One can imagine that Mary Ann's life as a young, single professional was a whirlwind of seeing patients, preparing lectures, teaching courses, attending staff meetings, and keeping up with professional and personal correspondence.[59] She made a living but undoubtedly had to live frugally. In 1878 she started a joint private practice with fellow doctor Sarah McNutt, and a year later the two rented a house together at 238 E. 13th Street in New York, just blocks from the Woman's Medical College building. Although Mary Ann complained to her mother that "it does take such a sight of money to furnish a house," she could not disguise her excitement at starting a household.[60] To help with expenses they rented out rooms to a young male lawyer, a troublesome tenant who refused to pay his share of the gas bill and soon moved out.[61] He was replaced by "two young ladies," one of whom was Eleanor Kilham, a "quiet but energetic and industrious" medical student from Massachusetts who was a member of the "Home Study Club," had "a very choice selection of books," and "likes to go with us to see patients in tenement houses."[62] Later Julia McNutt, Sarah's sister, joined the household while she attended the Woman's Medical College.

In addition to the private practice and adventurous house calls, Mary Ann's life revolved around teaching and other duties at the college. She proudly reported to her mother that she was earning sufficient money to support herself, having "made by practice $457.95 and by teaching $325.00" that year.[63] The following year the college enrolled a bigger class, and because faculty compensation depended on the number of students they taught, Mary Ann earned $400 from teaching.[64] It was a balancing act that might have made her wonder if she had correctly described school teaching as a more difficult profession. She related her schedule to her mother:

My lecture hour is from 12 to 1, on Mondays, Tuesday, Thursdays, & Fridays. On Mondays & Thursday I do not go down until 12 o'clock. that is my leisure time. Tuesday & Fridays I go down at 9 o'clock to the Dispensary, which is in the basement of the College building. . . . By 12 o'clock I am through seeing patients & go up stairs and lecture. Wednesday & Saturdays from 9 to until through I am in the examining room, treating the disease of women. Saturday at 11:1/2 I go into the surgical clinic room. Examine the patients, write out their histories & get things ready for Prof. Stimson's lecture on practical surgery. He closes at one, & then I dress the wounds & ulcers put on the splints or do whatever else has been ordered, and send off the patients. When I go into the Surgical clinic Saturday, Dr. West, my assistant finishes my clinic. From two to four in the afternoon we see patients at our office.[65]

Living on the Lower East Side of Manhattan, one of the most densely populated square miles on earth at the time, residing in a house with other professional women, Mary Ann Wattles enjoyed circumstances nearly opposite those of her sister, Sarah Wattles Hiatt. Whereas Sarah lived in a rural setting and had no close female friends with similar outlooks, Mary Ann was surrounded both by the general humanity of New York's poorest neighborhood and by other educated women like herself devoted to the needs of poor women and children. Collaboration came naturally among these women even in the business of setting up a household. Soon after Mary Ann and Sarah McNutt had moved into their new house, a number of friends came to visit and lend a hand. Mary Ann put them to work, telling her mother, "One young lady read aloud while the rest hemmed eight single bed sheets—a dozen table napkins & a table cloth. . . . We have several small figured gray carpets, which were $.65 a yard, made by our guests." Other longtime friends lived close enough that they could provide material and emotional support. Eugenia Morgan, Mary Ann's friend from Oberlin who was teaching at Wellesley, lent furniture and sent a box of bedding plants so that Mary Ann and Sarah could start a garden. Another friend had "gone South to teach and has left her nice upright piano and several other things here for us to take care of." Mary Ann declared, "We are the most fortunate persons in having things fall to us."[66] Fortune perhaps, but the cooperative efforts of women working together sustained female professionals just as it had nurtured the reform endeavors of Mary Ann's mother's generation.

Ellen More and Cora Marrett, among other historians, have pointed out the importance of the women's medical society for women physicians in the nineteenth century. Medical societies gave members a sense of community and professional identity. Modeled on male medical societies, which served to establish professional standards and enhance collegiality, women's medical societies emerged across the country wherever substantial medical communities existed. Many of the new women's societies arose out of the early alumnae associations of the medical colleges, often founded by a group of alumnae from a particular school. The Alumnae Association of the Woman's Medical College of the Infirmary of New York, established in 1873, was one of the earliest of these organizations and continued on as the Women's Medical Association of New York City after the college's closure in 1899.[67] While she was associated with the college and beyond, Mary Ann Wattles remained active in the Alumnae Association of the Woman's Medical College, serving as corresponding secretary in 1884–1885. Years later, after moving west, Mary Ann remained in touch with the Women's Medical Association and continued to receive updates on its activities.[68]

When these women gathered for alumnae reunions and meetings, they certainly talked about the latest scientific developments in medicine, but their camaraderie also had meaning for defining the balance between their professional and personal lives. Men and women, both within the medical community and outside, debated the question of marriage for professional women. Elizabeth Blackwell felt strongly that a woman doctor could not also be a wife and mother, and she remained single all her life. Her sister Emily seemed more ambivalent on the issue, accepting married women on the staff at the college and infirmary and supporting her students' and colleagues' decisions to take any option available to them. Both Emily and Elizabeth adopted children to raise, and Emily lived with another single woman, Elizabeth Cushier, displaying, as Regina Morantz-Sanchez has said, some of the "creatively diverse solutions to the problem of loneliness and the hunger for connection" these first women professionals chose. Morantz-Sanchez estimates that in the nineteenth century between one-fifth and one-third of women physicians appear to have married, whereas Ellen More found slightly higher rates of marriage among women doctors in Rochester, New York.[69]

Mary Ann Wattles's circle of friends, at least those represented in the extant correspondence, reflects these rates. Of the ten women doctors in this sample, two married and five remained single but established households with women. We do not have enough information about three of them to know of their circumstances. Mary Ann Wattles married in 1882, at the age of thirty-seven, and had three children. Sarah Wattles Hiatt married a doctor and had one adopted daughter. Emily Blackwell and Elizabeth Cushier lived and worked together for almost forty years. Annie Angell, Mary Ann's classmate and closest friend, never married and lived with another single woman. Christiana Isidore "Issie" Faunce, Mary Ann's student and sister-in-law, never married and lived for forty-two years with Helen Marshall, a high school English teacher and curator of the Slater Museum in Norwich, Connecticut. Eliza B. Phelps never married and lived with another Woman's Medical College alumna, Emma F. Ward, in East Orange, New Jersey. If this small sample tells us anything about professional women in the late nineteenth century, it is that most found alternatives to a heterosexual married life that allowed them to continue their careers without sacrificing the benefits of domestic partnership. A more conventional marriage was not out of the question, however, as Mary Putnam Jacobi and Mary Ann Wattles proved by marrying, having children, and continuing to work as physicians.

For a time, it looked as if Mary Ann Wattles would be satisfied with a female-centered home life and a career. However, at the age of thirty-seven she married Sylvanus Carroll Faunce, an artist ten years her junior. Mary Ann met her future husband through "Issie" Faunce, Carroll's sister and a student of Mary Ann's, who graduated from the Woman's Medical College in 1880. The Faunce siblings hailed from Duxbury, Massachusetts, from a long line of Faunces that went back to some of the earliest English settlers of Massachusetts. Carroll Faunce wanted to be a portrait painter but was working as a designer of textile patterns. He had attended some art school classes and was associated with the Art Students League of New York. His sister Issie often joined Carroll in social activities with his circle of friends, and it is likely she introduced him to Mary Ann. Mary Ann also took some sculpture classes, so the little leisure time she had seemed to be devoted to artistic pursuits and, not incidentally, some romance.[70] On July 4, 1882, Mary Ann Wattles and Carroll Faunce married and left for a honeymoon cruise up the Hudson River to Lakes George and Champlain. They made a pilgrimage to North Elba, where Carroll painted watercolors of the house of John Brown that would later hang in their own home.[71] A year later their first child, Theodore Wattles Faunce, was born, followed by daughters Eugenia in 1885 and Hilda in 1887.[72] The new family moved to Brooklyn in 1883, and Mary Ann commuted to Manhattan across the newly completed Brooklyn Bridge. She continued to teach at the Woman's

Medical College through 1889 and worked at the Infirmary until 1892.[73] It was a very full life, as her mother Susan acknowledged with some good-natured complaining on Christmas 1884, writing, "I have been expecting a letter from you every day since I began this. But as you are a college Professor, house keeper, wife, and Mother, I ought not to expect a letter very often, so I will be patient."[74]

Mary Ann Wattles Faunce found herself shouldering the burdens of the "double shift." One of the greatest challenges for working women of the time, as for working women of today, was how to take care of the domestic responsibilities of childcare and household chores while working outside of the home. It was important for Mary Ann to find workable solutions that would allow her to continue her career and defy mainstream convention, which disparaged married women with children for working outside the home. Being able to hire servants allowed her to meet this practical objective while emphasizing the professional status she wanted as a female physician, broadcasting her standing as a solid member of the middle class who could afford to employ working-class women in her household. Having hired help also satisfied a desire to assist women in hard straits. The women who worked for the Faunces came from troubled marriages or were widows, and some brought children with them. A "Mrs. Collins" worked for the Faunces while Mary Ann was pregnant with Theodore in 1883, left the following year, but returned to live with them in 1889 after divorcing "a worthless husband." Mrs. Collins's two children, a girl of eight and a boy of six, also came to live in the Faunce household.[75] In between Mrs. Collins's stints Mary Ann employed a "young English woman who lost her husband 3 wks. after she was married. She has a baby 5 weeks old, & in consideration of this 'encumbrance' she works for six dollars a month. She is not yet quite strong but will be very superior 'help' in time."[76] This arrangement worked for less than a year, when the young woman left to live with an aunt who could care for the child while she worked in a shop or factory. This seemed to be a less-than-desirable outcome for the young woman, but as Mary Ann explained, "Since her baby has been learning to walk & cutting double teeth, he has become too numerous to handle. . . . He is a most wonderful child, bright & strong, but a *terror*! He & Sister [Eugenia] are constantly squabbling when near each other."[77] Mary Ann also hired a professional nurse to help with the birth of her daughter Hilda in March 1887. Relating the events of the birth to her sister Emma, Mary Ann reported, "At 10 pm we retired, and at 12 Carroll started over to New York for my nurse, and at one pm the next day, Miss Hilda arrived."[78] The nurse stayed three weeks in the Faunce home and fed Mary Ann so well that she "was fatter when I got up than I have been before in many years."[79]

The other doctors associated with the Woman's Medical College supported Mary Ann's decision to start a family and seemed eager to offer advice on childrearing. Eliza B. Phelps, an 1870 graduate of the college who practiced in East Orange, New Jersey, sent her pages of information about Fröebelianism and kindergartens. Phelps urged Faunce to acquire colorful toys for the children and recommended books for Mary Ann to read. For Phelps, who never married or had children, Mary Ann's children posed a veritable laboratory of scientific discovery. "Do you see Babyhood?" she asked Mary Ann. "You are just one of the ones who should keep a record of the children's development—Have you seen those books for mothers? Have their pictures taken once a year—& note down every fact with the date of psychological interest."[80] There is no evidence that Mary Ann kept a scientific record of her children's growth—or even a sentimental baby book for that matter—but she did send them all to kindergarten, provided them vast quantities of reading material, and monitored their health very carefully.

Even with hired help and scientific advice, however, Mary Ann found the burdens of domesticity challenging. She solved this problem by calling upon her mother, Susan Wattles, who came east to help when Mary Ann was pregnant with her second child. Susan stayed with the Faunces from late 1884 until early 1892, when Mary Ann retired to devote herself full time to domestic life and the family moved to Massachusetts. It turned out Susan herself could present an extra burden for Mary Ann—Susan suffered from a recurring knee problem that left her "lame" on numerous occasions, and not surprisingly for someone her age, she often caught the same afflictions that befell the children. However, on the whole, Mary Ann treasured the time Susan was able to spend with the family, and Susan was able to offer crucial assistance even though Mary Ann worried about overtaxing her. After Mary Ann gave birth to Eugenia at home in June 1885, Sarah Wattles Hiatt wrote to her,

> I do love to think of mother's being with you through your confinement
> to put you up and take care of the babies and, though you do think it was

pretty hard on her and Carroll, I am sure they were both happier to have you in the house with them than to have had your place vacant during those weeks, even if they did have to lose some sleep.[81]

Mary Ann's reliance on Susan derived not merely from the domestic help that Susan could provide. Susan's spirit and zest for life uplifted Mary Ann and made her a welcome guest in the homes of Mary Ann's social and professional circle. Not long after Susan came to stay with the Faunces, she and Mary Ann were invited for lunch at the home of Emily Blackwell and Elizabeth Cushier. Susan's description of the Blackwell household demonstrates her easy acceptance of unconventional domestic arrangements. She wrote to Emma, "This family consists of two women physicians and a house patient, a house keeper, two hired girls, and Dr. Blackwell's youngest girl—the other is at school near Boston."[82] Everyone who met Susan felt drawn to her, and Mary Ann basked in the glow, telling Emma,

I don't know what we should do without Mother. The baby depends upon her to put him to sleep every day and goes as willingly as can be, while for me he would fret & struggle for half an hour. Then she reads the papers & renews, by her enthusiasm, my interest in the progress of the world. She greatly enjoyed a visit of a few days at Dr. McNutt's, and they enjoyed it too. And want her to come once a month anyway, while she stays here. Miss Chevalier—professor of chemistry—was so pleased with the interest Mother showed in her Laboratory, I have received many complements on my resemblance to her.[83]

For her part, Susan enjoyed being in New York and took advantage of as many opportunities as her health and household duties allowed. She attended plays and lectures, caught up with old friends, and went to temperance and suffrage meetings. Once she went to listen to a lecture given to women by Dr. Anna Longshore Potts, who "had pictures of different organs and explained what diseases often affected them and mentioned some simple remedies."[84] After her many years of living in rural Kansas, Susan was happy to see old friends living on the East Coast. In 1885 she visited with Emeline Bishop Mattison, one of the other Cincinnati Sisters who had worked with Susan teaching black pupils in the 1830s. Following the death of her husband, Emeline had moved in with her daughter in Brooklyn. "She is in her eightieth year," Susan reported to Emma, and "has not been able to see to read for three years, but her health is excellent. We could not see any of our girls looks in each other."[85]

As usual, Susan's main interest was women's rights, and she found many ways to feel connected to the movement. She attended several meetings of the Brooklyn WCTU before she "ascertained that they do not belong to Miss Willard's division but to the Evangelical." She told Emma that she would "try to find a W.C.T.U. who will work for Woman Suffrage."[86] In early 1886 the New York State Woman's Suffrage Association met in New York City, and Carroll went with Susan for an evening session. "He took the best of care of me," Susan wrote Emma, adding, "Susan B. Anthony was one of the speakers and I had a few minutes chat with her before the meeting was called to order."[87] In 1888 Susan could hardly contain her excitement when Carroll offered to pay her way to attend the organizing meeting of the International Council of Women in Washington, DC. Initially Susan said she would not go unless one of her daughters accompanied her but decided to attend when Esther Wattles offered to meet her there.[88] Organized by Elizabeth Cady Stanton and Susan B. Anthony to celebrate forty years of the women's rights movement, the Washington meeting brought together women from around the world to form a permanent organization dedicated to international issues of concern to women.[89] Susan and Esther had the pleasure of seeing and hearing many of the leading lights of the women's rights movement, including Stanton, Anthony, Lucy Stone, Willard, Julia Ward Howe, Isabella Beecher Hooker, Matilda Joslyn Gage, Clara Barton, Frederick Douglass, and Robert Purvis as well as dozens of lesser known speakers and delegates.[90] The *Women's Tribune* reported on the conference, and afterward Esther sent copies of the journal to Sarah Wattles Hiatt. Sarah summed up what it meant to the women who attended: "What a wonderful gathering that was. Each one of those women workers is, somewhere—a radiating center of beneficences & I cannot but think how the power of each one must be intensified by the stimulus & inspiration of contact with all the others. I am so glad mother could be there—and in company with Aunt Esther too." Sarah had heard from other Kansas women who had attended as well, telling Emma,

Annie Diggs, who was there sent the Tribune to Ida. Ida writes me, "I was much interested in the proceedings of the Council, and Oh I was so glad Aunt Susan was there, what a treat it was for her. Our Mrs Dr Hall was there. I presume you remember her; she is so very prominent in the suffrage work here, & she and one other lady, were elected on our school board this Spring. We heard after her return that she had made Aunt Susan's acquaintance so Maud & I called on her. She seems to have fallen in love with your mother, said she went to everything, including all the receptions."[91]

The Washington meeting underscored the value of organizing and networking for the women's movement, and Susan participated with the grateful appreciation born of years of living in the isolation of rural Kansas.

Mary Ann also understood the importance of working within a community of supportive women and benefited from the opportunities available in a cosmopolitan city. With the challenge of maintaining both career and family, however, she did not have much energy or time to participate in activism or urban entertainments. She continued to work at the woman's infirmary until 1891 but began to experience a series of nagging illnesses that sapped her energy for long periods. In early 1892 Mary Ann and Carroll left New York and moved to Newtonville, Massachusetts, a suburb of Boston. The existing letters do not make it clear why they moved, although Carroll had been worried about "fluctuations" in his firm and expressed concerns about maintaining his position.[92] Because Mary Ann's health most likely led to her leaving the infirmary for good, they might simply have seen it as a good time to make a change. After Mary Ann settled into her new home in Massachusetts, she sent Emily Blackwell a photograph of her children. Emily wrote back, wishing her well and acknowledging the difficulties of managing a profession and parenthood at the same time:

> I was quite pleased to receive your photograph of the three children. They are a very nice looking group. I should think the little girl would be very pretty, and they all look bright. I hope they will be a constantly increasing interest and satisfaction to you. I am very sorry to learn that you have been having trouble with your health. I think you were wise to take absolute rest. I quite agree with you that active practice is quite incompatible with active domestic duty.[93]

Even after leaving New York, Mary Ann lived in an urban environment full of social and artistic opportunities, circumstances that greatly contrasted with those of her sister Sarah. Through Mary Ann, however, Sarah could tap into the resources and opportunities available to her younger sister. In return Sarah gave Mary Ann advice on a range of topics and shared family stories their father used to tell. Sarah also acknowledged Mary Ann's superior medical knowledge and relied upon her for advice when it came to the latest medical technology and difficult diagnoses. In 1879 Sarah hastily wrote to Mary Ann:

> I have been trying for three or four days to write to you, not that I owe you a letter for strange to say I do not but I have a question to ask. Doctor has a patient whom he is treating for ulceration of the uterus. There is also anteversion, . . . the os directed backward & upward is reached with difficulty. It is easy to replace the uterus but it will not remain in position even while the woman lies quite still on her back unless it is supported. None of the pessaries which we have seem exactly adapted to her case & Lundy wants to try a stem pessary or uterine supporter, and he wants your advice as to what one is likely to be best in such a case. Have you ever used Dr McIntosh's uterine supporter & what do you think of it?[94]

Mary Ann scribbled a picture of the desired pessary on the back of the envelope and undoubtedly sent advice and perhaps even the item itself to her sister. Often Mary Ann purchased goods and equipment for Sarah, including cloth material, readymade clothing, and a microscope.[95] Both Sarah and Mary Ann understood how critical their connection was in combating the isolation of Sarah's life. Mary Ann was only too happy to help find a microscope for Lundy and Sarah's practice, telling Emma she was "so glad I had the chance to get her so good a microscope at so reasonable a price. It will do them worlds of good. No physicians office is complete without one nowadays."[96] For her part Sarah added, "I regard the possession and use of a microscope as one of the means of preventing that deterioration which those who are isolated have to guard against and I will sacrifice other things to that."[97]

Whereas Mary Ann provided Sarah information and amenities not readily available in Texas, Sarah freely offered advice on any topic imaginable, including housekeeping. Sarah sometimes had a servant to help her around the house but not always. The amount of housework Sarah did, along with her duties connected to the medical practice, seems overwhelming. She cooked, churned butter, made bread, sewed and ironed clothing (heating the irons in a fire even in the middle of Texas summers), raised gardens, canned garden products, cut up quarters of meat, salted and canned meat, did laundry, cleaned the house, stitched together rag rugs, and beat the carpets. Sarah's regimen of housework helps us to understand why rural women had so little time and energy for paid labor outside the home or unpaid reform efforts and reminds us why the ability to hire servants was so crucial for women pursuing careers. Mary Ann apparently also had a great deal of housework to do and complained about it, prompting Sarah to respond with her philosophy of housework:

And so you are wrestling with the housework problem. I try desperately to simplify the plan of procedure, to minimize the innumerable little things that crowd all those margins of leisure that—it seems—should lie white and clear around each day's special work. But my house keeping is not a model to be held up before an aspirant to fame in that line. My kitchen stove sometimes goes weeks without blacking; my windows ditto without washing. & sometimes when I have my glasses on and stand where I get an unusual light I see spider webs where such drapery is not to be desired. Three things I attend to strictly, I am careful about my table & cooking; three meals daily for three cranky stomachs and fastidious palates take thought & time as well as work, especially when many desirable things are not to be had and the need for economy in all is a part of the problem. I try to cook what each of us can eat, and not a great variety at one meal, but vary the meals, as much as I can. I am particular about the beds, to have them fresh sweet & clean as well as warm and comfortable. I am faithful in the use of the broom tho shy of the mop & scrubbing brush—then the laundry work—one must have clean clothes, table linen &c, these absolute essentials to healthy existence I am conscientious about, the rest I can drop in favor of a sick neighbor or a fascinating magazine or a buggy ride with Doctor, And "the rest" is multitudinous and quite fills up every bit of the afore-mentioned margin if it is allowed to. It has just struck 10-30 & I must go to bed.[98]

Reading this description of household duties, one is amazed that Sarah had time for any doctoring at all, but she seemed to have managed to do both. "Doctor," as she liked to call Lundy, had a sporadic practice, with a heavy load during the "sick season" and spare time in between to do a little farming and tend to some livestock. Many of his patients must have been poor dirt farmers who had difficulty coming up with cash to pay the medical bills. Sarah often refers to money owed them and outstanding accounts that might be collected after the cotton harvest. Lundy obviously depended upon her not just to keep up the household but also to assist in his practice. Writing to Emma in 1881, Sarah reported, "For more than a month past Doctor has been very busy professionally, and is so still, & that always makes a little extra work for me. In all surgery & in women's diseases that require local treatment I am his assistant so I have had to give several half days & some whole days in that way."[99]

Sarah seemed quite happy in her life with Lundy, lamenting only that she never had enough time or money to visit family or do more good in society. After Lundy died in March 1892, she tried to keep up his medical practice but also traveled more to see family.[100] She lived for a few years in Texas near her daughter, Minnie, who married Paul Crowder in 1893 and had a child of her own the following year. In early 1893 Sarah took her mother for a visit with family in Ohio.[101] Later that year she made an extended visit to her brother, Theodore, and his family in Mancos, Colorado, helping to care for him through a long illness.[102] In September 1894, she returned to Colorado when Theodore suffered a relapse. Through correspondence Sarah and Mary Ann mulled over the symptoms of Theodore's illness.[103] When Theodore failed to recover completely, Sarah took him to Massachusetts to stay with Mary Ann until they could figure out what was wrong with him. It might not have helped him that much, for he complained that the air was "low and damp" and that he caught cold every time the wind blew in from the east.[104] In 1896 Sarah traveled again to Massachusetts to spend several months with Mary Ann and some of their cousins in Connecticut.[105]

At times during this period Sarah seemed at a loss as to what she should do. On one of her visits to Colorado, she looked over the town of Durango and wondered if a woman physician could prosper there. She thought she might be too old to start a practice from scratch, but if her sister Mary Ann would go into a partnership with her, they might re-create the arrangement she had had with Lundy. She floated the idea with Mary Ann, saying,

> If the day ever comes when you and I can go into partnership, my dear sister, I will take charge of the housekeeping and the children and leave you quite free to devote yourself to professional work and to give your

leisure to your husband, and I will take care of you as I used to of Lundy. That is what a doctor needs. For the present I can see nothing better for me to do than to stay right here and work away. It is not very much but it is a living, & in such a time as this that is not to be despised. If we ever should do that it would have to be a permanent partnership because, at my age, I could hardly resume practice, if I once gave it up.[106]

With Mary Ann tied down with her own family and retired from the medical profession, nothing came of Sarah's proposal, steeped in ambivalence as it was. In many ways Sarah became the emotional center of her family, a role Susan Wattles had always filled. The mantle passed once and for all from mother to daughter during Susan's last illness in late 1897 and early 1898. Sarah seemed to know that Susan's time might be near when she stopped in Mound City in January 1897 on her return from visiting relatives in the East. She decided to stay and even opened an office to see patients.[107] She got involved in the local WCTU chapter, kept up with developments in the single-tax movement, and joined other Kansas women in founding a Woman's Relief Corps to memorialize the Civil War.[108] However, increasingly her time focused on caring for Susan, who was living with Emma. Again Sarah drew upon Mary Ann's superior medical knowledge, dutifully reporting symptoms and treatments as the two sisters discussed through correspondence how to care for their mother. Sarah considered it a privilege to have been present for Susan's last days, and Mary Ann regretted not being there herself. Mary Ann wrote to Susan, "I wish rapid transit were rapid enough to bring me there too—so that we could all be together for a little while." Although that dream could not be realized, Mary Ann was happy Susan's last years had been relatively pain free and "brightened by Faith and Hope." She told her mother, "If it should be that this is the last that I shall write directly to you here, let me say how much I love you, and how thankful I am that I am your daughter. And that I do try to live up to the standard of your example and teaching."[109]

Sarah had also tried to live up to the standards Susan set. It was a high bar, and Sarah seemed the one who most regretted her inability to attain it as she had wished. After Susan's death in January 1898, Sarah returned to Texas to take up practice again in Denton County. Sometime after 1901, she moved back to Mound City and lived with Emma and Eaton. In 1910 she went again to Colorado to minister to Theodore, suffering yet another bout of his recurring illness. Returning on the train from that visit, Sarah Wattles Hiatt fell ill and was taken in by relatives in Kansas City, where she died on November 2, 1910.[110]

Sarah, Mary Ann, and other professional women of their time felt a great sense of duty to make the world a better place, using the education they had been privileged to attain. Sarah's circumstances situated her in places lacking in those features essential for organized reform by women, but she did try though gentle persuasion to improve the moral and political condition of her patients and neighbors. She was in effect a carpet-bagger carrying Northern ideas about moral improvement and women's rights into hostile territory, and she had no choice but to tread lightly. Mary, on the contrary, lived in an urban environment with a variety of opportunities for organized reform activities as well as educational and artistic culture but required assistance from her mother so that she could maintain both a career and family. Many of their contemporaries, especially those who attended the first women's colleges or the state schools in the West that had accepted women, felt frustrated that there were so few occupations open to them where they could apply their newly acquired skills and knowledge. Some of these women, such as Jane Addams and Florence Kelley, started settlement houses and invented the field of social work so that they could bring their energies and talents to bear upon the problems of US society. Like women physicians, they also banded together in cooperative networks to support each other. All of these women labored at a time when the vote was denied them and gender expectations limited their activities and often took a heavy personal toll.

Members of this generation of women doctors were highly conscious of their identities as professional women and wanted to be taken seriously. They thought deeply about the curricula of their schools, the scientific bases of their medical work, and their special mission to address the medical concerns of women and children. Like other women across generations, they faced the dilemma of whether to choose a career or a family. Some married and had children, but many more chose to remain single or live in lifelong partnerships with other single professional women. Some became members of professional organizations and active citizens in their urban communities. Some went to the South or West to live and practice in small rural communities, where they spread progressive ideas while treating disease and injury. Few of them achieved an ideal balance of career, social service, and family life, but rather they cobbled together lives as best that they could within a society that defined no role for a working mother. Their endeavors exposed the obstacles professional women faced in the late nineteenth century and pointed to some of the solutions women would continue to explore.

7

A WESTERING FAMILY:
THE WATTLES-FAUNCES AS
SETTLER COLONISTS

Theodore Wattles must have been suffering from a little cabin fever that day in January 1880 when he "took a notion" to go out for some newspapers. He was spending the winter in a small log cabin, twelve feet by sixteen feet, with three other men on a homestead along the Mancos River, in southwestern Colorado. He set off on snowshoes for the nearest settlement, Parrott City, about fifteen miles away. After a two-day walk, he reached Parrott City, where he spent the night at a friend's house. Then he decided he "would go down on the Lower Laplata to look for an ax" he had lost the previous spring. He "had to snow shoe down to Browns six miles, stayed there all night and the next day walked 25 miles to the settlements below the Indian reservation." He said, "It snowed all day but I was going south and [away] from the mountains and after it got four or five inches deep of fresh snow did not gain on me any. The old snow was packed in the road the first part of the way and had gone off the last part, before this storm came." He stayed there four or five days, then caught a ride with "some teams coming up to Animas City" and camped out with them one night. It was twenty-five degrees below zero, and he "took a terable cold." When he got to Animas City, he found it "prety lively on account of there being a fiew soldiers there yet." He "stayed in Animas one day and then came home walking and snow shoeing," a journey of about thirty miles. He thought, "Snow Shoeing is very nice on level ground but up or down hill I had rather walk if the snow is not too deep."[1] Theodore, a Civil War veteran and the son of abolitionists, had become a rugged western pioneer.

The story of the Wattles family was always one of a westering family. Members of the family moved west in every generation, from when Augustus and Susan Wattles moved from New York to Ohio in the 1830s and then to Kansas in the 1850s. When Mary Ann Wattles went east for schooling and stayed to pursue her career, her backtracking did not break the usual pattern for Americans but reinforced it. Migration back and forth across the continent typified that mobility. When Mary Ann, her husband, Carroll, and their children moved to Colorado from Massachusetts in the late 1890s, they reflected the choices many Americans made in that decade, going west in response to an economic setback. Even though the circumstances under which Mary Ann moved west differed greatly from those of twenty years previously when Theodore Wattles became the first of the family to pass beyond the Hundredth Meridian, both of them went west as settlers in search of better fortunes, in contrast with their parents, who migrated in order to create a better society. Theodore Wattles and Mary Ann Wattles Faunce and their families participated in the great national project of transforming the West into a region of rugged, self-reliant individuals, free to tame and exploit the land in the interest of improving their families' chances in life. This narrative reflected the favorite image Americans had of themselves at the turn of the twentieth century. As historian Margaret Jacobs has argued, the story of hardy pioneers taking great risks and undergoing tremendous hardship obscured the reality of the conquest and dislocation of Native American peoples. In this narrative, the sacrifice made by settlers justified their claim to the land and entitled them to displace and dominate the original inhabitants.[2]

If we see western expansion and settlement through the lens of settler colonialism, it seems almost ironic to define some of the Wattleses as "settler colonists," as indeed they must be if we accept that settler colonies were those that displace native inhabitants so that the colonists could take the land. As Patrick Wolfe has said, "Settler colonialism destroys to replace."[3] Indigenous populations are deprived of their lands, either eliminated or pushed aside, so that white people may come in and settle the land. The settlers might not be the actual persons who eliminate the native presence, but they do benefit from their removal from those lands. In this sense Augustus and Susan certainly reaped the benefit of the removal of Native Americans from Ohio, though they saw little of the actual process themselves. When they moved to Kansas, the process of elimination was still going on all around them, with tribes removed from east of the Mississippi mingling with those native to the area and all of them under threat of further dispossession as white settlers poured into the territory.[4] The authors of the Kansas-Nebraska Act of 1854 had not wanted to wait until the troublesome issues of Indian title to the land had been sorted out to open Kansas land to settlement.

Preoccupied with the issue of black slavery, the Wattleses had little to say about Indians until the Civil War broke out and Augustus temporarily became an Indian agent. Like other abolitionists who occasionally noticed the plight of indigenous peoples, he recognized that the Indians were being cheated and abused and devoted his energies to publicizing the mistreatment. Although he did sympathize with their plight, such humanitarian concern could still occur under the purview of his purposes as a settler colonial. As Adele Perry has pointed out, liberal humanitarianism could and did coexist with the business of empire by critiquing how colonialism was carried out but failing to question colonialism itself.[5] Neither Susan nor Augustus ever seemed to question their right as white Americans to move onto lands taken from Indians. However, this is a complicated business in which one people's dispossession can become another's enfranchisement. One of the great accomplishments of the Wattles family in moving to Kansas came when their daughter Sarah Grimké Wattles took out a claim on a piece of that land. The ability to own property in her own name was a great step forward for the rights of white women, but it came at the expense of native people's possession of the land. This is the great paradox of western expansion: looking at the entire picture we see a massive project of settler colonialism, but focusing on the settlers themselves, we find families making choices we can respect and on occasion admire.

If the Wattles family's venture into Kansas revealed somewhat ingenuous participation in settler colonialism, Theodore Wattles's migration to Colorado after the war was much less so. Theodore consciously rejected the liberal humanitarianism of his parents and embraced the identity of a settler in its most individualistic and acquisitive sense. He went west to make his fortune and to acquire land, and he trusted his government to move the native population out of the way so that he could accomplish those goals. In making a choice about where he could settle, and in believing that he had an absolute right to settle wherever he wanted, Theodore was not merely a quintessential westerner but also the essence of a settler colonialist. In moving west, he also drew after him other members of his family, thus further engaging the Wattles family in the larger project of settling the country and alienating the land from its original inhabitants.

When Theodore Wattles mustered out of the US Army for the final time in 1866, he was a disillusioned man. Having grown accustomed to and perhaps fond of military life, he did not adjust to civilian routines as easily as his comrade and brother-in-law, Eaton Morse. Eaton had married Emma Wattles in October 1864; settled down in Mound City, Kansas; and welcomed his first child in 1866, Wilton Lowe Morse. In contrast, the quotidian joys of domestic life did not appeal to Theodore, not yet. During this period, he enrolled in a bookkeeping course somewhere, perhaps in Chicago, though we do not know if he tried to work at the practice. He probably spent time helping out on the family farm in Moneka. However, in the spring of 1875 he decided to depart for the territories and found his way to Fort Defiance on the border between Arizona and New Mexico, in the heart of Navajo country.

Constructed as a US Army fort in 1851, Fort Defiance now served as the first Indian agency on Navajo land. Theodore got work there inspecting, weighing, and shipping wool produced by the Navajos.[6] Whether by chance or design, Theodore had run across an old associate of his father's, W. F. M. Arny, formerly the agent of the National Kansas Committee in the 1850s. Augustus and Arny had worked together to distribute donated items to free-state settlers, and certainly Theodore had known him at that time as well. In 1875 Arny was serving as Indian agent at Fort Defiance and had become a highly controversial figure. Described by western historian Frank McNitt as "a hypocritical rascal, a Bible-pounding moralist who plotted larceny," Arny had irritated nearly everyone he met in New Mexico and Arizona.[7] He had a bad habit of pilfering dry goods destined for the Navajos' annuity payments, and to make matters worse, he was trying to get the US government to renegotiate the boundaries of the reservation to remove the choicest arable lands along the San Juan River from Navajo control. Arny had so antagonized the Navajos that they seized the fort and threatened to kill him unless the government replaced him with another agent. Arny resigned in July 1875, and a new agent arrived that fall.[8] The US Army sent Major William Redwood Price to Fort Defiance to sort through the agency's supplies, looking for the goods Arny had confiscated for himself. According to McNitt, "Ledgers were consulted, warerooms inspected, and lists of Arny's personal things, or those he claimed as his, were compared with lists of agency orders, furnishings, and supplies. A dry, dusty business."[9] Working in the fort's warehouses, Theodore Wattles was probably on hand to witness and perhaps participate in cleaning up Arny's mess.

By the end of all the turmoil, Theodore found himself out of a job. Writing to his mother in December, he reported,

> There has been quite a change in the aspect of affares here since I wrote last. Then it was reported that the new agent Mr Irwin had resigned, the department would not accept of his resignation and he has come on and Captain Clary has brought two employes with him and there are one or two more coming and Beardsly and I and some others have got to leave be discharged the first of Jan. Mr. Swain says Arny had more men employed than the appropriation would pay and he must discharge some.[10]

Although Theodore had spent less than a year at Fort Defiance, the experience exposed him to the culture of the Navajos and their most important livelihood, producing wool and woven items. Arny had reported that 60,000 pounds of wool had passed through the fort from Navajo trade in 1875, and his successor, Agent Irvine, related that the Navajos traded in 200,000 pounds of wool and blankets in 1877.[11] Wool was a thriving trade in the wholesale market, and soon woolen blankets rose in demand as well. Fascinated with Navajo weaving, the usually terse Theodore wrote three full pages to his mother describing how the Navajo women wove their blankets. He also sent her a Navajo rug, explaining to her why it was an item of high quality.[12]

After leaving Fort Defiance, Theodore and his friend Beardsley made their way north to the mining districts of the La Plata Mountains of southwestern Colorado. In October 1876, needing a grubstake, they borrowed $100 from John Moss, one of the original miners in the district, and Tiburcio Parrott, a San Francisco banker who lent Moss the capital for his ventures. Moss had founded the town of Parrott City in 1874. At the time it looked as if Parrott City would be the center of business for the La Plata mining district and certainly the future county seat. Theodore took a house in Parrott City and with a friend from Kansas, Frank Morgan, staked several claims in the surrounding mountains.[13]

Theodore's new home lay in the shadow of the La Plata Mountains, a subrange of the San Juan Mountains. Parrott City stood at the mouth of the La Plata Canyon. The La Plata and several other tributaries of the San Juan River, including the Mancos, Animas, and Los Piños, begin in the San Juan Mountains on the western side of the Continental Divide. Eventually the San Juan River joins the Colorado River in southeastern Utah. On the eastern side of the divide the waters drain into the Rio Grande, which flows into the San Luis Valley, gathering up the waters of the Alamosa and Conejos Rivers before flowing on down to New Mexico and eventually the Gulf of Mexico. From the slopes of 14,000-foot-plus Sneffels and Uncompahgre Peaks, the San Miguel River and the tributaries of the Gunnison River flow north before dumping into the Colorado. From the heart of the San Juan Mountains the Dolores River flows southwest, west, then north to meet the Colorado. These rivers became the major entry points into the San Juan Mountains for prospectors seeking gold and silver. Yet even these numerous waterways did not guarantee easy access to the San Juans, which offered some of the most challenging terrain in the Rocky Mountains. Jagged peaks, steep inclines, and deep, narrow canyons awaited the traveler. Weather could also pose its challenges. It could snow during any month of the year, and several feet of snow and drifts three times that high were almost guaranteed from October to May. Yet the abundance of minerals lured Spanish prospectors as early as 1765, and by the 1870s American miners came in droves, establishing camps throughout the rugged, narrow canyons. Many of these men were, like Theodore Wattles, veterans of the Civil War, bachelors, seeking fortune and adventure and a new life.[14]

The first wagon roads into the San Juan Mountains came through the San Luis Valley, up the Rio Grande River, and across the Continental Divide over Stony Pass, dropping down into Baker's Park, where the mining town of Silverton got its start in 1871. Gold was discovered near Lake San Cristobal in 1874, leading to the rise of Lake City, and a road was built to connect Saguache in the northwest corner of the San Luis Valley with Lake City and the mining district around it. From the south hopeful miners followed the Animas and La Plata Rivers into the high mountains and soon discovered strikes that led to the settlements of Animas City, Parrott City, and Rockwood. Just to the west and north, within the watersheds of the

Dolores and San Miguel Rivers, the mining camps of Rico, Ophir, Telluride, and Ouray all sprang up by the end of the decade.[15]

The Mancos River begins high in the La Platas on the slopes of Hesperus Mountain, a 13,232-foot peak the Navajos consider their sacred mountain of the North. After leaving the mountains, the Mancos River flows in a southwesterly direction through first a broad valley and then cutting canyons between high mesas, including Mesa Verde, before joining the San Juan River on its way to the Colorado. Down on the relatively level floor of the Mancos River Valley the community of Mancos started in the winter of 1875–1876, when seven prospectors erected some cabins in which to spend the winter. Most of them stayed on, building permanent homes and developing farms and ranches across the valley. Theodore Wattles joined them the following year, when he too came out of the mountains for the winter, then decided to settle in the valley as a homesteader.[16] Although he continued to work on his mining claims, he quickly discovered freighting offered a better opportunity for a steady income than mining did, and he went into the teamster business with some friends from Kansas. Working with teams of oxen, he hauled lumber, coal, machinery, and other materials to and from assorted mining towns in the La Plata Mountains. From their "trading point" of Animas City, "a place of 2 or 3 hundred inhabitants," they hauled freight to Rico, Parrott City, Rockwood, and Silverton over breathtakingly treacherous mountain passes.[17] Between freighting runs Theodore worked his land on the Mancos River, planting wheat and learning how to irrigate in that arid country. Until his own cabin was completed, he hunkered down with other bachelor settlers in Mancos for the winter. During the winter of 1879, he stayed in the home of Alex Ptolemy, a naturalized Canadian. It was a cozy arrangement, as he described to his mother:

> There are four of us here in this little cabin 12 X 16. Alex Ptolemy Ed his brother John Reid and my self the others are all from Canada. . . . There is a good floor in the house and a cook stove and a four light window there is a two story bunk Alex and I sleep in the upper one there is a sellar under the house with lots of potatoes and flour in it I can make just as good light bread with sour dough Alex has a lot of earthan dishes and we live like white folks only we use wheat coffee.[18]

He had partially completed his own cabin, having cut and hauled the house logs before winter set in. He still had to cut and peel the roof poles, as he reported to his mother. "It is to be a dirt roof," he told Susan, "and the poles are layed close together and daubed with mud and then loose dirt throwed on till it will turn rain. It makes a very warm and substantial roof and one that will not easily take fire."[19]

As an early settler in the region Theodore witnessed the first stages of development in the Mancos Valley and surrounding communities. When he first arrived, he had to travel great distances over poor roads through rugged mountain terrain. The nearest railroad terminus was located in Alamosa, which the Denver & Rio Grande Railroad (D&RG) reached in 1878 by building over La Veta Pass from Walsenburg. To get to Alamosa Theodore and other Mancos Valley settlers had to travel by horse or wagon over 10,015-foot Cumbres Pass, along the Colorado-New Mexico border, entering the San Luis Valley from the south, a trip of just more than 200 miles. When the D&RG extended the line over Cumbres and northward in 1881, it stopped two and a half miles short of Animas City at a spot named Durango, forcing the residents of Animas City to abandon their town site and move everything over to the new settlement growing up around the railroad depot. Parrott City missed out entirely on a railroad connection and dwindled to a ghost town by the turn of the century. Prior to the railroad's extension, Theodore and his friends endured some hair-raising adventures traveling between Mancos and Alamosa. During the winter of 1878–1879 Theodore's partner, Frank Morgan, took four yoke of oxen (i.e., eight oxen) to Alamosa to get supplies for winter but got caught in mountain snows on his return and could not get back to Mancos until the spring thaw. Theodore had to make a trip to Animas City, some thirty miles away, so he could get enough supplies to make it through the winter. He described the journey, and the grocery list, to his sister Mary Ann:

One of my neighbors was going with three yoke of oxen and I got him to take fifteen bushels of wheat for me to the mill 10 miles beyond Anamas. We started the day after new years it took ten days to make the trip. The day we started home from the mill it snowed about eight inches and there was a foot of snow there. Before that I was afraid we would not be able to get home but it did not snow as much over this way. On the La Plata divide the snow was up to the front end of the wagon for five miles but we made it with out any mishap. In Anamas City I got a fiew necessities such as bacon salt soda and soap and a pair of rubber boots.

They are a long way ahead of lether when one has to be out in the snow all day.[20]

Such arduous journeys became a way of life, especially in the winter. When spring rolled around, however, Theodore ranged far and wide. As soon as the weather warmed, he headed south to the San Juan River to round up cattle that had grazed there through the winter. During the spring season he also had to get his crops in on his ranch while waiting for the snow to melt in the mountains so they could commence the hauling business to the mining camps. Sometimes he hired men to tend the ranch while he was freighting, but he came back to Mancos for the harvest. In addition to his farming and teamster work, he also put in time on his mining claims when he could.[21] Developments in the region could force a change in his plans, as happened in the summer of 1879 when the freighting business came to a standstill as two railroad companies—the D&RG and the Atchison, Topeka & Santa Fe—fought a shooting war over the right to build a line through the Royal Gorge. Theodore found himself stranded in Alamosa, then the terminus of the D&RG, with five yoke of oxen and three wagons with a carrying capacity of 9,000 to 10,000 pounds, looking for some freight to haul. The railroad hired him "to guard the Road for three dollars a day and board," but that job lasted only two weeks. Finally, some freighting work came along, and he took a load to Lake City, a journey of 120 miles that took him three weeks to complete. Along the way he observed some of the features that would make the Rio Grande a tourist mecca in the lifetime of the next Wattles generation:

> The road to Lake is up the Rio Grand about eighty miles, through Wagon Wheel Gap where there are some very fine hot springs. It is quite a resort for tourests. There are an abundance of trout in the Rio Grand up there and deer and elk are quite plenty in the Mts. and it is cool enough to have frost most every night and in the forenoon it is pretty hot and now that the rainy season has set in it rains most every after noon.[22]

In nearly every regard Theodore was the quintessential settler. His motives for being in Colorado were clearly and unceremoniously to make his fortune in the best way he could find and perhaps to experience a little adventure along the way. He envisioned this region as wide open for possibilities and opportunities, some of which he would benefit from directly and some that would bring forth flourishing new towns and burgeoning trade. He undertook daunting physical feats under extreme conditions, and he lived under primitive conditions requiring great physical and psychological endurance. There is much in his exploits that deserves admiration and astonishment. At the same time, we remember that he and all the other white settlers in southwestern Colorado were taking out homesteads on land that had only very recently been the territory of the Utes.

The Ute Nation was well established in the mountains of Colorado by AD 1400. By the time the Spanish encountered the twelve Ute bands in the early seventeenth century, they lived within clearly defined territories throughout Colorado, Utah, and northern New Mexico. The Weenuche (or Weminuche) Band occupied the mountains and river valleys of the San Juan Mountains of southwestern Colorado. Now known as the Southern Utes, the Muaches and Capotes lived east of the Continental Divide in the southern San Juans, the San Luis Valley of Colorado, and northern New Mexico. The first treaty between the Utes and the United States came in 1849 when twenty-eight chiefs signed an X to indicate their agreement to live in peace with the white people. White captives were released, and the Utes promised to allow travelers and military personnel to cross their lands. They gave up no land, and no reservations were yet established. The treaty failed to guarantee peace as the Utes, US military personnel, and settlers negotiated developments on the ground. Mormons moving into Utah and gold rushers filtering into the Colorado Rockies pushed the Utes into a core territory of western Colorado by the 1860s. In 1861 President Abraham Lincoln created reservations for the Utes both in southern Colorado and southeastern Utah, but removal to them was not strictly enforced. Under an 1868 treaty the Utes gave up two-thirds of their land and could live only in the western one-third of Colorado. Agencies were established, annuities were promised, and the Utes who did not go along with the new arrangements, such as Chief Colorow's band, were treated as renegades.

However, as with most treaties with Indian tribes, white settlers who failed to respect treaty agreements suffered no such sanction, and in fact, the blatant disregard for the tribes' rights by intruders and squatters pushed government officials to make new treaties, drawn up to further restrict native domain in favor of settlers. In 1872, with miners pouring into the San Juan Mountains, Chief Ouray of the Southern Utes demanded that the government expel the trespassers. Instead, government agent Felix Brunot negotiated the cession of the San Juans for $500,000 in 1873. Over the next few years, the Utes lost more lands, and individual Utes expressed their anger and frustration by haranguing and attacking white settlers. The hostilities came to a climax in September 1879 when members of Chief Colorow's band killed Agent Nathan Meeker of the White River Agency, ten employees, and thirteen soldiers, and abducted the employees' wives and children. Meeker had been an arrogant agent much like Arny and tried to bend the Utes to his will by destroying their horse-racing track and other attempts to eradicate their traditional practices. Also, a white sheriff's posse had killed Colorow's son Tabernash when he visited their horse-racing track in Middle Park the previous year. Chief Ouray negotiated the release of the prisoners and surrender of Colorow, and there was a trial resulting in the removal of Colorow's band to the reservation in Utah in 1881. Following the Meeker Massacre, the US government further reduced the tribe's reservation lands.[23]

As one of the white men encroaching on Ute territory, Theodore's attitude regarding this profound land acquisition was just what we would expect. Like other Colorado settlers, Theodore saw no reason to nurture friendly or cooperative relationships with Native Americans. He had no motivation whatsoever to marry into an Indian family as white fur traders had once done to ensure allies and helpmates. His freighting business would not depend upon Indian customers, and he would not even need to curry personal favor with tribes as the price for traveling the roads safely.[24] He took it for granted that the land would be available for white settlement and that the federal government would guarantee the safety of the settlers. He closely followed transactions between government officials and the tribes. In November 1878, he told his mother, "This country is settling up considerable this fall. The fifteen mile strip and a 100 miles long on the south side of this Co. that the Indians had has been treted for and is opened for settlement. There is not much farming land on it but most of it is good stock country."[25] In the spring of 1880, following the Meeker Massacre the previous autumn, he reported, "We don't apprehend any trouble this spring with the Utes. There will be no difficulties unless the Govt. trys to move them or to take the White River murderers and in that case probably they will put troops enough in here to protect the settlers befor they commence."[26]

Any typical settler would assume whites had the right to expect their government to eliminate the native presence on any lands desired for settlement. However, Theodore was the son of Augustus and Susan Wattles, reformers who had devoted their lives to humanitarian causes, including the welfare of Native Americans. In choosing to think like a typical settler, Theodore turned his back almost entirely on his parents' idealism. Except for one statement of appreciation for Navajo weaving, Theodore never had a word of sympathy for Native Americans and, at times, almost seemed to be goading his mother with his contempt for them. In 1885, after a report of an Indian attack on a settler, Theodore wrote to his mother, "We feal no fear of the Indians," adding derisively, "of course they will not be punished. The humanatarians back east would howl and that would scare Congress."[27] Theodore sounds very much the westerner, scorning the government and everyone back East in one breath, indifferent to his own father's role as a humanitarian. As if to underscore his contempt for the "misplaced" sympathy reformers held for these peoples, Theodore made sure to tell Susan the gory details of the Indian attack on the settlers:

A week ago last night the Indians set fire to a house in Montezuma Valey and when the man (Mr. Gentner) came out to put the fire out shot him. His wife ran to help him and they shot her in the shoulder. He told his wife to let him alone and save the children which [she] succeeded in doing, getting out the back while they wer finishing her husband. They shot him seven times. She wandered around through the sage brush and cactus with her four little ones just as they had jumped out of bed till nearly day light. She carried the baby in her arms or rather her arm for the bone in her shoulder was all shattered. The Dr. says there is not more than one chance in ten for her to live. It was nearly two days before the Dr. could reach her. This happened June 20th About ten oclock on the morning of that day there wer six Indians killed across the Dolores river on the head of Beaver Creek twenty five miles from this murder. They had been killing cattle and told the cattlemen if they made any fuss about it they would whip them again like they did last summer. The day before they went to a house where there wer two women and tried to outrage them. They were frightened away. The whites attact them next morning at day light killed four men one child and one squaw. One man and one squaw got away. The soldiers are over here now from Ft. Lewis and I don't know what will happen next.[28]

Theodore seemed unconcerned that a Native American child and woman, who could only have been innocent of the crimes committed, had been murdered, but surely Susan would have noticed and cared. Although Susan was not one to engage in confrontation with her only son, she might have conspired with Mary Ann (with whom she was living at the time) to send a copy of *Ramona* by Helen Hunt Jackson, an advocate for native peoples, to Theodore for Christmas that year. When Theodore's wife, Mell, opened the package, she "had a good laugh," she said, writing to Mary Ann. "If you think you could induce Theo to read anything of Helen Hunt Jackson's writing, you are mistaken. The Indians are a thorn in his side and anything in their favor is a similar sensation in the other side."[29] Theodore's sentiments about Native Americans did not come from his upbringing, but he had thoroughly absorbed them. He might have adopted the views of other settlers in Kansas, or perhaps succumbed to peer pressure in the military, or grew to hate Indians after he lived in Colorado. Maybe he just took a contrarian view to his father's beliefs. Perhaps, as with the vast majority of Americans, he ingested the cultural messages and imperatives of the time and went along without much thought to it, satisfied that the great national project of colonizing the West was justified and right.

Cultural imperatives are difficult to withstand, which is one reason, after it had been set in motion, settler colonization of the continent had such momentum. It is not difficult to understand why Theodore rebuffed his father's humanitarian view toward Native Americans, given his circumstances. When it came to women's rights, another of the family's cherished reform ideas, Theodore carried on the family tradition in supporting woman's suffrage, a position not uncommon in his western environs. However, when his mother pushed for Theodore to adopt her views on sex reform, he put his foot down, firmly. Susan Wattles had become intrigued with the idea of radical sex reform in the early 1880s when some women's rights proponents suggested women would have more control over their lives if they could manage their own reproduction. Controlling one's sexuality, however, was difficult at a time when contraception was not reliable or widely available. This was not an entirely new notion for Susan because her brother and sister-in-law, John and Esther Wattles, had publicly advocated and privately practiced sexual moderation in the 1850s. In later years Esther told her daughters she and John had had sexual intercourse only three times in their entire married life; it was well planned and resulted in the birth of the three girls, two years apart, all born within the first two weeks of February.[30] Few reformers of the 1850s, however, had followed the example of John and Esther. The later sex reform movement owed much to the efforts of an ex-Quaker named Elmina Drake Slenker, who equated sexual excess with the same degradation of women and the home that alcohol caused. Advocates of sex reform published a newspaper called the *Alpha,* in which they argued for greater access to contraception for women. Until women had more reliable birth control, they had few options other than abstinence within marriage to determine the size of their families.[31]

Theodore might have remained blissfully unaware of these developments but for his mother's good intentions upon his marriage in early 1885. On January 22 of that year, Theodore married Melvina J. Hammond, a young woman whose family had come from Canada to settle in southwestern Colorado. Melvina, or Mell, taught school in Durango when she first met Theodore, but she had been raised in some rough mining camps, possibly with an alcoholic father, and was not particularly drawn to the prospects of domesticity. It took Theodore many months to persuade Mell to marry him. As he told Susan, "I had a pretty hard time, encountered many adverse winds that it is not worth while to speak of now that we are safe in port."[32] He was not nearly as securely moored as he thought. While negotiating their marriage prospects, Mell thought she had made it very clear to Theodore that she did not want to give birth to one child after another, so their sex life would be quite limited. After they were married, Theodore's understanding of that agreement did not match that of Mell. Unfortunately for Theodore, his mother decided to intervene. It had always been a practice of Susan's to send literature to her friends and family to enlighten and educate them. Shortly after hearing about Theodore's marriage, Susan began sending Mell copies of the *Alpha.* Mell loved it. She wrote to thank Susan, saying,

> I would like so much to talk personally to you of the matter it contains.
> So few people aim so high in their standard of moral excellence that if

one has any ideas they dare not express them. Theodore . . . thinks I am
fanatical. He did say, however, that in all your talk of Woman's Rights,
the point in question never entered his head. Don't you think, Mother,
that if children were better born, in later life they would require less
legislation? Voting is woman's right, of course, but far superior to that
is the right to bring into the world children not quite so closely.[33]

Theodore added his own perspective in a postscript: "Mell says I am to
give my views on the 'Alpha' They will have to be some what brief for this
small space. I think it is too extream all together. I am afraid it is going to
make trouble in this family, so you better don't send it some more. Mell is
a born fanatic and when she believes anything she believes it as hard as she
can."[34] Neither Susan nor Mell gave up easily. Six weeks later Mell wrote to
Susan to say, "The Alpha was not the beginning of our trouble. That began
the first night of our married life. I said the other day that I would rather be
killed by the Indians than live as my nearest neighbor does, Who married
at 14 and now at 21 has four children and complains of being 'so tired' and
more than that, has a white savage for a husband."[35] Theodore again added
a postscript, sharing more information than we might assume would be
provided to a mother by a son in the Victorian era:

> Your last letter came some time ago when Mell read it she put her arms
> around my neck and kissed me and said "your Mother is an awfull good
> woman" I don't see why men and women was made so different now
> I think I am very moderate it seames to me that two or three times a
> week is not exsessive indulgence but Mell thinks twice a month often
> enough but realy I cant stand that perhaps I will have to come to it. Mell
> don't have the backache or complain of any physical inconvienance but
> [she says] "it aint right"—and "it is our duty to do what we can for the
> reform" I don't care a straw for reform I want to do what is best and
> agreeable for ourselves.[36]

The last we hear of the subject came just a month later when Theodore
pulled out all the stops, resorting to phrenological science, nearly begging
his mother to understand his plight:

> I see Mell has been righting to you and as the letter has not gon yet I will
> put in a fiew lines about this subject that mars our perfect bliss. Mell

gave me to understand what her views wer before we wer married but she was allways hinting up some bugerboo to scare me from marrying her and we did not know whether our desires would correspond to our theories or not till we wer married a while and tryed it. We have a little round up every fiew weeks. I make all sorts of promices and then coaks her to brake them After I have abstained for four or five days the back of my head wher amativeness is located begins to ache at first only a dul pain and it jumps and throbs and Mell says I go around like a ghost and I can't think of anything else and she takes pity on me and then she is provoked with her self not because of the injurious effect on her but for fear of the effect on the coming man and it aint right. God did not intend it to be so and it is our duty to reform the world. When a man is in that fix he don't care much for the reformation of the world and he is liable to think irreverent thought.[37]

Theodore and Mell worked it out somehow and soon had two children (no more!).

For Theodore, his vision of what his life should contain and his mother's idea of what might be achieved in life were two incompatible dreams. Theodore had conventional goals, and although he never broke off contact with his family, he cast aside the reformer identity his parents had constructed and his sisters Sarah and Mary Ann felt compelled to emulate. Theodore wanted material success and thought the world he lived in would be improved through material development. He believed that white farmers and ranchers settling the country would greatly improve on the ways Native Americans had used the land and built their societies. He epitomized western settlers in his support for indigenous displacement and in attracting other settlers to the West to help get the job done. Settler colonialism required a constant stream of fresh recruits to fill in the vast spaces of western country and to ensure a continual flow of new capital. Throughout the West local boosters tried to lure settlers with the promise of fertile lands and wide-open opportunities. Embellished descriptions of prairie and desert drew the ambitious and striving, and families used the bonds of emotive and economic ties to lure kinfolk westward. The Wattles family embodied this pattern of chain migration, with a single individual going on ahead of the rest of the family, figuring out the new circumstances, then encouraging and assisting others to come along. Theodore forged the way, set down roots, and then enabled other members of the family to become established in the same locale. In drawing family to the West, he was also enlisting them in the colonizing and settling project.

The first member of the family to follow him to Colorado was his nephew Wilton Morse, son of Emma and Eaton Morse. Born in 1866, Wilton grew up on the family farm in Mound City, Kansas, the oldest of five sons and one daughter. After attending the State Agricultural College of Kansas (later Kansas State University), Wilton went to Mancos, Colorado, in 1890 and stayed with Theodore and his family. In December 1890, a few months after his arrival, he attended a three-day teachers institute so that he could teach in Colorado.[38] He did a variety of work, including helping Uncle Theodore on the ranch, working for the railroad surveying crew, and teaching school. On October 1, 1891, he wrote to his grandmother, Susan Wattles, saying, "I have been in Colo. a little over a year now, came to Mancos the 23 of Sept. a year ago, and I can't say that I like it as well as I do Kansas." Susan had asked him about his school, so he reported:

> Well, I had quite a nice school frame, and ceiled. It was well sealed, and I got some good maps a little while before school closed. My enrollment was a little over thirty and nine families were represented. The school was out the first of last March and I haven't taught since. Do not like teaching very well but will teach again this winter. I think this will be the last one I will try. When I commenced last winter I was told that I had a very hard school to teach but did not find it so. There were no boys older than 15 and they were not large enough to make much trouble, that is serious trouble. They were not bad but rather mischevious.[39]

Wilton stayed in Colorado, teaching when he could find no other work and picking up other jobs when he could. He did farm work for Theodore and neighboring ranchers, including the Wetherills, the Wattleses' neighbors.[40] Wilton was a great help to Theodore's family when Theodore became ill in 1895 and his sister Sarah came to Colorado to escort him back east to Massachusetts, where she and Mary Ann could tend to him. Much more than ranch work, however, Wilton enjoyed carpentering. In 1891 he had gone to Durango to buy some tools and soon had several jobs building barns for people around Mancos. He built one barn that was "100 x 22 ft and is 14 ft to the eaves, it has a beamed roof and no sides."[41] Wilton stayed in Mancos and made a career as a builder and architect, even though he never had any formal training. He built the Mancos High School and many houses in the Mancos area.[42]

Wilton was not the only member of the family to follow Theodore to Colorado. Mary Ann and Carroll Faunce began buying land in the Mancos Valley in 1889, while they were still living in Brooklyn. The land, adjacent to Theodore's ranch, came up for sale, and Theodore tried to interest Eaton and Emma in buying it before suggesting that the Faunces purchase it. "I wrote to Emma about a very cheap farm there is for sale," he wrote to Susan, who was living with Mary Ann:

> It has to be sold to pay the debts and I am the administrator. There are three hundred and twenty acres nearly all fenced, ten acres in alfalfa, 10 in timothy, 70 in wheat & oats, log barn 20 x 40 with basement stable cheap frame house with five rooms all for five thousand dollars or 160 acres with the houses and alfalfa on it for $3000.00 or the other 160 for $2000. A purchaser could borrow $3000. on it at 10 percent if he did not have the money to pay down. If I owned the property and was out of debt—would not take three times that for it. But a man has got to work it and spend some more to make it pay & Mary knows what working on a farm is, a good manager could make it pay and higher the work done.[43]

Mary Ann and Carroll responded positively to the offer, not only purchasing the ranch but also taking out a mortgage on it that enabled them to lend some money to Theodore.[44] Carroll especially became very excited about the prospect of becoming a western farmer. Mell Wattles, who did not always appreciate her rough circumstances, exercised a little reverse boosterism on her brother-in-law. Writing to Susan, Mell said,

> If Mr. Faunce could go through our routine for a month his western fever would be succeeded by a chill. A good taste of Colorado dust and some of the water the people are using now on the Mancos would reduce his pulse in no time. Please understand I am not trying to discourage your western trip—we will receive you with open arms, but this ranch business is not the nicest in the world.[45]

The Faunces were unable to make the trip out to Colorado to see the land or take care of any paperwork, so Theodore assisted them by placing legal notices in the county office. Because they did not move to Mancos until 1900, Theodore managed the ranch for nearly a decade, making arrangements to have work done on their land, selling the crops, or renting the land to tenants.[46] He must have felt a strong sense of familial devotion to care for their interests for such a long time even as his health was deteriorating and his own ranch began to suffer from neglect.

When Mary Ann and Carroll Faunce finally did go to Colorado, their economic circumstances had changed, and the move seemed more like a last resort than an exciting opportunity. In 1889, when they bought the Colorado ranch, they were living in Brooklyn and both of them were employed. They were financially secure enough that they could buy the ranch in Colorado and lend money to Theodore by taking out a mortgage on the ranch. Susan Wattles was living with them and taking care of the children so that Mary Ann could work. The arrangement seemed to suit all involved, and the Faunces probably felt as prosperous as they ever would again. Circumstances changed quickly for them, however, reminding us that very few people ever have complete control over their destinies. At the end of 1892 poor health forced Mary Ann to resign from her position with the New York Infirmary.[47] Carroll might have lost his job as a textile designer around the same time. He had been worried about "fluctuations" in the industry and feared that his firm might succumb.[48] Whatever the reason, he secured a new position in Newtonville, Massachusetts, a suburb of Boston, and the family moved in early 1893. Susan Wattles returned to Kansas at this time, probably confident Mary Ann could take care of her children and household because she would not be working. But Mary Ann's health problems persisted, and in September 1894 she asked a cousin to come to stay with her to help with the household while she had a "surgical operation," possibly a hysterectomy.[49] Following this, the Faunce family seemed happy enough in their domestic circle but worried by developments in society at large. Both Mary Ann and Carroll felt deeply distressed by the great malaise that had struck the country with the Panic of 1893 and ensuing economic depression.

Caused by the failures of major railroad companies, the panic led to a plunge in the stock market, widespread bank collapses, pervasive unemployment, and depressed agricultural, mining, and industrial sectors. The Panic of 1893 occurred at a time of great income disparity spawned by decades of laissez-faire policy that allowed some individuals to amass huge fortunes while laborers languished under a parsimonious wage structure, long hours, and dangerous workplace conditions. Many people deplored these circumstances, leading to a wide variety of reform efforts, from campaigns to organize workers to schemes for changing the foundation of the capitalist system. Many believed scarcity of currency circulating in the economy contributed to the economic stagnation, and the monetization of silver would solve the currency shortage.[50] Colorado's economy suffered a severe shock from the panic that lasted the entire decade and into the new century. To no avail westerners sounded the call for silver in hopes of reviving moribund mining districts, banks, and farms.[51] The depression of the 1890s gave impetus to Progressive reformers, who would eventually construct a basic social safety net that included maximum hours, minimum wages, workplace safety regulations, and the regulation of financial institutions. However, for Mary Ann and Carroll and their contemporaries, none of these provisions existed, and people who called for such measures were considered radicals and troublemakers by the vast majority of middle-class citizens.

Mary Ann and Carroll were comfortably middle class themselves, but they could feel no certainty that the broken system around them would be fixed or that they would be spared the calamity. They felt much anxiety for themselves and for loved ones affected by the downturn. They worried about Theodore, whose health was failing and whose livelihood depended upon the depressed agricultural and mining sectors. They worried about cousins facing destitution when financial institutions collapsed. They could not help but feel anxiety when Sarah wrote in July 1893 that she "had a letter from Ida tonight giving me some of the particulars as to the effect on them of the closing of the first National Bank of Ft. Scott. Our cousins have lost *everything* . . . neither Charley nor Joe know what they will do next. . . . The drugstore was in debt to the bank & so when the crash came *had* to turn everything over to the bank."[52] As the Panic of 1893 and its aftermath swept across the country, even those who kept their jobs had to deal with the unease and apprehension on a daily basis.

It cannot surprise us, therefore, that Mary Ann and Carroll would support some of the many reform causes that flourished in the stressful atmosphere of the 1890s. Mary Ann had always supported woman's suffrage and temperance, as did Susan, Sarah, and Emma. (It would have been strange indeed if a Wattles did not—even Theodore supported woman's suffrage and temperance.) The particular economic reform idea that seized Mary Ann and Carroll was the Single Tax. A panacea in the eyes of believers, the

Single Tax was the brainchild of Henry George, a California journalist and economic theorist who argued that all the economic woes of capitalism came from the control of land by the few and the ability of property owners to accrue wealth from rent without producing anything. Governments, therefore, should tax land, and land only, so that rent could not accrue as unearned wealth. In effect, property owners would be paying a tax to use the land, keeping as their profit whatever they were able to produce using that land. Wealth would be distributed evenly throughout society because there would be no taxes on production, interest, or wages, thus benefiting capitalists and workers alike. George laid out his theories in his book *Progress and Poverty,* published in 1879, and the Single Tax idea gained a wide following in the 1890s. The Single-Tax philosophy was not a true socialist idea in George's thinking because it retained private property, but many people at the time viewed it as a dangerous socialist scheme that aimed to supplant private property with common property ownership.[53]

Mary Ann and Carroll both believed fervently in the Single Tax, as did Sarah. Mary Ann belonged to a "Single Tax class and club" in Boston, officially called the Massachusetts Single-Tax League, and she took Sarah to meetings and a "single tax reception & supper" when she came to visit. Sarah and Mary Ann exchanged ideas and clippings about the Single Tax. Sarah wrote that she was going to "send you mother's last 'Woman's Journal' and two clippings from the Union Signal—the organ of the W.C.T.U.— of the same week because of references in them to the single tax. Just to show how the single tax idea has been seized upon by thinking minds in many lines of reform work."[54] Mary Ann was asked to write a paper to present to the Newton Social Sciences Club on the Single Tax. After having Carroll critique it, she told Sarah, "He seemed to think it would do. But that I might have enlarged a little upon its temperance aspect." When they attended the next single-tax reception and supper, she "made the pleasant acquaintance of a lady from Wellesley—belongs to the Grange there— and she feels a desire to know why the town of Wellesley should exempt the large fields of Wellesley College from taxation thus increasing the rate of others." Mary Ann offered no evaluation of this single-tax enthusiasm run rampant but did comment on meeting "Prof Hays of W, who I believe is Eugenia Morgan's Assistant, Has lectured to their Club—And is in favor of the Single Tax—if that is the complexion of thought in Wellesley I am very glad to hear it."[55]

Sarah also waded fully into the fray of Single-Tax furor while staying in Kansas to care for Susan in her final illness. She wrote a "pretty long" letter to the editor of the *Labor Leader* in which she tried "to tell all I knew." Attending a WCTU meeting at which the discussion centered on the issue of "the obstacles in the way of effective temperance work," she brought up the Single Tax and "tried, in a few remarks, to show them how the single tax would deprive [the liquor] business of all special legal protection and destroy its monopolistic power." Excitedly, Sarah told Mary Ann about meeting Mr. and Mrs. W. H. Wakefield. Wakefield,

whose name is sometimes in Single Tax papers, or in other publications favorable to the single tax," was the "son of old Judge Wakefield whom we used to know in Douglas Co, in 1855–56. He is a very enthusiastic worker for the single tax & presents the subject clearly and forcibly. He was very much interested when I spoke about the banquets given by the Mass. single tax league. He had read full reports of them.[56]

The excitement generated by activism and recalling the old days of the antislavery movement certainly animated the correspondence of the Wattles sisters as well as the Faunce household. Unfortunately, it also led to disaster for Carroll Faunce's career. Unlike Mary Ann, Carroll had always been an argumentative person. As Mary Ann once said, "He likes to find someone to disagree with."[57] In 1898, his confrontational personality cost him his job as a textile designer. Carroll and Mary Ann decided to deal with this adversity by moving to Colorado, but their circumstances required them to do so in stages. They could not move immediately to their Mancos ranch because it was occupied by a renter. Carroll also hoped to get another job so that they could take up ranching with some capital in hand. So Mary Ann and the children moved to Fort Collins, Colorado, while Carroll stayed behind in Boston, moving into smaller living quarters and looking for work. He was desperately unhappy while separated from his family and unable to take care of them. He was worried and left "wondering how this sudden bursting of our affairs is going to effect us and how you are feeling about it, how the children are going to be influenced for their future. I hate to be so far from my responsibilities." He went on to say,

It was bad enough when things were running with some smoothness, but my present sensations are decidedly new to me, the being out of work & very slim prospects of getting any, is not what I am used to. After I hear from you . . . I shall go to New York. (I may go before) and see what can be done but I do not think I shall be able to get in any where. It is known all over the trade now or will be when I get to N. Y. and it is something that will not be treated lightly. I have no direct hints, but I kind of feel that my Silver & Taxation views have had not a little to do with the decided feeling against me in the firm's view.[58]

Possibly blacklisted for his political views—and his tendency to impose them upon anyone in listening distance—Carroll Faunce did what many men did when facing adversity. He headed west, planning to "fall back on the ranch." He told Mary Ann, "If I do not get work here I shall telegraph you 'Coming' then you can write to [Theodore] & he can get Wms off the place as soon as he can."[59]

In the meantime, Mary Ann and the children settled down in Fort Collins. A notice in the local paper indicated they were "stopping with Mr. and Mrs. Stratton until they can find a suitable house to move into," and Mr. Faunce would come "as soon as he can close up his business in the east." The Faunces had "noticed Dr. McHugh's professional card in the *Courier,* they wrote him inquiring about the climate, church and school advantages and were so well pleased with his reply that they packed up at once and started for this city."[60] Once again old Kansas connections came to bear on the fortunes of the family. Harris Stratton had been a Kansas pioneer in the 1850s and had known the Wattles family. Now that his family had settled in Fort Collins, his daughter had married a doctor, P. J. McHugh.[61] Mary Ann chose to settle in Fort Collins on the first leg of the journey to Mancos because of these old acquaintances. She and the children remained in Fort Collins until the summer of 1899, when Carroll finally joined them and they moved to the ranch in Mancos.[62] The circumstances of their migration west had not gone exactly as hoped, but having faced a calamity that might have devastated another family in the tumultuous 1890s, they were very fortunate. The circumstances were such, however, that they began their ranching enterprise with very little available capital. This might have contributed to their lack of success in agriculture.

Farming is a precarious occupation, dependent upon weather, pests, availability of water, and above all, the markets. Theodore Wattles struggled to make a go of his ranch in the Mancos Valley, and he had been raised on farms. Carroll Faunce had never been a farmer prior to taking over his ranch, and he discovered no great talent for the business. His ranch did have certain advantages, especially in having good water rights for irrigation. His nephew Wilton Morse had wisely judged the prospects for the Faunce ranch in 1891 when he wrote his grandmother, telling her,

> I think he has the best red land ranch in the Valley. There are two kinds of land, the "red" and "adobe" which is a sort of drab colored clay. Underneath the red land are granite boulder beds and very often they crop out and no land of this kind is entirely clear from them. Uncle Carroll's ranch has fewer of them than any other one in the Valley. The red land is the best for alfalfa and the 'dobe for grain. . . . The two ranches touch as I have shown them but Uncle Theodore's just barely touches the river with its southeast corner. Uncle Carroll's ranch is the nicest one to irrigate in the Valley, it is almost as even as a table top and has a good slope to the Southwest. However I do not believe he would like farming out here if he was here. Drinking water that is good water is a scarce article out here as there are no wells and the river or ditch water gets very alkali during the irrigating season. However this could be overcome by putting up ice and making cisterns. I don't think he and aunt Mary would like the society here, and to my notion it isn't just the best place to raise a family.[63]

Despite the advantages of his land in comparison with neighboring ranches, Carroll failed as a farmer. Another economic panic hit in 1907, plunging the country into recession and hurting agricultural markets. Carroll's financial losses led him to send out circulars advertising the ranch as an investment prospect. He sent circulars to family across the country, including cousins in Boston and the Morses in Kansas.[64] Somehow Carroll became angry with Eaton and Emma over some aspect of this investment scheme. Perhaps Eaton failed to cooperate with the advertising or might have refused to invest or loan money to Carroll. Whatever the cause, a family rift developed between Carroll and Mary Ann's siblings, forcing Mary Ann to take the side of her husband. The episode was especially tragic because the Morses' only daughter, Eleanor, had contracted tuberculosis and Eaton had brought her to Colorado in hopes that the dry mountain air would help her to recover. Mary Ann recommended Eleanor spend the summer in an open-air camp, living out of a tent, where she might benefit from a robust lifestyle. However, during the summer Mary Ann, deferring to Carroll's wishes, had refused to allow Emma to come to stay with her on the Faunce ranch. Although she apologized to Eaton for her lack of hospitality, Mary Ann could not heal the breach between Carroll and her family. She hoped Eaton's "clear insight & sound judgment might be able to clear up some of the tangle of business misapprehension, and set us all straight again," but apparently it was not to be so. Obliquely, she continued, "It seems to me now impossible to punish the wrong, without hurting the innocent more than the wrong doer."[65] It must have been a bitter and difficult few years on the farm for Mary Ann, at odds with her family because of Carroll.

Carroll's ranch continued to go downhill, and finally he was forced to sell out by 1910. He had grown wheat and alfalfa and raised pigs and cows. Mary Ann kept bees and produced honey. When they sold out, she advertised to sell thirty beehives.[66] The loss of the farm was devastating to Carroll and Mary Ann. Once again, they parted ways hoping that Carroll could find a job to earn money to support them. He returned to New York, where he found a position as a textile designer. Mary Ann moved to Denver for a few years, then lived for a time in Estes Park. Writing in 1935, Mary Ann recalled, "My husband after having lost a lifes savings on a Western farm, returned to his former business after 60 years of age & in ten years made enough to keep us in our declining years."[67] Carroll lived and worked in New York City until late 1923, when he returned to Colorado and helped his daughter Eugenia build a guest ranch. In the meantime, however, he corresponded regularly with Mary Ann, always railing against an economic system that was stacked against the little guy. He was particularly concerned about agriculture, convinced as he was that farmers were being squeezed out of their livelihood by an unjust market system. He sent packages full of newspapers and magazines to Mary Ann, imploring her to read them and educate herself on the situation. "If you will particularly read in today Sunday 'March of Events,' Senator Borah's article," he wrote in a typical letter, "it may inform you and the children what I was up against and which I doubt if you ever appreciated."[68] Hilda Faunce Wetherill had little sympathy with her father during this time, as she expressed to Mary Ann:

> The publics & clippings you sent from papa had lots of good stuff in them, but it surely does take the courage out of a person to believe any

of it. What would they have us do—lay down till some one changed the laws—or go ahead & show them what we could do if we had a chance? Farming can't stop because it doesn't pay, tho any other business can—and it stands a better chance of paying now than it ever did. Papa failed because he was not a rancher, not because ranching does not pay.[69]

The move to Colorado might have been disruptive for the Faunce children at the time, but in later life they showed no regrets, and all embraced the identity of Westerners. Only Mary Ann seems to have expressed any regret that might have been related to the move to Colorado, specifically regarding the lack of educational opportunities for her children. She once wrote of her children that they "were all educated in the University of 'Hard Knocks,' & are all reliable citizens."[70] Surely she referred to the setbacks and hardships she and Carroll experienced as a result of moving to Colorado. They had hoped to send their children to college but were unable to do so after Carroll lost his job and the ranch failed. At the time of the move to Colorado in 1898, Theodore Faunce was fifteen, Eugenia was thirteen, and Hilda was eleven. They attended school in Fort Collins but did not attend school in Mancos. Their cousin Ruth Wattles recalled that Mary Ann had collected a large library of classics the children read. According to Ruth, Mary Ann believed her children were already educated beyond what the Mancos schools could teach them.[71] Mary Ann Kipp Hairgrove recalled her grandmother, Eugenia Faunce Wetherill, saying she had been "home-schooled."[72]

The Faunce children and their Wattles cousins all remained in the West. Theodore Faunce helped out on his father's ranch, hired out to the Wetherills on Alamo Ranch, and probably worked on his Uncle Theodore's place as well. He and his cousin Howard Wattles, Theodore's son, became fast friends and enjoyed some adventures together. A local paper posted a note about the two in 1908, saying, "Howard Wattles and Theodore Faunce, two enterprising dryland farmers, were out at their claims near Mesa Verde last week. They tell us they spent the stormy days with one Mr. Ersken Mallet of some musical fame and that the trio spent three days in singing."[73] Theodore Faunce enjoyed at least one big adventure with Clayton and Win Wetherill when he helped them drive a herd of burros across Utah and Nevada to sell to miners in Tonopah, Nevada. For much of his young adulthood Theodore Faunce went from job to job and place to place, helping out his sister Eugenia on her ranch or John Wetherill with an expedition out of Kayenta. During World War I he served with the Arizona Cavalry at the rank of corporal. In 1927 he married Laura Rutherford, and they had one daughter, Helen Rose. They settled down in Wells, Nevada, where he had a fish farm and a popcorn shop in his old age. He died in 1968.[74]

Howard Wattles, son of Theodore and Melvina Wattles, continued to work the family farm in Mancos after the death of his father in 1912. Melvina lived with him until she went to live with her daughter, Ruth Jocelyn Wattles, in Fort Collins in the late 1920s. Melvina died in 1935 at the age of eighty.[75] Howard also worked for Mesa Verde National Park as a road maintenance worker and supervisor. He retired in the 1950s and went to Fort Collins to live with Ruth. He died in 1974 at the age of eighty-eight. Ruth attended the University of California at Berkeley where she received a master's degree in English. She taught for a few years at Fort Lewis school, outside of Durango, before it became Fort Lewis College. Then she joined the faculty of Colorado A&M College (later Colorado State University), where she was a professor of English and theater until the 1950s. She died in 1985 at the age of ninety-seven. Ruth Wattles is credited with creating the CSU Archives through her collection of school records she used to write the history of the college.[76] In many ways Ruth Wattles carried on her family legacy in her devotion to education. Neither she nor Howard ever married.

Except for young Theodore Faunce's embrace of western exploits, the Mancos experience left the Faunce family with few happy memories. By 1907 both Faunce daughters, Eugenia and Hilda, had left the ranch and the family behind. In August 1905, just after turning eighteen, Hilda Faunce eloped with Win Wetherill, a barely divorced man sixteen years her senior. Her father was so angry with her that he refused to speak to her for years. Two years later Eugenia Faunce married Clayton Wetherill, the brother of Hilda's husband. What had been a family identity based on the generational experiences of Augustus and Susan Wattles now changed, and for the Faunce sisters, their family identity would become associated with the family into which they married, the Wetherills.

This transformation of family identity had something to do with the westering experience of the Wattleses and Faunces. By moving west, Theodore Wattles shed almost all vestiges of his parents' idealism. Away from the influences of his family he became a typical settler, making up his own mind about reforms he would adopt for himself based on his own criteria. He kept only what seemed to make sense to him in his new circumstances, which placed him more in line with the settlers around him. Starting out on his new homestead in the Mancos Valley, Theodore wanted Native Americans moved out of the way, so he rejected the humanitarianism that had motivated his parents. Only woman's suffrage continued to make sense to him, but that reform idea appealed to many western settlers who wanted to encourage women to participate in settlement. In the 1890s Theodore joined many other Coloradans in supporting William Jennings Bryan for president, thus abandoning the Republican Party, his political home since the Civil War. This shift also made sense to a western settler outraged that silver had been demonetized by an eastern conspiracy of fat cat bankers and corrupt Republican politicians, or so it seemed to him. Settlers engaged in the project of colonization were nothing if not resilient in their relentless drive for material success, which makes it all the more ironic so many of them were destined for failure. Too many factors were stacked against individualistic small farm agriculture or prospecting; they could not overcome the harsh environment, a globalizing market, corporate competition, or tight credit. Carroll and Mary Ann Wattles Faunce thought the West truly was their safety valve, but their idyllic western farm chewed up their capital, ruptured their family bonds, and broke their indomitable pioneer spirit.

Settler colonialism helps us to understand the big story of US history in ways other narratives failed to do. Settler colonialism reveals the harsh reality of the dislocation of Native American societies as Euro-American settlers imposed cultural and political sovereignty upon the land. It forces us to acknowledge the impact of conquest in ways romanticized and mythologized histories allow us to ignore. A paradox lies at the heart of this history, however, because families are not disinterested observers of these developments. Descendants like to think the ancestors who endured hardships and took great risks did so to improve the prospects of their children and grandchildren, and this was not a disgraceful motive. Acknowledging those efforts does not necessarily romanticize them. Families also see and understand the results of what their ancestors did in ways historians often fail to recognize. Individual families know how the story turned out, whether their ancestors succeeded or failed, and many western families failed. Both families and historians could reach a more realistic assessment of this history if all parties could recognize the very human motivations that operated in settler families and at the same time acknowledge the great hurt and harm done to Native Americans through that conquest as well as the disadvantages Native Americans continue to experience as a result. These contradictory narratives both have truth in them, and the challenge for everyone is to see the truth that exists in others' perspectives.

A WESTERN IDENTITY: THE WETHERILL WOMEN

Born in Brooklyn, New York, in 1885 and 1887, Eugenia and Hilda Faunce spent the first years of their lives under the tutelage and care of their grandmother, Susan Lowe Wattles, while their mother, Mary Ann Wattles Faunce, went to work as a physician and professor of medicine. Their father, Sylvanus Carroll Faunce, was an artist and a staunch socialist committed to the cause of woman's suffrage. Eugenia and Hilda could not have known at such a young age that it was a rare experience for little girls like them to be raised by a former abolitionist, a female physician, and a socialist, all feminists to the core. One might have thought, as their parents hoped, Eugenia and Hilda would grow up to get good educations and pursue professional careers of their own. They would have had tremendous opportunities for good schools and rich cultural experiences living in urban New York City. Thirty years later, however, Eugenia Faunce Wetherill and Hilda Faunce Wetherill were living in rural Colorado and Arizona, respectively, married to brothers who were cowboys, wilderness guides and outfitters, and traders with the Native Americans. Eugenia helped her husband, Clayton Wetherill, operate a fish hatchery and outfit expeditions for hunting and archaeological forays across the Four Corners area of Colorado, Utah, Arizona, and New Mexico. Hilda found herself assisting her husband, Win Wetherill, in running a trading post on the Navajo Reservation in northeastern Arizona. Neither woman had attended school much beyond the elementary level, yet they were well read, practical, adaptable, and strong-willed. They had adopted their husbands' family occupations as their own, and they would tend to associate themselves with the

Wetherill family reputation more than with their own family history. They had become thoroughly western women.

The livelihoods of the Wetherill women depended upon western myths and mystiques. The West has always existed in the imagination as a beacon of hope and possibility. For the Wattles and Faunce families, the western experience turned out to be full of disappointments, but that made them no less western in their self-image. If anything, being western meant overcoming immense obstacles, and sometimes that involved merely getting through the inevitable hard times. A select few always struck it rich, and everyone else muddled along the best they could, just happy to be living in God's country. When Carroll and Mary Ann Faunce lost their life savings on the failing Mancos Valley ranch, Carroll returned to the East to find a job to support them, but notably, Mary Ann did not go with him. She stayed in Colorado, determined to remain a westerner. Her three children also remained in the West all their lives, despite their early beginnings on the East Coast. Eugenia and Hilda Faunce married men who were quintessentially western in their identities and who pursued occupations possible only because of the public's interest in western stereotypes. In marrying into the Wetherill family, the Faunce sisters embraced an identity based on a western narrative quite different from their own family story of progressive reform activism. They would continue to cherish the Wattles legacy—and importantly, to do their part to save the family letters—but they layered upon that another narrative that derived from their association with the Wetherills. Like their grandmother and mother before them, they challenged traditional gender roles but not out of devotion to the cause of women's rights. Later, as women without husbands, one a widow and the other a divorcée, they had to struggle to make a living for themselves in a man's world. Eugenia became a lady rancher, and Hilda became the "Desert Wife." Their identity as western women owed much to the family into which both had married.

The Faunce sisters married Wetherill brothers. The Wetherills had homesteaded the ranch next to Theodore Wattles's place. Benjamin Kite "B. K." Wetherill and his wife Marian Tompkins Wetherill had arrived in the Mancos Valley in 1880 after having lived in Leavenworth, Kansas, and Joplin, Missouri. They had five sons—Richard, Al, John, Clayton, and Winslow—and a daughter, Anna. The family expanded in 1885 when an old friend from Kansas, Charlie Mason, married Anna.[1] Theodore Wattles quickly befriended the Wetherill family, becoming especially fond of Marian. He even asked his mother to send some *Woman's Journals* to Mrs. Wetherill, telling Susan that Marian was "my neighbor here and my good friend and the mother of six children. They are from Levenworth Kas. She is a very religious woman a Baptist and her children are a grate credit to her. She reminds me of Aunt Esther."[2] Marian was the sort of pioneer woman who would go to a neighbor's house in the middle of a blizzard to deliver a baby. When Theodore's wife, Mell, gave birth to their first child, it was snowing so badly that the doctor could not come, so Marian came over to help. It was a difficult delivery; Mell was in labor for twenty-four hours and "suffered terribly," according to Theodore. "Mrs. Wetherell thought the baby was dead at first the cord was wraped around its neck and its eyes wer protruding."[3] Two years later, Marian came back and helped to deliver the Wattleses' second child. Mell called her "my Dr., my nurse, and my friend."[4] As with many rural families in the West, this sort of collaboration among neighbors was vital to their survival.

Unlike Theodore Wattles and almost all other settlers in the Mancos Valley, B. K. Wetherill had a favorable impression of the local Utes and made an effort to befriend them. He had served as an Indian agent in Oklahoma, where he had helped to diffuse some tense situations between Native Americans and whites. As a devoted Quaker, he thought all individuals deserved respect and consideration, and he instilled this instinct in his children. The Utes responded to these gestures and gave the Wetherills permission to graze the family's cattle on the tribal lands, which included the deep canyons that cut into Mesa Verde. In pursuit of these wandering cattle, the Wetherill boys came across the remnants of the ancestral Pueblo civilization, called the Cliff Dwellers because of the houses they built in recessed cavities high up in the canyon walls. As early as 1885 Al Wetherill might have first seen the most spectacular of these sites, Cliff Palace, and in 1888 Richard Wetherill and Charlie Mason first climbed into the immense ruin. Over the next decade, the Wetherill brothers excavated numerous sites on Mesa Verde, collected and sold thousands of relics, and guided a number of archeologists and tourists to see and work in the ruins.[5]

The Wetherills' excursions into the canyons of Mesa Verde coincided with a great upsurge of interest in indigenous southwestern peoples in the 1880s and 1890s. Living in a rapidly modernizing world, many people were drawn to "primitive" cultures, romanticized as more authentic and imaginative than the industrialized and urbanized society the United States was becoming. Collecting Native American artifacts became a trend, and enterprising individuals in southwestern Colorado began to grasp the potential of marketing relics.[6] The Wetherills were among numerous local individuals who actively excavated ruins with commercial intent beginning as early as the mid-1880s. By 1891 the Wetherills had sold several collections, the largest for $3,000 to the Colorado Historical Society. They had also escorted many parties of tourists to the ruins at Mesa Verde, thus establishing themselves as well-known guides and outfitters of such expeditions. However, as they guided and collected, they also expanded their understanding of archaeological methods and came to see themselves as caretakers of the Mesa Verde sites. They wrote to the Smithsonian Institution to urge the federal government to send someone into Mesa Verde to excavate the ruins properly. Smithsonian officials responded that the institution was unable to support such an expedition at that time, but the Wetherills should continue with the work themselves, using accurate recording methods.[7] The Wetherills learned to be more cautious excavators from Gustaf Nordenskiöld, a Swedish scientist who had been a client and became their tutor when they escorted him into the ruins in 1891. Although their association with Nordenskiöld increased their awareness of scientific methods, it also earned them an unwanted notoriety. When Nordenskiöld tried to leave Durango with the large collection of artifacts acquired on this outing, he was arrested by local officials, who charged him with attempting to steal valuable artifacts. A judge released Nordenskiöld and dropped all charges after determining that no laws existed to prevent the removal of artifacts.[8]

The Wetherills' collecting continued as they branched out to explore other sites in Utah, Arizona, and New Mexico. Richard Wetherill moved with his family to Chaco Canyon in New Mexico, where he excavated the giant ruins of Pueblo Bonito and opened a trading post for the Navajos. John Wetherill took his family to the far northern part of the Navajo Reservation and started a trading post at Ojato, later moving it to Kayenta. From there he reconnoitered the vast country around them in search of ancient ruins. Over time he became a much-sought-after guide to sites such as Kiet Siel and Betatakin along with geographical features such as Rainbow Bridge. Al Wetherill, the last of the brothers to live on Alamo

Ranch in Mancos, operated several trading posts around the Navajo Reservation before moving to Gallup to work for the US Post Office. Clayton became indispensable to both Richard and John as a guide, outfitter, and digger of relics, until he married and joined his brother-in-law, Charlie Mason, in the fish business on the upper Rio Grande.

Winslow "Win" Wetherill was the youngest of the brothers, born in 1871 in Leavenworth, Kansas. Win assisted his brothers in excavations of the Mesa Verde ruins and in outfitting expeditions into the ruins. His obituary claimed, "During the winters of 1889, 1890 and 1891 he lived in Spruce Tree House and Cliff Palace while working at the excavations."[9] In 1896 Win went to Iowa to work for an uncle, and there he met Mattie Pauline Young of Oskaloosa, Iowa. After a short courtship, they married in Oskaloosa on September 16, 1896.[10] Two children, Milton and Helen, were born to Win and Mattie Pauline. In 1898 they returned to the Four Corners area, where Win took over a trading post at Tiz-na-tzin on the Navajo Reservation in New Mexico. Located about twenty miles north of Chaco Canyon, the post was one of a half dozen owned by the Hyde Exploring Expedition, a company founded by Talbot Hyde and Fred Hyde Jr. of New York. The Hydes also underwrote the trading post run by Richard Wetherill at Chaco Canyon.[11] In 1901 Win received a license to trade at Two Grey Hills in the Chuska Mountains, west of Chaco. In 1903 Win and his brother Al tried unsuccessfully to get a retail business going to sell Navajo rugs and blankets, opening a store in downtown Denver. The business ended when Win and Clayton took the merchandise to the St. Louis World's Fair of 1904, where they set up a booth to display and sell Navajo artifacts. By that time, Win's wife, Mattie Pauline, had returned to her family in Iowa, not wanting to raise their two children on the reservation. Win charged her with abandonment and filed divorce proceedings against her.[12]

When Win returned to Colorado after the fair, he showed up in Mancos claiming to be divorced. In May 1905, he joined a group of men from Mancos, including his brother Clayton, going out to Goldfield, Nevada, "to dig up a fortune in the next few weeks," according to the local paper.[13] The prospecting turned out not as fruitful as they had hoped, but they learned miners were willing to pay a good price for burros. So the Wetherills returned to Colorado to organize a burro drive to Nevada. Back in Mancos, Win's attentions turned to Hilda Faunce, who had just turned eighteen. Hilda found herself smitten with Win, seventeen years her senior. He was a very handsome man—a rugged outdoorsman, a crack marksman—and he obviously charmed her. He seemed much less attractive to her parents, who heartily disapproved of the courtship and forbade the marriage. However, one day when Mary Ann, Carroll, and Eugenia had gone to Durango for a few days, Win and Hilda eloped. On August 21, 1905, witnessed by two Montezuma County clerks, they were married in Cortez. It took a long time before Carroll forgave her.[14] The newlyweds took off for Tonopah, Nevada, with Win driving a wagon and Hilda driving a buggy. Clayton Wetherill, in the meantime, gathered up a crew for the burro drive. He recruited Hilda's twenty-two-year-old brother, Theodore Faunce, and a couple of young Navajo men, and they set off across Utah with a herd of burros. When they finally reached Tonopah, they sold more than seventy-five burros for $35 to $45 each, or so Theodore claimed in his old age.[15]

In 1906, Win, Hilda, and Clayton all went out to California because they wanted to see what San Francisco looked like following the big earthquake in April.[16] Then Hilda and Win headed up the coast to Oregon, where Win went to work for a lumber company in North Bend.[17] After spending eight years in Oregon, Win and Hilda returned to the Southwest in 1914 and leased a small trading post at Black Mountain on the Navajo Reservation. Located about twenty-five miles west of Chinle, the Black Mountain Trading Post was owned by Lorenzo Hubbell.[18] Hubbell had started his original store at Ganado around 1878 and owned numerous trading posts across that part of the reservation. Hubbell epitomized trading on the reservation, an activity that played a central role in the acculturation of Navajos to white ways.

The Navajo Reservation, established by the Treaty of 1868, covers about 3.5 million acres across northwestern New Mexico and northeastern Arizona. At the time of its creation some 7,000 Navajos had recently returned to their homeland from a harrowing internment at Bosque Redondo, in southeastern New Mexico. This experience and the colonizing efforts that followed profoundly affected the Navajo Nation. A part of that colonization project was the integration of the Diné into the capitalist economy, a process monitored by the US government through granting trading licenses, mining leases, and other allowances to private citizens to operate on the reservation. Navajos learned to be vigilant in guarding their land and resources against unscrupulous exploitation by outsiders. The trading post became an important institution on the reservation from the

1880s through the 1930s. Anglo traders became cultural brokers, agents of change who introduced the goods of a modern society but worked and lived in a Navajo world. Traders had to understand and respect the ways of Navajos in order to succeed there. They brought in imported and manufactured goods they exchanged for Navajo wool, sheep, blankets, and crafts, thus creating economic opportunities for Navajos but also introducing paternalistic patterns that complicated Navajos' desire for autonomy.[19]

In joining Win Wetherill in running a trading post, Hilda Faunce Wetherill adopted the occupation and identity of her in-laws. She was not alone in making such a choice. Her sisters-in-law, Marietta Palmer Wetherill and Louisa Wade Wetherill, also formed their identities in part through the activities of their husbands. None of these women would have ended up at trading posts on the Navajo Reservation had they not married Wetherill men. Although they were more than mere appendages to their husbands, they came to live under these circumstances through their husbands. Yet each experienced those circumstances and encountered the Navajos in her own unique way. In their relationships with the Navajos all three women displayed tremendous curiosity about and sympathy for the Navajo way of life, which reflected the general approach all the Wetherills took toward Native Americans. Like other sympathetic observers, Hilda, Louisa, and Marietta might have been well meaning in their relationships with Navajos, but they still participated in a process intended to ease the Native Americans into white life. Navajos would lose control over much of their culture in the process, and whites would decide which aspects of Navajo culture were worth saving. Much of this endeavor was focused upon indigenous art and religious artifacts and included efforts to bring Navajo culture to the attention of the larger society.[20]

During the late nineteenth and early twentieth centuries, collectors of "primitive" art acquired numerous articles of value, and anthropologists gathered cultural information from indigenous peoples. Collectors and anthropologists often expressed a perceived fear that indigenous peoples were disappearing and that the younger generations were not learning and perpetuating the knowledge of the culture. To these white observers, they were doing a vital service for native peoples by preserving cultural artifacts and knowledge that otherwise would be lost forever. Seen in its best light, such collecting did save much important material culture and information from Native American societies. At its worst, cultural collection can be seen as another form of colonial control in which whites assume a right to collect indigenous culture without according native people authority over their own images, arts, knowledge, and economic production.[21] The three Wetherill women all participated in publicizing Navajo culture to the larger society and making it possible for whites to acquire Navajo objects and products. Each did so for different reasons and displayed varying degrees of understanding of its implications for Navajos.

Hilda's sister-in-law Louisa "Lula" Wade Wetherill showed great empathy and devotion for the Navajo and seems to have genuinely won their trust and admiration. Born in 1877 in Wells, Nevada, Louisa was the daughter of an itinerant miner who moved the family to Mancos, Colorado, in 1879. In 1896 she married John Wetherill, who was ranching and guiding archaeologists throughout the Four Corners region. In 1900 the Hyde Exploring Expedition hired John to run a trading post at Ojo Alamo, north of Chaco Canyon.[22] Louisa moved into the trading post with her two small children and her younger brother, and John left for months at a time guiding expeditions. When her brother became deathly ill, Louisa had no one to turn to except the neighboring Navajo, with whom she could not communicate. Help came eventually, and the boy recovered, but Louisa resolved to learn the Navajo language and make them her friends so that she would never again feel so isolated. She quickly became a fluent Navajo speaker, learning the language so readily her Navajo friends thought she must have been a long-lost Navajo herself or descended from the Navajo. They gave her a Navajo nickname, "Asthon Sosi," the Slim Woman.[23]

In 1907 Louisa and John moved to the remote northern region of the reservation, first building a trading post at Ojo Oljato in Monument Valley and later one at Kayenta. There they settled down and operated their trading post until their deaths in the 1940s. The Wetherills became loyal allies to their Navajo neighbors, often helping them to negotiate with government officials. John and Louisa informed Indian agents about the conditions of the Navajo and lobbied on their behalf. They spoke often of the need for schools on the reservation, arguing, "The Navajo children are as dear to their parents as white children and . . . it is wrong to take them from their homes and keep them until they have forgotten how to live on the reservation."[24] They procured medicines at their own expense to give to Navajo families and gained a reputation as fair dealers who would listen to the Navajo perspective and represent them honestly.[25] They never made much money at trade and died poor.[26] Their great interests in life were the Navajo people and the land.

Louisa Wetherill wanted to know everything about Navajo culture. Over time she became well acquainted with medicinal herbs and plants, traditional creation narratives, healing ceremonials, sand paintings, weaving, and more. Louisa established a friendly relationship with a number of the Navajos, including the influential leader Hoskinini and his son Hoskinini-begay, and an elder healer, Wolfkiller, who became her particular friend. These associations opened the door for Louisa. Her friends, especially Wolfkiller, told her the traditional stories, showed her the use of medicinal plants, and invited her into their hogans.[27] After witnessing a healing ceremony, she became fascinated with sand paintings and decided that despite the traditional Navajo prohibition against preserving them, the colorful designs should be recorded. She feared that as the old healers aged, the younger generation was abandoning the traditional practices. She persuaded a Navajo healer, Yellow Singer (Sam Chief) to make crayon drawings of the paintings, which she had copied in watercolor paintings. Over time she collected hundreds of sand paintings and specimens of medicinal plants, to which she added written descriptions of their uses and the ceremonies with which they were associated.

As her reputation for expertise on Navajo culture grew, she began to share her knowledge with the wider Anglo world. As early as 1909 Louisa's collection of sand painting drawings had attracted the attention of art collectors and anthropologists. Among others, Edgar L. Hewett of the School of American Archaeology in Santa Fe tried to purchase Louisa's collection of drawings of sand paintings as well as the descriptive notes she had made.[28] She refused to sell her original drawings. When archaeologist and family friend Byron Cummings found a potential buyer for the original drawings in Europe, Louisa offered copies instead.[29] In response to another inquiry she said the originals were worth $10,000 but would not part with them even at that price.[30] Although she held on to her original sand painting collection for many years, she was not opposed to publicizing Navajo culture. Eventually she donated some sand painting originals to Arizona museums during her lifetime, and the bulk of her collection went to the Arizona State Museum after her death.[31] She also encouraged her friend Yellow Singer to donate sand paintings to the University of Arizona, and she helped the Fred Harvey Company organize a display of Navajo ceremonials and paintings in its Gallup hotel.[32]

Louisa's collecting of traditional ceremonial designs paralleled the activity of other trading-post wives working in tandem with private collectors and anthropologists of the time. Frances "Franc" Johnson Newcomb, who operated a trading post at Two Grey Hills with her husband, collaborated with Navajo healer Hosteen Klah in the same way Wetherill worked with Yellow Singer. Newcomb and Klah worked with Mary Cabot Wheelwright to create a museum to house the paintings and weavings depicting the designs.[33] Like Newcomb, Louisa Wetherill believed members of the public would see value in Navajo culture if they could understand it as she did. She believed it was important to preserve Navajo culture even while introducing Navajos to American education and economic practices. In this respect she performed the role of a cultural broker in trying to facilitate their transition to modern society without completely obliterating the traditional culture. Louisa Wetherill seemed to pay more attention to certain cultural aspects than others did, showing a great interest in traditional narratives, medicinal plants, and the healing arts. Perhaps the perspective of her gender influenced her in this direction, or perhaps because she was a woman, she was regarded as a less threatening observer and given more access. Other trading-post wives seemed to have enjoyed a similar trust, but not all of them faithfully upheld that confidence as well as Louisa did.

Marietta Palmer Wetherill, who married the oldest Wetherill brother, Richard, was a difficult personality. She endured tragedy and suffering in her life, but family lore depicts her as self-centered, manipulative, and needy. She went to great lengths to create a sympathetic self-portrait, even to the point of outright fabricating stories about herself. Much of what we think we know about Marietta Wetherill comes from her own claims, and because her veracity has been proven suspect so often, we are left wondering what we can trust. What is clear and demonstrable is she claimed to be an authority on Native Americans and their culture, and she was actually in a position to learn much about them. Unfortunately, she used this knowledge in an unashamedly self-serving manner.

Born in 1876 to a family of traveling musicians, Marietta grew up as the center of her parents' attention and the highlight of the family show. Every year the Palmers would leave their home base in Burdett, Kansas, and travel in a modified bandwagon around the country, performing musical shows that showcased Marietta's talents on harp and guitar. In 1895 the family showed up at the Wetherill ranch in Mancos, Colorado, asking to be shown the Cliff Dweller ruins. Richard Wetherill took a shine to eighteen-year-old Marietta and spent a full year squiring the entire family around the Four Corners region to see every conceivable sight. In 1896 Richard proposed to Marietta, and soon the two had married and moved to Chaco Canyon, where Richard dug in the ruins and built a trading post. In 1901 he was forced to abandon his excavations and relied exclusively on ranching and trading to support his growing family. In 1910 Richard was killed by a Navajo under circumstances never fully understood. Marietta moved with her five young children to Cuba, New Mexico, gradually losing touch with the rest of the Wetherill family. She spent the rest of her life living in various places around New Mexico and trying to create a reputation as an authority on the Native Americans.[34]

In 1932 Marietta Wetherill published an article in *Scribner's Magazine*, "Death of a Medicine Man." She began her amazing tale by saying, "For three consecutive nights my wrist was cut as was the wrist of my foster father, and the two wounds were bound together." With this ceremony, she claimed, she was adopted into the Navajo nation at the age of two. When she reached puberty, she contended, red-hot coals were placed under each of her armpits in "an ordeal that very few of the Indian girls care to attempt." After that she was "given a good many more privileges in the tribe. They felt I was all right." Even these outlandish assertions pale in comparison with the main focus of the article, a lurid description of the ritual execution of an unsuccessful medicine man accused by the tribe of possession by devils.[35]

Soon after its publication, the article caught the attention of a number of defenders of Native American rights. Michael Harrison, the assistant superintendent of the Northern Pueblos Agency in Santa Fe, and Philip Johnston, an engineer and photographer who had grown up as a missionary's son on the Navajo Reservation, organized a campaign to demand that *Scribner's* retract the article and correct the misunderstandings produced by it. Johnston wrote to the editor of *Scribner's,* stating, "The story 'Death of a Medicine Man' is the most amazing collection of misstatements that I have ever seen." Even if Marietta Wetherill intended the story to be fictitious, which she did not, the criticisms would apply with equal force, Johnston argued. "Such a tale paints a false picture of America's aborigines, ascribing to them qualities which they do not possess in the remotest degree. Impressions thus gained by the public may ultimately prove highly prejudicial and harmful to the welfare of these splendid people."[36]

Harrison and Johnston contacted a number of people to corroborate Marietta's information, including Oliver La Farge, Sam Day, Talbot Hyde, and Louisa Wetherill.[37] Louisa answered his questions forthrightly, saying the article was "such a collection of bunk I have never read before." Furthermore, she went on to say, "The so called Mrs. Wetherill has no right to use the name of Wetherill," having been remarried twice since the death of Richard Wetherill.[38] Harrison also contacted Thomas H. Dodge, chair of the Navajo Tribal Council. Dodge wrote to *Scribner's* himself, declaring Marietta's story a fake. "At best," he wrote, "it is nothing more than a horrible nightmare and, perhaps, she has lived with her nightmare for so long a time that she has actually come to believe in it." One by one, Dodge dissected Marietta's assertions, pointing out how the story violated every tenet of Navajo belief and practice. Perhaps, Dodge mused sarcastically, Marietta Wetherill had discovered that "an entirely new tribe of Indians is living in our midst, in fact, in Northern New Mexico. Lo, the poor Indian. Now they will be besieged by scientists, Government agents, politicians, exploiters and even bootleggers. Their happy isolation is at an end."[39] *Scribner's* responded by printing several letters of protest, including one from A. H. Gardner, a Navajo from the Leupp Agency whose father and grandfather were medicine men. Of Marietta's story he said, "Every sentence . . . betrays the fact that it was written by a person who knew little or nothing about the Navajos."[40]

Marietta, given the opportunity to rebut her detractors by the *Scribner's* editors, countered that her experiences with Navajos had taken place decades before and that present generations of both Navajos and Anglos had no idea of the cultural changes over time. The editors at *Scribner's* seemed bamboozled by this argument and declined to retract Marietta's story, stating that they had presented both sides of the story and members of the public could "draw their own conclusions." They did, however, refuse permission to *Reader's Digest* to reprint the article.[41]

For Marietta the article in *Scribner's* was only one instance in a long career of storytelling that tarnished the reliability of her word. She had a remarkable ability to charm people with her tales, and one after another, writers and scholars stepped forward to help her publicize her views. Writer Grace French Evans helped write the *Scribner's* article. Two decades later, another southwestern writer, Mabel C. Wright, completed an entire manuscript on the life of Marietta Wetherill, only withdrawing it from publication at the last minute because of the doubts raised by Marietta's stories.[42] In the early 1950s a journalist named Lou Blachley recorded over seventy-five hours of Marietta's stories, giving her ample license to embellish, exaggerate, fabricate, and expropriate. She changed the story "Death of a Medicine Man," but only slightly, claiming that her adoption into the Navajo Nation occurred when she was twenty-two, not two.[43] Kathyrn Gabriel, who edited and published the stories, said, "Marietta told a good story and a valid one. I don't believe she purposely misrepresented the Navajos, although she places them in a light that might draw criticism. Marietta may have inserted herself into a story where she didn't belong, but that doesn't mean the story didn't happen, with or without her."[44] Personal memoirs do not have to be true, of course, but Marietta often used her association with the Navajos to make herself seem more important.

Sadly and ironically, Marietta Wetherill as a white woman immersed in reservation life was in a position to learn a great deal about Navajo culture, and she probably did acquire much good knowledge, but she intertwined that information in a web of outright fabrications. She did not merely perpetuate stereotypes; she created new ones. She did so for the worst possible reasons, to draw attention to herself. It is quite likely Marietta was aware her sisters-in-law Louisa and Hilda, as well as other trading-post wives such as Franc Newcomb, were receiving attention in the 1920s and early 1930s for their promotion of Navajo culture. Certainly, she knew the public craved stories about Native Americans. For her own self-serving reasons, she sought to capitalize on that trend.

Hilda Faunce Wetherill spent much less time on the Navajo Reservation than either Marietta or Louisa did, living at the Black Mountain Trading Post from 1914 to 1918. Her relationships with Navajos were not as deep as those of Louisa, and she did not learn as much of the language and culture as did her sister-in-law. Yet Hilda was an astute observer who wrote vivid descriptions of the personalities and situations of trading-post life. Helping Win with the business, Hilda became drawn into the lives of her Navajo customers and wrote about them in letters to her family. Some of these letters were written to her cousin, Ruth Jocelyn Wattles, who saved them and persuaded Hilda she should publish them. Ruth, a graduate student in English at the University of California at Berkeley in the mid-1920s, helped Hilda edit an article based on the letters, which appeared in the *Atlantic Monthly,* and then a book, *Desert Wife,* both published in 1928.[45] By this time Hilda had left Win but was still married to him. He was in the process of filing divorce papers, charging her with abandonment, and she was afraid he might seek to share in the profits of the book if he or any of the other Wetherills were identified. So she used pseudonyms throughout the book: Win was "Ken," Al Wetherill was "Fred," John Wetherill was "Jo," and Lorenzo Hubbell was "Mr. Taylor." Hubbell's trading post at Ganado was called Lugontale, the Salina Springs trading post was referred to as Saluni, and the Black Mountain Trading Post itself was "Covered Water." The town of Mancos was called "Del Rio."[46]

Desert Wife is both a narrative and a compilation of lively stories full of rich descriptions of the land and people of the Navajo Reservation. Ruth Wattles, who had a keen sense of the dramatic, certainly influenced the structure of the book, and Hilda's keen power of observation was evident throughout.[47] Both Ruth and Hilda reflected awareness of the cultural trends that underlay the appeal of Native American themes. Aficionados of Indian stories as well as art and relics were drawn by the supposed primitivism of the southwestern tribes. As Erika Bsumek has shown, traders and vendors of Navajo rugs and jewelry used the labels "primitive" and "exotic" to promote sales. Traders themselves revealed that often they viewed their Navajo customers as primitive bargainers because they insisted on various methods of trade, such as bartering, that had long since lost their place in modern business transactions. Trading posts were seen as relics of a bygone era, venues where "frontier commerce" took place as in the Old West. Traders viewed their business practices from their own perspective, often believing they manipulated their Navajo customers, whom they depicted as naïve and childlike. However, as Bsumek has argued, the Navajos felt they controlled the trade, knew how to get what they wanted, and often thought they got the better of the traders.[48]

In *Desert Wife* Hilda Faunce Wetherill never fully overcame a tendency to view her customers in the stereotypical terms of the day, but she also expressed deep admiration for the Navajos. To her they were happy, childlike savages, innocent in their superstitions but, at times, dangerous and frightening. She became immensely interested in them and showed great concern for their welfare, especially in times of sickness and family crisis. She concluded that their way of life worked well for them and expressed concern that the modern world would prove destructive to their culture, sensing that the trading post itself served as a conduit for some of the harmful aspects of modernity. *Desert Wife* nevertheless revealed important insights about how whites viewed their interactions with Navajos during the trading-post era. Hilda portrayed Win Wetherill as being fair, firm, and honest in his dealings with Navajos and as demonstrating an uncanny understanding of Navajo psychology. He taught Hilda how to trade with them by withstanding personal entreaties for handouts and bargains. The Navajo way of bargaining most impressed Hilda when she recalled, "The Indians were one hundred per cent. good as beggars, and it was the lingo with which they tried to wheedle us out of everything movable on the place that I first learned." The Navajos addressed her as "grandmother" and "my pretty younger sister," as they told tales of woe and promised to repay debts as soon as the sheep would be sheared or a blanket finished.[49] To Hilda, these Navajo solicitations appeared comical and quaint but did not prevent her from ultimately making business deals with her customers that satisfied them and made a profit for her store. Other Navajo customs worried her. Invited to a hogan to witness the birth of a child, Hilda was appalled at the proceedings and wondered "how any Indian woman escaped blood poisoning." Yet she "could not admire enough the strength and fortitude of the women."[50] Hilda cultivated her relationships with Navajo women. She went to visit them in their own homes and took a real interest in their children. Although she criticized many aspects of Navajo culture, she defended polygamy as a practice that made sense in the Navajo context. She came to understand much about the important role of women in Navajo culture, something that not all whites or government policy makers managed to do. She often spoke of women's ownership of sheep, explaining that a man had to consult the woman whose wool was being sold before sealing a deal.[51]

Hilda spent only a short time on the Navajo Reservation, and her primary purpose in being there was to save money for a life off the reservation. Yet she did stake a claim to authority on Navajo culture by publishing her memoir and issuing a short book of Navajo songs. In doing so she joined the ranks of a number of whites, including her sisters-in-law, who expropriated Navajo culture as something they could publicize in response to popular appetite for the primitive and romantic. Hilda certainly grasped the public interest in Native Americans and wanted to share what she considered her expertise. Her awareness that her livelihood contributed to the breakdown of Navajo culture and the possible supplanting of their way of life with modern white culture reflects the irony and tragedy of settler colonialism. Neither Hilda nor her husband were mean-spirited persons, and neither intended to do any harm to the Navajos—quite the opposite. They saw an opportunity to stake a claim for themselves as the societal structure of the time encouraged them to do. However, the terms of the colonial nature of her society allowed them to think it was their prerogative to do business on Navajo land, to observe Navajo life, and to pass their own judgments, all without asking Navajo permission to do so. The Navajos responded in their own ways to do the best they could for themselves. Navajos negotiated with the traders, befriended them, assisted them at times, and struck the best bargains they could, whether or not an observer like Hilda recognized their actions as rational and appropriate.

Trading-post business was brisk during these years largely because of the demands for beef and wool created by the war in Europe. In the spring of 1918 Hilda reported that the Navajos were starting to bring in their wool to sell. She explained, "Some of the hungry ones are beginning to shear wool in small bits—sometimes not even all over one sheep, and sometimes two or three sheep—wool will be higher than ever this spring—yarn is $3.00 a pound wholesale."[52] World War I raged well beyond the boundaries of the reservation, but Hilda and Win kept up with events in part because Mary Ann Faunce sent them newspapers. "Our quiet life was disturbed again and again," said Hilda in *Desert Wife*, "by the mail sack as Hosteen Sendol-zhi brought the roll of rotogravure sheets which Mother sent us from the *New York Times*. These brought the war nearer to us than anything else."[53] Hilda always shared the newspapers with the Navajos congregated in the "bull pen." They showed intense interest in the descriptions of artillery and pictures of the streets of Paris. "They pointed and marveled," Hilda wrote.

I marveled, too, at the real intelligence with which they studied the picture. Not one of them had ever been farther from the reservation than the railroad towns a hundred miles to the south and east, but of course they recognized the buildings. They counted the stories and the windows and guessed that a particular building would be as high as such and such a rock or bluff. They recognized cars and automobiles and identified soldiers by the uniforms, and they counted all of them.[54]

One Navajo looked at the pictures of ambulances and wounded soldiers and told Hilda, "*'Dechi do hiyia a-sun al-so de-chi,'* meaning 'Much weeping. All the women will cry.'"[55] However, when an order came for the Navajo men to go to Fort Defiance to register for the draft, the response was not at all sympathetic. A story got around that they would be enlisted in the US Army and sent to France, where "they would be put in the front and shot first to save the white man." For several weeks the Navajos conferred angrily amongst themselves, some threatening to kill all the white men on the reservation and hole up in defense of their homes and families when the army came to get them. Win ultimately diffused the situation by telling the Navajos that if they had to join the military, it would only be to defend the reservation against a Mexican invasion and that he would go with them as their leader. Hilda claimed everyone settled down after that.[56]

By 1918 Win and Hilda had saved enough money from the trading-post business to buy a small farm outside Farmington, New Mexico. Leaving in November, just as the armistice was announced, Hilda realized, "We had woven so many threads of friendship that it hurt to break them. I stopped often to think that in all my life these four years were the most isolated and the most colorful."[57] They were also the happiest years of her marriage with Win. After they settled down in Farmington, their relationship changed and he became physically abusive toward her. Although Win had never been an amiable person, his new erratic behavior probably resulted from a brain injury suffered when a mule kicked him in the head. However, Hilda was not one to endure abusive behavior, and she reluctantly left him in 1922. She went to California, where she attended nursing school, and after graduation she got a position as the school nurse at the California School for the Deaf and Blind in Berkeley.[58]

Hilda's sister, Eugenia Faunce, also married a Wetherill brother. Like all the Wetherill wives, Eugenia's identity was shaped by the influence of her husband and in-laws. Although Eugenia and her husband did not operate a trading post, they followed the example of other family members in pursuing occupations relating to western tourism. Eugenia Faunce's livelihood catered to a romanticized image of the Old West and the public desire for authentic wilderness experiences. The appeal of these western motifs had underwritten Wetherill family activities since the 1880s. Eugenia's romance with a Wetherill brother began after her sister, Hilda, ran off with Win Wetherill. Win's brother, Clayton Wetherill, was a frequent visitor to Mancos, even after the family's Alamo Ranch was sold in 1902.[59] Clayton just loved to roam around, and until he married Eugenia in 1907, he traveled from one brother's home to another, helping with the outfitting work that became the family business after the discovery of Cliff Palace. Clayton, or "Clate," was indispensable as the Wetherills developed an expertise in archaeological tourism. It seemed as if everyone wanted to go see the ruins at Mesa Verde, but no roads existed to get there in the 1890s, so the Wetherill brothers packed people in on horseback and set up camps for them in the wilderness. Packing tents and food for groups of people was a routine skill in the nineteenth century, but the Wetherill men became proficient at packing delicate artifacts on horse- or mule-back. Everyone who visited the ruins wanted to take out a pot or two, but the archeologists who came to excavate, especially Baron Gustaf Nordenskiöld, took out crates' worth, all packed on the backs of mules and horses.[60] Clayton helped to outfit the expeditions for Nordenskiöld in and out of Mesa Verde and later outfitted the expeditions of other scientists, including T. Mitchell Prudden, George Pepper, Aleš Hrdlička, A. V. Kidder, and Samuel Guernsey, who visited archeological sites around the Four Corners region. Clayton spent much time at Chaco Canyon, where Richard and Marietta Wetherill and their children lived and ran a trading post while excavating the ruins. He helped his other brother John take archeologists and adventurers to various ruins or to Rainbow Bridge.[61] When it came to packing horses and outfitting camps, Clayton was considered the best in the business.

Clayton was also a very nice man, or so thought Eugenia Faunce. He was very deferential to her parents, unlike his younger brother Win, who had soured the Faunces on Wetherill men by eloping with Hilda. Clayton, in contrast, sent a stiffly worded letter asking for Eugenia's hand in marriage. "My dear Mr & Mrs Faunce," he wrote from a camp at Moonlight, Utah, "Eugenia has honored me with her promise to become my wife—it is not necessary for me to say how I regard her, with your consent, my treatment of her in the future will speak for itself." He signed the letter, "Respectfully yours, Clayton Wetherill."[62] Carroll and Mary Ann agreed, and on May 9, 1907, Eugenia Faunce and Clayton Wetherill were married at the Methodist parsonage in Mancos.[63]

The newly married couple went to live at Hermit Lakes, on the eastern side of the Continental Divide. Their new home lay at 9,850 feet in elevation, just twenty-five miles due east of Silverton as the crow flies. Had they traveled by road, they would have had to go by wagon or railroad south out of Durango to Cumbres Pass, over the Divide to Antonito, then north to Alamosa, then up the Rio Grande to Creede, then by wagon thirty miles up above Creede, a journey of more than 200 miles. Instead they went on horseback from Mancos directly over the Continental Divide either by Stony Pass or Weminuche Pass to reach their new home. They packed their belongings in panniers on the backs of horses, and they trailed after them a cow the Faunces gave them as a wedding present. After they arrived at Hermit Lakes, they moved into a little log cabin Clayton had built for them, near the cabin of his sister, Anna, brother-in-law Charlie Mason, and their family. Clayton planned to join Charlie in the fish hatchery business.

Eugenia's leaving home must have felt like an escape for her. At that time her father, Carroll Faunce, was desperately trying to save his farm. He had been sending out flyers to friends and family, hoping to recruit investors who would infuse the ranch with cash. It might have been a somewhat harebrained scheme because Eaton Morse, a careful financial manager, had apparently turned him down. The ensuing family flap so enraged Carroll that he forbade Mary Ann even to allow her sisters to come into their home, and Mary Ann acquiesced, unhappily.[64] Tensions ran high in the Faunce household, and Eugenia wrote about it to a cousin in Massachusetts, who wrote back to say,

> It seems as though you must admire and respect and love your husband or husband-to-be, better than your father, to be willing to give up what seems to me to be a certainty for an uncertainty filled with some trouble as well as some happiness. . . . "Home" means something sacred to me, and if the one you have just left has not seemed so to you, then may the one you will help to make satisfy you better.[65]

Eugenia embraced her new life with gusto, even though it must have seemed she could not have moved any farther from civilization than to live at Hermit Lakes. Charlie Mason, who first built a cabin there on South Clear Creek around 1890, called the place Hermit Lake because he felt like a hermit living so far from any other people. Mason had chosen the isolated mountain valley because he wanted to start raising fish, and his uncle Justus Tompkins told him this would be just the place to do it. Tompkins had gone up Clear Creek while working as a guide for William H. Jackson, the photographer for the Hayden Geological Survey of 1874.[66] South Clear Creek flowed into the Rio Grande about fifteen miles downstream, but here it meandered through a beautiful canyon cut into Finger Mesa. With the help of Clayton, Charlie had laid a dam across the creek to make a little lake and built a small cabin. Later he bought an old homestead with a natural lake on it upstream and added another cabin so that he could bring his family over from Mancos in the spring of 1899. Charlie and Anna had five daughters who came and went at Hermit as they married and began their own families. They also adopted two boys. When Clayton brought Eugenia to Hermit Lakes in 1907, she became "Aunt Genie" to an assortment of Charlie and Anna's children and grandchildren.[67] In April 1908, Eugenia gave birth to her own son, Gilbert Faunce Wetherill. Her mother, Mary Ann Faunce, came over from Mancos to assist with the birth.[68]

Charlie Mason was the first person to start raising fish on the upper Rio Grande. At first he thought he would raise the native cutthroat trout, but he claimed they refused to stay in his lakes, so he imported the first eastern brook trout to the upper Rio Grande in 1901. He had 100,000 eastern brook trout eggs shipped from Massachusetts, and when this batch proved successful, he ordered another 200,000 the following year. Mason was responsible for starting the brook trout population on the upper Rio Grande that still flourishes today.[69] Fish hatching and stocking had only recently become a significant activity throughout the Rocky Mountains. Historian Jen Corinne Brown has pointed out that artificial propagation of fish in hatcheries was a new development in fish culture, starting in the mid-nineteenth century on the East Coast. As described by Brown, the process was basically the same in all hatcheries, starting with the "fish culturalist," or fish farmer, taking live spawning fish from streams or lakes, mixing the eggs and sperm, and then incubating the fertilized eggs in a "controlled environment with running water." After they are hatched, the small fish feed off their yolk sacs until the sacs disappear, at which stage the fish, now referred to as fry, must be fed by the fish farmer. The fry can then be planted in lakes or ponds or kept in raceways at the hatchery and raised to adult size. As Brown observed, "Hatcheries required clean running water, a fair amount of daily labor, fish food, and a belief in human superiority over nature."[70] Fish culturalists, Brown argues, were replacing native fish species with imported species just as human settler colonialists were supplanting Native American populations. Throughout the West these new hatcheries turned out browns, brooks, and rainbows to create a new "trout culture," all so that a new leisure class of fishermen could come to the Rocky Mountains to enjoy the sport of fishing. An entire new industry of fishing tourism was based upon this widespread phenomenon.[71]

Charlie and Clayton could not imagine any grave consequences that might accrue from the development of their fish business. They were looking for fish that would serve their purposes, and the native cutthroat had not worked out, so they resorted to using imported species. In their minds, this was no different than introducing a new breed of cattle to a western ranch. Clayton had been involved in Charlie's operation almost from the start, and the two probably collaborated in planning a new hatchery a year after Clayton and Eugenia moved to Hermit. They built a house and fish hatchery about seven miles downstream from Hermit, on land Clayton had purchased from Lora Officer, twenty miles upriver from the town of Creede. Officer's ranch, now the San Juan Ranch, was located right at the junction where the road from Creede split, with one branch following the Rio Grande over Stony Pass to the top of the Divide and down to Silverton and the other road going over Slumgullion Pass into Lake City. Because their own house was not quite ready, and Clayton and Eugenia wanted to get moved before too much snow fell, they lived in one room of Officer's cabin for the winter of 1908–1909. In mid-October 1908, in the middle of moving, Eugenia wrote to her mother from Hermit. A "heavy wet snow" was falling, and she could not see the mountain across the lake. There were seven inches on the ground, but Clayton had taken a load down to the new location and "is coming back tomorrow & will take Baby & me down if it is not too stormy."[72] Their new house had four rooms upstairs, and in the basement Clayton constructed a fish hatchery. His daughter, Hilda Wetherill Kipp, described the operation:

It was just a small hatchery. The hatching troughs were built at ground level below the framed portion of the house. There were 12 troughs and a spring was piped down to the house and water ran year around. There was a tank that was hand dug and boarded up inside and then there was another one behind the stone house and it had baffles in it and it was twelve feet long and 8 feet wide and the water was an ideal fifty two degrees year around.[73]

The cold water ran through the troughs, where the fish eggs had to lie undisturbed until they "eyed," the stage when the eye of the embryo is visible and the egg is nearly ready to hatch. At that point the eyed eggs could be hatched or taken out and planted in streams or lakes. Clayton would pack the eggs or freshly hatched fish "fry" into kegs that he would load onto the back of a mule and take up to Charlie's ponds. When the fish grew to marketable size, they were netted, cleaned, and packed in ice, then taken down to Creede on a wagon to be shipped out on the railroad to Denver and Colorado Springs. Clayton and Charlie's fresh trout could be served in a fancy restaurant in "the Springs" within twenty-four hours of being taken from Hermit Lake.

As the fish business expanded, so did the family. Clayton and Eugenia's second son, Carroll Clayton Wetherill, was born January 5, 1911. Again, Mary Ann Faunce came to stay with them for the birth and signed her grandson's birth certificate as the attending physician.[74] Mary Ann was living with the Wetherills when a daughter, Hilda Theano Wetherill, was born on March 5, 1920. When the children were old enough for school, they went down the road to Officer's Ranch, where a cabin had been converted to a schoolhouse. L. S. "Lora" Officer and Charlie Mason worked out an arrangement to establish a small school for their children and to pool their resources to hire a teacher. They had a short school session at Hermit Lakes in the summer and another short one in the winter at Officer's. Officer, who had ten children, later bought a house in Creede, and his entire family would go to live in town for the winter so his children could attend school there.[75] The Wetherill children also went to school in Creede.

As the Wetherill family grew, Eugenia's responsibilities expanded, all the more so because Clayton often left for weeks or months at a time to guide and outfit archaeological expeditions. Eugenia went with him as often as she could, when she could take the children. Clayton probably continued to work at guiding and outfitting because he enjoyed it, but he might also have felt an obligation to help his brothers. Richard still lived at Chaco Canyon in 1910, although his critics had tried to uproot him from his homestead and prevent him from doing any further excavating there. Richard carried on despite his difficulties, maintaining a trading post and ranch near Pueblo Bonito. On June 22, 1910, Richard Wetherill was shot dead in a dispute with several Navajos on his ranch. Clayton and John Wetherill were 200 miles away, at a digging near Marsh Pass in Arizona, with the archaeologist T. Mitchell Prudden. The two Wetherills and Prudden hurried to Chaco, where they comforted Richard's widow and tried to help sort out a controversial and tangled investigation into the murder. Clayton spent most of the rest of the summer traveling back and forth to Chaco, Aztec, Farmington, and Durango attending hearings and tending to the needs of his brother's family.[76] His travels over the next few years were not so fraught with tragedy. He took Prudden on several more expeditions, guided Samuel Guernsey, and even helped his brother John squire former president Theodore Roosevelt around northern Arizona. Roosevelt was so impressed by the wilderness skills of the Wetherills that he sent his son Quentin out to stay with Clayton and Eugenia over the summer of 1914. Quentin helped Clayton build some guest cabins at Ruby Lake. Clayton had stocked the lake with fish for tourists who wanted to catch "wild" trout.[77] As the children got old enough to travel, Eugenia and the boys sometimes accompanied Clayton on his treks. In June 1916, the Durango newspaper noted:

Clayton Wetherill, his wife and two children, two helpers with camp outfits and several driving, riding and pack animals are in the city. Mr. Wetherill and party arrived overland from their home at Creede and yesterday outfitted here to go overland to Farmington, where he will meet a party of Smithsonian archeologists and guide them to the famous archeological fields of Western New Mexico and in Arizona. Mr. Wetherill is one of the most famous guides in the country. They leave today.[78]

Unfortunately, Clayton could not keep up such an active life. He had a heart condition stemming from a bout of rheumatic fever he had suffered as a young man. In April 1920 Eugenia and Mary Ann were summoned by telegram to Farmington, where Clayton had taken ill.[79] As Clayton's condition worsened over the next few months, Mary Ann recommended that Clayton move to a lower elevation to ease the strain on his heart. However, on October 20, 1921, Clayton died of heart disease.[80] He was fifty-three years old. He had been widely respected by the many people he had guided on expeditions across the Four Corners region. S. J. Guernsey of the Peabody Museum of Harvard wrote to Eugenia with condolences:

> I do not know of any one for whom I had a greater fondness. We seemed to have such kindred interests. I remember in 1920 when I was just going into the field and wrote him from Gallup & really at the time had lost interest in the work because Clate was not going along.
>
> It would be a great satisfaction to you if you could hear the many fine things such men as Dr. Prudden, Kidder and others have said about him.[81]

Eugenia Faunce Wetherill was now a widow at the age of thirty-six, with three children at home. Gilbert was the oldest at thirteen. Her second son, Carroll, was ten, and the baby, Hilda, was twenty months old.[82] Eugenia had to find a way to support her family. They had few close neighbors in the secluded valley in the heart of the San Juan Mountains. Only a handful of cattle and dude ranches straddled the Rio Grande above Creede in the early 1920s. Living at over 9,000 feet in elevation, the residents of the upper Rio Grande could raise few crops in the short growing season and were developing livelihoods dependent on the summer tourist trade. Whereas Clayton's business had been to market fish to restaurants over the mountains and to guide tourists on fishing, hunting, or archeological expeditions, Eugenia decided to cater to tourists by building a dude ranch.

Eugenia cashed in Clayton's life insurance policy, about $4,000, and bought an old homestead a few miles away, right on the river. There was an old cabin there, and over the next decade Eugenia built a dozen more cabins, outbuildings, and corrals and acquired a small herd of horses. She called the place "Wetherill Ranch." In 1924 Carroll Faunce returned to Colorado from New York. He and Mary Ann settled on the ranch, moving into a little cabin. Carroll went to work helping to build some of the guest cabins. His great-granddaughter, Mary Ann Kipp Hairgrove, who grew up on Wetherill Ranch, remembered Eugenia telling her stories about building the cabins. "They built [the cabins] from logs they skidded off the hillside," Hairgrove recalled, "and the logs, they were down, and they had been cured in the fire that the Utes had set in the country, when they chased the Utes out of that country." She knew Carroll Faunce had done much of the work building the cabins but was not sure how he lifted or sawed the logs. "I don't know if Grandpa Faunce did that or not," she said.

> He was notoriously difficult to work with, and so he ended up doing all the work by himself, and . . . I don't know how he lifted one log on top of the other, using a fulcrum type thing or exactly. But he did most of the work. If he had to have somebody help, I guess he would ask. But he was so difficult to work with that nobody wanted to help him.[83]

Guests came to Wetherill Ranch to stay in rustic cabins, ride horses, fish the river and lakes, and hunt for game. The first cabin was rented to a family from Wichita Falls, Texas, for the summer of 1923.[84] Eugenia managed the ranch, hiring cowboys to guide tourists to local high mountain lakes where they would fish for trout. To ensure good fishing, Eugenia continued Clayton's practice of stocking lakes and streams with farm-raised fish, except that she relied on someone else to raise and stock the fish.[85] Her son Carroll, ten when his father died, was operating the family fish hatchery by the age of sixteen. A friend recalls that as teenagers he and Carroll ran the hatchery by themselves for two years. "Every fall," he remembered, "we took a million brook eggs at Wright's lower lake next to the headquarters. Brook trout was the only fish we hatched in that hatchery. We only hatched eggs and fry. Carroll and I built the middle dam on Wright's Ranch with 'V' handled shovels and a team of white horses."[86] Carroll taught the business to his future son-in-law, Floyd Getz, who recalls that Carroll routinely gathered eggs from small timberline lakes and brought them back to his hatchery on horseback. Carroll raised fish all his life, eventually building a dude ranch of his own and several different hatcheries.[87] One of the lakes Carroll stocked was Ruby Lake, located above Wetherill Ranch, where Quentin Roosevelt had helped Clayton Wetherill build cabins. Guests from Wetherill Ranch could ride up to Ruby Lake to fish and stay in the cabins.

The story of Eugenia Faunce Wetherill offers an interesting example of a widow who remained independent and self-reliant by adopting the livelihood of her husband's family after his death. Eugenia knew the business of raising and stocking fish from her life with Clayton, but she had also learned the business of catering to tourists from her in-laws. Charlie and

Anna Mason had provided cabins for tourists who came to fish in Hermit Lake. Anna had learned about taking care of guests from her mother, Marian Wetherill, who had hosted hundreds of visitors at Alamo Ranch who had come to visit the ruins at Mesa Verde. Marietta Wetherill was known to have shared the campsite duties on expeditions and was depicted in a buckskin riding outfit sitting in camp as part of the outfitting team. The women might well have taken a turn at digging in an archeological site, but their primary roles in the family business were those of cook and caretaker for the guests.[88] The role of women in archaeological tourism easily translated into similar domestic roles in dude ranching. Yet it was very difficult work. Mary Ann Kipp Hairgrove remembered all the labor involved in keeping up a dude ranch, work she was expected to help with while growing up there in the 1950s. "And of course a dude ranch is just a woman killer," she recalled, "because there's all the washing and the cleaning and the cabins and the cooking, and it's just, there's so much to it. And it's just not fun."[89] Mary Ann enjoyed working with the horses more than doing the work designated for the women. However, in many ways, dude ranching was an occupation women could do because so much of the work was perceived as the purview of women.

Dude ranching had its origins in North Dakota, Montana, and Wyoming as early as the 1880s, when cattle ranchers discovered that wealthy easterners would willingly pay good money to stay for a few weeks on a ranch, eat ranch food, and take a turn at herding a few cows. Visitors, or "dudes," as the typically eastern, urban-based tourists came to be called, found leisure activities such as hunting and fishing even more alluring than actual ranch work. Dude ranchers learned they could "sometimes make more money by herding tourists down a trail than by herding cattle," as Patricia Nelson Limerick observed. This was western adventure without the dangers of the Old West.[90] Dude ranching was not actual ranching, and real stock ranchers often disdained both the dudes and the dude ranchers for not producing anything of value. Serving guests did not seem to be as substantive as producing beef or wool.[91] There is in this attitude more than a hint of suggestion that dude ranching was an effeminate enterprise compared with real ranching. Dude ranching appealed to a more romantic image of the West, cultivated by Owen Wister's writing and Frederick Remington's art at the turn of the century. Eastern tourists could participate in the "cowboy West" just as Teddy Roosevelt had done on his own Dakota ranch. As Frieda Knobloch said, dude ranching offered "the spectacle of western adventure," promising "the scenic appeal of the Rocky Mountain West . . . , the abundance of big game . . . , and the temporary primitivism of camp life" for the wealthy tourists.[92] Just as collecting Native American relics reflected whites' fascination with a romanticized and tamed primitive culture, dude ranching relied upon a yearning for Old West stereotypes and safe wilderness experience.

Owning and operating a dude ranch might have afforded Eugenia and other female ranchers more opportunities for roles beyond hostess, but the work of managing ranch personnel, supervising construction projects, keeping the books, and overseeing financial matters might all be understood as extensions of the role of managing a large household. Fish farming, however, seemed firmly a male activity in the Wetherill family tradition. Eugenia cleaned and cooked fish for family consumption but never helped with the cleaning of fish for market, done entirely by the men. Other activities associated with fish farming seemed even more clearly designated for men if only because of the physical exertion required. In the winter large quantities of ice had to be cut from the lakes and stored for use in packing fish over the summer. Taking eggs in mountain streams required the men to stand in icy running water for hours at a time, grabbing fish and squeezing out eggs and semen by hand. Except for taking a wagon of fish to Creede, which Eugenia was known to do, most travel and freighting was done by packing horses and mules. Charlie and Clayton packed fish on horseback across the Continental Divide from the Pine River to the Rio Grande watershed. They hauled fish fry by mule to high mountain lakes. Wrangling and packing horses and mules required not only great physical strength but also skill in handling animals, rope, and harnesses, not to mention the ability to shoe the beasts on the trail. Kegs and barrels of water, eggs, and fish had to be carefully lifted and securely fastened onto the backs of the pack animals. It would have been easy to presume women lacked the physical ability to do such work given assumptions about the relative strength of men and women.[93]

Eugenia Wetherill might have chosen dude ranching over fish farming for a number of different reasons. The business of dude ranching was just beginning to develop on the upper Rio Grande in the 1920s. Eugenia's granddaughter, Carol Ann Wetherill Getz, believes her grandmother recognized that dude ranching offered a better business opportunity than the more limited prospects of trout farming. Eugenia had five or six neighbors living along the Rio Grande who had already begun the transition from working cattle ranches to dude ranching, and several of these ranches were run by widows. She thus had a support network of independent and practical-minded women around her. Although some of these women did remarry, Eugenia never married again, preferring to keep the company of several "gentlemen friends" who shared her interests. One of these men, Frank Wills, worked for her as a wrangler and guide on the ranch. Another, L. C. Oppey, was a shell-shocked World War I veteran who drifted around the mountains, living off the land and doing odd jobs for various ranches. For Eugenia, the main attraction of both men was apparently their willingness to help her look for lost gold mines.[94]

In the late 1940s Eugenia started to ease out of the ranch work after her daughter, Hilda, and her husband, Charley Kipp, took over the operation of Wetherill Ranch. Eugenia was able to spend more time with her sister, Hilda Faunce Wetherill, who had been working at the California School for the Deaf and Blind in Berkeley since 1925. Sister Hilda traveled to Colorado for summer vacations whenever she could, staying at Wetherill Ranch. As a younger woman she had enjoyed riding horses and going on camping trips with "Genia," as all the family called her. In 1932 they took turns taking photographs of each other skinny-dipping in a high mountain lake above timberline.[95] After the death of their mother, Mary Ann Faunce, in 1935, Eugenia had the responsibility of taking care of their father, Carroll. Carroll and Mary Ann had lived in a small house in Creede during the winters and in a cabin on Wetherill Ranch during the summers, a routine Carroll continued as long as he was able. In 1947 Carroll saw his three children together for the last time. Upon returning to California, Hilda wrote in her diary, "Back from summer vacation Sept 3rd—Had visits with Theodore & family in Wells, Nev—drove with them to Genia's—many happy days. Papa well but feeble. Children all well & everybody busy."[96] In the summer of 1949 Hilda saw her father for the last time. She recorded that September,

> In June I went on to Creede & found Papa as feeble but he has had no stroke, Genia doing 3 peoples work to keep the family together & fed & Papa cared for in a home near Center Colo. I stayed only 3 weeks about the shortest visit ever but by July 1 their work increased so my visit

would be over done. I had a room in the Hathaway cabin—& built a fire to dress by mornings.[97]

On December 13, 1949, she wrote simply, "Wire from Genia. Papa died Sat. AM Dec 3—I've not heard since—Sent $200.00 to help last expenses anyway."[98] Sylvanus Carroll Faunce was ninety-four years of age when he passed.

Hilda enjoyed visiting with other friends in the Four Corners region as well. In 1935 she took a trip with Agnes Morley Cleaveland to visit Mesa Verde.[99] Hilda and Agnes had much in common in their love of the Southwest and their desire to write about it. Cleaveland grew up on a ranch in New Mexico, then married a California engineer and settled down in Berkeley to raise a family. Agnes went every year to spend some time at her family's ranch in Datil, New Mexico, and while residing in California she was an active member of the California Writers' Club, various women's organizations, and the Republican Party. She wrote short stories and in 1941 published *No Life for a Lady*, a popular memoir about her youth on the family ranch.[100] Hilda probably first met Agnes in Berkeley, where they lived only blocks from each other and both belonged to the California Writers' Club.[101] Hilda visited Agnes at the Datil ranch in the 1930s, and they visited Mesa Verde together. Hilda also became friends with Agnes's niece, Faith Morley Reed. When Hilda came out to Colorado on summer trips, she usually took the train into Albuquerque. Several times Faith picked up Hilda in Albuquerque and drove her to Alamosa, where someone from Hilda's family would come down from the ranch to get her. In 1965 Faith picked up Hilda in Santa Fe and took her for a visit to the Morley ranch in Datil. Hilda recorded, "We drove to Datil 200 miles south & west of Santa Fe, after 30 years it had changed completely. Faith's home is there a fine big house. We stayed there 2 nights & drove around & to the pass on the hill where Ray Morley's ashes were scattered & his stone marker are."[102]

In 1950 Hilda retired from the School for the Deaf and Blind and moved to an ocean-side house in Cambria, just northwest of San Luis Obispo. Eugenia went out to California to spend the winters with her there, driving out by herself as long as she was able. Eugenia and Hilda took many driving trips together, traveling around the Southwest in Eugenia's 1955 Chevy. They became tourists themselves, enjoying the Grand Canyon and other iconic sites that offered the same appeal as *Desert Wife* or a visit to

Wetherill Ranch. Hilda was devoted to her family and cherished her connections to Colorado. She also valued her association with the Wetherills and might never truly have gotten over her attachment to Win Wetherill. Her great-niece Carol Ann Wetherill Getz always thought Hilda remained in love with Win long after she left him. She never remarried or developed any attachment to another man. On August 21, 1952, the anniversary of her wedding to Win, she wrote an odd little note in her diary: "A memorable date 47 yrs! No comment. Just gratefull."[103] Hilda maintained contact with other members of the Wetherill family, writing to John and Louisa Wetherill and stopping to see them in Kayenta, Arizona. John and Louisa and their son Ben visited Hilda in 1938 when they were in Berkeley for medical reasons.[104] In 1944, after John died, Hilda wrote to Louisa to send condolences. Ben Wetherill, Louisa's son, had stopped in Berkeley to see Hilda, and she "was so glad Ben could stop & tell me how you all were." Hilda reminisced about old times with the family. "I've often lived over the period I was with Win," she said, "and knew you all better—the things about Win that resembled John were the best traits he had. I wish there had been more of them."[105] In 1953, several years after Louisa had also died, Hilda and Eugenia drove through Kayenta on one of their trips and stopped to visit with an old friend of the family who "gave us more information on John & Lula—Ben, etc."[106]

Of all her family Hilda was closest to Eugenia. Throughout the 1950s Eugenia spent all her winters in California with Hilda, sometimes with other family members or friends along the way. In the winter of 1959–1960 Eugenia fell ill while in California and had to be hospitalized. Eugenia's daughter-in-law, Ina Wetherill, went out to California to drive Eugenia and Hilda back to Colorado. The next winter Eugenia again drove herself to California and again became so ill she had to go into the hospital. This time her daughter, Hilda, and son Carroll flew out to California to drive her home. The following year, Eugenia Faunce Wetherill died on August 5, 1962, aged seventy-seven. Hilda wrote in her diary, "Now in February 1963 I'm remembering those hard months & missing her & thinking of her pluck & courage—& the many things we talked of—our lives & trips & friends. She did not dread dying—but said 'I've lived long enough.'"[107] When Hilda returned again to Wetherill Ranch, she said, "The ranch looked so good to me, but no Genia—how I missed her!"[108]

In 1965 Hilda attended a Wetherill family reunion held at Mesa Verde. It seemed important to her to go, and it seemed important to her that the Wetherills would acknowledge her as part of the family. She wrote in her diary, "A Wetherill family reunion is planned at Mesa Verde Park. . . . Carol Ann & Marion got the idea & already have heard from 100 members—I don't know that many Wetherills—& wonder how many have ever heard of me."[109] In all, more than 125 members of the Wetherill family showed up, most of whom Hilda did not know. Win's daughter, Helen, and son, Milton, were there with their families; Hilda was not introduced to them, but they were pointed out to her. She enjoyed the gathering and appreciated the effort made by the National Park Service to welcome the descendants of the original Wetherill brothers, who had done so much to explore Mesa Verde. The Wetherill family valued this heritage and came together to share an identity based on a common history. Hilda also valued that heritage and identity, even though she had left the family and made her own way in the world after the end of her marriage to Win Wetherill. In 1966 Hilda moved into a retirement home in Pacific Grove, where she spent her remaining years; she passed away April 9, 1979, at the age of ninety-two. As she was settling her affairs, she might have given some thought to her legacy. One of the last things she did was to send some items to Bertha Dutton "for her museum in Santa Fe," Hilda said. Included were a book on Navajo weaving, a copy of *Desert Wife,* "also squaw belt, corn planting stick, Blanket making comb stick, wool horse hobble, photographs of Sand paintings."[110] It was a collection fitting a western woman.

Both Eugenia and Hilda Faunce Wetherill considered themselves western women, even though they had been born in Brooklyn and lived the first decade of their lives on the East Coast. Moreover, they both embraced the identity of their husbands' family, even though Hilda had left Win Wetherill and Clayton Wetherill had died prematurely. In the years following Win's divorce from her, Hilda led a life that by most women's criteria would have been one of accomplishment; she earned a nursing degree and pursued a career in which she helped many children with disabilities. Yet that career never seemed the focus of her life. She loved to return to Colorado, ride horses, and enjoy the mountains. She loved writing about her western experience and nature. Her family mattered to her, as it did to her sister. Eugenia's story confirms the importance of family influence in determining how well a woman adjusts to widowhood. Eugenia relied on family and neighbors for assistance, but the examples set by her own family and her in-laws also influenced what she did as a widow. Her upbringing in a nonconventional family expanded her sense of women's roles, but her husband's family introduced her to the tourist industry that would become her livelihood. Eugenia made choices that reflected the important role these family legacies played in her struggle to support herself and her children. The Faunce-Wetherill sisters built meaningful lives while constructing identities based on both western myths and realities.

EPILOGUE

In 2007 I traveled to the Boston area to do research for this book. While there, I went out to Duxbury to look for information on the Faunces. Carroll Faunce's family was still a bit of a mystery to me. Carol Ann Wetherill Getz told some intriguing stories about the Faunces, saying that her first relative to land on American soil was "a little indentured servant" who came to Plymouth in 1623. The Faunces eventually moved up the shoreline a few miles north to the town of Duxbury, and the Faunces had lived there well into the twentieth century. Carol Ann thought there had been a number of sailors in the family, and one of the Faunces was said to have been lost at sea sailing from Shanghai to Calcutta in the 1860s. By the mid-twentieth century the family line had petered out somewhat, and when the last Duxbury cousin, Vercy Hathaway Hill, died in 1958, Hilda Faunce Wetherill had made a trip east to help close up the family house because there were no other relatives left in Massachusetts. While there, she gathered some old letters and assorted family memorabilia, and she did some genealogical research, finding evidence tracing the Faunce line back to John Faunce, who at the age of thirteen had arrived in Plymouth on the *Anne* in 1623. Hilda later recorded this genealogy in a large leather ledger that Carol Ann now keeps.[1]

On my own visit to Duxbury, I was sure I would find some sort of archival trace of Faunces. I contacted the Duxbury Historical Society to no avail. I spent some time at the Duxbury Public Library and found a copy of the Faunce family genealogy, perhaps the same copy Hilda had used to compile her genealogy. Thanks to her work, I already had that information, and besides, family history is more than just the genealogy. The genealogy is the scaffolding of the family history; it is crucial, but it is only the beginning of the story. I needed context. The search was fruitless, and I had run out of time. Before I left, however, I thought I should visit Plymouth. I am an American historian, after all, and I had never been to Plymouth. So I drove the eleven miles from Duxbury to Plymouth and parked down on the waterfront, feeling like the all-American tourist as I walked the tree-lined path toward Plymouth Rock. Plymouth Rock itself, a somewhat smallish boulder with a large crack and the date "1620" chiseled into it, was itself a great letdown, but the edifice that protects it, a tall marble structure of ten classical columns, was quite impressive. All in all, I was a bit underwhelmed, but as a loyal supporter of public history, I made sure to read all the interpretive signs outlining the history of Plymouth Rock. And there it was. Faunce. Thomas Faunce had been the first person to tell the story of Plymouth Rock. I had finally found some Faunce context, and it was not at all what I had expected.

Historical research is like that. One never knows when an exciting discovery will come along, and one must doggedly pursue every lead knowing that much of the evidence we need is likely to have gone missing. We are always limited by the availability of sources from the past, so we have to imagine all the possible places where sources might have been saved. Finding family records can be quite a challenge because records are preserved only if each successive generation has the same commitment to keeping the family history alive. To track down the family records I needed, I had to imagine what each member of the family would have done with the letters and deeds and other documents generated by a person in a lifetime. The nineteenth century was the great era of letter writing because of increased literacy and mobility, but not all great letter-writers were great stewards of letters. Augustus Wattles wrote hundreds of letters, many of which were saved by other people, but he did not keep letters sent to him. Susan Lowe Wattles saved everything she could, including her own school papers. Sarah Grimké Wattles Hiatt was that bane of the historian's existence, the letter-burner. She would write to someone that she was on a massive letter-burning spree, sitting by the open fire and reading letters from bygone days as she chucked them one by one into the flames. Then she would write to someone and tell him or her to burn her letter immediately after reading it. We are thankful some persons ignored her wishes. Neither Theodore nor his wife, Melvina Wattles, seemed concerned with keeping letters. Only the letters they wrote to others have survived. Little personal correspondence survives from either of their children, not even college archivist Ruth Wattles. Emma Wattles Morse and Mary Ann Wattles Faunce, however, took after their mother in saving every letter and scrap of paper they thought had any significance. Mary Ann's trove of records even included utility bills, bless her heart. We know what happened to her records. She carried them from New York to Boston; to Mancos, Colorado; to Denver and Estes Park; and then to Creede, Colorado, where she left them tucked away somewhere on the Wetherill Ranch. Her daughter Eugenia Faunce Wetherill and granddaughter Hilda Wetherill Kipp left them largely safe and untouched, looking at them occasionally just for fun. When Eugenia's sister Hilda Faunce Wetherill (the names do get confusing) died in 1979, her niece Hilda Wetherill Kipp cleaned out Aunt Hilda's apartment in California and brought back a collection of papers and letters to Colorado. After the death of Hilda Kipp in 1997, the collections of Mary Ann Wattles Faunce and Hilda Faunce Wetherill passed to Carol Ann Wetherill Getz (Eugenia's granddaughter), who persuaded me to take a look at them one summer in the early 2000s.

The fate of Emma Wattles Morse's family papers, which included many of Susan Lowe Wattles's papers, involved a bit more mystery. When Emma died in 1929, she was survived by five sons: Wilton, John, Theodore, Stuart, and Orlin. She had lived in the old family home in Mound City with John and his wife, Sadie, who had no children. Emma's sons apparently divided her papers among themselves soon after her death, perhaps when they gathered for her funeral. Wilton Morse, who lived in Mancos, Colorado, seems to have taken the largest batch of letters because he got the letters his father, Eaton Morse, wrote to Emma during the Civil War as well as the letters Susan and Mary Ann Wattles Faunce wrote to Emma when Susan lived in Brooklyn with the Faunces. His collection also included a large number of letters written by his brother John when he served in the Philippines during the Spanish-American War and the letters his sister, Eleanor, wrote home while she was a student at the University of Kansas at the turn of the century. Eleanor died in 1910 of tuberculosis. After Wilton's death in 1939, his share of the family papers passed to his son, Stanley, and then to Stanley's niece, Patti Morse Curtis, of Colorado Springs.

John Otis Morse, a lawyer who served in the Kansas State Legislature, and Theodore Wattles Morse, the editor and publisher of the *Emporia Times,* both seem to have inherited some of their father's papers, and they knew what to do with them. They gave all the family records they had to the Kansas State Historical Society in Topeka. Of all the brothers, they had remained citizens of Kansas and had a stake in being identified with the history of Kansas. John died in 1939, and Theodore died in 1953.

That leaves the remaining two sons, Stuart Tellson Morse and Orlin Raymond Morse, both of whom left Kansas to pursue their careers elsewhere. Stuart worked variously as a livestock broker and a farmer and was living in Florida when his mother died in 1929. He did not return home for Emma's funeral and died in 1932 in Florida. It is unlikely he received any of the family's papers. Orlin R. Morse became a civil engineer and settled in Fort Worth, Texas, where he died in 1953. He was close to his mother and returned home for her funeral, so it is likely he might have acquired some of her papers. Someone in the family inherited a portion of Susan Lowe Wattles's papers and letters that included her school compositions and baby journal as well as Theodore Wattles's letters to his parents during the Civil War, making this collection valuable for Civil War collectors. At some point, someone sold this collection to a private collector, who later sold the records to the National Park Service. This collection is now housed at the Wilson's Creek National Battlefield in Republic, Missouri.

This long foray into the fate of the family papers reveals to us something about the family's interest in their history. Certainly, there were members of the family who did not care about preserving old papers and letters. One of those was Theodore Wattles, who did not care about carrying on the family legacy in other respects as well. With the exception of Sarah Wattles Hiatt, who curiously could burn letters and value the family identity at the same time, most of the family members who preserved letters also cared deeply about the family history. Some of them understood the value of placing family collections in archives, and the two who made an effort to do so were arguably the most public-spirited of the Morse sons. Wilton Morse did not give his collection to an archive, but keeping them in the family must have been important to him. His granddaughter, Patti Morse Curtis, had a deep interest in her family's history and felt pride in what her family had done as settlers in Kansas and Colorado and as abolitionists before that. She was committed to preserving the letters and intent upon trying to get her own children and grandchildren interested in the family history through them.

If future generations were interested in this history, what would interest them, and why? The letters themselves have an intrinsic, physical appeal; they are fascinating to hold, touch, and examine. Many of the letters are still contained in the original envelopes, with nineteenth-century stamps and postmarks. The handwriting seems both elegant and foreign. How long will future generations be able to casually read nineteenth-century cursive writing without some special training? If reading original letters requires the equivalent of learning a foreign alphabet, will future family members be motivated enough to make the effort to read old letters? Clearly, the greatest value of collections such as these will be to historians, and the value for historians will be much different than for families. Families might find the stories of the people who wrote the letters interesting and exciting because families want to think of their ancestors as interesting and exciting. However, few family members will go to the trouble of contextualizing old documents to fill out the stories of their ancestors. Historians will have to do that. The story historians are likely to tell, however, will not be simple narratives of the lives of family members. Historians will be even less likely to embellish the stories to make the family look good. Historians have other concerns, many of which will have no interest whatsoever for families.

As the historian, I return to the question with which I began: How does looking at a family change the way we look at history? What the Wattles-Faunce-Wetherill family story does, I think, is to help us understand better how social change happens and why change does not occur as a continuous progression going forward. Through the nineteenth century important social reform movements arose because of the agency of certain individuals. In many cases, however, when we look at those individuals, we really should see families. Many abolitionists acted not as single individuals alone but as members of families. John Brown's many sons, and even his daughters and daughters-in-law, were critical in supporting him in his antislavery activities. He honed his reformist zeal as the patriarch of his family. For many abolitionists, it is difficult to separate what they did from something that happened within their families. Women such as Angelina Grimké gave up active reform work in part to raise a family, whereas others, such as Elizabeth Cady Stanton, came later to reform work after attending to significant family obligations. The Wattleses participated in the abolitionist movement as a family, and they would not have accomplished what they did if it had been Augustus Wattles or Susan Wattles working alone. The nature of the way they worked together reflected the family identity they themselves forged. They did not sit idly by but jumped right in and enthusiastically, vigorously, and with all their hearts *participated* in the abolitionist movement. It was a family trait to work at things even to the point of exhaustion and broken health. Their work ethic became a model for their children, but it was not the only family trait they constructed. They shared and reinforced in each other certain ideas. Susan and Augustus had been attracted to one another because of similar backgrounds, having spent their youth and early adulthood in the burned-over district of Oneida County, New York. Their fiery passion for reform came from that experience. They believed in progress, both moral and material, and thought all Americans, white and black, male and female, should have an equal chance to pursue it. They passed these family values from one generation to the next by raising their children to follow their examples and by maintaining a family memory that kept certain traditions alive. Thus, they constructed a family identity that emphasized activism, independent thinking, and social justice. When they acted upon these ideas, which individual members of the family did to varying degrees, they helped to make the circumstances of American life different from one generation to the next.

The story of this family also shows the limits of agency in bringing about social change. Few individuals or families determine their own destiny entirely. Plans go astray. It is difficult to maintain a high degree of intensity of spirit over a long period of time and from one generation to the next. Children do not always grow up the way their parents intend. The Wattles-Faunce-Wetherill families found themselves buffeted about by the great events and developments of their times. The Civil War might have brought the realization of the dream of emancipation, but it also scattered the family. Devastating economic downturns in the 1890s and 1900s ruptured well-laid plans. Divorce and death could not be predicted. The members of these families responded to these challenges as best they could, and some of them had to jettison social reform for simple survival. The combination of individual agency and outside influences make up a life, and as Elizabeth Cady Stanton once pointed out, each of us live "under circumstances peculiar to ourselves."[2] Even the support of family could not always provide sufficient foundation to exercise agency under some circumstances. Sarah Wattles Hiatt felt great pressure to measure up to the standards of her parents and her mentor, Sarah Grimké, but she found herself in such limiting circumstances she was unable to be the social activist she thought she should be. Although her life was hardly a moral failure, she had hoped to do more. Mary Ann Wattles Faunce, in contrast, accomplished much for the cause of professional women in her career as a physician only to suffer a great setback later in her life for reasons largely beyond her control. Her daughters, Eugenia Faunce Wetherill and Hilda Faunce Wetherill, made statements simply by living as independent women and seemed to have no inclination for social activism.

The ability of other abolitionist families to carry on with social activism depended equally upon circumstances. After John Brown's execution, his family found the notoriety too overwhelming to remain in the public eye, but members of the family did maintain their faith that their father's cause had been right. For the most part they tried to live quietly, speaking out only to make the occasional, futile attempt to defend their father's reputation.[3] William Lloyd Garrison's children faithfully carried on the ideals of their father, although one son came near to embracing the racist politics of Reconstruction, much to the chagrin of his father. Fanny Garrison Villard more than made up for her brother; she was able to rely upon her husband's resources to pursue her reform goals, contributing much energy to the woman's suffrage movement. She also acted as a solid influence on her own son, who then carried the mantle of idealism in the next generation by embracing women's rights and writing a sympathetic biography of John Brown.[4] The Grimké-Weld family, however, saw a diminishment of reform fervor in the second generation, while at the same time discovering new family members who challenged and ultimately heightened their own idealism. After the Civil War Sarah Grimké and Angelina Grimké Weld found that their brother in South Carolina had fathered three sons with his slave mistress. Sarah and Angelina welcomed their nephews into the family and offered them what help they could. By acknowledging their family connections, Sarah and Angelina embodied the ideal of racial reconciliation without ever stepping back into the public sphere.[5]

Families able to offer wide-ranging connections and mutual aid contribute to the ability of family members to lead successful lives and shape the course of events. The second generation of Wattles children ran into and were assisted by an amazing number of their parents' acquaintances from the abolitionist movement. All her life Sarah Grimké Wattles Hiatt cherished the mentorship she had received from Sarah Grimké and valued the network of friends she had made while attending the Eagleswood School. Having once known such comradeship and progressive idealism made it all the more poignant for her when she lamented the lack of such company as an adult, but she still felt privileged to have had such benefits from her family connections. Other family connections helped the Wattles children as they made their way in the world. Theodore Wattles seems to have gotten a job at Fort Defiance because an old ally of his father's, W. F. M. Arny, was the Indian agent there. Too bad Mr. Arny was so corrupt that Theodore lost that job when Arny was ousted. Theodore was able to land on his feet in the San Juan mining district in part because he partnered up with old friends from Kansas. Emma Wattles learned about James Caleb Jackson and his water-cure establishment through the reform circles of her parents and Uncle John Otis Wattles. The Blackwells, a family with an extensive reform record of their own, were known to the Wattleses from the 1830s, and that influenced Mary Ann Wattles's choice of medical school. Later, when Mary Ann took her own children to Colorado, she went first to Fort Collins, where old family friends from the heady days of Bleeding Kansas welcomed her and helped her get settled. And when Mary Ann's daughter Hilda Faunce Wetherill left an abusive husband with nowhere to go, she went to California to a nursing school because of her mother's old acquaintance who was a doctor there.

Family connections do matter, sometimes even more than family money. However, family money is also important. Neither Augustus nor John Wattles ever had any money, but their brother-in-law, David Ripley, had a very successful sawmill and box-making plant in Newark, New Jersey. David took great interest in the reform work of his brothers-in-law and gave them money when they needed it for travel. The next generation also benefited from David's generosity. Ripley financed the education and European travel of Mary Ann Wattles as well as John's daughters, Celestia, Harmonia, and Theano and, at one time or another, welcomed each of the Wattles girls into his home for extended stays.

Connections and resources thus contribute to family success, hardly a new revelation but one certainly reinforced by the Wattles family story. This was a reform family, however, and the material success of the family was almost always secondary to its ideals. Susan and Augustus Wattles, along with John and Esther, were certainly on the cutting edge of gender reform. They knew it, and they consciously chose to embrace women's rights. Susan never abandoned her commitment to women's rights and expected her children, even Theodore, to construct their lives to accommodate progressive ideas on gender. She did not have to worry about her daughters—or sons-in-law, for that matter—on this score, but she found she could not interfere too much in Theodore's domestic life. Theodore, however, had married a headstrong woman who seemed to have practical ideas on the relations of the sexes and who probably bent the gender rules in the direction of equality even without Susan's help. Living in frontier conditions encouraged women to be strong-willed and tough-minded, and that experience merely reinforced ideals of gender equity that had arisen from within the abolitionist movement. The Wattles family members certainly paid attention to the feminist theorizing of their East Coast friends, but their lives on the Ohio and Kansas frontiers stretched gender boundaries through necessity and practice. The formation of identity derives from many sources, and sometimes it can be difficult to pinpoint exactly where certain features originate.

The experience of Mary Ann Wattles Faunce offers a particular lesson about family and gender equity. Of all the Wattles children and grandchildren, Mary Ann most embodied the progress her parents hoped to see for all women, but Mary Ann's success depended upon family support. Mary Ann had educational opportunities because her aunt, Esther Whinery Wattles, took Mary Ann east along with her own daughters so that the girls could get an education at Oberlin College. The aspiration to become a doctor might have been nurtured through the books Sarah Grimké sent the family when Mary Ann was a young girl, and the medical school she chose to attend was founded and operated by old acquaintances from the abolitionist movement. Her wealthy uncle financed her entire education. However, perhaps the most important contribution from her extended family came when Mary Ann's mother, Susan Lowe Wattles, moved in with the family and took care of her young children so that Mary Ann could continue to work as a physician and professor. Of all the obstacles to women working outside of the home and pursuing careers, the most daunting and intractable was and remains child care. It was almost unthinkable in Mary Ann's time that a middle-class woman would continue to work after having children, but she could do it because Susan approved of her career and helped her to manage it. If historians only looked at the public work of Mary Ann Wattles Faunce and failed to examine her domestic and family circumstances, we would miss possibly the most important lesson her life holds for us today. She did not do it alone. The support of extended family enabled her to succeed, and in the absence of family support, other forms of support must be available for working women.

Many developments become clearer when family circumstances are considered. The Wattles family identity as social reformers waned as family members moved west in the late nineteenth century. The shift in identity to western ranchers and Indian traders seems abrupt and incongruous until we consider that the Faunce women who married into the Wetherill family embraced a western identity reflecting the occupational choices of their in-laws. The activities of the Wetherill family appealed to Eugenia and Hilda Faunce, as they spoke to a yearning in the US public and many around the world for a romanticized version of the American West. This particular development could only have happened in a specific time, the late nineteenth and early twentieth century, when certain features of the West were disappearing or at least in the form they had taken up to that point. Native Americans, as free-roaming and self-determining peoples, were vanishing, and quite a number of artists, writers, and anthropologists were hammering home this idea, with at least two important consequences. First, the specter of a vanishing race caused white people, especially those living far away from real indigenous peoples, to begin to romanticize everything about the doomed Native Americans. The western world was rushing headlong into full-blown modernity, and nostalgic notions about the moral superiority, innocence, and simplicity of less-complicated times and peoples abounded. The Native Americans, even as they were being crushed economically and deprived of their culture in real life, were being romanticized as nature's noblemen in popular culture. The second consequence was that it began to be fashionable in the 1880s and 1890s to own a piece of this vanishing culture as a sort of keepsake of an authentic primitive culture that soon would disappear. Neither of these trends, romanticizing or collecting, have ever really disappeared, and happy to say, Native Americans themselves have survived and now participate in the dialogue about these issues.

The Wetherills happened to be in a place at exactly the right time to make occupations based on these trends. Because of the interest in the "vanishing race," they could dig up relics to sell to interested buyers, or they could guide people to the places where these relics lay, or they could operate trading posts where they could trade for items such as blankets and jewelry that could be sold to eager collectors. A different occupation, the dude ranch, traded on another romanticized notion of the disappearing Old West, the life of the cowboy. The lure of the western wilderness experience, an itch that could be scratched by going hunting and fishing in a scenic Rocky Mountain tableau, also grew out of a disappearing reality. There was no more frontier, but tourists could still experience something of what that frontier life must have been. The Faunce sisters, whose childhoods had been spent in Brooklyn and Boston, took to these western livelihoods as if they had been born to it. Many family identities changed when people arrived in the West.

The great irony of this family trajectory is that for all the idealism devoted to racial equality and the sincere humanitarianism with which many family members viewed the Native Americans, their progress through the generations and across the continent came at the expense of Native Americans. What was happening to Native Americans did not go unnoticed by members of the family, but there seemed to be little acknowledgment of any responsibility on their part. This seems odd in part because they had so much sensitivity to and sympathy for the plight of the slaves and freed blacks. Augustus Wattles recounted the retreat of the tribes in his history of Kansas written for the *Herald of Freedom,* but he blamed their demise on the slaveocracy's insatiable appetite for land. He also documented the miserable conditions under which Native Americans lived in Kansas during the Civil War but again blamed Southern politicians. It was not that sympathy for the Native Americans was nonexistent within the family. Susan Wattles and Mary Ann Wattles Faunce read Theodore's reports about conflicts between whites and Utes in Colorado and in response sent him a book by Helen Hunt Jackson. The Wetherills saw Native Americans as human beings and treated them with respect. Yet even so, all of these families continued to move west and continued to improve their own families' chances by settling on land previously held by Native American families. This is not to single out these families for any particular blame. This is the story of America. When we wonder how this continent could be so callously taken from Native Americans, how Americans could be *settler colonists,* we should think about families and how powerful the human motivation is to improve the lives of their children and grandchildren. We do not like to juxtapose families and settler colonialism because the history of families is our own history, the story of *our ancestors,* who undertook hardship *on our behalf.* It is supposed to be a noble and edifying story, not a story of cynical, racist conquest. However, that is ultimately the lesson of family history, that our own families making self-interested but well-meaning and even ennobling decisions were the same people who supported policies that dispossessed Native Americans and settled on their lands. We can live with that in part because we compartmentalize our history and are able to think about family history on the one hand and what happened to the Native Americans on the other. We should not, however, forget one history in order to honor the other. We need to remember both in order to understand the humanity of settler colonists as well as the humanity of dispossessed native families. Acknowledging the former helps us to understand the past, and remembering the latter helps us to acknowledge our present responsibilities to the descendants of Native Americans.

Family history, ultimately, is like any other history in bringing to light the complexities and contradictions of the human condition. Looking at families in the past draws this history closer to home, nearer to our own lived experience. We are all members of a family of one sort or another at some point in our lives, and this we have in common with people in the past. This common ground allows us a place to stand while we contemplate the differences that separate us.

NOTES

PROLOGUE: FROM PLYMOUTH ROCK TO CREEDE, COLORADO

1. John Seelye, *Memory's Nation: The Place of Plymouth Rock* (Chapel Hill: University of North Carolina Press, 1998), 34.

2. Faunce family genealogy, compiled by Hilda Faunce Wetherill, in Faunce Collection, private possession of Carol Ann Wetherill Getz, Alamosa, Colorado, and Hilda Faunce Wetherill, estate papers, Faunce Collection.

3. William Cronon, "Foreword," in Richard White, *Remembering Ahanagran: A History of Stories* (Seattle: University of Washington Press, 1998), viii–x.

4. Victoria Freeman, *Distant Relations: How My Ancestors Colonized North America* (South Royalton, VT: Steerforth, 2000); Annette Gordon-Reed, *The Hemingses of Monticello: An American Family* (New York: Norton, 2009); Joseph Amato, *Jacob's Well: A Case for Rethinking Family History* (St. Paul: Minnesota Historical Society Press, 2009); Andrew Graybill, *The Red and the White: A Family Saga of the American West* (New York: Norton, 2014); Anne Hyde, *Empires, Nations, and Families: A New History of the North American West, 1800–1860* (New York: HarperCollins, 2012).

5. For an overview of trends in family history, see George C. Alter, "Generation to Generation: Life Course, Family, and Community," *Social Science History* 37, no. 1 (Spring 2013): 1–26.

6. Maurice Halbwachs, *On Collective Memory*, ed., trans., intro. Lewis A. Coser, translation of *Les cadres sociaux de la mémoire* (Chicago: University of Chicago Press, 1992); Marianne Hirsch, *Family Frames: Photography, Narrative, and Postmemory* (Cambridge, MA: Harvard University Press, 1997).

7. Susan E. Gray, *The Yankee West: Community Life on the Michigan Frontier* (Chapel Hill: University of North Carolina Press, 1996).

8. Joan M. Jensen, *Calling This Place Home: Women on the Wisconsin Frontier, 1850–1925* (St. Paul: Minnesota Historical Society Press, 2006).

9. Freeman, *Distant Relations*, xvii.

10. Mary S. Hartman, *The Household and the Making of History: A Subversive View of the Western Past* (New York: Cambridge University Press, 2004), 30–33, 40, 48–51, 69, 243, 249–250, 259–261, 267.

11. Elizabeth Jameson, "Halfway across That Line: Gender at the Threshold of History in the North American West," *Western Historical Quarterly* 47, no. 1 (Spring 2016): 16.

12. For instance, in majority male settings such as mining camps, men arrange themselves into groups in which domestic duties are assigned and the members take responsibility for the welfare of all members. See Susan Lee Johnson, *Roaring Camp: The Social World of the California Gold Rush* (New York: Norton, 2000), 99–140.

13. Tamara K. Hareven, *Families, History, and Social Change: Life-Course and Cross-Cultural Perspectives* (Boulder, CO: Westview Press, 2000), 18, 324–327.

14. Joseph A. Amato, "Rethinking Family History," *Minnesota History* 60, no. 8 (Winter 2007/2008): 328.

CHAPTER 1. SUSAN AND AUGUSTUS: PARTNERS FOR REFORM

1. *Letters of Theodore Dwight Weld, Angelina Grimké Weld, and Sarah Grimké, 1822–1844*, ed. Gilbert H. Barnes and Dwight L. Dumond (Gloucester, MA: Peter Smith, 1965), 178 (hereafter *Weld-Grimké Letters*); Gilbert Hobbs Barnes, *The Anti-Slavery Impulse, 1830–1844* (New York: Harcourt, Brace, 1964; orig. 1933), 227, fn11.

2. Mrs. O. E. (Emma) Morse, "Sketch of the Life and Works of Augustus Wattles," *Collections of the Kansas Historical Society* 17 (1928): 291.

3. Mary Ann Wattles Faunce, "Recollections of a Grandmother," (1920s), handwritten manuscript, Faunce Collection, in private possession of Carol Ann Wetherill Getz, Alamosa, Colorado (hereafter Faunce Collection).

4. Susan E. Lowe Wattles, "Autobiography," Folder 1, Wattles Family Collection, Wilson's Creek National Battlefield, Republic, Missouri (hereafter WCNB).

5. Elizabeth Stone, *Black Sheep and Kissing Cousins: How Our Family Stories Shape Us* (New Brunswick, NJ: Transaction, 2004), 17.

6. Mary P. Ryan, *Cradle of the Middle Class: The Family in Oneida County, New York, 1790–1865* (New York: Cambridge University Press, 1981), 8–13, 52–59; Robert H. Abzug, *Passionate Liberator: Theodore Dwight Weld and the Dilemma of Reform* (New York: Oxford University Press, 1980), 34–35.

7. Lowe family genealogy, compiled by Hilda Faunce Wetherill, Faunce Collection; "Descendants of William Low," http://www.walcat.concentrichost.com /LOW.htm, accessed January 31, 2011; Susan Lowe Wattles, "Autobiography," Folder 1, Wattles Family Collection, WCNB; Susan Lowe to Laura, September 28, 1831, Folder 1, Wattles Family Collection, WCNB.

8. Mary Kelley, *Learning to Stand and Speak: Women, Education, and Public Life in America's Republic* (Chapel Hill: University of North Carolina Press, 2006), 2–4, 17–19, 37–41.

9. Ibid., 25.

10. Ibid., 26–27.

11. Chris Dixon, *Perfecting the Family: Anti-Slavery Marriages in Nineteenth-Century America* (Amherst: University of Massachusetts Press, 1997), 4; Carl Degler, *At Odds: Women and the Family in America from the Revolution to the Present* (New York: Oxford University Press, 1980), 26–29; Barbara Welter, "The Cult of True Womanhood, 1820–1860," *American Quarterly* 18 (Summer 1966): 133–155; Nancy F. Cott, *The Bonds of Womanhood: "Woman's Sphere" in New England, 1780–1835* (New Haven, CT: Yale University Press, 1977), 70–74, 80–87; Linda Kerber, "Separate Spheres, Female World, Woman's Place: The Rhetoric of Women's History," *Journal of American History* 75 (June 1988): 9–39.

12. Carol Lasser, "How Did Oberlin Women Students Draw on Their College Experience to Participate in Antebellum Social Movements, 1831–1861?" *Women and Social Movements in the United States, 1600–2000,* May 2002; http://womhist.binghamton.edu/oberlin.htm (accessed February 3, 2006); Stacey M. Robertson, *Hearts Beating for Liberty: Women Abolitionists in the Old Northwest* (Chapel Hill: University of North Carolina Press, 2010); Anne M. Boylan, *The Origins of Women's Activism: New York and Boston, 1797–1840* (Chapel Hill: University of North Carolina Press, 2002), 16–17, 32–37; Michael D. Pierson, *Free Hearts and Free Homes: Gender and American Antislavery Politics* (Chapel Hill: University of North Carolina Press, 2003), 11–12; Nancy A. Hewitt, *Women's Activism and Social Change: Rochester, New York, 1822–1872* (Ithaca, NY: Cornell University Press, 1984), 39.

13. Hewitt, *Women's Activism,* 40–41.

14. Barnes, *Anti-Slavery Impulse,* 9–12.

15. Gretchen Townsend Buggeln, *Temples of Grace: The Material Transformation of Connecticut's Churches* (Lebanon, NH: University Press of New England, 2003), 147.

16. Thomas D. Hamm, *God's Government Begun: The Society for Universal Inquiry and Reform, 1842–1846* (Bloomington: Indiana University Press, 1995), 23; New London County, Connecticut, Archives History, Town Poor in Lebanon Town Treasurer's Records, 1818–1882, http://files.usgwarchives.net/ct/newlondon/history/other/townpoor86 (accessed February 5, 2011); Faunce family genealogy, compiled by Hilda Faunce Wetherill, in private possession of Carol Ann Wetherill Getz, Alamosa, Colorado; "Spirit Knocking in Cincinnati," *Cleveland Plain Dealer,* October 26, 1850, 2.

17. George W. Gale, *Autobiography of George Washington Gale (1789–1861), Founder of Galesburg, Illinois, and Knox College* (New York: n.p., 1964), 276–278.

18. Abzug, *Passionate Liberator,* 61–67.

19. Paul Goodman, "The Manual Labor Movement and the Origins of Abolitionism," *Journal of the Early Republic* 13, no. 3 (Autumn 1993): 362.

20. Ibid., 363–364.

21. Abzug, *Passionate Liberator,* 52–73, 87; "Intelligence: Auxiliary Societies," *African Repository and Colonial Journal* 9, no. 7 (September 1833): 215.

22. Milton C. Sernett, *Abolition's Axe: Beriah Green, Oneida Institute, and the Black Freedom Struggle* (Syracuse, NY: Syracuse University Press, 1986), xiii.

23. *History of the Foundation and Endowment and Catalogue of the Trustees, Alumni, and Students of the Lane Theological Seminary* (Cincinnati, OH: Ben Franklin Printing House, 1848), 11–12; Lawrence Thomas Lesick, *The Lane Rebels: Evangelism and Antislavery in Antebellum America* (Metuchen, NJ: Scarecrow, 1980), 35–51; Walter R. Keagy, "The Lane Seminary Rebellion," *Bulletin of the Historical and Philosophical Society of Ohio* 9, no. 2 (April 1951): 141–145.

24. *New York Evangelist*, March 3, 1832; Sernett, *Abolition's Axe*, 40; Asa A. Stone to Theodore Weld, in *Weld-Grimké Letters*, 106–108; Robert Samuel Fletcher, *A History of Oberlin College from Its Foundation through the Civil War*, vols. 1 and 2 (New York: Arno, 1971), 54–55.

25. *A Statement of the Reasons Which Induced the Students of Lane Seminary to Dissolve Their Connection with That Institution* (Cincinnati, OH: n.p., 1834), 3, pamphlet, Cincinnati Historical Society. This copy had been given by Augustus Wattles to an acquaintance. It is inscribed with "Mr. A. C. Wright from your friend, A. Wattles" on the title page.

26. Lesick, *Lane Rebels*, 72.

27. Henry Mayer, *All on Fire: William Lloyd Garrison and the Abolition of Slavery* (New York: St. Martin's Griffin, 1998), 110–112, 173–177.

28. Lesick, *Lane Rebels*, 75.

29. Abzug, *Passionate Liberator*, 79–88; Lesick, *Lane Rebels*, 72–79.

30. Lesick, *Lane Rebels*, 78–79.

31. "From the Western Recorder: Lane Seminary," *Emancipator* 1, no. 16 (March 6, 1834): 3.

32. Ibid.

33. Oliver Johnson, *William Lloyd Garrison and His Times; or, Sketches of the Anti-Slavery Movement in America and of the Man Who Was Its Founder and Moral Leader* (Boston: B. B. Russell, 1880), 169–170.

34. Augustus Wattles, "Statement in Regard to Cincinnati," in *Proceedings of the Ohio Anti-Slavery Convention Held at Putnam on the Twenty-Second, Twenty-Third, and Twenty-Fourth of April 1835* (New York: American Anti-Slavery Society, 1835), 22.

35. Wendell P. Dabney, *Cincinnati's Colored Citizens: Historical, Sociological, and Biographical* (New York: Negro Universities Press, 1970; orig. 1926 Dabney), 101–102.

36. Lesick, *Lane Rebels*, 92–93; Leonard L. Richards, *"Gentlemen of Property and Standing": Anti-Abolition Mobs in Jacksonian America* (New York: Oxford University Press, 1970), 41–42.

37. *A Statement of the Reasons Which Induced the Students of Lane Seminary to Dissolve Their Connection with That Institution*, 24.

38. Ibid.

39. Ibid., 25.

40. Ibid.

41. Benjamin Quarles, *Black Abolitionists* (New York: Oxford University Press, 1969), 47–49; Weld quoted on 51.

42. Augustus and Susan Wattles to Mary Lukens, June 25, 1838, Lukens-Gilbert Papers, Western Reserve Historical Society, Cleveland, Ohio (hereafter WRHS).

43. Barnes, *Anti-Slavery Impulse*, 154–157.

44. Henry Blackwell, quoted in Chris Dixon, *Perfecting the Family: Anti-Slavery Marriages in Nineteenth-Century America* (Amherst: University of Massachusetts Press, 1997), 94–95.

45. Virginia Scharff, "Lighting Out for the Territory: Women, Mobility, and Western Place," in *Power and Place in the North American West*, ed. Richard White and John M. Findlay (Seattle: University of Washington Press, 1999), 296.

46. Carolyn G. Heilbrun, *Writing a Woman's Life* (New York: Ballantine Books, 1988), 23. The expenses of the Cincinnati Sisters were paid by Arthur Tappan, who would later resist the efforts of female abolitionists to take a greater role in public antislavery work. Johnson, *William Lloyd Garrison*, 170–171.

47. Susan Lowe to Theodore Dwight Weld, March 1835, in *Weld-Grimké Letters*, 215–216.

48. S. Wells, J. A. Thome, Wm. T. Allan, Marius E. Robinson, and J. T. Pierce to Theodore D. Weld, December 15, 1834, in *Weld-Grimké Letters*, 178–179.

49. Ibid.

50. Johnson, *William Lloyd Garrison*, 171.

51. *Proceedings of the Ohio Anti-Slavery Convention Held at Putnam, 1835*, 18.

52. Augustus Wattles to Susan E. Lowe, April 28, 1835, Wattles Family Collection, WCNB.

53. Ibid.

54. Ibid.

55. Keith P. Griffler, *Front Line of Freedom: African Americans and the Forging of the Underground Railroad in the Ohio Valley* (Lexington: University Press of Kentucky, 2004), 33, 69–70, 75, 141.

56. Theodore D. Weld to Lewis Tappan, December 22, 1835, in *Weld-Grimké Letters*, 248.

57. Theodore D. Weld to Lewis Tappan, February 22, 1836, in *Weld-Grimké Letters*, 265; Theodore D. Weld to Lewis Tappan, April 5, 1836, in *Weld-Grimké Letters*, 287.

58. Elizur Wright Jr. to Theodore D. Weld, August 5, 1836, in *Weld-Grimké Letters*, 323; John L. Myers, "Antislavery Activities of Five Lane Seminary Boys in 1835–1836," *Bulletin of the Historical and Philosophical Society of Ohio* 21 (April 1963): 111; Quarles, *Black Abolitionists*, 51.

59. Letter to editor from Augustus Wattles, *Liberator*, May 14, 1836; Robert Price, "The Ohio Anti-Slavery Convention of 1836," *Ohio State Archaeological and Historical Society Quarterly* 45 (1887): 173–188; Ann Hagedorn, *Beyond the River: The Untold Story of the Heroes of the Underground Railroad* (New York: Simon and Schuster, 2002), 102–109; Robertson, *Hearts Beating for Liberty*, 18–19.

60. Nikki M. Taylor, *Frontiers of Freedom: Cincinnati's Black Community, 1802–1868* (Athens: Ohio University Press, 2005), 109–112.

61. *Narrative of the Late Riotous Proceedings against the Liberty of the Press in Cincinnati, with Remarks and Historical Notes Relating to Emancipation, Addressed to the People of Ohio by the Executive Committee of the Ohio Anti-Slavery Society* (Cincinnati, OH: n.p., 1836), 31, 39–41, pamphlet, Ohio Historical Society, Columbus, Ohio.

62. Ulrich F. Mueller, *Red, Black, and White* (Cartagena, OH: Author, 1935) in Special Collections and Archives, Wright State University, Dayton, Ohio, http://corescholar.libraries.wright.edu/cgi/viewcontent.cgi?article=1015&context=special_books (accessed March 24, 2017), 58; *Weld-Grimké Letters*, 178.

63. *Weld-Grimké Letters*, 178.

64. Mark Perry, *Lift Up Thy Voice: The Grimké Family's Journey from Slaveholders to Civil Rights Leaders* (New York: Penguin, 2001), 172–173; Elizabeth Cady Stanton, *Eighty Years and More: Reminiscences of Elizabeth Cady Stanton* (New York: Sourcebooks, 1970), 43–44.

65. Degler, *At Odds*, 8, 36–42.

66. Lillian Schlissel, *Women's Diaries of the Westward Journey* (New York: Schocken, 1982), 14, 28, 111, 115; John Mack Faragher, *Women and Men on the Overland Trail* (New Haven, CT: Yale University Press, 1979), 163.

67. Leonard I. Sweet, *The Minister's Wife: Her Role in Nineteenth-Century American Evangelicalism* (Philadelphia, PA: Temple University Press, 1982), 184–197.

68. A number of historians have shown the importance of women's home production in gradually integrating nineteenth-century families into the market economy. See Joan M. Jensen, *Loosening the Bonds: Mid-Atlantic Farm Women, 1750–1850* (New Haven, CT: Yale University Press, 1986), 111–112, 207; Susan Sessions Rugh, *Our Common Country: Family Farming, Culture, and Community in the Nineteenth-Century Midwest* (Bloomington: Indiana University Press, 2001), 20–21, 65–67; Jeanne Boydston, *Home and Work: Housework, Wages, and the Ideology of Labor in the Early Republic* (New York: Oxford University Press, 1990), 156–159; and Catherine E. Kelly, *In the New England Fashion: Reshaping Women's Lives in the Nineteenth Century* (Ithaca, NY: Cornell University Press, 1999), 42–50.

69. Ronald G. Walters, *The Antislavery Appeal: Abolitionism after 1830* (Baltimore, MD: Johns Hopkins University Press, 1976), 101–110.

70. Robert H. Abzug, *Cosmos Crumbling: American Reform and the Religious Imagination* (New York: Oxford University Press, 1994), 6. Other discussions of ultraism can be found in Hamm, *God's Government Begun*, 57; Hewitt, *Women's Activism and Social Change*, 41; and Lori D. Ginzberg, *Women and the Work of Benevolence: Morality, Politics, and Class in the Nineteenth-Century United States* (New Haven, CT: Yale University Press, 1990), 67–97.

71. Dixon, *Perfecting the Family*, 16–17, 82–87, 144.

72. Augustus Wattles to Angelina Grimké, May 7, 1838, *Weld-Grimké Letters*, 666.

73. Jean Fagan Yellin, *Women and Sisters: The Antislavery Feminists in American Culture* (New Haven, CT: Yale University Press, 1989), 38–39; Karen Sánchez-Eppler, *Touching Liberty: Abolition, Feminism, and the Politics of the Body* (Berkeley: University of California Press, 1993), 111.

74. "Letter of Condemnation," *Liberator*, February 28, 1840.

75. Hamm, *God's Government Begun*, 115.

76. Esther Wattles, "Memoir of Esther (Whinery) Wattles, 1819–1908," 1905, John O. Wattles Collection, WRHS, 1–3.

77. John Otis Wattles, *A Few Thoughts on Marriage* (Salem, OH: J. H. Painter, 1844), 3, 4, 12–16, 25–26.

78. Hamm, *God's Government Begun*, 114–115.

79. Wattles, *Memoir*, 3. Another contemporary observer explained that the reputed cause of the failure of Prairie Home was that the community leased rather than owned its land, though he doubted Prairie Home would have succeeded even if it owned the land because the community had no government of any sort. John Humphrey Noyes, *Strange Cults and Utopias of Nineteenth-Century America* (New York: Dover, 1966), 327.

80. *Herald of Progression* 1, no. 6 (October 1845): 4. John O. Wattles Collection, WRHS.

81. Wattles, *Memoir*, 11.

82. Ibid., 9.

83. John L. Myers, "American Anti-Slavery Society Agents and the Free Negro, 1833–1838," *Journal of Negro History* 52, no. 3 (July 1967): 212–214; Gerda Lerner, *The Grimké Sisters from South Carolina: Pioneers for Women's Rights and Abolition*, rev. ed. (Chapel Hill: University of North Carolina Press, 2004), 101; Augustus Wattles to Asa Mahan, July 29, 1836, Correspondence 1, 1822–1866, Treasurer's Office, Box 2, Oberlin College Archives, Oberlin, Ohio; *Report of the Second Anniversary of the Ohio Anti-Slavery Society Held in Mount Pleasant, Jefferson County, Ohio on the Twenty-Seventh of April, 1837* (Cincinnati, OH: Anti-Slavery Society, 1837), 4; "Colored Schools in Ohio," *Philanthropist*, September 15, 1837; Augustus Wattles to Marius Robinson, November 1, 1837, Marius R. Robinson Papers, WRHS. In late 1836 or early 1837 Augustus might have been in Connecticut for family business, perhaps to receive some sort of inheritance. Gilbert Barnes, in *Anti-Slavery Impulse*, mentions that Augustus received an inheritance that enabled him to buy land (226), and Augustus did begin to buy his own land in Mercer County in March 1837, after his return from the East. The origin of such an inheritance is not clear, but it is highly unlikely that it resulted from the death of his father. Family records differ on the date of Erastus's death, giving both 1835 and 1839 as the date, but it is not likely Erastus had any money to bequeath. He was given a pauper's burial in an unmarked grave and had been listed among the Lebanon Town Poor in 1831; see New London County, Connecticut, Archives History, Town Poor in Lebanon Town Treasurer's Records, 1818–1882, http://files.usgwarchives.net/ct/newlondon/history/other/townpoor86 (accessed February 5, 2011.

84. "Good News from Ohio," *Liberator*, May 9, 1835.

85. Morse, "Sketch of the Life," 291–293; Patent No. OH0680_.379; Patentee: Augustus Wattles, March 15, 1837, Bureau of Land Management Government

Land Office Records, http://www.glorecords.blm.gov (accessed April 15, 2007); Augustus Wattles, letter, in Henry Howe, *Historical Collection of Ohio; Containing a Collection of the Most Interesting Facts, Traditions, Biographical Sketches, Anecdotes, etc. Relating to Its General and Local History: with Descriptions of Its Counties, Principal Towns, and Villages* (Cincinnati, OH: Derby, Bradley, 1847), 355.

86. Wattles to Robinson, November 1, 1837, WRHS.

87. *Biographical and Historical Record of Jay and Blackford Counties, Indiana* (Chicago: n.p., 1887), 252–253; Julia Ann Lowe Weber to David P. Lowe, July 28, 1867, Lowe Papers, Mound City Historical Society, Mound City, Kansas (hereafter MCHS).

88. Charles Theodore Greve, *Centennial History of Cincinnati and Representative Citizens*, vol. 1 (Chicago: Biographical Publishing, 1904).

89. Jonathan Lowe to David P. Lowe, September 19, 1858, David P. Lowe Papers, MCHS; Augustus and Susan Wattles to David P. Lowe, October 5, 1853, David P. Lowe Papers, MCHS; Augustus and Susan Wattles to David P. Lowe, February 15, 1856, David P. Lowe Papers, MCHS; Faunce, "Recollections of a Grandmother"; "Obituary: Hon. D. P. Lowe," *Linn County Clarion*, April 14, 1882, Clippings File, Linn County Historical Society (hereafter LCHS).

90. Elizabeth Lowe Byrd to David P. Lowe, April 26, 1855, in David P. Lowe Papers, MCHS; Elizabeth Lowe Byrd to David P. Lowe, April 18, 1858, David P. Lowe Papers, MCHS.

91. Susan E. Wattles, quoted in Mueller, *Red, Black, and White*, 58.

92. Wattles to Robinson, November 1, 1837, Marius R. Robinson Papers, WRHS.

93. Augustus and Susan Wattles to Mary Lukens, June 25, 1838, Lukens-Gilbert Papers, WRHS.

94. J.S.H. letter to the editor, *Xenia Free Press*, November 28, 1840.

95. Ibid.

96. Lucretia Mott to James Miller McKim, July 19, 1839, in *Selected Letters of Lucretia Coffin Mott*, ed. Beverly Wilson Palmer (Urbana-Champaign: University of Illinois Press, 2002), 57; Lucretia Mott to Elizabeth Pease, February 18, 1841, in ibid., 86. See also "A Colored Settlement," *Liberator,* January 1, 1841; "Colored Settlements in Ohio," *New Bedford Mercury*, January 1, 1841.

97. "Colored Settlement in Mercer County," *Herald of Progression* 1, no. 5 (September 1845), 3, John O. Wattles Collection, WRHS.

98. "Augustus Wattles Again," *Pennsylvania Freeman,* December 29, 1841.

99. Ibid. Although it was dangerous for participants in the Underground Railroad to admit to "conducting" fugitives before the Civil War, Susan Lowe Wattles acknowledged having done so in an 1881 letter to Susan B. Anthony published in *History of Woman Suffrage*, vol. 2, ed. Elizabeth Cady Stanton, Susan B. Anthony, and Matilda Joslyn Gage (New York: Arno/*New York Times*, 1969), 255.

100. Howe, *Historical Collections of Ohio*, 504.

101. Augustus Wattles to John Wattles, December 27, 1845, printed in *Herald of Progression* 1, no. 9 (January 1846): 2, John O. Wattles Collection, WRHS.

102. Gerda Lerner, *The Feminist Thought of Sarah Grimké* (New York: Oxford University Press, 1998), 96.

103. Susan E. Lowe Wattles to "My Dear Husband" (Augustus Wattles), (1863?), Folder 6, Wattles Family Collection, WCNB.

104. Susan E. Lowe Wattles, Journal of Her Children, 1838–1846, Folder 1, Wattles Family Collection, WCNB, 1.

105. Ibid., 9.

106. Ibid., 13.

107. Ibid., 19.

108. Ibid., 16.

109. Mary Ann Wattles Faunce recalled in "Recollections of a Grandmother" that as a child traveling through the Ohio woods, she would hear the howling of wolves.

110. Wattles, Journal of Her Children, 8–9.

111. Ibid., 3–4. Susan incorrectly spelled "paregoric" in her diary, but here and throughout the book, I have left the original spelling as found in the documents, without cluttering up the quotations with [*sic*]. Nineteenth-century spelling was not fully standardized, and many of the family members used unique and often inconsistent forms of spelling.

112. Ibid., 11.

113. Ibid., 14.

114. Ibid., 15.

115. Susan E. Wattles to Betsy Cowles, June 30, 1838, Betsy Mix Cowles Collection, Kent State University Special Collections and Archives, Kent State University, Kent, Ohio.

116. Hamm, *God's Government Begun*, 175.

117. Augustus Wattles to David Lowe, October 3, 1853, Wattles Family Papers, MCHS.

118. Augustus Wattles to David Lowe, August 26, 1853, Wattles Family Papers, MCHS.

CHAPTER 2. FOR FREEDOM AND EQUALITY:
THE WATTLES FAMILY IN KANSAS

1. Oswald Garrison Villard, *John Brown, 1800–1859: A Biography Fifty Years Later* (New York: Knopf, 1943), 371.

2. Kristen Tegtmeier Oertel, *Bleeding Borders: Race, Gender, and Violence in Pre–Civil War Kansas* (Baton Rouge: Louisiana State University Press, 2009), 40–41; Michael A. Morrison, *Slavery and the American West: The Eclipse of Manifest Destiny*

and the *Coming of the Civil War* (Chapel Hill: University of North Carolina Press, 1997), 142–143, 161; James A. Rawley, *Race and Politics: "Bleeding Kansas" and the Coming of the Civil War* (Philadelphia, PA: Lippincott, 1969), 79–90.

3. Augustus Wattles to David P. Lowe, October 5, 1853, Wattles Family Papers, Mound City Historical Society, Mound City, Kansas (hereafter MCHS).

4. Kansas Territorial Census, 1859, Kansas State Historical Society, Topeka, Kansas (hereafter KSHS). The territorial census asked each family to state their date of settlement in Kansas, and other sources of family memory restate 1855 as their date of arrival in Kansas. One source unfortunately confuses this point: Sarah Grimké addressed a letter to the Wattleses in response to their arrival in Kansas on which she wrote the date, April 2, with no year indicated. The editors of the Grimké letters put the year 1854 in brackets. This has to be an error because all other sources point to 1855 as the date of their settling in Kansas. The Grimké letter was probably written in 1856, and this is the date I will use in brackets. Sarah Grimké to Augustus Wattles, April 2, [1856], Weld-Grimké Papers, William L. Clements Library, University of Michigan, Ann Arbor, Michigan (hereafter UM).

5. Edward Daniels, "Letter from Mr. Daniels," *Milwaukee Sentinel,* April 17, 1856. Daniels was obviously indulging in some boosterism because the Wattleses would have had to travel at the breakneck speed of thirty-five miles per day to cover seven hundred miles in twenty days. A more typical wagon speed would have been around ten to fifteen miles per day without any delays or incidents.

6. Thomas Goodrich, *War to the Knife: Bleeding Kansas, 1854–1861* (Lincoln: University of Nebraska Press, 2004; orig. Stackpole Books, 1988), 9–22; Samuel A. Johnson, *The Battle Cry of Freedom: The New England Emigrant Aid Company in the Kansas Crusade* (Lawrence: University Press of Kansas, 1954), 3–8, 74–75.

7. Nicole Etcheson, *Bleeding Kansas: Contested Liberty in the Civil War Era* (Lawrence: University Press of Kansas, 2004), 48–54.

8. Goodrich, *War to the Knife,* 27–42; Etcheson, *Bleeding Kansas,* 56–62; *Herald of Freedom,* May 26, 1855.

9. Etcheson, *Bleeding Kansas,* 72–76.

10. Robert H. Abzug, *Cosmos Crumbling: American Reform and the Religious Imagination* (New York: Oxford University Press, 1994), 6; Thomas D. Hamm, *God's Government Begun: The Society for Universal Inquiry and Reform, 1842–1846* (Bloomington: Indiana University Press), 57.

11. Daniels, "Letter from Mr. Daniels."

12. *Herald of Freedom,* June 30, 1855, July 21, 1855; "Doings of the Kansas Legislature," *Baltimore Sun,* July 30, 1855; "Kansas Legislature," *Liberator,* June 3, 1855.

13. Susan Wattles to David Lowe, September 30, 1855, in Wattles Family Papers, MCHS.

14. Goodrich, *War to the Knife,* 47–48; Etcheson, *Bleeding Kansas,* 76–77.

15. Charles Robinson to Eli Thayer, April 2, 1855, in Eli Thayer Collection, #519, Box 1, Folder 1, KSHS.

16. "Free-State Emigrants' Battery," daguerreotype, 1856, Item 90323, KSHS, www.kansasmemory.org/item/90323 (accessed July 6, 2011. I am indebted to Ola Mae Earnest, curator of the Linn County Historical Museum, who identified Augustus Wattles in the photograph. The photograph has been reproduced often, recently used as the cover photograph of Nicole Etcheson's book and in Ken Burns's documentary on the Civil War.

17. Sarah Moore Grimké to Augustus, Susan, and Sarah Wattles, April 2, [1856], in Weld-Grimké Papers, UM.

18. David S. Reynolds, *John Brown, Abolitionist: The Man Who Killed Slavery, Sparked the Civil War, and Seeded Civil Rights* (New York: Knopf, 2005), 132–133.

19. *Herald of Freedom*, June 30, 1855.

20. Reynolds, *John Brown*, 136.

21. US Congress, Senate Select Committee on the Harpers Ferry Invasion, *Invasion at Harpers Ferry* (New York: Arno, 1969), 213.

22. Richard J. Hinton, *John Brown and His Men; With Some Account of the Roads They Traveled to Reach Harpers Ferry* (New York: Funk and Wagnalls, 1894), 9–12.

23. Richard O. Boyer, *The Legend of John Brown: A Biography and a History* (New York: Knopf, 1973), 257; Robert Samuel Fletcher, *A History of Oberlin College from Its Foundation through the Civil War*, vol. 1 (New York: Arno, 1971), 155.

24. Reynolds, *John Brown*, 124–134.

25. Elizabeth L. Byrd to David Lowe, April 26, 1855, in Wattles Family Papers, MCHS.

26. Julia Ann Weber to David P. Lowe, October 27, 1856, Wattles Family Papers, MCHS. Territorial Governor John W. Geary was appointed governor in the summer of 1856. Geary arrived in Kansas in time to preside over the freeing of the "treason prisoners," but the order to drop charges of treason had come from President Franklin Pierce. Etcheson, *Bleeding Kansas*, 126–131. It is not clear, however, that John Byrd was actually one of the "treason prisoners" freed at this time. More likely he was the victim of the random and widespread violence in Kansas, many acts of which did not make it into national newspapers.

27. Augustus and Susan Wattles to David Lowe, February 15, 1856, in Wattles Family Papers, MCHS.

28. Ibid.

29. Susan Wattles to David Lowe, February 15, 1856, in Wattles Family Papers, MCHS.

30. Goodrich, *War to the Knife*, 73–85.

31. Rawley, *Race and Politics*, 129–133.

32. Reynolds, *John Brown*, 171–182.

33. Ibid., 196–205.

34. Morse, "Life and Work of Augustus Wattles," 296.

35. Augustus Wattles to Mr. Brown, October 15, 1856, in James Blood Collection, Correspondence 1854–1861, KSHS.

36. James C. Malin, *John Brown and the Legend of Fifty-Six* (New York: Haskell House, 1971), 498–499.

37. *Herald of Freedom*, November 1, 1856; G. W. Brown, *The Truth at Last: Reminiscences of Old John Brown—Thrilling Incidents of Borderlife in Kansas* (Rockford, IL: Abraham E. Smith, 1880), 40.

38. *Herald of Freedom*, November 8, 1856.

39. George W. Brown, *False Claims of Kansas Historians Truthfully Corrected* (Rockford, IL: Author, 1902), 78.

40. *Herald of Freedom*, November 22, 1856.

41. *Herald of Freedom*, December 27, 1856.

42. *Herald of Freedom*, November 21, 1857, November 28, 1857, January 16, 1858.

43. Kansas State Central Committee Record Book, July 4, 1856, Item 90311, Henry Miles Moore Collection #450, Box 18, Folder 1, KSHS, 8.

44. Ibid., November 27, 1856, 48.

45. Johnson, *Battle Cry of Freedom*, 214–220.

46. W. F. M. Arny to William Barnes, October 25, 1856, in William Barnes Collection, #269, Box 2, Folder 1, KSHS.

47. A. Curtiss to William Hutchinson, December 21, 1856, in William Hutchinson Collection #400, Box 1, Folder 2, KSHS.

48. *Herald of Freedom*, January 24, 1857; W. F. M. Arny to William Hutchinson, October 28, 1856, in William Hutchinson Collection, KSHS.

49. Augustus Wattles to Thaddeus Hyatt, January 9, 1857, in Thaddeus Hyatt Papers, KSHS.

50. Johnson, *Battle Cry of Freedom*, 251–253.

51. US Congress, *Invasion at Harpers Ferry*, 214.

52. F. B. Sanborn, *The Life and Letters of John Brown, Liberator of Kansas, and Martyr of Virginia* (Boston: Roberts Brothers, 1891), 391.

53. Nelson Hawkins [John Brown] to Augustus Wattles, April 8, 1857, in Sanborn, *Life and Letters of John Brown*, 391.

54. Augustus Wattles to James Smith [John Brown], June 18, 1857, in Sanborn, *Life and Letters of John Brown*, 394.

55. Etcheson, *Bleeding Kansas*, 143–150.

56. Augustus Wattles to Dear Sir (John Brown), August 21, 1857; *Herald of Freedom*, October 17, 1857; Augustus Wattles to Cyrus K. Holliday, November 8, 1857, in Cyrus K. Holliday Papers, KSHS.

57. James H. Holmes to John Brown, August 16, 1857, in Sanborn, *Life and Letters of John Brown*, 395.

58. John O. Wattles, "Slavery in Kansas," *Herald of Freedom*, January 13, 1855.

59. William Ansel Mitchell, *Linn County, Kansas: A History* (Kansas City, MO: Campbell-Gates, 1928), 135–136.

60. "Railroad Meeting at Emporia," *Herald of Freedom*, August 8, 1857.

61. Charles Wesley Goodlander, *Memoirs and Recollections of the Early Days of Fort Scott* (Fort Scott, KS: Monitor Books and Printers, 1900), 6.

62. James Redpath, *Hand-book to Kansas Territory and the Rocky Mountains' Gold Region: Accompanied by Reliable Maps and a Preliminary Treatise on the Pre-emption* (New York: J. H. Colton, 1859), 83.

63. Hinton, *John Brown and His Men*, 206.

64. Ibid., 209–210; Goodrich, *War to the Knife*, 213–215; G. Murlin Welch, *Border Warfare in Southeastern Kansas, 1856–1859* (Pleasanton, KS: Linn County Historical Society, 1977), 15–16, 38–50.

65. Augustus Wattles to Friend (William) Hutchinson, April 28, 1858, William Hutchinson Collection, KSHS.

66. Reynolds, *John Brown*, 268–269; Etcheson, *Bleeding Kansas*, 197.

67. Hinton, *John Brown and His Men*, 215; Susan E. Wattles to Emma Wattles Morse, July 1887, Curtis Collection, private possession of Patti Morse Curtis, Colorado Springs, Colorado.

68. US Congress, *Invasion at Harpers Ferry*, 217.

69. Articles of Agreement for Shubel Morgan's Company, July 12, 1858, in John Brown Collection, #299, KSHS. Shubel Morgan was one of John Brown's aliases in Kansas.

70. US Congress, *Invasion at Harpers Ferry*, 217. Brown's recurring illness might have been advanced malaria. See Robert E. McGlone, *John Brown's War against Slavery* (New York: Cambridge University Press, 2009), 180–181.

71. Etcheson, *Bleeding Kansas*, 197–198; Tom L. Holman, James Montgomery, 1813–1871, EdD diss., Oklahoma State University, Stillwater, Oklahoma, 1973, 78–82.

72. Hinton, *John Brown and His Men*, 230–231.

73. US Congress, *Invasion at Harpers Ferry*, 215.

74. Villard, *John Brown*, 371.

75. Hinton, *John Brown and His Men*, 222; Holman, James Montgomery, 98.

76. Hinton, *John Brown and His Men*, 222.

77. "John Brown Parallels," in Hinton, *John Brown and His Men*, Appendix, 645–646.

78. US Congress, *Invasion at Harpers Ferry*, 219.

79. "An Attempted Rescue of John Brown from Charlestown, Va., Jail: An Address by O. E. Morse of Mound City, before the Kansas State History Society, at the Twenty-Eighth Annual Meeting, December 1, 1903," *Kansas State Historical Society Collections* 8 (1903–1904): 213–225.

80. US Congress, *Invasion at Harpers Ferry*, 219–222.

CHAPTER 3.

SARAH: THE MAKING OF A FEMINIST CONSCIOUSNESS

1. John Brown to Mary Brown, November 16, 1859, John Brown Collection, #299, Box 2, Folder 5, Kansas State Historical Society (KSHS), Topeka, Kansas.

2. Robert H. Abzug, *Passionate Liberator: Theodore Dwight Weld and the Dilemma of Reform* (New York: Oxford University Press, 1980), 273; David S. Reynolds, *John Brown, Abolitionist: The Man Who Killed Slavery, Sparked the Civil War, and Seeded Civil Rights* (New York: Knopf, 2005), 389; Bonnie Laughlin-Schultz, *The Ties That Bound Us: The Women of John Brown's Family and the Legacy of Radical Abolitionism* (Ithaca, NY: Cornell University Press, 2013), 71.

3. Susan E. Lowe Wattles, Journal of Her Children, 1838–1846, Folder 1, 1840–1850s, Wattles Family Collection, Wilson's Creek National Battlefield, Republic, Missouri, 3 (hereafter WCNB).

4. Ibid., 6.

5. Ibid., 15.

6. Ibid., 30.

7. Susan E. Wattles to Augustus Wattles, August 29, [1847], Folder 6, Wattles Family Collection, WCNB.

8. Biographical information on the Grimké sisters can be found in Gerda Lerner, *The Grimké Sisters from South Carolina: Pioneers for Women Rights and Abolition* (Chapel Hill: University of North Carolina Press, 1998); Mark Perry, *Lift Up Thy Voice: The Grimké Family's Journey from Slaveholders to Civil Rights Leaders* (New York: Penguin, 2001); Catherine Birney, *The Grimké Sisters, Sarah and Angelina Grimké: The First American Women Advocates of Abolition and Woman's Rights* (Westport, CT: Greenwood, 1969; orig. 1885); Robert H. Abzug, *Passionate Liberator: Theodore Dwight Weld and the Dilemma of Reform* (New York: Oxford University Press, 1980). In a recent fictional portrayal of Sarah and Angelina Grimké, *The Invention of Wings* (New York: Viking, 2014), Sue Monk Kidd dramatically captures the conflict and challenge of the Grimké sisters' decision to reject their slaveholding family and embrace abolitionism.

9. Lerner, *Grimké Sisters from South Carolina*, 101.

10. Wedding invitation list, Marriage of Angelina Grimké and Theodore Dwight Weld, May 1838, in Weld-Grimké Papers, William L. Clements Library, University of Michigan, Ann Arbor, Michigan (hereafter UM); Augustus Wattles to Angelina Grimké, May 7, 1838, *Letters of Theodore Dwight Weld, Angelina Grimké, and Sarah Grimké, 1822–1844*, ed. Gilbert H. Barnes and Dwight L. Dumond (Gloucester, MA: Peter Smith, 1965), 666.

11. Sarah Moore Grimké to Augustus and Susan Wattles, April 10, 1850, in Weld-Grimké Papers, UM. It is also not clear if the Grimké-Welds knew the Ripleys through other circumstances or perhaps just became acquainted with them through the Wattles, but a relationship did develop. Sarah Grimké consulted David Ripley on a legal matter at least once. Sarah Moore Grimké to David Ripley, May 16, 1861, Weld-Grimké Papers, UM.

12. Lerner, *Grimké Sisters of South Carolina*, 134.

13. Sarah Grimké, *Letters on the Equality of the Sexes and Other Essays*, ed. Elizabeth Ann Bartlett (New Haven, CT: Yale University Press, 1988), 21–21, 32–34, 38.

14. Ibid., 23–25.

15. Sarah Moore Grimké to Augustus Wattles, February 1, 1852, in Weld-Grimké Papers, UM.

16. Sarah Moore Grimké to Sarah Wattles, November 12, 1853, in Weld-Grimké Papers, UM.

17. Sarah Moore Grimké to Augustus and Sarah Wattles, May 11, 1854, in Weld-Grimké Papers, UM.

18. Sarah Moore Grimké to Augustus and Sarah Wattles, March 23, 1854, in Weld-Grimké Papers, UM.

19. "Paulina Kellogg Wright," *American National Biography Online*, http://www.anb.org.

20. Alison M. Parker, *Articulating Rights: Nineteenth-Century American Women on Race, Reform, and the State* (DeKalb: Northern Illinois University Press, 2010), 91; National Register of Historic Places Nomination Form: Mary Birdsall House, Indiana Division of Historic Preservation and Archaeology, 4.

21. Sarah Moore Grimké to Sarah Wattles, June 1, 1856, in Weld-Grimké Papers, UM.

22. Harriot Kezia Hunt, *Glances and Glimpses; or Fifty Years Social, Including Twenty Years Professional Life* (Boston: John P. Jewett, 1856), 44.

23. Ibid., 71.

24. Linn County, Kansas, Tax Records, April 30, 1857, Linn County Historical Society, Pleasanton, Kansas (hereafter LCHS); Bureau of Land Management, General Land Office Records, Warrant No. 46645, June 27, 1862, www.glorecords.blm.gov (accessed November 2, 2012).

25. Secretary's Book of the Moneka Woman's Rights Association, KSHS, 2–10.

26. Joseph G. Gambone, "The Forgotten Feminist of Kansas: The Papers of Clarina I. H. Nichols, 1854–1885," *Kansas Historical Quarterly* 39 (Spring 1973): 12–15; Marilyn S. Blackwell and Kristen T. Oertel, *Frontier Feminist: Clarina Howard Nichols and the Politics of Motherhood* (Lawrence: University Press of Kansas, 2010), 62–77.

27. Michael D. Pierson, *Free Hearts and Free Homes: Gender and American Antislavery Politics* (Chapel Hill: University of North Carolina Press, 2003), 93.

28. Blackwell and Oertel, *Frontier Feminist*, 138–145, 169–172.

29. Gambone, "Forgotten Feminist of Kansas," 413; Wendell Phillips to Mrs. S. E. Wattles, April 16, 1860, in Wattles Collection, KSHS.

30. Elizabeth Cady Stanton, Susan B. Anthony, and Matilda Joslyn Gage, eds., *History of Woman Suffrage*, vol. 1: *1848–1861* (New York: Arno, 1969; orig. Fowler and Wells, 1881), 193.

31. Lori D. Ginzberg, *Women and the Work of Benevolence: Morality, Politics, and Class in the Nineteenth-Century United States* (New Haven, CT: Yale University Press, 1990), 157–167.

32. Sarah M. Grimké to Susan and Sarah Wattles, January 27, 1859, in Weld-Grimké Papers, UM.

33. See Richard White, *Railroaded: The Transcontinentals and the Making of Modern America* (New York: Norton, 2011), 1–3, for a description of the US antebellum railroad system.

34. Sarah Wattles to Susan E. Wattles, April 27, [1859], Folder 14, Wattles Family Collection, WCNB.

35. Abzug, *Passionate Liberator*, 259–263; Lerner, *Grimké Sisters of South Carolina*, 235–239; Perry, *Lift Up Thy Voice*, 197–200.

36. Carol Berkin, *Civil War Wives: The Lives and Times of Angelina Grimké Weld, Varina Howell Davis, and Julia Dent Grant* (New York: Knopf, 2009), 92.

37. Eagleswood School, "Statement of Particulars," brochure, enclosure to Angelina Grimké Weld from Theodore Weld, ca. 1860, Weld-Grimké Papers, UM.

38. Ibid.

39. Berkin, *Civil War Wives*, 80.

40. Sarah Moore Grimké to Sarah Wattles, November 12, 1853, in *Weld-Grimké Letters*, UM.

41. Sarah M. Grimké to Sarah Wattles, April 1, 1859, in Weld-Grimké Papers, UM.

42. Lerner, *Grimké Sisters of South Carolina*, 242–243.

43. Augustus Wattles to Emma Wattles, July 22, 1860, in Curtis Collection, private possession of Patti Morse Curtis, Colorado Springs, Colorado.

44. Sarah G. Wattles to Susan E. Wattles, October 11, 1859, Folder 6, Wattles Family Collection, WCNB.

45. Ibid.

46. Abzug, *Passionate Liberator*, 267.

47. Benjamin P. Thomas, *Theodore Weld: Crusader for Freedom* (New York: Octagon, 1973), 229–234.

48. Sarah M. Grimké to Sarah Wattles, December 10, 1861, in Weld-Grimké Papers, UM.

49. Lerner, *Grimké Sisters of South Carolina*, 242–243.

50. Richard J. Hinton, *John Brown and His Men* (New York: Arno, 1968), 210–222.

51. Reynolds, *John Brown, Abolitionist*, 244–246, 299–311, 321–322, 370–374.

52. Rebecca Spring to Mrs. Mary Brown, March 23, 1862, John Brown Papers, MS 1246 1859–1904, KSHS.

53. Hinton, *John Brown and His Men*, 559.

54. Sarah Wattles to Augustus Wattles, February 9, 1862, Folder 8, 1861–1865, Wattles Family Collection, WCNB.

55. Ibid.

56. Spring to Brown, March 23, 1862.

57. Sarah M. Grimké to Sarah Wattles, March 17, 1861, in Weld-Grimké Papers, UM.

58. William Ansel Mitchell, *Linn County, Kansas: A History* (Kansas City, MO: Campbell-Gates, 1928), 331–332.

59. Sarah G. Wattles to Susan E. Wattles, December 25, 1859, Folder 6, Wattles Family Collection, WCNB.

60. Ruth Bordin, *Frances Willard: A Biography* (Chapel Hill: University of North Carolina Press, 1986), 6–13, 189; Jed Dannenbaum, "The Origins of Temperance Activism and Militancy among American Women," *Journal of Social History* 15, no. 2 (Winter 1981): 235–238.

CHAPTER 4. THE WATTLES FAMILY IN THE CIVIL WAR, PART I:
A SCATTERED HOME FRONT

1. Mary Ann Wattles to Sarah G. Wattles, May 20, 1860, Folder 10, Wattles Family Collection, Wilson's Creek National Battlefield, Republic, Missouri (hereafter WCNB).

2. Mary Ann Wattles to Sarah G. Wattles, July 8, 1860, Folder 10, Wattles Family Collection, WCNB.

3. Albert Castel, *A Frontier State at War: Kansas 1861–1865* (Lawrence: Kansas Heritage Press, 1992, orig. 1958), 14–15.

4. Michael Fellman, *Inside War: The Guerrilla Conflict in Missouri during the American Civil War* (New York: Oxford University Press, 1990), v.

5. Michael Fellman, "I Came Not to Bring Peace, but a Sword": The Christian War God and the War of All against All on the Kansas-Missouri Border," in *Bleeding Kansas, Bleeding Missouri: The Long Civil War on the Border,* ed. Jonathan Earle and Diane Mutti Burke (Lawrence: University Press of Kansas, 2013), 13.

6. Castel, *Frontier State at War,* 102–109, 124–132, 136, 143, 214.

7. US Census Bureau, Decennial Census, www.census.gov/prod/www/decennial.html.

8. Emma Wattles to Sarah G. Wattles, February 17, 1861, Folder 3, Wattles Family Collection, WCNB.

9. Castel, *Frontier State at War,* 42–43.

10. Emma Wattles to Sarah G. Wattles, June 9, 1861, Folder 3, Wattles Family Collection, WCNB.

11. Castel, *Frontier State at War,* 50.

12. Alisse Portnoy, *Their Right to Speak: Women's Activism in the Indian and Slave Debates* (Cambridge MA: Harvard University Press, 2005), 89–113.

13. Kristen Tegtmeier Oertel, *Bleeding Borders: Race, Gender, and Violence in Pre–Civil War Kansas* (Baton Rouge: Louisiana State University Press, 2009), 17–18, 35–40.

14. Ibid., 11–13.

15. John O. Wattles, "Slavery in Kansas," *Herald of Freedom,* January 13, 1855.

16. "The History of Kansas," *Herald of Freedom,* January 24, 1857.

17. Richard J. Hinton, *John Brown and His Men; with Some Account of the Roads They Traveled to Reach Harpers Ferry* (New York: Funk and Wagnalls, 1894), 67.

18. Elliott West, *The Contested Plains: Indians, Goldseekers, and the Rush to Colorado* (Lawrence: University Press of Kansas, 1998), 145–146.

19. S. W. Cone to F. R. Ford, May 12, 1860, Folder 10, Wattles Family Papers, WCNB. It is not clear what Park City referred to in the letter of introduction. A number of temporary mining camps were called Park City, especially in the early days of the Colorado gold rushes. There was a Park City, Colorado, located in Jackson County, but it began as a mining town after the Civil War. http://www.ghost towns.com/states/co/parkcity.html.

20. LeRoy R. Hafen, *Colorado and Its People: A Narrative and Topical History of the Centennial State*, vol. 1 (New York: Lewis Historical Publishing, 1948), 195. The Union Mining District was located in Clear Creek County near Empire. *Place Names of Colorado: A Genealogical and Historical Guide to Colorado* (Denver: Colorado Council of Genealogical Societies, 1999), 478, 654. http://digital.denver library.org/cdm/compoundobject/collection/p16079c01125/id/706/rec/2.

21. Mining Claim, September 15, 1860, Folder 10, Wattles Family Collection, WCNB.

22. Mining Claim, September 16, 1860, Folder 10, Wattles Family Collection, WCNB.

23. West, *Contested Plains*, 228–235, 258–263; Ned Blackhawk, *Violence over the Land: Indians and Empires in the Early American West* (Cambridge, MA: Harvard University Press, 2006), 205–208.

24. Emma Wattles to Sarah G. Wattles, May 30, 1861, Folder 3, Wattles Family Collection, WCNB.

25. Augustus Wattles to W. P. Dole, May 20, 1861, in Annie Heloise Abel, *The American Indian as Participant in the Civil War*, vol. 2 (Cleveland, OH: Arthur H. Clarke, 1919), 46–47 fn91.

26. David A. Nichols, *Lincoln and the Indian: Civil War Policy and Practices* (Columbia: University of Missouri Press, 1978), 22.

27. Augustus Wattles to W. P. Dole, September 25, 1861, *Supplement to the Official Records of the Union and Confederate Armies: Part I—Reports*, vol. 1, Serial No. 1 (Wilmington, NC: Broadfoot, 1994), 250–251.

28. Augustus Wattles to Susan E. Wattles, November 26, 1861, Curtis Collection, private possession of Patti Morse Curtis, Colorado Springs, Colorado (hereafter CC).

29. Augustus Wattles to Emma Wattles, December 5, 1861, CC.

30. "How the Indians Have Been Treated," *Sunday Mercury,* December 15, 1861.

31. E. B. French to Augustus Wattles, May 17, 1862, Folder 11, Wattles Family Collection, WCNB; Theodore W. Wattles to Augustus Wattles, March 8, 1863, Wattles Family Collection, WCNB; Emma Wattles to Augustus Wattles, April 1 1863, Folder 3, Wattles Family Collection, WCNB.

32. Stephen D. Andrews, "Which Threatens to Tear Our Fabric Asunder: The Opposition to American Spiritualism, 1848–1860," PhD diss., Stanford University, Palo Alto, California, 2005, 8–10; Ernest Joseph Isaacs, "A History of

Nineteenth-Century American Spiritualism as a Religious and Social Movement," PhD diss., University of Wisconsin, Madison, Wisconsin, 1975, 15–23; R. Laurence Moore, *In Search of White Crows: Spiritualism, Parapsychology, and American Culture* (New York: Oxford University Press, 1977), 6–7.

33. Drew Gilpin Faust, *This Republic of Suffering: Death and the American Civil War* (New York: Vintage, 2008), 180–185; Ann Braude, *Radical Spirits: Spiritualism and Women's Rights in Nineteenth-Century America* (Bloomington: Indiana University Press, 2001), xv–xxiii, 32–34, 38–40, 56–61, 70–71.

34. Mark Perry, *Lift Up Thy Voice: The Grimké Family's Journey from Slaveholders to Civil Rights Leaders* (New York: Penguin, 2001), 200–201.

35. Isaacs, "History of Nineteenth-Century American Spiritualism," 114; Harvey Wickes Felter, *Historical Sketch of the Eclectic Medical Institute, Cincinnati* (Cincinnati, OH: Lloyd Library, 1912); Braude, *Radical Spirits,* 19; "Spirit Knocking in Cincinnati," *Cleveland Plain Dealer,* October 26, 1850, 2.

36. Sarah M. Grimké to Augustus Wattles, February 1, 1852 in Weld-Grimké Papers, William L. Clements Library, University of Michigan, Ann Arbor, Michigan (hereafter UM). Mary Ann Wattles to Augustus Wattles, March 24, [1873], Folder 12, Wattles Family Collection, WCNB.

37. Braude, *Radical Spirits,* 145–146.

38. Moore, *In Search of White Crows,* 119–121.

39. Sarah M. Grimké to Augustus Wattles, February 1, 1852, in Weld-Grimké Papers, UM.

40. Augustus Wattles to Emma Wattles, December 5, 1861, CC. Emma Morrison was a family friend in Kansas who died in February 1861. Emma Wattles to Sarah Wattles, February 17, 1861, Folder 3, Wattles Family Papers, WCNB. Harriett Howells might have been the wife of Henry C. Howells, a member of several Fourierist communities and of the Raritan Bay Union, where Sarah Wattles came to know him. "Henry C. Howells," Peggy Jean Townsend and Charles Walker Townsend, *Milo Adams Townsend and Social Movements of the Nineteenth Century,* http://www.bchistory.org/beavercounty/booklengthdocuments/AMilobook /default.nclk; Dorothy Sterling, *Ahead of Her Time: Abby Kelley and the Politics of Anti-Slavery* (New York: Norton, 1991), 307.

41. Augustus Wattles to Susan Lowe Wattles, November 26, 1861, CC.

42. Susan Lowe Wattles to Augustus Wattles, December 22, 1861, Folder 16, Wattles Family Collection, WCNB.

43. Emma Wattles to Augustus Wattles, November 10, 1861, Folder 3, Wattles Family Collection, WCNB.

44. Susan Wattles to Augustus Wattles, December 10, 1862, Folder 16, Wattles Family Collection, WCNB.

45. Mary Ann Wattles to Augustus Wattles, April 17, 1864, Folder 11, Wattles Family Collection, WCNB.

46. Susan Wattles to Augustus Wattles, December 26, 1861, Folder 16, Wattles Family Collection, WCNB.

47. Mary Ann Wattles to Augustus Wattles, July 6, [1863], Folder 3, Wattles Family Collection, WCNB.

48. Both women apparently managed their farms quite well during the war. In the 1865 Kansas state census, Esther is listed as having real estate worth $4,080, and Augustus and Susan's real estate value stood at $3,000. This made Esther the seventh wealthiest property owner in Paris Township and the wealthiest female head of household. Because the vast majority of households held less than $500 in real estate, even Augustus and Susan were better off than most of their neighbors. Kansas State Census Collection, 1855–1925, Kansas State Historical Society (KSHS).

49. Susan Wattles to Augustus Wattles, November 17, 1861, Folder 16, Wattles Family Collection, WCNB.

50. Ibid.

51. Susan Wattles to Augustus Wattles, December 10, 1862, Folder 16, Wattles Family Collection, WCNB.

52. Susan Wattles to Augustus Wattles, December 28, 1862, Folder 16, Wattles Family Collection, WCNB. "Mr. Stearns" may have been John H. Stearns, about thirty years of age in 1862, originally from Vermont. He had been a member and president of the Moneka Women's Rights Association in 1858 and would remain in Mound City after the war, working as a schoolteacher. Secretary's Book for Moneka Woman's Rights Association, KSHS; Kansas State Census Collection; US Census 1870, 1910.

53. "Overview of Scrofula," http://emedicine.medscape.com/article/858234-overview.

54. Paul Starr, *The Social Transformation of American Medicine: The Rise of a Sovereign Profession and the Making of a Vast Industry* (New York: Basic Books, 1982), 30–31, 42.

55. Sarah M. Grimké to Augustus Wattles, February 1, 1852, in Weld-Grimké Papers, UM; Mary Ann Wattles to Augustus Wattles, March 24, [1873], Folder 12, Wattles Family Collection, WCNB.

56. Starr, *Social Transformation of American Medicine,* 53; "The Signs of the Times! Or a Complete History of the Mysterious Rappings in Cincinnati," *Cleveland Plain Dealer,* November 7, 1850, 2.

57. Starr, *Social Transformation of American Medicine,* 51; Jennifer J. Connor and J. T. H. Connor, "Thomsonian Medical Literature and Reformist Discourse in Upper Canada," *Canadian Literature: A Quarterly of Criticism and Review* 131 (Winter 1991): 141–142.

58. Susan E. Wattles to Augustus Wattles, August 29, 1847, Folder 6, Wattles Family Collection, WCNB; Susan E. Cayleff, *Wash and Be Healed: The Water Cure Movement and Women's Health* (Philadelphia, PA: Temple University Press, 1987), 83.

59. Cayleff, *Wash and Be Healed,* 2–3, 6–11, 23–24.

60. Ibid., 30, 85, 95, 114.

61. Jane B. Donegan, *"Hydropathic Highway to Health": Women and Water-Cure in Antebellum America* (New York: Greenwood, 1986), 56.

62. Cayleff, *Wash and Be Healed*, 94, 114.

63. William D. Conklin, *The Jackson Health Resort: Pioneer in Its Field as Seen by Those Who Knew It Well* (Dansville, NY: Dansville Public Library, 1971), 27.

64. Donegan, *"Hydropathic Highway to Health,"* 57.

65. Conklin, *Jackson Health Resort*, 17–18.

66. Emma Wattles to Augustus Wattles, April 1, 1863.

67. Ibid.

68. Emma Wattles to Augustus Wattles, November 19, 1862, Folder #3, Wattles Family Collection, WCNB.

69. Ibid.

70. Augustus Wattles to Emma Wattles, November 24, 1862, CC.

71. Emma Wattles to Augustus Wattles, November 28, 1862, Folder 3, Wattles Family Collection, WCNB.

72. Emma Wattles to Sarah Wattles, December 7, 1862, Folder 3, Wattles Family Collection, WCNB.

73. Augustus Wattles to Emma Wattles, 18 May 1863, CC.

74. Emma Wattles Morse to Susan E. Wattles, January 9, 1865, Folder 3, Wattles Family Collection, WCNB.

75. William Ansel Mitchell, *Linn County, Kansas: A History* (Kansas City, MO: Campbell-Gates, 1928), 130; Susan E. Wattles to Augustus Wattles, December 2, 1864, Folder 16, Wattles Family Collection, WCNB.

76. Sarah Wattles Hiatt to Susan E. Wattles, July 11, 1865, CC.

77. Susan E. Wattles to Augustus Wattles, March 2, 1863, Folder 16, Wattles Family Collection, WCNB.

78. Judith Giesberg, *Army at Home: Women and the Civil War on the Northern Home Front* (Chapel Hill: University of North Carolina Press, 2009), 10, 17–34; Elizabeth D. Leonard, *Yankee Women: Gender Battles in the Civil War* (New York: Norton, 1994), 169–166, 196–201.

79. Nina Silber, *Daughters of the Union: Northern Women Fight the Civil War* (Cambridge, MA: Harvard University Press, 2005), 248, 250–251, 263–264.

80. Elizabeth Cady Stanton, Susan B. Anthony, and Matilda Joslyn Gage, eds., *History of Woman Suffrage*, vol. 2: *1861–1876* (Rochester, NY: Susan B. Anthony, 1881), 255–256.

CHAPTER 5. THE WATTLES FAMILY IN THE CIVIL WAR, PART II:
FIGHTING FOR UNION AND MEMORY

1. Eaton Morse to Sarah Wattles, August 15, 1862, Curtis Collection, private possession of Patti Morse Curtis, Colorado Springs, Colorado (hereafter CC).

2. Ibid.

3. Emma Wattles to Sarah Wattles, March 25, 1860, Folder 10, Wattles Family Collection, Wilson's Creek National Battlefield, Republic, Missouri (hereafter WCNB); Theodore Wattles Morse, Application to the Sons of the American Revolution, 1925, Folder 20, Wattles Family Collection, WCNB; Moneka Woman's Rights Association, Preamble and Constitution, 1858, Kansas State Historical Society, Topeka, Kansas (KSHS).

4. Sarah Wattles to Augustus Wattles, February 9, 1862.

5. I am using the masculine here because the vast majority of soldiers in the Civil War were male. This is not to diminish the role of women who participated in the Civil War, whether dressed as male soldiers or as nurses or in other roles. It is certainly not meant to diminish the role of women as soldiers in modern warfare. Now that women share that responsibility, they too are subject to the transformational influences of war, some of which disproportionately affect women, such as sexual assault.

6. Sarah Wattles to Susan Wattles, August 25, 1861, Folder 8, Wattles Family Collection, WCNB.

7. Henry Mayer, *All on Fire: William Lloyd Garrison and the Abolition of Slavery* (New York: St. Martin's, 1998), 520, 551; Harriet Hyman Alonso, *Growing Up Abolitionist: The Story of the Garrison Children* (Amherst: University of Massachusetts Press, 2002), 2, 163.

8. Sarah Wattles to Susan Wattles, September 12, 1861, Folder 8, Wattles Family Collection, WCNB; Emma Wattles to Augustus Wattles, May 4, 1862, CC.

9. Susan Wattles to Augustus Wattles, May 25, 1862, Folder 16, Wattles Family Collection, WCNB.

10. Susan and Mary Wattles to Augustus Wattles, December 22, 1861, Folder 16, Wattles Family Collection, WCNB.

11. Susan Wattles to Augustus Wattles, May 4, 1862, Folder 16, Wattles Family Collection, WCNB.

12. Theodore W. Wattles to Augustus Wattles, November 26, 1862, Wattles Family Collection, WCNB.

13. William H. Burnside, *The Honorable Powell Clayton* (Conway: University of Central Arkansas Press, 1991), 11.

14. Ibid., 12; James McPherson, *The Battle Cry of Freedom: The Civil War Era* (New York: Oxford University Press, 1988), 578–579.

15. Theodore W. Wattles to Susan E. Wattles, December 17, 1862, Wattles Family Collection, WCNB.

16. Emma Wattles to Sarah Wattles Hiatt, March 17, 1863, Folder 3, Wattles Family Collection, WCNB.

17. Emma Wattles to Augustus Wattles, March 25, 1863, Folder 3, Wattles Family Collection, WCNB

18. Theodore W. Wattles to Susan Lowe Wattles, June 12, 1863, Wattles Family Collection, WCNB.

19. Thomas A. DeBlack, "1863: "We Must Stand or Fall Alone," in *Rugged and Sublime: The Civil War in Arkansas,* ed. Mark K. Christ (Fayetteville: University of Arkansas Press, 1994), 78–82; Thomas A. DeBlack, *With Fire and Sword: Arkansas, 1861–1874* (Fayetteville: University of Arkansas Press, 2003), 89–92.

20. Theodore W. Wattles to Augustus Wattles, July 15, 1863, Wattles Family Collection, WCNB.

21. DeBlack, "1863," 84.

22. DeBlack, *With Fire and Sword,* 90–97; *Encyclopedia of Arkansas History and Culture,* http://www.encyclopediaofarkansas.net/encyclopedia/entry-detail.aspx?entryID=908 (accessed August 15, 2015).

23. DeBlack, *With Fire and Sword,* 99–101.

24. Emma Wattles to Augustus Wattles, December 5, 1863, Folder 3, Wattles Family Collection, WCNB.

25. *Encyclopedia of Arkansas History and Culture,* http://www.encyclopediaof arkansas.net/encyclopedia/entry-detail.aspx?entryID=94 (accessed April 7, 2015).

26. Emma Wattles to Augustus Wattles, May 4, 1862.

27. Susan Wattles to Augustus Wattles, May 25, 1862, Folder 3, Wattles Family Collection, WCNB. It is not clear when Clayton stopped sending slaves back to their masters, but certainly he ceased to do so after the Emancipation Proclamation came into effect on January 1, 1863. In Pine Bluff in late 1863, Clayton set up "contraband camps" to accommodate the hundreds of former slaves seeking the protection of the Union forces. DeBlack, *With Fire and Sword,* 99.

28. Emma Wattles to Augustus Wattles, November 28, 1862, Folder 3, Wattles Family Collection, WCNB.

29. Eaton wrote to Emma, "I have a recommendation from Col Clayton that of itself almost pays me for my three years since I shall presume it as one of my laurels. When I have more time I will send you a copy of it I value it because the Col was disinterested in giving it and was sincere what he sais regarding me." O. E. Morse to Emma Wattles, August 24, 1864, CC.

30. O. E. Morse to Emma Wattles, February 2, 1864, CC.

31. Burnside, *Powell Clayton,* 15.

32. Eaton Morse to Emma Wattles, July 31, 1864, CC.

33. Burnside, *Powell Clayton,* 116.

34. Eaton Morse to Emma Wattles, June 26, 1864, CC.

35. Ibid.

36. Stephen V. Ash, *When the Yankees Came: Conflict and Chaos in the Occupied South, 1861–1865* (Chapel Hill: University of North Carolina Press, 1995), 84–85.

37. Ibid., 25–29, 42–43, 50–51.

38. Drew Gilpin Faust, *Mothers of Invention: Women of the Slaveholding South in the American Civil War* (Chapel Hill: University of North Carolina Press, 1996), 196.

39. Ibid., 198–200.

40. Ash, *When the Yankees Came,* 30.

41. Cita Cook, "The Practical Ladies of Occupied Natchez," in *Occupied Women: Gender, Military Occupation, and the American Civil War,* ed. LeeAnn Whites and Alecia P. Long (Baton Rouge: Louisiana State University Press, 2009), 122.

42. Faust, *Mothers of Invention,* 209–210.

43. LeeAnn Whites and Alecia P. Long, "Introduction," in *Occupied Women: Gender, Military Occupation, and the American Civil War,* ed. Whites and Long (Baton Rouge: Louisiana State University Press, 2009), 9; Alecia P. Long, "(Mis)Remembering General Order No. 28: Benjamin Butler, the Woman Order, and Historical Memory," in ibid., 17; LeeAnn Whites, "'Corresponding with the Enemy': Mobilizing the Relational Field of Battle in St. Louis," in ibid., 105.

44. Whites and Long, "Introduction," *Occupied Women,* 7.

45. Ash, *When the Yankees Came,* 76–77.

46. O. E. Morse to Emma Wattles, January 20, 1864, CC.

47. O. E. Morse to Emma Wattles, January 31, 1864, CC.

48. O. E. Morse to Emma Wattles, February 13, 1864, CC.

49. O. E. Morse to Emma Wattles, January 31, 1864.

50. O. E. Morse to Emma Morse, March 11, 1864, CC.

51. O. E. Morse to Emma Morse, April 10, 1864, CC.

52. Nina Silber, *Daughters of the Union: Northern Women Fight the Civil War* (Cambridge, MA: Harvard University Press, 2005), 252–256.

53. O. E. Morse to Emma Wattles, March 11, 1864.

54. O. E. Morse to Emma Wattles, April 10, 1864.

55. DeBlack, *With Fire and Sword,* 104–108.

56. United Confederate Veterans of Arkansas, *Confederate Women of Arkansas in the Civil War 1861–1865: Memorial Reminiscences* (Little Rock: United Confederate Veterans of Arkansas, 1907), 27.

57. DeBlack, *With Fire and Sword,* 112.

58. United Confederate Veterans of Arkansas, *Confederate Women of Arkansas,* 143.

59. Ibid.

60. O. E. Morse to Emma Wattles, January 10, 1864, CC.

61. Theodore W. Wattles to Augustus Wattles, April 7, 1863, Wattles Family Collection, WCNB.

62. Eric T. Dean Jr., *Shook over Hell: Post-Traumatic Stress, Vietnam, and the Civil War* (Cambridge, MA: Harvard University Press, 1997), 61–62.

63. Emma Wattles to Augustus Wattles, May 4, 1862, Folder 3, Wattles Family Collection, WCNB.

64. O. E. Morse to Emma Wattles, January 20, 1864.

65. Theodore W. Wattles to Augustus Wattles, January 24, 1864, Wattles Family Collection, WCNB.

66. DeBlack, *With Fire and Sword,* 108–115.

67. O. E. Morse to Emma Wattles, May 1, 1864, CC.

68. O. E. Morse to Emma Wattles, June 26, 1864, CC.

69. O. E. Morse to Emma Wattles, August 24, 1864, CC.

70. Augustus Wattles to Emma Wattles, October 17, 1864, CC.

71. Theodore W. Wattles to Augustus Wattles, October 5, 1865, Wattles Family Collection, WCNB.

72. Theodore W. Wattles to Augustus Wattles, April 15, 1865, Wattles Family Collection, WCNB.

73. Theodore W. Wattles to Augustus Wattles, May 14, 1865, Wattles Family Collection, WCNB.

74. Alan T. Nolan, "The Anatomy of the Myth," in *The Myth of the Lost Cause and Civil War History*, ed. Gary W. Gallagher and Alan T. Nolan (Bloomington: Indiana University Press, 2000), 14–21.

75. David S. Reynolds, *John Brown, Abolitionist: The Man Who Killed Slavery, Sparked the Civil War, and Seeded Civil Rights* (New York: Knopf, 2005), 486–487; Julie Roy Jeffrey, *Abolitionists Remember: Antislavery Autobiographies and the Unfinished Work of Emancipation* (Chapel Hill: University of North Carolina Press, 2008), 155–163; David W. Blight, *Race and Reunion: The Civil War in American Memory* (Cambridge, MA: Harvard University Press, 2001), 89–97, 138–139.

76. Bonnie Laughlin-Schultz, *The Tie That Bound Us: The Women of John Brown's Family and the Legacy of Radical Abolitionism* (Ithaca, NY: Cornell University Press, 2013), 115–116; Merrill D. Peterson, *John Brown: The Legend Revisited* (Charlottesville: University of Virginia Press, 2002), 60–65.

77. G. W. Brown, *The Truth at Last. History Corrected. Reminiscences of Old John Brown. Thrilling Incidents of Border Life in Kansas* (Rockford, IL: Abraham E. Smith, 1880), 1.

78. George W. Brown, *False Claims of Kansas Historians Truthfully Corrected* (Rockford, IL: G. W. Brown, 1902).

79. Laughlin-Schultz, *Tie That Bound Us*, 126–128.

80. F. G. Adams to O. E. Morse, July 14, 1887, Note A in O. E. Morse, "An Attempted Rescue of John Brown from Charlestown, VA, Jail," *Kansas State Historical Society Collections* 8 (1903–1904), 224.

81. Ibid., 213–225.

82. Ibid., 220.

83. US Congress, Senate. Select Committee on the Harper's Ferry Invasion, "Invasion at Harper's Ferry" (New York: Arno, 1969), 219–222.

84. Theodore Botkin to Franklin G. Adams, June 16, 1887, Franklin G. Adams Papers, KSHS.

85. Susan E. Wattles to Emma Wattles Morse, July 1, 1887, CC.

86. Sarah G. Wattles Hiatt to Emma Wattles Morse, October 3, 1887, CC.

87. Ibid.

88. Mrs. O. E. [Emma Wattles] Morse, "Sketch of the Life and Work of Augustus Wattles," *Collections of the Kansas State Historical Society* 17 (1926–1928), 298–299.

89. Powell Clayton to Capt. O. E. Morse, August 11, 1887, O. E. Morse Papers, KSHS.

90. Blight, *Race and Reunion*, 66–67, 171–175, 255–256.

91. "Written for the W. R. C. Presidents Part of the Ritual at the Memorial Services in the Cemetery of M'd City Kans on May 30th 1906, by Mrs Sarah G. W. Hiatt, Pres, W.R.C.," O. E. Morse Papers, KSHS.

CHAPTER 6. "MY DEAR DOCTOR":
THE MEDICAL CAREERS OF THE WATTLES SISTERS

1. Emily Blackwell to Elizabeth Blackwell, August 12, 1878, Container 93, Blackwell Family Papers, Library of Congress, Washington, DC.

2. Carla Bittel, *Mary Putnam Jacobi and the Politics of Medicine in Nineteenth-Century America* (Chapel Hill: University of North Carolina Press, 2009), 100–109; Carla Bittel, "Science, Suffrage, and Experimentation: Mary Putnam Jacobi and the Controversy over Vivisection in Late Nineteenth-Century America," *Bulletin of the History of Medicine* 79 (2005): 664–694; Regina Morantz-Sanchez, *Sympathy and Science: Women Physicians in American Medicine* (New York: Oxford University Press, 1985), 184–202; Susan Wells, *Out of the Dead House: Nineteenth-Century Women Physicians and the Writing of Medicine* (Madison: University of Wisconsin Press, 2001), 146–192.

3. "Autobiography of Elizabeth Cushier," in *Medical Women of America: A Short History of the Pioneer Medical Women of America and Their Colleagues in England,* ed. Kate Campbell Hurd-Mead and Elizabeth Burr Thelberg (New York: Froben Press, 1933), 85–95; Lillian Faderman, *To Believe in Women: What Lesbians Have Done for America—A History* (Boston: Mariner, 2000), 278, 289.

4. Sarah J. McNutt, *Medical Women Yesterday and Today* (New York: William Wood, 1918), 4; S. S. Horn and G. G. Goetz, "The Election of Sarah McNutt as the First Woman Member of the American Neurological Association," *Neurology* 59, no. 1 (2002): 113–117.

5. Woman's Medical College of the New York Infirmary, *Sixteenth Annual Catalogue and Announcement, June 1884* (G. P. Putnam's Sons, 1884), 21–22.

6. Ellen S. More, *Restoring the Balance: Women Physicians and the Profession of Medicine, 1850–1995* (Cambridge, MA: Harvard University Press, 1999), 2–3, 23–24.

7. Lundy's parents, Eli and Hannah Morrow Hiatt, were Quaker abolitionists originally from Guilford County, North Carolina. They moved first to Ohio, then to Indiana, where their widowed daughter Tilney married David Lowe, brother of Susan Lowe. David Lowe adopted Tilney's son, Eli, who took the Lowe name. David and Tilney had two children of their own. Hiatt family genealogy, Linn County Historical Society, Pleasanton, Kansas.

8. "Obituary: Eli Hiatt," *Pleasanton Observer,* April 10, 1886; "Obituary: Sarah Wattles Hiatt," *Pleasanton Observer,* November 5, 1910, Clippings Book, Sommer-

ville Library, Mound City, Kansas; Lundy B. Hiatt to David P. Lowe, November 30, 1864, David P. Lowe Papers, Mound City Historical Society, Mound City, Kansas (hereafter MCHS).

9. Kenneth M. Ludmerer, *Learning to Heal: The Development of American Medical Education* (Baltimore, MD: Johns Hopkins University Press, 1985), 11–24; Arleen Marcia Tuchman, *Science, Medicine, and the State in Germany: The Case of Baden, 1815–1871* (New York: Oxford University Press, 1993), 5–11.

10. Leslie B. Arey, *Northwestern University Medical School, 1859–1959: A Pioneer in Educational Reform* (Evanston, IL: Northwestern University Press, 1959), 32–36.

11. Lundy B. Hiatt to David P. Lowe, November 30, 1864.

12. Sarah Grimké to Sarah Wattles Hiatt, January 19, 1865, in Weld-Grimké Papers, William L. Clements Library, University of Michigan, Ann Arbor, Michigan (hereafter UM).

13. James D. Ivy, *"No Saloon in the Valley": The Southern Strategy of Texas Prohibitionists in the 1880s* (Waco, TX: Baylor University Press, 2003), 8–9; Alwyn Barr, *Reconstruction to Reform: Texas Politics, 1876–1906* (Austin: University of Texas Press, 1971), 9–15.

14. Cathy Luchetti, *Medicine Women: The Story of Early-American Women Doctors* (New York: Crown, 1998), 97–99, 109–116.

15. Sarah Wattles Hiatt to Esther Wattles, March 6, 1887, John O. Wattles Papers, Western Reserve Historical Society, Cleveland, Ohio (hereafter WRHS).

16. Sarah Wattles Hiatt to Mary Ann Wattles, February 26, 1878, David P. Lowe Papers, MCHS.

17. Mary Kelley, *Learning to Stand and Speak: Women, Education, and Public Life in America's Republic* (Chapel Hill: University of North Carolina Press, 2006), 123–132, 144–145.

18. Elizabeth Cady Stanton, Susan B. Anthony, and Matilda Joslyn Gage, eds., *History of Woman Suffrage*, vol. 3 (New York: Arno/New York Times, 1969), 803.

19. James D. Ivy, "'The Lone Star Surrenders to a Lone Woman': Frances Willard's Forgotten 1882 Texas Temperance Tour," *Southwestern Historical Quarterly* 102, no. 1 (July 1998), 45–46, 51.

20. Ivy, *"No Saloon in the Valley,"* 4, 10, 21–25.

21. Sarah Wattles Hiatt to Emma Wattles Morse, February 11, 1887, Curtiss Collection, private possession of Patti Morse Curtis, Colorado Springs, Colorado (hereafter CC).

22. Sarah Wattles Hiatt to Emma Wattles Morse, June 21, 1880, CC.

23. US Census Bureau, US Census, 1880, Denton County, Texas.

24. Sarah G. Wattles Hiatt to Emma Wattles Morse, May 6, 1888, CC.

25. On the growth of opportunities for higher education for women, see Barbara Miller Solomon, *In the Company of Educated Women: A History of Women and Higher Education in America* (New Haven, CT: Yale University Press, 1985).

26. Mary Ann Wattles Faunce, "Recollections of a Grandmother," (1920s), handwritten manuscript, in Mary Ann Wattles Faunce Collection, private

possession of Carol Ann Wetherill Getz, Alamosa, Colorado (hereafter Faunce Collection).

27. Carol Ann Wetherill Getz, interview with Lynne Getz, January 30, 2007, Alamosa, Colorado.

28. Mary Ann Kipp Hairgrove, interview with Lynne Getz, May 22, 2012, Del Norte, Colorado.

29. Mary Ann Wattles to Sarah Wattles, July 8, 1860, Folder 10, Wattles Family Collection, WCNB.

30. Thomas D. Hamm, *God's Government Begun: The Society for Universal Inquiry and Reform, 1842–1846* (Bloomington: Indiana University Press), 224.

31. Mary Ann Wattles Faunce Alumnae File, Oberlin College Alumni Records 28, Oberlin College Archives, Oberlin, Ohio.

32. Anna Eugenia Morgan and Elizabeth Mary Anne Morgan Alumnae Files, Oberlin College Alumni Records 28, Oberlin College Archives, Oberlin Ohio.

33. Helen Goodwin Renwick Alumnae File, Oberlin College Alumni Records 28, Oberlin College Archives.

34. Ruth Jocelyn Wattles to Leila Deborah Smith, undated, Wattles Family Collection, WRHS.

35. Mary Ann Wattles to Susan E. Wattles, [1879], Folder 17, Wattles Family Collection, WCNB.

36. Emily Blackwell to Elizabeth Blackwell, October 11, 1869, Box 11, Folder 164, Blackwell Papers, Schlesinger Library, Harvard University, Cambridge, Massachusetts.

37. Dorothy Clark Wilson, *Lone Woman: The Story of Elizabeth Blackwell, the First Woman Doctor* (Boston: Little, Brown, 1970), 99–100.

38. Morantz-Sanchez, *Sympathy and Science*, 49, 70; Steven J. Peitzman, *A New and Untried Course: Woman's Medical College and Medical College of Pennsylvania, 1850–1998* (New Brunswick, NJ: Rutgers University Press, 2000), 5–13.

39. Woman's Medical College of the New York Infirmary, *Sixteenth Annual Catalogue and Announcement*, 6.

40. Morantz-Sanchez, *Sympathy and Science*, 70–76; Annie Sturgeon Daniel, "'A Cautious Experiment': The History of the New York Infirmary for Women and Children and the Woman's Medical College of the New York Infirmary; Also Its Pioneer Founders, 1853–1899," *Medical Woman's Journal* 46 (May–December 1939): 196–202 (hereafter *MWJ* with volume number); Bittel, *Mary Putnam Jacobi*, 104–106.

41. Annie Sturgeon Daniel, "'A Cautious Experiment,': The History of the New York Infirmary for Women and Children and the Woman's Medical College of the New York Infirmary; Also Its Pioneer Founders, 1853–1899," *Medical Woman's Journal* 48 (April 1941), 102 (hereafter *MWJ* with volume number).

42. Mary A. Wattles, *Valedictory Address Delivered at the Second Annual Commencement of the Woman's Medical College of the New York Infirmary, March 28th, 1871* (New York: S. Angell, 1871), 3–12.

43. Woman's Medical College of the New York Infirmary, *Sixteenth Annual Catalogue and Announcement*, 7.

44. Daniel, "'A Cautious Experiment,'" *MWJ* vol. 48, 36, 272.

45. Thomas Neville Bonner, *To the Ends of the Earth: Women's Search for Education in Medicine* (Cambridge, MA: Harvard University Press, 1992), 7–8, 26–27.

46. Mary Ann's study in Europe was financed by her uncle, David Ripley, husband of Mary Ann Wattles Ripley. Ripley owned a large sawmill and packing-box plant in Newark, New Jersey, and frequently gave money to both Augustus and John Wattles for their travels and activities. After the death of John Wattles, David Ripley promised to pay for the education of John's daughters. Celestia, Harmonia, and Theano Wattles all attended Oberlin College and later studied and traveled in Europe with David Ripley's assistance.

47. Elizabeth M. Cushier to Mary Ann Wattles, December 12, 1875, Faunce Collection.

48. Bonner, *To the Ends of the Earth*, 35.

49. Cushier to Wattles, December 12, 1875.

50. Ibid.

51. Ibid.

52. E. B. Ryder to Mary Ann Wattles, November 12, 1876, Faunce Collection.

53. Ibid.

54. E. B. Ryder to Mary Ann Wattles, February 6, 1877, Faunce Collection.

55. Roy Porter, *The Greatest Benefit to Mankind: A Medical History of Humanity* (New York: Norton, 1997): 370–373.

56. Mary Ann Wattles to Emily Blackwell, January 8, 1876, Box 13, Blackwell Papers, MC411, Schlesinger Library, Harvard University, Cambridge, Massachusetts.

57. A. D. H. Kelsey to Mary Ann Wattles, November 8, 1875, Faunce Collection.

58. Ibid.; Samuel Willetts to David Ripley, November 29, 1875; David Ripley to Mary Ann Wattles, December 1875, Faunce Collection.

59. Daniel, "'A Cautious Experiment,'" *MWJ* 48, 36, 235, 273, 276–277; Woman's Medical College of the New York Infirmary, *Annual Catalogue and Announcement*, 1869–1889; Board of Trustees of the New York Infirmary, Minutes, Annual Meetings, Cornell University Medical Center Archives, New York, New York. Mary Ann Wattles Faunce was reappointed to work in the infirmary and dispensary annually from 1872 to 1891, with the exception of 1875–1876, when she studied in Europe.

60. Mary Ann Wattles to Susan E. Wattles, September 8, 1879, Folder 12, Wattles Family Collection, WCNB.

61. Edward B. Hill to Drs. Wattles and McNutt, May 1, 1879, Faunce Collection.

62. Mary Ann Wattles to Susan E. Wattles, October 13, 1879, Folder 12, Wattles Family Collection, WCNB.

63. Mary Ann Wattles to Susan E. Wattles, September 8, 1879.

64. Mary Ann Wattles to Susan E. Wattles, May 11, 1880, Folder 4, Wattles Family Collection, WCNB.

65. Mary Ann Wattles to Susan E. Wattles, October 13, 1879.

66. Mary Ann Wattles to Susan E. Wattles, September 8, 1879.

67. Ellen More, "The Blackwell Society and the Professionalization of Women Physicians," *Bulletin of the History of Medicine* 61 (1987): 603–608; Cora Bagley Marrett, "On The Evolution of Women's Medical Societies," *Bulletin of the History of Medicine* 53 (1979): 434–435, 445.

68. Ellen A. Wallace to Mary Ann Wattles, March 30, 1885; Gertrude A. Farwell to Mary Ann Wattles Faunce, February 1, 1886; Invitation, Women's Medical Association of New York City, Memorial in Honor of Dr. Elizabeth Blackwell and Dr. Emily Blackwell, January 1911, Faunce Collection.

69. Morantz-Sanchez, *Sympathy and Science*, 126–136; More, *Restoring the Balance*, 23–24.

70. L. Celestia Wattles to Mary Ann Wattles, September 9, 1880, Faunce Collection; Isidore Faunce to Mary Ann Wattles Faunce, December 16, 1883, Faunce Collection; Ruth J. Wattles to Hilda Wetherill Kipp, undated, Faunce Collection.

71. Mary Ann Wattles Faunce to Theodore W. Wattles, July 26, 1882, Faunce Collection; Mary Ann Wattles Faunce to Emma Wattles Morse, May 10, 1887, CC.

72. Wattles-Faunce-Wetherill family genealogy, compiled by Hilda Faunce Wetherill, Faunce Collection.

73. Board of Trustees of the New York Infirmary, Minutes, Annual Meeting, November 12, 1891; Woman's Medical College of New York, *Annual Catalogue and Announcement*, 1888–1889.

74. Susan E. Wattles to Mary Ann Wattles Faunce, December 24, 1884, Faunce Collection.

75. Mary Ann Wattles Faunce to Emma Wattles Morse, April 16, 1888, CC; Mary Ann Wattles Faunce to Emma Wattles Morse, March 15, 1889, CC.

76. Mary Ann Wattles Faunce to Emma Wattles Morse, May 10, 1887.

77. Mary Ann Wattles Faunce to Emma Wattles Morse, April 16, 1888.

78. Mary Ann Wattles Faunce to Emma Wattles Morse, May 10, 1887.

79. Mary Ann Wattles Faunce to Emma Wattles Morse, April 16, 1887, CC.

80. Eliza B. Phelps to Mary Ann Wattles, August 31, 1885, Faunce Collection.

81. Sarah Wattles Hiatt to Mary Ann Wattles Faunce, July 2, 1885, Faunce Collection.

82. Susan E. Wattles to Emma Wattles Morse, January 25, 1885, CC.

83. Mary Ann Wattles Faunce to Emma Wattles Morse, February 1, 1885, CC.

84. Susan E. Wattles to Emma Wattles Morse, November 15, 1887, CC.

85. Susan E. Wattles to Emma Wattles Morse, October 4, 1885, CC.

86. Ibid.

87. Susan E. Wattles to Emma Wattles Morse, March 26, 1886, CC.

88. Susan E. Wattles to Emma Wattles Morse, March 7, 1888, CC.

89. Leila J. Rupp, *Worlds of Women: The Making of an International Women's Movement* (Princeton, NJ: Princeton University Press, 1997), 15–21; Susan B. Anthony and Ida Husted Harper, eds., *The History of Woman Suffrage*, vol. 4, (Indianapolis: Hollenbeck, 1902), 124–128.

90. Anthony and Husted, *History of Woman Suffrage*, vol. 4, 136–137.

91. Sarah Wattles Hiatt to Emma Wattles Morse, May 6, 1888, CC. Annie Diggs was a prominent Populist, temperance leader, and suffragist who lived in Lawrence, Kansas. She was president of the Women's Alliance in Washington, DC, the Kansas Woman's Free Silver League, and the Kansas Equal Suffrage Association among other organizations. She lectured across the United States on Populism, temperance, and suffrage.

92. Susan E. Wattles to Emma Wattles Morse, January 26, 1890, CC.

93. Emily Blackwell to Mary Ann Wattles Faunce, November 7, 1893, Faunce Collection.

94. Sarah Wattles Hiatt to Mary Ann Wattles, July 23, 1879, Faunce Collection.

95. Sarah Wattles Hiatt to Mary Ann Wattles Faunce, July 3, 1885, Faunce Collection.

96. Mary Ann Wattles Faunce to Emma Wattles Morse, November 15, 1885, CC.

97. Sarah Wattles Hiatt to Mary Ann Wattles Faunce and Susan E. Wattles, October 16, 1885, Faunce Collection.

98. Sarah Wattles Hiatt to Mary Ann Wattles Faunce, January 10, 1892, Faunce Collection.

99. Sarah Wattles Hiatt to Emma Wattles Morse, January 15, 1888, CC.

100. Lundy B. Hiatt gravestone, Chinn's Chapel Cemetery, Copper Canyon, Denton County, Texas.

101. Sarah Wattles Hiatt to Mary Ann Wattles Faunce, February 21 1893, Faunce Collection.

102. Sarah Wattles Hiatt to Mary Ann Wattles Faunce, July 31, 1893, Faunce Collection.

103. Sarah Wattles Hiatt to Mary Ann Wattles Faunce, September 7, 1894, Faunce Collection.

104. Theodore W. Wattles to Susan E. Wattles, June 25, 1895, CC.

105. Sarah Wattles Hiatt to Mary Ann Wattles Faunce, July 25, 1896, Faunce Collection.

106. Sarah Wattles Hiatt to Mary Ann Wattles Faunce, August 2, 1893, Faunce Collection.

107. Sarah Wattles Hiatt to Mary Ann Wattles Faunce, July 30, 1896, Faunce Collection; Sarah Wattles Hiatt to Mary Ann Wattles Faunce, January 20, 1897, Faunce Collection.

108. Sarah Wattles Hiatt to Mary Ann Wattles Faunce, February 24, 1897, Faunce Collection; Sarah Wattles Hiatt to Mary Ann Wattles Faunce, June 12, 1897, Faunce Collection.

109. Mary Ann Wattles Faunce to Susan E. Wattles, December 27, 1897, CC.

110. "Sarah Wattles Hiatt," November 5, 1910, obituary, Clippings File, Sommerville Public Library, Mound City, Kansas.

CHAPTER 7. A WESTERING FAMILY:
THE WATTLES-FAUNCES AS SETTLER COLONISTS

1. Theodore W. Wattles to Susan E. Wattles, February 13, 1880, Curtis Collection, private possession of Patti Morse Curtis, Colorado Springs, Colorado (hereafter CC).

2. Margaret D. Jacobs, *White Mother to a Dark Race: Settler Colonialism, Maternalism, and the Removal of Indigenous Children in the American West and Australia, 1880–1940* (Lincoln: University of Nebraska Press, 2009), 2–7.

3. Patrick Wolfe, "Settler Colonialism and the Elimination of the Native," *Journal of Genocide Research* 8, no. 4 (December 2006): 388.

4. Kristen Tegtmeier Oertel, *Bleeding Borders: Race, Gender, and Violence in Pre–Civil War Kansas* (Baton Rouge: Louisiana State University Press, 2009), 10–15.

5. Adele Perry, *Colonial Relations: The Douglas-Connolly Family and the Nineteenth-Century Imperial World* (New York: Cambridge University Press, 2015), 128–130.

6. "Theodore W. Wattles," obituary, 1912, Clippings File, Linn County Historical File, Pleasanton, Kansas.

7. Frank McNitt, *The Indian Traders* (Norman: University of Oklahoma Press, 1962), 144; Martha Blue, *Indian Trader: The Life and Times of J. L. Hubbell* (Walnut, CA: Kiva Press, 2000), 22–23.

8. McNitt, *Indian Traders*, 154–160.

9. Ibid., 162.

10. Theodore Wattles to Susan Wattles, December 16, 1875, CC.

11. Kathy M'Closkey, *Swept under the Rug: A Hidden History of Navajo Weaving* (Albuquerque: University of New Mexico Press, 2002), 31.

12. Theodore Wattles to Susan Wattles, December 16, 1875.

13. "Draft to Messrs. Wattles & Beardsley," Parrott City, Colorado, October 18, 1876; Quit Claim Deed, Benjamin Ford to Theodore W. Wattles & Frank Morgan, September 5, 1877, La Plata County, Colorado, Folder Wattles Family Papers, Box 2, Ruth Jocelyn Wattles Collection, Special Collections, Colorado State University, Fort Collins, Colorado; Sarah Platt Decker Chapter of the Daughters of the American Revolution, *Pioneers of the San Juan Country*, vol. 1 (Colorado Springs, CO: Out West Printing and Stationary, 1942), 72.

14. Robert L. Brown, *An Empire of Silver: A History of the San Juan Silver Rush* (Caldwell, ID: Caxton, 1965), 27–30.

15. Ibid., 57–74; Phyllis Flanders Dorset, *The New Eldorado: The Story of Colorado's Gold and Silver Rushes* (New York: Macmillan, 1970), 208–209.

16. Fern D. Ellis, *Come Back to My Valley: Historical Remembrances of Mancos, Colorado* (Cortez, CO: Southwest Printing, 1976), 1–3; Theodore Wattles to Susan Wattles, August 16 1878, CC.

17. Theodore W. Wattles to Susan Wattles, May 23, 1879, CC.

18. Theodore W. Wattles to Susan Wattles, February 4, 1879, CC.

19. Ibid.

20. Theodore W. Wattles to Mary Ann Wattles, January 19, 1879, Faunce Collection.

21. Theodore W. Wattles to Susan E. Wattles, April 6, 1882, CC.

22. Theodore W. Wattles to Susan Wattles, July 26, 1879, CC.

23. Virginia McConnell Simmons, *The Ute Indians of Utah, Colorado, and New Mexico* (Boulder, CO: University Press of Colorado, 2000), 14–23, 86–87, 131–132, 179–191; Ned Blackhawk, *Violence over the Land: Indians and Empires in the Early American West* (Cambridge, MA: Harvard University Press, 2006), 219–225.

24. Elliot West, *The Contested Plains: Indians, Goldseekers, and the Rush to Colorado* (Lawrence: University Press of Kansas, 1998), 189–191.

25. Theodore W. Wattles to Susan Wattles, November 24, 1878, CC.

26. Theodore W. Wattles to Susan Wattles, March 3, 1880, CC.

27. Theodore W. Wattles to Susan Wattles, July 26, 1885, Folder 4, Wattles Family Collection, Wilson's Creek National Battlefield, Republic, Missouri (hereafter WCNB).

28. Theodore W. Wattles to Susan Wattles, June 28, 1885, Folder 4, Wattles Family Collection, WCNB.

29. Melvina H. Wattles to Mary Ann Wattles Faunce, January 3, 1886, Folder 4, Wattles Family Collection, WCNB.

30. Thomas Hamm, *God's Government Begun: The Society for Universal Inquiry and Reform, 1842–1846* (Bloomington: Indiana University Press, 1995), 220.

31. Joanne E. Passet, *Sex Radicals and the Quest for Women's Equality* (Urbana: University of Illinois Press, 2003), 148–149; Hal D. Sears, *The Sex Radicals: Free Love in High Victorian America* (Lawrence: Regents Press of Kansas, 1977), 204–208.

32. Theodore W. Wattles to Susan E. Wattles, February 5, 1885, Folder 4, Wattles Family Collection, WCNB.

33. Melvina H. Wattles to Susan Wattles, May 8, 1885, Folder 4, Wattles Family Collection, WCNB.

34. Ibid.

35. Melvina H. Wattles to Susan Wattles, June 28, 1885, Folder 13, Wattles Family Collection, WCNB.

36. Theodore W. Wattles to Susan Wattles, June 28, 1885, Folder 13, Wattles Family Collection, WCNB.

37. Theodore W. Wattles to Susan Wattles, July 26, 1885.

38. Melvina H. Wattles to Susan Wattles, December 21, 1890, Folder 2, Wattles Family Collection, WCNB.

39. Wilton L. Morse to Susan Wattles, October 1, 1891. Although Wilton did not say so, the school building where he taught was called the Wattles School because Theodore had been on the school board and had hauled the lumber to build it. Ellis, *Come Back to My Valley*, 92–97.

40. Sarah Wattles Hiatt to Mary Ann Wattles Faunce, September 7, 1894, Faunce Collection; Melvina H. Wattles to Mary Ann Wattles Faunce, February 17, 1895, Faunce Collection.

41. Wilton Morse to Susan Wattles, October 1, 1891.

42. Patti Morse Curtis, interview with Lynne Getz, May 17, 2012, Colorado Springs, Colorado; Ellis, *Come Back to My Valley*, 97.

43. Theodore W. Wattles to Susan Wattles, June 16, 1889, CC.

44. Sarah Wattles Hiatt to Mary Ann Wattles Faunce, March 20, 1894, Faunce Collection.

45. Melvina H. Wattles to Susan Wattles, July 29, 1889, CC.

46. Theodore W. Wattles to Mary Ann Wattles Faunce, May 1, 1891, Faunce Collection; Theodore W. Wattles to Mary Ann Wattles Faunce, October 27, 1891, Faunce Collection; Montezuma County (Colorado) Deed Book No. 1, Admx. Deed, December 20, 1889, 425.

47. Emily Blackwell to Mary Ann Wattles Faunce, November 7, 1893, Faunce Collection.

48. Susan Wattles to Emma Wattles Morse, January 26, 1890, CC.

49. Sarah Thomas to Mary Ann Wattles Faunce, September 2, 1894, Faunce Collection.

50. Robert H. Wiebe, *The Search for Order, 1877–1920* (New York: Hill and Wang, 1967), 91–94.

51. Robert G. Athearn, *The Coloradans* (Albuquerque: University of New Mexico Press, 1976), 189–191.

52. Sarah Wattles Hiatt to Mary Ann Wattles Faunce and S. C. Faunce, July 31, 1893, Faunce Collection.

53. Henry George, *Progress and Poverty: An Inquiry into the Cause of Industrial Depression and of Increase of Want with Increase of Wealth* (New York: Walter J. Black, 1942), 221–230, 333–348, 364–366, 379; Paul F. Boller Jr., *American Thought in Transition: The Impact of Evolutionary Nationalism, 1865–1900* (Chicago: Rand-McNally, 1969), 104–107; Dominic Candeloro, "The Single Tax Movement and Progressivism, 1880–1920," *American Journal of Economic and Sociology* 38, no. 2 (1979): 113–127. To be fair, there have been many adherents to the ideas of Henry George, sometimes called Georgism, and among the multiple permutations of this philosophy many socialist ideas exist. Candeloro and others argue, however, that George's proposals offered a "reformed and purified capitalism" that influenced the Progressive movement.

54. Sarah Wattles Hiatt to Mary Ann Wattles Faunce, January 20, 1897, Faunce Collection; Sarah Wattles Hiatt to Mary Ann Wattles Faunce, February 24, 1897, Faunce Collection.

55. Mary Ann Wattles Faunce to Sarah Wattles Hiatt, February 21, 1897, CC.

56. Sarah Wattles Hiatt to Mary Ann Wattles Faunce, June 12, 1897, CC.

57. Mary Ann Wattles Faunce to Susan Wattles, March 9, 1892, Folder 2, Wattles Family Collection, WCNB.

58. S. C. Faunce to Mary Ann Wattles Faunce, February 5, 1899, Faunce Collection.

59. Ibid.

60. Fort Collins *Courier*, August 18, 1898.

61. "Mrs. Harris Stratton, Pioneer Here, Laid to Last Rest Wednesday," Fort Collins *Courier*, October 20, 1922.

62. Alumnae File, Mary Ann Wattles Faunce, Oberlin College Archives, Oberlin, Ohio.

63. Wilton Morse to Susan Wattles, October 1, 1891.

64. Vercy Hathaway Hill to Eugenia Faunce Wetherill, July 11, 1907, Faunce Collection; Emma Wattles Morse to Mary Ann Wattles Faunce, March 23, 1915, Faunce Collection.

65. Mary Ann Wattles Faunce to Orlin Eaton Morse, September 5, 1907, CC; Orlin Eaton Morse to John Otis Morse, September 22, 1907, CC. From Colorado Eaton took Eleanor to New Mexico for a time, then finally back to Kansas, where she died in 1910.

66. Mancos *Times-Tribune*, August 28, 1908; Durango *Democrat*, September 15, 1909; Montezuma *Journal*, August 4, 1910; Mancos *Times-Tribune*, December 9, 1910.

67. 1935 Quinquennial Report Blank, Alumnae File, Mary Ann Wattles Faunce, Oberlin College Alumni Records, Group 28, Oberlin, Ohio.

68. S. C. Faunce to Mary Ann Wattles Faunce, September 30, 1923, Faunce Collection.

69. Hilda Faunce Wetherill to Mary Ann Wattles Faunce, March 6, 1918, Faunce Collection.

70. 1935 Quinquennial Report Blank, Alumnae File, Mary Ann Wattles Faunce.

71. Ruth Jocelyn Wattles to Leila Deborah Smith, n.d., Wattles Papers, Western Reserve Historical Society, Cleveland, Ohio.

72. Mary Ann Kipp Hairgrove, interview with Lynne Getz, May 22, 2012, Del Norte, Colorado.

73. Mancos *Times-Tribune*, Feb. 21, 1908, Mancos, Colorado.

74. Jean McElrath, *Aged in Sage* (Wells, NV: Recorder Press, 1964), 163–166.

75. 1920 U.S. Census; 1930 U.S. Census; and Find-a-Grave-Index. Howard and Ruth Wattles were buried together in the Resthaven Memory Gardens in Fort Collins. Because their names were both placed on the same marker, Find-A-Grave Index incorrectly lists them as husband and wife.

76. Ruth J. Wattles, "Oral Interview," June 20, 1978, Charlene Tresner, interviewer, typewritten transcript, Fort Collins Public Library, Colorado.

1. Fred Blackburn, *The Wetherills: Friends of Mesa Verde* (Durango, CO: Durango Herald Small Press, 2006), 9–14.

2. Theodore W. Wattles to Susan Wattles, June 22, 1884, Folder 4, Wattles Family Collection, Wilson's Creek National Battlefield, Republic, Missouri (hereafter WCNB). Theodore was mistaken about Marian Wetherill's religious affiliation; she and B. K. were Quakers.

3. Theodore Wattles to Susan Wattles, January 22, 1886, Folder 4, Wattles Family Collection, WCNB.

4. Melvina Hammond Wattles to Susan Wattles, July 23, 1886, Curtis Collection, personal collection of family letters in possession of Patti Morse Curtis, Colorado Springs, Colorado (hereafter CC).

5. Frank McNitt, *Richard Wetherill: Anasazi, Pioneer Explorer of Southwestern Ruins*, rev. ed. (Albuquerque: University of New Mexico Press, 1966), 8–12, 16, 22–27, 30–37; Melinda Elliott, *Great Excavations: Tales of Early Southwestern Archaeology, 1888–1939* (Santa Fe, NM: School of American Research Press, 1995), 3–14.

6. *Collecting Native America, 1870–1920*, ed. Shepard Krech III and Barbara A. Hail (Washington, DC : Smithsonian Institution Press, 1999), v, 11; T. J. Jackson Lears, *No Place of Grace: Antimodernism and the Transformation of America Culture, 1880–1920* (New York: Pantheon, 1981), 142–149.

7. David Harrell, "'We Contacted Smithsonian': The Wetherills at Mesa Verde," *New Mexico Historical Review* 63 (July 1987): 234.

8. James E. Snead, *Ruins and Rivals: The Making of Southwest Archaeology* (Tucson: University of Arizona Press, 2001), 3–21.

9. "Obituary: Winslow Wetherill," 1939, Clippings File, Wetherill Family, Farmington Museum, Farmington, New Mexico.

10. Certificate of Marriage, Winslow Wetherill and Mattie Pauline Young, September 16, 1896, Oskaloosa, Iowa, Wetherill Family Papers, Anasazi Heritage Center, Dolores, Colorado (hereafter AHC).

11. Teresa J. Wilkins, *Patterns of Exchange: Navajo Weavers and Traders* (Norman: University of Oklahoma Press, 2008), 70; Robert P. Powers and Miranda Warburton, "Historic Artifacts of the Chaco Additions Inventory Survey," in *The Chaco Additions Survey: An Archaeological Survey of the Additions to Chaco Culture National Historical Park*, eds. Robert P. Powers and Ruth M. Van Dyke, Reports of the Chaco Center No. 14 (Santa Fe, NM: National Park Service, 2015), 66, www.chacoarchive.org/ChacoAdditionsSurvey/.

The Hydes, wealthy heirs of the Babbitt Soap Company, developed a fascination with the Navajo and Anasazi ruins through Richard Wetherill. From 1893 to 1903 they made annual trips to the Four Corners region to visit remote archeological sites, guided by one of the Wetherills. McNitt, *Richard Wetherill*, 57, 112–113, 140–151, 173–178.

12. McNitt, *Richard Wetherill*, 214; Carol Ann Wetherill Getz, interview with Lynne Getz, June 25, 2004, Creede, Colorado; Lease from Addie Ludlow Bingham and Harry Ludlow to the Navajo Indian Blanket Stores Co., August 15, 1903, Win Wetherill Collection, Museum of Northern Arizona, Flagstaff, Arizona.

13. *Mancos Times.*

14. Carol Ann Wetherill Getz, phone interview with Lynne Getz, March 15, 2012; Certificate of Marriage, Winslow Wetherill and Hilda Faunce, August 21, 1905, Montezuma County, Cortez, Colorado.

15. Jean McElrath, *Aged in Sage* (Wells, NV: Recorder Press, 1964), 163–166.

16. Getz, phone interview, March 15, 2012.

17. US Census Bureau, US Census, 1910.

18. Frank McNitt, *The Indian Traders* (Norman: University of Oklahoma Press, 1962), 204.

19. Erika Marie Bsumek, *Indian-Made: Navajo Culture in the Marketplace, 1868–1940* (Lawrence: University Press of Kansas, 2008), 47–75; Peter Iverson, *Diné: A History of the Navajos* (Albuquerque: University of New Mexico Press, 2002), 66–69, 76–81; Willow Roberts Powers, *Navajo Trading: The End of an Era* (Albuquerque: University of New Mexico Press, 2001), 3–5; McNitt, *Indian Traders*, 68–86.

20. Bsumek, *Indian-Made*, 23–33, 114–124; Nancy J. Parezo and Karl A. Hoerig, "Collecting to Educate: Ernest Thompson Seton and Mary Cabot Wheelwright," in *Collecting Native America*, 203–206, 216–225; Lesley Poling-Kempes, *Ladies of the Canyons: A League of Extraordinary Women and Their Adventures in the American Southwest* (Tucson: University of Arizona Press, 2015), 305–309.

21. *Collecting Native America*, 11; Louise Lamphere, "The Internal Colonization of the Navajo People," *Southwest Economy and Society* 1, no. 1 (1976): 6–8.

22. Frances Gillmor and Louisa Wade Wetherill, *Traders to the Navajo: The Story of the Wetherills of Kayenta* (Albuquerque: University of New Mexico Press, 1953; orig. 1934), 48–49; the Hyde brothers, Talbot and Fred Jr., were the heirs to the Babbitt Soap fortune and spent a considerable amount of money financing archaeological expeditions in the Southwest. The Hydes underwrote Richard Wetherill's excavations and trading post at Chaco Canyon and hired several of the Wetherill brothers to outfit trips in Arizona and Utah. The Hydes established retail stores in New York and other cities as outlets for Native American blankets and other crafts. Most of the antiquities collected under Hyde sponsorship were donated to the American Museum of Natural History. See Bsumek, *Indian-Made*, 124–125, 145; Blackburn, *Wetherills*, 57–60.

23. Gillmor and Wetherill, *Traders to the Navajo*, 50–51, 53–54.

24. Louisa Wetherill to Mrs. Pool, (1928), 2003.35.D.66.0, in Wetherill Family Papers, AHC.

25. Louisa Wetherill to Commissioner of Indian Affairs Cato Sells, January 31, 1916, 2003.D.90.0, in Wetherill Family Papers, AHC; McNitt, *Indian Traders*, 270–273. The Wetherills also maintained good relations with the Utes, with whom the Navajo often conflicted. For instance, in 1914–1915 Louisa Wetherill

intervened when a young Ute, Everett Hatch, was accused of murdering a Mexican. Louisa made sure Hatch received fair treatment and helped to persuade reluctant witnesses to come forward on Hatch's behalf. Hatch was found not guilty of the charges. Mary Apolline Comfort, *Rainbow to Yesterday: The John and Louisa Wetherill Story* (New York: Vantage, 1980), 107–109.

26. Apparently none of the Wetherills made great profits at trading. At the time of Richard Wetherill's death, he was $3,000 in debt, very little of which was collected by his estate. His widow, Marietta, was forced to sell many prized items in order to support her family. Kathy M'Closkey reports that Herman Schweizer of the Fred Harvey Company purchased a number of textile items from Marietta for $692 and sold them at a 500 percent increase. See M'Closkey, *Swept under the Rug: A Hidden History of Navajo Weaving* (Albuquerque: University of New Mexico Press, 2002), 52–53, 294. Hilda Wetherill claims the money they saved to purchase a farm was augmented by her side businesses, sewing clothes for Navajos and selling eggs. Wetherill, *Desert Wife* (Lincoln: University of Nebraska Press, 1981; orig. Little, Brown, 1928), 133; Hilda Wetherill to Mary Ann Faunce, March 12, 1918, Faunce Collection, private possession of Carol Ann Wetherill Getz, Creede, Colorado.

27. Gillmor and Wetherill, *Traders to the Navajo*, 82.

28. Edgar L. Hewett to John and Louisa Wetherill, May 15, 1912, 2001.18.D.38.0, Wetherill Family Papers, AHC.

29. Byron Cummings to John Wetherill, March 29, 1911, 2001.18.D.316.0, Wetherill Family Papers, AHC.

30. Louisa Wetherill to Joseph E. Pogue, June 17, 1912, Wetherill Family Papers, AHC.

31. Comfort, *Rainbow to Yesterday*, 80–85.

32. Ibid., 82–83; Mary E. J. Colter to Louisa Wetherill, March 24, 1923, 2001.18D.823.0, Wetherill Family Papers; Mary E. J. Colter to Louisa Wetherill, May 18, 1923, 2001.18.D.824.0, Wetherill Family Papers, AHC.

33. Franc Johnson Newcomb, *Hosteen Klah: Navaho Medicine Man and Sand Painter* (Oklahoma City: University of Oklahoma Press, 1964), 157–164, 187–188, 202; Parezo and Hoerig, "Collecting to Educate," 216–221.

34. Kathryn Gabriel, "Introduction," in *Marietta Wetherill: Reflections on Life with the Navajos in Chaco Canyon,* ed. Kathryn Gabriel (Boulder, CO: Johnson Books, 1992), 1–15; McNitt, *Richard Wetherill*, 99–116, 313–317.

35. Marietta Wetherill and Grace French Evans, "Death of a Medicine Man," *Scribner's Magazine* 91 (May 1932): 304–308.

36. Philip Johnston to Robert Bridges, Editor *Scribner's Magazine,* November 5, 1932, File: Marietta Wetherill, "Death of a Medicine Woman," Michael Harrison Collection, unprocessed, Archives, University of California at Davis Library.

37. Michael Harrison to Philip Johnston, February 13, 1933, Box 1, Folder 6, MS 033, Thomas H. Dodge Collection, Special Collections, Arizona State University, Tempe, Arizona.

38. Louisa Wetherill to Michael Harrison, February 6, 1933, File: Marietta Wetherill, "Death of a Medicine Man," Michael Harrison Collection, University of California–Davis.

39. Thomas H. Dodge to Editor, *Scribner's Magazine*, February 25, 1933, Box 1, Folder 6, Thomas H. Dodge Collection, Arizona State University, Tempe, Arizona.

40. A. H. Gardner, to the Editor, *Scribner's Magazine* 93 (March 1933): 17.

41. K. S. Crichton to Michael Harrison, February 17, 1933, Box 1, Folder 6, Thomas H. Dodge Collection, Arizona State University, Tempe, Arizona.

42. Mabel C. Wright to Elizabeth Wetherill Watson, January 10, 1958, 2004..84..D.137.o, Wetherill Family Papers, AHC; Joseph Schmedding to Mabel C. Wright, August 28, 1954, 2004..84..D.151.o, Wetherill Family Papers, AHC; Joseph Schmedding to Mabel C. Wright, February 18, 1955, 2004..84..D.152.o, Wetherill Family Papers, AHC; Mabel C. Wright, "Asthanne (Little Woman): The Story of Marietta Wetherill," unpublished manuscript, 2004..84..D.103.o, Wetherill Family Papers, AHC.

43. Gabriel, *Marietta Wetherill*, 21.

44. Ibid., 17.

45. Hilda Wetherill, "The Trading Post: Letters from a Primitive Land," *Atlantic Monthly* (September 1928): 289–300; Faunce, *Desert Wife*, 104–109, 303; Ruth J. Wattles, "Oral Interview" with Charlene Tresner, June 20, 1978, typewritten transcript, Fort Collins Public Library, Fort Collins, Colorado.

46. Carol Ann Wetherill Getz, interview with Lynne Getz, August 20, 2008, Creede, Colorado. Hilda had good reason to be concerned Win might want to take some credit for her writing about the trading post. In a collection of his papers there is an offprint of the *Atlantic Monthly* article, with "+ Win Wetherill" in his handwriting scribbled under her byline. Win Wetherill Papers, Museum of Northern Arizona, Flagstaff, Arizona.

47. Ruth Jocelyn Wattles Collection, College Archives, Colorado State University, Fort Collins, CO.

48. Bsumek, *Indian-Made*, 76–79, 89–96.

49. Faunce, *Desert Wife*, 99–101.

50. Ibid., 158–163.

51. Ibid., 146.

52. Hilda Faunce Wetherill to Mary Ann Wattles Faunce, March 6, 1918, Faunce Collection.

53. Faunce, *Desert Wife*, 285–286.

54. Ibid., 286–287.

55. Ibid., 289.

56. Ibid., 289–295.

57. Ibid., 305.

58. Carroll Faunce to Mary Ann Wattles Faunce, October 29, 1922, Faunce Collection; Carol Ann Wetherill Getz interview, August 20, 2008. According to Carol

Ann Getz, Hilda went to California because a doctor friend of Mary Ann Faunce was associated with the nursing school Hilda attended.

59. *Montezuma Journal*, March 29, 1901; *Mancos Times*, June 21, 1901; *Farmington Times*, January 10, 1902; *Mancos Times*, December 6, 1906.

60. McNitt, *Richard Wetherill*, 38–44.

61. Ibid., 8–12, 16, 22–27, 30–37; Blackburn, *The Wetherills*, 138–143.

62. Clayton Wetherill to S. C. Faunce and Mary Ann Wattles Faunce, March 1, 1907, Faunce Collection.

63. Certificate of Marriage, Clayton Wetherill and Eugenia Faunce, May 9, 1907, Montezuma County, Cortez, Colorado; "Wetherill-Faunce," *Mancos Times-Tribune*, May 10, 1907.

64. Mary Ann Wattles Faunce to Orlin Eaton Morse, September 5, 1907, CC.

65. Vercy Hathaway Hill to Eugenia Faunce Wetherill, July 11, 1907, Faunce Collection.

66. William Henry Jackson, *Time Exposure: The Autobiography of William Henry Jackson* (New York: G. P. Putnam's Sons, 1940), 236–242.

67. Ralph D. Bent, *Four Families* (Redondo Beach, CA.: Ralph Bent, 1988), 73–79. The Masons' daughters were Alice, born 1886; Debby, born 1888; Marion, born 1890; Olive, born 1892; and Luella, born 1895.

68. *Mancos Times-Tribune*, May 22, 1908.

69. Glen A. Hinshaw, *Crusaders for Wildlife: A History of Stewardship in Southwestern Colorado* (Ouray, CO: Western Reflections Publishing, 2000), 49–50.

70. Jen Corinne Brown, *Trout Culture: How Fly Fishing Forever Changed the Rocky Mountain West* (Seattle: University of Washington Press, 2015), 42.

71. Ibid., 66–90.

72. Eugenia Faunce Wetherill to Mary Ann Wattles Faunce, October 20, 1908, Faunce Collection.

73. Hilda Wetherill Kipp quoted in Hinshaw, *Crusaders for Wildlife*, 58–59.

74. Certificate of Birth, Carroll Clayton Wetherill, January 5, 1911, Faunce Collection.

75. "L. S. Officer's Story, (As told to Iola Officer without corrections or additions)," typewritten manuscript, Special Collections, Adams State College, Alamosa, Colorado.

76. McNitt, *Richard Wetherill*, 5–7, 277, 289, 294.

77. *Creede Candle*, August 15, 1914, 4.

78. *Durango Democrat*, June 17, 1916.

79. *Creede Candle*, April 17, 1920.

80. Death Certificate, Clayton Wetherill, October 20, 1920, Mineral County, Colorado.

81. S. J. Guernsey to Eugenia Faunce Wetherill, December 5, 1921, Faunce Collection.

82. Faunce-Wetherill family genealogy, Faunce Collection.

83. Mary Ann Kipp Hairgrove, interview with Lynne Getz, May 22, 2012, Del Norte, Colorado.

84. Carol Ann Getz, "The Wetherill Ranch Is Completed Dream of a Widowed Pioneer Lady," *Monte Vista Journal*, July 31, 1969, 5.

85. Carol Ann Wetherill Getz, interview with Lynne Getz, February 9, 2007, Alamosa, Colorado; Floyd Getz, interview with Lynne Getz, January 23, 2007, Phoenix, Arizona.

86. Howard Kennell quoted in Hinshaw, *Crusaders for Wildlife*, 59.

87. Floyd Getz interview, January 23, 2007.

88. Blackburn, *The Wetherills*, 64, 99–100.

89. Hairgrove interview, May 22, 2012.

90. Patricia Nelson Limerick, "Seeing and Being Seen: Tourism in the American West," in *Over the Edge: Remapping the American West*, ed. Valerie J. Matsumoto and Blake Allmendinger (Berkeley: University of California Press, 1999), 21.

91. Hal Rothman, *Devil's Bargain: Tourism in the Twentieth-Century West* (Lawrence: University Press of Kansas, 2000), 128–129. On western dude ranching, see also Lawrence R. Borne, *Dude Ranching: A Complete History* (Albuquerque: University of New Mexico Press, 1983), 1–46; and Elizabeth Clair Flood, *Old-Time Dude Ranches Out West: Authentic Ranches for Modern-Day Dudes* (Salt Lake City, UT: Gibbs-Smith, 1995), 5–15.

92. Frieda Knobloch, "Creating the Cowboy State: Culture and Underdevelopment in Wyoming since 1867," *Western Historical Quarterly* 32, no. 2 (Summer 2001): 210, 212.

93. Carol Ann Wetherill Getz interview, February 15, 2007; Hinshaw, *Crusaders for Wildlife*, 51.

94. Carol Ann Wetherill Getz, interview with Lynne Getz, June 15, 1998, Creede, Colorado; Janis Jacobs, *Ribs of Silver, Hearts of Gold: The Story of Homesteading, Ranching, and Dude Ranching in Mineral County and the Upper Rio Grande*, vol. 2 (Creede, CO: Creede Historical Society, 1994), 23–28.

95. Hilda Faunce Wetherill, photo album, Faunce Collection.

96. Hilda Faunce Wetherill, diary, September 4, 1947, Faunce Collection.

97. Ibid., September 1949.

98. Hilda Faunce Wetherill, diary, December 13, 1949.

99. Hilda Faunce Wetherill, photo album.

100. Darlis A. Miller, *Open Range: The Life of Agnes Morley Cleaveland* (Norman: University of Oklahoma Press, 2010), 57–59, 94, 119–126.

101. "Wetherill, Hilda Faunce," *American Women, 1935–1940: A Composite Biographical Dictionary*, vol. 2: M–Z (Detroit, MI: Gale, 1981), 966; Hilda Faunce Wetherill to John and Louisa Wetherill, November 3, 1938, 200618.D.429.o, Wetherill Family Papers, AHC.

102. Hilda Faunce Wetherill, diary, June 18, 1965.

103. Ibid., August 21, 1952.

104. Hilda Faunce Wetherill to Martha Wetherill, March 26, 1940, 2000.19.D, Wetherill Family Papers, AHC.

105. Hilda Faunce Wetherill to Louisa Wetherill, December 11, 1944, 2001.18.D.470.0, Wetherill Family Papers, AHC.

106. Hilda Faunce Wetherill, diary, May 6, 1953.

107. Ibid., February 1963.

108. Ibid., June 3, 1964.

109. Ibid., June 16, 1965.

110. Ibid., June 30, 1966.

EPILOGUE

1. Carol Ann Wetherill Getz, August 20, 2008, interview with Lynne Getz, Creede, Colorado.

2. "Solitude of Self," *Elizabeth Cady Stanton/Susan B. Anthony: Correspondence, Writings, Speeches*, ed. Ellen Carol DuBois (New York: Schocken, 1981), 246–254.

3. Bonnie Laughlin-Schultz, *The Tie That Bound Us: The Women of John Brown's Family and the Legacy of Radical Abolitionism* (Ithaca, NY: Cornell University Press, 2013), 112–113, 136–152.

4. Harriet Hyman Alonso, *Growing Up Abolitionist: The Story of the Garrison Children* (Amherst: University of Massachusetts Press, 2002), 270–271, 278–292, 311–332.

5. Mark Perry, *Lift Up Thy Voice: The Grimké Family's Journey from Slaveholders to Civil Rights Leaders* (New York: Penguin, 2001), 227–230, 249–254.

BIBLIOGRAPHY

MANUSCRIPT COLLECTIONS AND ARCHIVES

Adams, Franklin G. Papers. Kansas State Historical Society. Topeka, Kansas.
American Medical Women's Association Archives. New York Hospital, Cornell Medical Center, Archives. New York, New York.
Ashtabula County Female Anti-Slavery Society Records. Western Reserve Historical Society. Cleveland, Ohio.
Barnes, William Collection. Kansas State Historical Society. Topeka, Kansas.
Blackwell Family Papers. Library of Congress. Washington, District of Columbia.
Blackwell Papers. Harvard University, Schlesinger Library. Cambridge, Massachusetts.
Blood, James Collection. Kansas State Historical Society. Topeka, Kansas.
Board of Trustees of the New York Infirmary, Minutes, Annual Meetings. New York Hospital, Cornell Medical Center, Archives. New York, New York.
Brown, John Collection. Kansas State Historical Society. Topeka, Kansas.
California School for the Deaf and Blind. Records. California State Archives. Sacramento, California.
Cowles, Betsy Mix Collection. Kent State University Special Collections and Archives. Kent, Ohio.
Cummings, Byron Collection. Arizona Historical Society. Tucson, Arizona.
Curtis Collection, in private possession of Patti Morse Curtis. Colorado Springs, Colorado.
Dodge, Thomas H. Collection. Arizona State University, Special Collections. Tempe, Arizona.
Faunce, Mary Ann Wattles Collection, in private possession of Carol Ann Wetherill Getz. Alamosa, Colorado.
Gillmor, Frances Papers. Arizona, University of Arizona. Tucson, Arizona.
Harrison, Michael Collection. University of California–Davis, Library, Archives. Davis, California.
Hiatt Family Files. Linn County Historical Society. Pleasanton, Kansas.
Higginson, Thomas Wentworth Papers. Kansas State Historical Society. Topeka, Kansas.
Hinton, Richard J. Papers. Kansas State Historical Society. Topeka, Kansas.

Holliday, Cyrus K. Papers. Kansas State Historical Society. Topeka, Kansas.

Hutchinson, William Collection. Kansas State Historical Society. Topeka, Kansas.

Hyatt, Thaddeus Papers. Kansas State Historical Society. Topeka, Kansas.

Lane Seminary Collection. Cincinnati Historical Society. Cincinnati, Ohio.

Lane Theological Seminary. Annual Reports. Ohio History Center. Columbus, Ohio.

Linn County History Collection. Kansas State Historical Society. Topeka, Kansas.

Lowe, David P. Papers. Mound City Historical Society, Somerville Library. Mound City, Kansas.

Lukens-Gilbert Papers. Western Reserve Historical Society. Cleveland, Ohio.

McNitt, Frank Papers. New Mexico Records Center and Archives. Santa Fe, New Mexico.

Moneka Woman's Rights Association Papers. Kansas State Historical Society. Topeka, Kansas.

Montgomery, James Papers. Kansas State Historical Society. Topeka, Kansas.

Moore, Henry Miles Collection. Kansas State Historical Society. Topeka, Kansas.

Morse, O. E. Papers. Kansas State Historical Society. Topeka, Kansas.

Oberlin College Alumni Files. Oberlin College Archives. Oberlin, Ohio.

Oberlin College Treasurer's Office Correspondence. Oberlin College Archives. Oberlin, Ohio.

Robinson, Marius Papers. Western Reserve Historical Society. Cleveland, Ohio.

Stearns, George L. Papers. Kansas State Historical Society. Topeka, Kansas.

Thayer, Eli Collection. Kansas State Historical Society. Topeka, Kansas.

Wattles, Augustus Collection. Kansas State Historical Society. Topeka, Kansas.

Wattles, John O. Papers. Western Reserve Historical Society. Cleveland, Ohio.

Wattles, Ruth Jocelyn Collection. Colorado State University, Special Collections. Fort Collins, Colorado.

Wattles Family Collection. Wilson's Creek National Battlefield. Republic, Missouri.

Wattles Family Files. Linn County Historical Society. Pleasanton, Kansas.

Wattles Family Papers. Mound City Historical Society, Somerville Library. Mound City, Kansas.

Weld-Grimké Papers. University of Michigan, William L. Clements Library. Ann Arbor, Michigan.

Wetherill, John Papers. Museum of Northern Arizona. Flagstaff, Arizona.

Wetherill, Louisa Papers. Museum of Northern Arizona. Flagstaff, Arizona.

Wetherill, Win Papers. Museum of Northern Arizona. Flagstaff, Arizona.

Wetherill, Win Papers. Northern Arizona University, Cline Library. Flagstaff, Arizona.

Wetherill Family Papers. Anasazi Heritage Center. Dolores, Colorado.

Anthony, Susan B., and Ida Husted Harper, eds. *History of Woman Suffrage*. Vol. 4. Indianapolis, IN: Hollenbeck, 1902.

Barnes, Gilbert H., and Dwight L. Dumond, eds. *Letters of Theodore Dwight Weld, Angelina Grimké Weld, and Sarah Grimké, 1822–1844*. Gloucester, MA: Peter Smith, 1965.

Bent, Ralph D. *Four Families*. Redondo Beach, CA: Ralph Bent, 1988.

Brown, George W. *False Claims of Kansas Historians Truthfully Corrected*. Rockford, IL: G. W. Brown, 1902.

———. *The Truth at Last. History Corrected. Reminiscences of Old John Brown. Thrilling Incidents of Border Life in Kansas*. Rockford, IL: Abraham E. Smith, 1880.

Confederate Women of Arkansas in the Civil War 1861–1865: Memorial Reminiscences. Little Rock: United Confederate Veterans of Arkansas, 1907.

Faunce, Hilda. *Desert Wife*. Lincoln, NE: Bison Books, 1981; original Boston: Little, Brown, 1928.

———. "The Trading Post: Letters from a Primitive Land." *Atlantic Monthly* (September 1928): 289–300.

Gabriel, Kathryn, ed. *Marietta Wetherill: Reflections on Life with the Navajos in Chaco Canyon*. Boulder, CO: Johnson, 1992.

George, Henry. *Progress and Poverty: An Inquiry into the Cause of Industrial Depression and of Increase of Want with Increase of Wealth*. New York: Walter J. Black, 1942.

Gillmor, Frances, and Louisa Wade Wetherill. *Traders to the Navajos: The Story of the Wetherills of Kayenta*. Albuquerque: University of New Mexico Press, 1967.

Goodlander, Charles Wesley. *Memoirs and Recollections of the Early Days of Fort Scott*. Fort Scott, KS: Monitor Books and Printers, 1900.

Grimké, Sarah. *Letters on the Equality of the Sexes and Other Essays*. Edited by Elizabeth Ann Bartlett. New Haven, CT: Yale University Press, 1988.

Herald of Freedom, Lawrence, Kansas, 1856–1859.

Hinton, Richard J. *John Brown and His Men; with Some Account of the Roads They Traveled to Reach Harpers Ferry*. New York: Funk and Wagnall's, 1894.

History of the Foundation and Endowment and Catalogue of the Trustees, Alumni, and Students of the Lane Theological Seminary. Cincinnati, OH: Ben Franklin Printing House, 1848.

Hunt, Harriot Kezia. *Glances and Glimpses; or Fifty Years Social, Including Twenty Years Professional Life*. Boston: John P. Jewett, 1856.

Jackson, William Henry. *Time Exposure: The Autobiography of William Henry Jackson*. New York: G. P. Putnam's Sons, 1940.

Johnson, Oliver. *William Lloyd Garrison and His Times; or Sketches of the Anti-Slavery Movement in America, and of the Man Who Was Its Founder and Moral Leader*. Boston: B. B. Russell, 1880.

McNutt, Sarah J. *Medical Women Yesterday and Today.* New York: William Wood, 1918.

Morse, Mrs. O. E. (Emma). "Sketch of the Life and Works of Augustus Wattles. *Collections of the Kansas Historical Society* 17 (1928): 290–299.

Morse, Orlin E. "An Attempted Rescue of John Brown from Charleston, Va., Jail." *Kansas Historical Collections* 8 (1903–1904): 213–226.

Mott, Lucretia. *Selected Letters of Lucretia Coffin Mott.* Edited by Beverly Wilson Palmer. Urbana-Champaign: University of Illinois Press, 2002.

Narrative of the Late Riotous Proceedings against the Liberty of the Press in Cincinnati, with Remarks and Historical Notes Relating to Emancipation, Addressed to the People of Ohio by the Executive Committee of the Ohio Anti-Slavery Society. Cincinnati: n.p., 1836. Ohio Historical Society, Columbus, Ohio.

Newcomb, Franc Johnson. *Hosteen Klah: Navaho Medicine Man and Sand Painter.* Oklahoma City: University of Oklahoma Press, 1964.

Proceedings of the Ohio Anti-Slavery Convention Held at Putnam on the Twenty-Second, Twenty-Third, and Twenty-Fourth of April 1835. New York: American Anti-Slavery Society, 1835.

Redpath, James. *Hand-book to Kansas Territory and the Rocky Mountains' Gold Region: Accompanied by Reliable Maps and a Preliminary Treatise on the Pre-emption.* New York: J. H. Colton, 1859.

Report of the Second Anniversary of the Ohio Anti-Slavery Society, Held in Mount Pleasant, Jefferson County, Ohio, on the Twenty-Seventh of April, 1837. Cincinnati: Ohio Anti-Slavery Society, 1837.

Robinson, Charles. *The Kansas Conflict.* New York: Harper and Brothers, 1892.

Robinson, Sara. *Kansas: Its Interior and Exterior Life.* Boston: Crosby, Nichols, 1856.

Sanborn, Frank B. *Life and Letters of John Brown.* Boston: Roberts Brothers, 1885.

Stanton, Elizabeth Cady. *Eighty Years and More: Reminiscences of Elizabeth Cady Stanton.* New York: Sourcebooks, 1970.

Stanton, Elizabeth Cady, Susan B. Anthony, and Matilda Joslyn Gage, eds. *History of Woman Suffrage.* Vol. 1: *1848–1861.* New York: Arno, 1969; original Fowler and Wells, 1881.

———, eds. *History of Woman Suffrage.* Vol. 3. New York: Arno/*New York Times*, 1969.

A Statement of the Reasons Which Induced the Students of Lane Seminary to Dissolve Their Connection with That Institution. Cincinnati, OH: n.p., 1834. Cincinnati Historical Society.

US Senate. Mason Committee Hearing on Harpers Ferry Raid. *United States Reports,* 36th Congress, 1st Session, No. 278, 1860.

Wattles, John Otis. *A Few Thoughts on Marriage.* Salem, OH: J. H. Painter, 1844.

Wattles, Mary A. *Valedictory Address Delivered at the Second Annual Commencement of the Woman's Medical College of the New York Infirmary, March 28, 1871.* New York: S. Angell, 1871.

Wattles, Ruth J. Oral interview with Charlene Tresner. June 20, 1978. Fort Collins Public Library. Fort Collins, Colorado.

Wetherill, Benjamin Alfred. *The Wetherills of Mesa Verde*. Cranbury, NJ: Associated University Presses, 1976.

Wetherill, Lulu Wade, and Byron Cummings. "A Navajo Folk Tale of Pueblo Bonito." *Art and Archaeology* (September 1922).

Wetherill, Marietta, and Grace French Evans. "Death of a Medicine Man." *Scribner's* 91 (May 1932): 304–308.

Woman's Medical College of the New York Infirmary. *Sixteenth Annual Catalogue and Announcement, June 1884*. New York: G. P. Putnam's Sons, 1884.

SECONDARY SOURCES

Abel, Annie Heloise. *The American Indian as Participant in the Civil War*. Vol. 2. Cleveland, OH: Arthur H. Clarke, 1919.

Abels, Jules. *Man on Fire: John Brown and the Cause of Liberty*. New York: Macmillan, 1971.

Abram, Ruth J., ed. *"Send Us a Lady Physician": Women Doctors in America, 1835–1920*. New York: Norton, 1985.

Abzug, Robert H. *Cosmos Crumbling: American Reform and the Religious Imagination*. New York: Oxford University Press, 1994.

———. *Passionate Liberator: Theodore Dwight Weld and the Dilemma of Reform*. New York: Oxford University Press, 1980.

Alonso, Harriet Hyman. *Growing Up Abolitionist: The Story of the Garrison Children*. Amherst: University of Massachusetts Press, 2002.

Alter, George C. "Generation to Generation: Life Course, Family, and Community." *Social Science History* 37, no. 1 (Spring 2013): 1–26.

Amato, Joseph. *Jacob's Well: A Case for Rethinking Family History*. St. Paul: Minnesota Historical Society Press, 2009.

———. "Rethinking Family History." *Minnesota History* 60, no. 8 (Winter 2007/2008): 326–333.

Andrews, Stephen D. "Which Threatens to Tear Our Fabric Asunder: The Opposition to American Spiritualism, 1848–1860." PhD diss., Stanford University, Palo Alto, California, 2005.

Arey, Leslie B. *Northwestern University Medical School, 1859–1959: A Pioneer in Educational Reform*. Evanston, IL: Northwestern University Press, 1959.

Ash, Stephen V. *When the Yankees Came: Conflict and Chaos in the Occupied South, 1861–1865*. Chapel Hill: University of North Carolina Press, 1995.

Athearn, Robert G. *The Coloradans*. Albuquerque: University of New Mexico Press, 1976.

Barnes, Gilbert Hobbs. *The Anti-Slavery Impulse, 1830–1844*. New York: D. Appleton-Century, 1933.

Barr, Alwyn. *Reconstruction to Reform: Texas Politics, 1876–1906*. Austin: University of Texas Press, 1971.

Berkin, Carol. *Civil War Wives: The Lives and Times of Angelina Grimké Weld, Varina Howell Davis, and Julia Dent Grant*. New York: Knopf, 2009.

Bigham, Darrel E. *On Jordan's Banks: Emancipation and Its Aftermath in the Ohio River Valley*. Lexington: University Press of Kentucky, 2006.

Birney, Catherine. *The Grimké Sisters, Sarah and Angelina Grimké: The First American Women Advocates of Abolition and Woman's Rights*. Westport, CT: Greenwood, 1969; original 1885.

Bittel, Carla. *Mary Putnam Jacobi and the Politics of Medicine in Nineteenth-Century America*. Chapel Hill: University of North Carolina Press, 2009.

——. "Science, Suffrage, and Experimentation: Mary Putnam Jacobi and the Controversy over Vivisection in Late Nineteenth-Century America." *Bulletin of the History of Medicine* 79, no. 1 (2005): 664–694.

Blackburn, Fred. *The Wetherills: Friends of Mesa Verde*. Durango, CO: Durango Herald Small Press, 2006.

Blackhawk, Ned. *Violence over the Land: Indians and Empires in the Early American West*. Cambridge, MA: Harvard University Press, 2006.

Blackwell, Marilyn S., and Kristen T. Oertel. *Frontier Feminist: Clarina Howard Nichols and the Politics of Motherhood*. Lawrence: University Press of Kansas, 2010.

Blight, David W. *Race and Reunion: The Civil War in American Memory*. Cambridge, MA: Harvard University Press, 2001.

Blue, Martha. *Indian Trader: The Life and Times of J. L. Hubbell*. Walnut, CA: Kiva Press, 2000.

Boller Jr., Paul F. *American Thought in Transition: The Impact of Evolutionary Nationalism, 1865–1900*. Chicago: Rand-McNally, 1969.

Bonner, Thomas Neville. *To The Ends of the Earth: Women's Search for Education in Medicine*. Cambridge, MA: Harvard University Press, 1992.

Bordin, Ruth. *Frances Willard: A Biography*. Chapel Hill: University of North Carolina Press, 1986.

Borne, Lawrence R. *Dude Ranching: A Complete History*. Albuquerque: University of New Mexico Press, 1983.

Boydston, Jeanne. *Home and Work: Housework, Wages, and the Ideology of Labor in the Early Republic*. New York: Oxford University Press, 1990.

Boyer, Richard O. *The Legend of John Brown: A Biography and a History*. New York: Knopf, 1973.

Boylan, Anne M. *The Origins of Women's Activism: New York and Boston, 1797–1840*. Chapel Hill: University of North Carolina Press, 2002.

Braude, Ann. *Radical Spirits: Spiritualism and Women's Rights in Nineteenth-Century America*. Bloomington: Indiana University Press, 2001.

Brown, Jen Corinne. *Trout Culture: How Fly Fishing Forever Changed the Rocky Mountain West*. Seattle: University of Washington Press, 2015.

Brown, Robert L. *An Empire of Silver: A History of the San Juan Silver Rush.* Caldwell, ID: Caxton, 1965.

Bsumek, Erika Marie. *Indian-Made: Navajo Culture in the Marketplace, 1868–1940.* Lawrence: University Press of Kansas, 2008.

Burnside, William H. *The Honorable Powell Clayton.* Conway: University of Central Arkansas Press, 1991.

Candeloro, Dominic. "The Single-Tax Movement and Progressivism, 1880–1920." *American Journal of Economics and Sociology* 38, no. 2 (1979): 113–127.

Castel, Albert. *A Frontier State at War: Kansas 1861–1865.* Lawrence: Kansas Heritage Press, 1992, original 1958.

Cayleff, Susan. *Wash and Be Healed: The Water-Cure Movement and Women's Health.* Philadelphia, PA: Temple University Press, 1987.

Christ, Mark K., ed. *Rugged and Sublime: The Civil War in Arkansas.* Fayetteville: University of Arkansas Press, 1994.

Comfort, Mary Apolline. *Rainbow to Yesterday: The John and Louisa Wetherill Story.* New York: Vantage, 1980.

Cott, Nancy F. *The Bonds of Womanhood: "Woman's Sphere" in New England, 1780–1835.* New Haven, CT: Yale University Press, 1977.

———. *Public Vows: A History of Marriage and the Nation.* Cambridge, MA: Harvard University Press, 2000.

Dabney, Wendell P. *Cincinnati's Colored Citizens: Historical, Sociological, and Biographical.* New York: Negro Universities Press, 1970.

Daniel, Annie Sturgis. "'A Cautious Experiment': The History of the New York Infirmary for Women and Children and the Woman's Medical College of the New York Infirmary; Also Its Pioneer Founders, 1853–1899." *Medical Woman's Journal* 46 (May–December 1939), 121–131, 168–174, 196–202, 229–238, 269–280, 295–309, 335–339, 357–360.

———. "'A Cautious Experiment': The History of the New York Infirmary for Women and Children and the Woman's Medical College of the New York Infirmary; Also Its Pioneer Founders, 1853–1899." *Medical Woman's Journal* 47 (January–December 1940), 10–12, 40–45, 67–69, 97–101, 135–139, 167–171, 199–204, 234–239, 263–268, 296–300, 323–329, 357–370.

———. "'A Cautious Experiment': The History of the New York Infirmary for Women and Children and the Woman's Medical College of the New York Infirmary; Also Its Pioneer Founders, 1853–1899." *Medical Woman's Journal* 48 (January–December 1941), 10–13, 33–39, 74–79, 102–103, 134–138, 167–173, 197–202, 233–240, 272–278, 301–307, 331–338, 364–371.

———. "'A Cautious Experiment': The History of the New York Infirmary for Women and Children and the Woman's Medical College of the New York Infirmary; Also Its Pioneer Founders, 1853–1899." *Medical Woman's Journal* 49 (January–August 1942), 12–15, 37–40, 71–74, 105–109, 137–138, 165–166, 208–212, 241–243.

———. *The New York Infirmary: A Century of Devoted Service, 1854–1854.* New York: New York Infirmary, 1954.

Dannenbaum, Jed. "The Origins of Temperance Activism and Militancy among American Women." *Journal of Social History* 15, no. 2 (Winter 1981): 235–252.

Dean Jr., Eric T. *Shook over Hell: Post-Traumatic Stress, Vietnam, and the Civil War.* Cambridge, MA: Harvard University Press, 1997.

DeBlack, Thomas A. *With Fire and Sword: Arkansas, 1861–1874.* Fayetteville: University of Arkansas Press, 2003.

Degler, Carl. *At Odds: Women and the Family in America from the Revolution to the Present.* New York: Oxford University Press, 1980.

Dixon, Chris. *Perfecting the Family: Anti-Slavery Marriages in Nineteenth-Century America.* Amherst: University of Massachusetts Press, 1997.

Dorset, Phyllis Flanders. *The New Eldorado: The Story of Colorado's Gold and Silver Rushes.* New York: Macmillan, 1970.

Drachman, Virginia G. *Hospital with a Heart: Women Doctors and the Paradox of Separatism at the New England Hospital, 1862–1969.* Ithaca, NY: Cornell University Press, 1984.

Earle, Jonathan, and Diane Mutti Burke, eds. *Bleeding Kansas, Bleeding Missouri: The Long Civil War on the Border.* Lawrence: University Press of Kansas, 2013.

Elliott, Melinda. *Great Excavations: Tales of Early Southwestern Archaeology, 1888–1939.* Santa Fe, NM: School of American Research Press, 1995.

Ellis, Fern D. *Come Back to My Valley: Historical Remembrances of Mancos, Colorado.* Cortez, CO: Southwest, 1976.

Etcheson, Nicole. *Bleeding Kansas: Contested Liberty in the Civil War Era.* Lawrence: University Press of Kansas, 2004.

Faderman, Lillian. *To Believe in Women: What Lesbians Have Done for America—A History.* Boston: Mariner, 2000.

Fagan, Jean, and John C. Van Horne, eds. *The Abolitionist Sisterhood: Women's Political Culture in Antebellum America.* Ithaca, NY: Cornell University Press, 1994.

Faragher, John Mack. *Women and Men on the Overland Trail.* New Haven, CT: Yale University Press, 1979.

Farley, Frances. "The New York Infirmary for Women and Children, 1870–1899: Women Doctors in Transition." Honors thesis, Duke University, Durham, North Carolina, 1983.

Faust, Drew Gilpin. *Mothers of Invention: Women of the Slaveholding South in the American Civil War.* Chapel Hill: University of North Carolina Press, 1996.

———. *This Republic of Suffering: Death and the American Civil War.* New York: Vintage, 2008.

Fellman, Michael. *Inside War: The Guerrilla Conflict in Missouri during the American Civil War.* New York: Oxford University Press, 1990.

Fletcher, Robert Samuel. *A History of Oberlin College: From Its Foundation through the Civil War.* 2 vols. Arno Press/New York Times, 1971.

Flood, Elizabeth Clair. *Old-Time Dude Ranches out West: Authentic Ranches for Modern-Day Dudes.* Salt Lake City, UT: Gibbs-Smith, 1995.

Fowler, Don. *A Laboratory for Anthropology: Science and Romanticism in the American Southwest, 1846–1930.* Albuquerque: University of New Mexico Press, 2000.

Fox, Nancy C., ed. *Prehistory and History of the Southwest: Papers in Honor of Alden C. Hayes.* Albuquerque: Archaeological Society of New Mexico, 1985.

Freeman, Victoria. *Distant Relations: How My Ancestors Colonized North America.* South Royalton, VT: Steerforth, 2000.

Gallagher, Gary W., and Alan T. Nolan, eds. *The Myth of the Lost Cause and Civil War History.* Bloomington: Indiana University Press, 2000.

Gambone, Joseph G. "The Forgotten Feminist of Kansas: The Papers of Clarina I. H. Nichols, 1854–1885," *Kansas Historical Quarterly* 39 (Spring 1973): 12–15.

Garceau, Dee. "Single Women Homesteaders and the Meanings of Independence: Places on the Map, Place in the Mind." *Frontiers* 15 (Spring 1995): 1–26.

Ginzberg, Lori D. *Untidy Origins: A Story of Woman's Rights in Antebellum New York.* Chapel Hill: University of North Carolina Press, 2005.

——. *Women and the Work of Benevolence: Morality, Politics, and Class in the Nineteenth-Century United States.* New Haven, CT: Yale University Press, 1990.

Goodman, Paul. "The Manual Labor Movement and the Origins of Abolitionism." *Journal of the Early Republic* 13, no. 3 (Autumn 1993): 355–388.

Goodrich, Thomas. *War to the Knife: Bleeding Kansas, 1854–1861.* Lincoln: University of Nebraska Press, 2004.

Gordon-Reed, Annette. *The Hemingses of Monticello: An American Family.* New York: Norton, 2009.

Gray, Susan E. *The Yankee West: Community Life on the Michigan Frontier.* Chapel Hill: University of North Carolina Press, 1996.

Graybill, Andrew. *The Red and the White: A Family Saga of the American West.* New York: Norton, 2014.

Greve, Charles Theodore. *Centennial History of Cincinnati and Representative Citizens.* Vol. 1. Chicago: Biographical Publishing, 1904.

Griffler, Keith P. *Front Line of Freedom: African Americans and the Forging of the Underground Railroad in the Ohio Valley.* Lexington: University Press of Kentucky, 2004.

Hafen, LeRoy R. *Colorado and Its People: A Narrative and Topical History of the Centennial State.* Vol. 1. New York: Lewis Historical Publishing, 1948.

Hagedorn, Ann. *Beyond the River: The Untold Story of the Heroes of the Underground Railroad.* New York: Simon and Schuster, 2002.

Halbwachs, Maurice. *On Collective Memory,* edited, translated, and introduced by Lewis A. Coser. Translation of *Les cadres sociaux de la mémoire.* Chicago: University of Chicago Press, 1992.

Haller Jr., John S. *Medical Protestants: The Eclectics in American Medicine, 1825–1939.* Carbondale: Southern Illinois University Press, 1994.

Hamm, Thomas D. *God's Government Begun: The Society for Universal Inquiry and Reform, 1842–1846.* Bloomington: Indiana University Press, 1995.

Hareven, Tamara K. *Families, History, and Social Change: Life-Course and Cross-Cultural Perspectives.* Boulder, CO: Westview Press, 2000.

Harrell, David. "'We Contacted Smithsonian': The Wetherills at Mesa Verde." *New Mexico Historical Review* 62, no. 3 (1987): 229–248.

Hartman, Mary S. *The Household and the Making of History: A Subversive View of the Western Past.* New York: Cambridge University Press, 2004.

Heilbrun, Carolyn G. *Writing a Woman's Life.* New York: Ballantine, 1988.

Hewitt, Nancy A. *Women's Activism and Social Change: Rochester, New York, 1822–1872.* Ithaca, NY: Cornell University Press, 1984.

Hinshaw, Glen A. *Crusaders for Wildlife: A History of Stewardship in Southwestern Colorado.* Ouray, CO: Western Reflections, 2000.

Hirsch, Marianne. *Family Frames: Photography, Narrative, and Postmemory.* Cambridge, MA: Harvard University Press, 1997.

Hoffert, Sylvia D. *When Hens Crow: The Woman's Rights Movement in Antebellum America.* Bloomington: Indiana University Press, 1995.

Holman, Tom L. "James Montgomery, 1813–1871." EdD diss., Oklahoma State University, Stillwater, Oklahoma, 1973.

Hyde, Anne. *Empires, Nations, and Families: A New History of the North American West, 1800–1860.* New York: HarperCollins, 2012.

Isaacs, Ernest Joseph. "A History of Nineteenth-Century American Spiritualism as a Religious and Social Movement." PhD diss., University of Wisconsin, Madison, Wisconsin, 1975.

Isenberg, Nancy. *Sex and Citizenship in Antebellum America.* Chapel Hill: University of North Carolina Press, 1998.

Iverson, Peter. *Diné: A History of the Navajos.* Albuquerque: University of New Mexico Press, 2002.

Ivy, James D. "'The Lone Star Surrenders to a Lone Woman': Frances Willard's Forgotten 1882 Texas Temperance Tour." *Southwestern Historical Quarterly* 102, no. 1 (July 1998): 44–61.

———. *No Saloon in the Valley: The Southern Strategy of Texas Prohibitionists in the 1880s.* Waco, TX: Baylor University Press, 2003.

Jabour, Anya. *Marriage in the Early Republic: Elizabeth and William Wirt and the Companionate Ideal.* Baltimore, MD: Johns Hopkins University Press, 1998.

Jacobs, Janis. *Ribs of Silver, Hearts of Gold: The Story of Homesteading, Ranching, and Dude Ranching in Mineral County and the Upper Rio Grande.* Vol. 2. Creede, CO: Creede Historical Society, 1994.

Jacobs, Margaret D. *White Mother to a Dark Race: Settler Colonialism, Maternalism, and the Removal of Indigenous Children in the American West and Australia, 1880–1940.* Lincoln: University of Nebraska Press, 2009.

Jameson, Elizabeth. "Halfway across That Line: Gender at the Threshold of History in the North American West." *Western Historical Quarterly* 47, no. 1 (Spring 2016): 1–26.

Jeffrey, Julie Roy. *Abolitionists Remember: Antislavery Autobiographies and the Unfinished Work of Emancipation.* Chapel Hill: University of North Carolina Press, 2008.

———. *The Great Silent Army of Abolitionism: Ordinary Women in the Antislavery Movement.* Chapel Hill: University of North Carolina Press, 1998.

Jensen, Joan M. *Calling This Place Home: Women on the Wisconsin Frontier, 1850–1925.* St. Paul: Minnesota Historical Society Press, 2006.

———. *Loosening the Bonds: Mid-Atlantic Farm Women, 1750–1850.* New Haven, CT: Yale University Press, 1986.

Johnson, Samuel A. *The Battle Cry of Freedom: The New England Emigrant Aid Company in the Kansas Crusade.* Lawrence: University Press of Kansas, 1954.

Johnson, Susan Lee. *Roaring Camp: The Social World of the California Gold Rush.* New York: Norton, 2000.

Keagy, Walter R. "The Lane Seminary Rebellion." *Bulletin of the Historical and Philosophical Society of Ohio* 9, no. 2 (April 1951): 141–145.

Kelley, Mary. *Learning to Stand and Speak: Women, Education, and Public Life in America's Republic.* Chapel Hill: University of North Carolina Press, 2006.

Kelly, Catherine E. *In the New England Fashion: Reshaping Women's Lives in the Nineteenth Century.* Ithaca, NY: Cornell University Press, 1999.

Kerber, Linda. "Separate Spheres, Female World, Woman's Place: The Rhetoric of Women's History." *Journal of American History* 75 (June 1988): 9–39.

Kidd, Sue Monk. *The Invention of Wings.* New York: Viking, 2014.

Knobloch, Frieda. "Creating the Cowboy State: Culture and Underdevelopment in Wyoming since 1867." *Western Historical Quarterly* 32, no. 2 (Summer 2001): 201–221.

Krech III, Shepard, and Barbara A. Hail, eds. *Collecting Native America, 1870–1920.* Washington, DC: Smithsonian Institution Press, 1999.

Lamphere, Louise. "The Internal Colonization of the Navajo People." *Southwest Economy and Society* 1, no. 1 (1976): 6–14.

Lasser, Carol. "How Did Oberlin Women Students Draw on Their College Experience to Participate in Antebellum Social Movements, 1831–1861?" Women and Social Movements in the United States, 1600–2000. May 2002. http://womhist.binghamton.edu/oberlin.htm. Accessed February 3, 2006.

Laughlin-Schultz, Bonnie. *The Tie That Bound Us: The Women of John Brown's Family and the Legacy of Radical Abolitionism.* Ithaca, NY: Cornell University Press, 2013.

Lears, T. J. Jackson. *No Place of Grace: Antimodernism and the Transformation of American Culture, 1880–1920.* New York: Pantheon, 1981.

Leavitt, Judith Walzer. *Brought to Bed: Child Bearing in America, 1750–1950.* New York: Oxford University Press, 1986.

Lerner, Gerda. *The Feminist Thought of Sarah Grimké.* New York: Oxford University Press, 1998.

———. *The Grimké Sisters from South Carolina: Rebels against Slavery.* Boston: Houghton Mifflin, 1967.

Lesick, Lawrence Thomas. *The Lane Rebels: Evangelicalism and Antislavery in Antebellum America.* Metuchen, NJ: Scarecrow, 1980.

Luchetti, Cathy. *Medicine Women: The Story of Early American Women Doctors.* New York: Crown, 1998.

Ludmerer, Kenneth M. *Learning to Heal: The Development of American Medical Education.* New York: Basic Books, 1985.

Malin, James C. *John Brown and the Legend of Fifty-Six.* New York: Haskell House, 1971.

Marrett, Cora Bagley. "On the Evolution of Women's Medical Societies." *Bulletin of the History of Medicine* 53 (1979): 434–445.

Matsumoto, Valerie J., and Blake Allmendinger, eds. *Over the Edge: Remapping the American West.* Berkeley: University of California Press, 1999.

Mayer, Henry. *All on Fire: William Lloyd Garrison and the Abolition of Slavery.* New York: St. Martin's, 1998.

McElrath, Jean. *Aged in Sage.* Wells, NV: Recorder, 1964.

McGlone, Robert E. *John Brown's War against Slavery.* New York: Cambridge University Press, 2009.

M'Closkey, Kathy. *Swept under the Rug: A Hidden History of Navajo Weaving.* Albuquerque: University of New Mexico Press, 2002.

McNitt, Frank. *The Indian Traders.* Norman: University of Oklahoma Press, 1962.

———. *Richard Wetherill: Anasazi.* Albuquerque: University of New Mexico Press, 1957.

McPherson, James. *The Battle Cry of Freedom: The Civil War Era.* New York: Oxford University Press, 1988.

Miller, Darlis A. *Open Range: The Life of Agnes Morley Cleaveland.* Norman: University of Oklahoma Press, 2010.

Mitchell, William Ansel. *Linn County, Kansas: A History.* Kansas City, MO: Campbell-Gates, 1928.

Moore, R. Laurence. *In Search of White Crows: Spiritualism, Parapsychology, and American Culture.* New York: Oxford University Press, 1977.

Morantz-Sanchez, Regina. *Sympathy and Science: Women Physicians in American Medicine.* New York: Oxford University Press, 1985.

More, Ellen S. "The Blackwell Society and the Professionalization of Women Physicians." *Bulletin of the History of Medicine* 61 (1987): 603–628.

———. *Restoring the Balance: Women Physicians and the Profession of Medicine, 1850–1995.* Cambridge, MA: Harvard University Press, 1999.

More, Ellen Singer, and Maureen A. Milligan, eds. *The Empathic Practitioner: Empathy, Gender, and Medicine.* New Brunswick, NJ: Rutgers University Press, 1994.

Morrison, Michael A. *Slavery and the American West: The Eclipse of Manifest Destiny and the Coming of the Civil War.* Chapel Hill: University of North Carolina Press, 1997.

Myers, John L. "American Anti-Slavery Society Agents and the Free Negro, 1833–1838." *Journal of Negro History* 52, no. 3 (July 1967): 212–214.

———. "Antislavery Activities of Five Lane Seminary Boys in 1835–1836." *Bulletin of the Historical and Philosophical Society of Ohio* 21 (April 1963): 95–111.

Myres, Sandra. *Westering Women and the Frontier Experience, 1800–1915*. Albuquerque: University of New Mexico Press, 1982.

Nichols, David A. *Lincoln and the Indian: Civil War Policy and Practices*. Columbia: University of Missouri Press, 1978.

Noyes, John Humphrey. *Strange Cults and Utopias of Nineteenth-Century America*. New York: Dover, 1966.

Oertel, Kristen Tegtmeier. *Bleeding Borders: Race, Gender, and Violence in Pre–Civil War Kansas*. Baton Rouge: Louisiana State University Press, 2009.

———. "'The Free Sons of the North' versus 'The Myrmidons of Border-Ruffianism': What Makes a Man in Bleeding Kansas?" *Kansas History* 25, no. 3 (Autumn 2002): 174–189.

Parker, Alison M. *Articulating Rights: Nineteenth-Century American Women on Race, Reform, and the State*. DeKalb: Northern Illinois University Press, 2010.

Passet, Joanne E. *Sex Radicals and the Quest for Women's Equality*. Urbana-Champaign: University of Illinois Press, 2003.

Peitzman, Steven J. *A New and Untried Course: Woman's Medical College and Medical College of Pennsylvania, 1850–1998*. New Brunswick, NJ: Rutgers University Press, 2000.

Perry, Adele. *Colonial Relations: The Douglas-Connolly Family and the Nineteenth-Century Imperial World*. New York: Cambridge University Press, 2015.

Perry, Mark. *Lift Up Thy Voice: The Grimké Family's Journey from Slaveholders to Civil Rights Leaders*. New York: Penguin, 2001.

Peterson, Merrill D. *John Brown: The Legend Revisited*. Charlottesville: University of Virginia Press, 2002.

Phillips, Roderick. *Putting Asunder: A History of Divorce in Western Society*. New York: Cambridge University Press, 1988.

Phipps, Sheila R. *Genteel Rebel: The Life of Mary Greenhow Lee*. Baton Rouge: Louisiana State University Press, 2004.

Pierson, Michael D. *Free Hearts and Free Homes: Gender and American Antislavery Politics*. Chapel Hill: University of North Carolina Press, 2003.

Poling-Kempes, Lesley. *Ladies of the Canyons: A League of Extraordinary Women and Their Adventures in the American Southwest*. Tucson: University of Arizona Press, 2015.

Porter, Roy. *The Greatest Benefit to Mankind: A Medical History of Humanity*. New York: Norton, 1997.

Portnoy, Alisse. *Their Right to Speak: Women's Activism in the Indian and Slave Debates*. Cambridge, MA: Harvard University Press, 2005.

Powers, Robert P., and Ruth M. Van Dyke, eds. *The Chaco Additions Survey: An Archaeological Survey of the Additions to Chaco Culture National Historical Park*.

Reports of the Chaco Center No. 14. Santa Fe, NM: National Park Service, 2015. www.chacoarchive.org/ChacoAdditionsSurvey/.

Powers, Willow Roberts. *Navajo Trading: The End of an Era.* Albuquerque: University of New Mexico Press, 2001.

Price, Robert. "The Ohio Anti-Slavery Convention of 1836." *Ohio State Archaeological and Historical Society Quarterly* 45 (1887): 173–188.

Quarles, Benjamin. *Black Abolitionists.* New York: Oxford University Press, 1969.

Rawley, James A. *Race and Politics: "Bleeding Kansas" and the Coming of the Civil War.* Philadelphia, PA: J. P. Lippincott, 1969.

Reynolds, David S. *John Brown, Abolitionist: The Man Who Killed Slavery, Sparked the Civil War, and Seeded Civil Rights.* New York: Knopf, 2005.

Richards, Leonard L. *"Gentlemen of Property and Standing": Anti-Abolition Mobs in Jacksonian America.* New York: Oxford University Press, 1970.

Robertson, Stacey M. *Hearts Beating for Liberty: Women Abolitionists in the Old Northwest.* Chapel Hill: University of North Carolina Press, 2010.

Rothman, Hal. *Devil's Bargain: Tourism in the Twentieth-Century West.* Lawrence: University Press of Kansas, 2000.

Rotundo, Anthony. *American Manhood: Transformations in Masculinity from the Revolution to the Modern Era.* New York: Basic Books, 1993.

Rugh, Susan Sessions. *Our Common Country: Family Farming, Culture, and Community in the Nineteenth-Century Midwest.* Bloomington: Indiana University Press, 2001.

Rupp, Leila J. *Worlds of Women: The Making of an International Women's Movement.* Princeton, NJ: Princeton University Press, 1997.

Ryan, Mary P. *Cradle of the Middle Class: The Family in Oneida County, New York, 1790–1865.* New York: Cambridge University Press, 1981.

Sahli, Nancy Ann. *Elizabeth Blackwell, M.D. (1821–1910): A Biography.* New York: Arno, 1982.

Sánchez-Eppler, Karen. *Touching Liberty: Abolition, Feminism, and the Politics of the Body.* Berkeley: University of California Press, 1993.

Sarah Platt Decker Chapter D.A.R. *Pioneers of the San Juan Country.* Vol. 1. Colorado Springs, CO: Out West, 1942.

Scharff, Virginia. "Lighting Out for the Territory: Women, Mobility, and Western Place," in *Power and Place in the North American West.* Edited by Richard White and John M. Findlay. Seattle: University of Washington Press, 1999.

Schlissel, Lillian. *Women's Diaries of the Westward Journey.* New York: Schocken, 1982.

Sears, Hal D. *The Sex Radicals: Free Love in High Victorian America.* Lawrence: Regents Press of Kansas, 1977.

Sernett, Milton C. *Abolition's Axe: Beriah Green, Oneida Institute, and the Black Freedom Struggle.* Syracuse, NY: Syracuse University Press, 1986.

Silber, Nina. *Daughters of the Union: Northern Women Fight the Civil War.* Cambridge, MA: Harvard University Press, 2005.

Sklar, Kathryn Kish. *Women's Rights Emerges within the Antislavery Movement, 1830–1870: A Brief History with Documents.* Boston: Bedford/St. Martin's, 2000.

Smith, Sherry L. "Single Women Homesteaders: The Perplexing Case of Elinor Pruitt Stewart." *Western Historical Quarterly* 22 (May 1991): 163–183.

Snead, James E. *Ruins and Rivals: The Making of Southwest Archaeology.* Tucson: University of Arizona Press, 2001.

Solomon, Barbara Miller. *In the Company of Educated Women: A History of Women and Higher Education in America.* New Haven, CT: Yale University Press, 1985.

Starr, Paul. *The Social Transformation of American Medicine.* New York: Basic Books, 1982.

Stoler, Anna Laura. *Along the Archival Grain: Epistemic Anxieties and Colonial Common Sense.* Princeton, NJ: Princeton University Press, 2009.

———, ed. *Haunted by Empire: Geographies of Intimacy in North American History.* Durham, NC: Duke University Press, 2006.

Stone, Elizabeth. *Black Sheep and Kissing Cousins: How Our Family Stories Shape Us.* New Brunswick, NJ: Transaction, 2004.

Sweet, Leonard I. *The Minister's Wife: Her Role in Nineteenth-Century American Evangelicalism.* Philadelphia, PA: Temple University Press, 1982.

Taylor, Nikki M. *Frontiers of Freedom: Cincinnati's Black Community, 1802–1868.* Athens: Ohio University Press, 2005.

Thomas, Benjamin P. *Theodore Weld: Crusader for Freedom.* New Brunswick, NJ: Rutgers University Press, 1950.

Tuchman, Arleen Marcia. *Science, Medicine, and the State in Germany: The Case of Baden, 1815–1871.* New York: Oxford University Press, 1993.

———. "Situating Gender: Marie E. Zakrzewska and the Place of Science in Women's Medical Education." *Isis* 95 (2004): 34–57.

Villard, Oswald Garrison. *John Brown: 1800–1859—A Biography Fifty Years After.* Cambridge MA: Riverside, 1911.

Walsh, Mary. *"Doctors Wanted: No Women Need Apply."* New Haven, CT: Yale University Press, 1977.

Walters, Ronald G. *The Antislavery Appeal: Abolitionism after 1830.* Baltimore, MD: Johns Hopkins University Press, 1976.

Welch, G. Murlin. *Border Warfare in Southeastern Kansas.* Pleasanton, KS: Linn County Historical Society, 1977.

Wells, Susan. *Out of the Dead House: Nineteenth-Century Women Physicians and the Writing of Medicine.* Madison: University of Wisconsin Press, 2001.

Welter, Barbara. "The Cult of True Womanhood, 1820–1860." *American Quarterly* 18 (Summer 1966): 133–155.

West, Elliot. *The Contested Plains: Indians, Goldseekers, and the Rush to Colorado.* Lawrence: University Press of Kansas, 1998.

White, Richard. *Railroaded: The Transcontinentals and the Making of Modern America.* New York: Norton, 2011.

———. *Remembering Ahanagran: A History of Stories.* Seattle: University of Washington Press, 1998.

White, Richard, and John M. Findlay, eds. *Power and Place in the North American West.* Seattle: University of Washington Press, 1999.

Whites, LeeAnn, and Alecia P. Long, eds. *Occupied Women: Gender, Military Occupation, and the American Civil War.* Baton Rouge: Louisiana State University Press, 2009.

Wiebe, Robert H. *The Search for Order, 1877–1920.* New York: Hill and Wang, 1967.

Wilkins, Teresa J. *Patterns of Exchange: Navajo Weavers and Traders.* Norman: University of Oklahoma Press, 2008.

Wilson, Dorothy Clarke. *Lone Woman: The Story of Elizabeth Blackwell, the First Woman Doctor.* Boston: Little, Brown, 1970.

Wissler, Clark. "Pueblo Bonito as Made Known by the Hyde Expedition." *Natural History* (July–August 1922): 343–354.

Wolfe, Patrick. "Settler Colonialism and the Elimination of the Native." *Journal of Genocide Research* 8, no. 4 (December 2006): 387–409.

Yellin, Jean Fagan. *Women and Sisters: The Antislavery Feminists in American Culture.* New Haven, CT: Yale University Press, 1989.

INDEX

abolitionist movement, 17, 45, 55
  immediatism, 17, 19–22
  racial equality and, 26–27
  split over women's rights, 26,
    287n46
  violence against, 28, 30–31
Abzug, Robert, 33
Adams, Franklin, 164
Addams, Jane, 208
Alamo Ranch, 235, 242–243, 256
Alcott, Bronson, 94
Alpha, 223–224
Amato, Joseph, 10
American Anti-Slavery Society
    (AASS), 21, 26, 28, 30, 39, 43, 83
American Colonization Society, 22
Ancestry.com, 3
Ancestry Roadshow, 4
Angell, Annie, 192, 198
Anthony, Susan B., 87, 89, 202,
    290n99
antislavery movement, 6, 12, 17, 21,
    32, 80
  Garrisonians in, 55
  Native Americans and, 105–106
Arizona State Museum, 247
Armitage, Susan, 8
Arny, William Frederick Milton
    (W. F. M.), 66–67, 213–214, 278
Art Students League of New York, 198
Association for the Advancement
    of the Medical Education for
    Women, 191

Atchison, Topeka & Santa Fe Railroad,
    218
Atlantic Monthly, 252
Austin, Harriet, 123, 124

Baker, Mercy, 177–178
Bancroft, Ashley, 30
Banks, Nathaniel P., 157
Barton, Clara, 202
Beecher, Catharine, 15, 35
Beecher, Lyman, 20–23
Berkin, Carol, 92
Billroth, Theodore, 192
Birdsall, Mary, 87
Birney, James, 31, 55, 94
Bishop, Emeline. *See* Mattison,
    Emeline Bishop
Blachley, Lou, 251
Black Jack, Battle of, 63
Black Mountain Trading Post, 244,
    251–255
  "Covered Water," 252
Blackwell, Elizabeth, 177, 188, 189,
    197, 278
Blackwell, Emily, 7, 177, 188, 189, 194,
    197–198, 201, 203, 278
Blackwell, Henry, 27
Bleeding Kansas, 51, 56, 63, 71, 72, 90,
    94, 104, 129, 137, 162, 163, 164,
    186
Bloomer, Amelia, 87, 185
Blue Lodges, 71
Blunt, James G., 110

Border Ruffians, 54–55, 60, 65, 66
Botkin, Amelia, 98
Botkin, Theodore, 165–166
Boylan, Anne, 16
Brown, Fanny Hurd, 123
Brown, Frederick (brother of John Brown), 58
Brown, George Washington (G. W.), 56, 63, 64, 65–66, 69, 70
  False Claims of Kansas Historians Truthfully Corrected, 163–164
  The Truth at Last: History Corrected, 163
Brown, Jason, 58, 63
Brown, Jen Corinne, 258
Brown, John, 6, 51, 57, 58, 69, 79–80, 95, 102, 104, 277
  activities in Kansas in 1858, 72–77, 90, 96, 187
  on Indian policy, 107
  "Parallels," 76, 90
  Pottawatomie Massacre and, 63, 68, 75, 163
  reputation following Civil War, 162–164
  Wattles family memory of, 162
Brown, John, Jr., 58, 63
Brown, Mary, 79–80, 95, 164
Brown, Owen, 58
Browning, Elizabeth Barrett, *Aurora Leigh*, 86
Brunot, Felix, 220
Bryan, William Jennings, 237
Bryant, William Cullen, 94
Bsumek, Erika, 252
Buchanan, Joseph R., 113, 121
Burns, Ken, 293n16
Burnside, William, 144–145
Butler, Benjamin, 147
Byrd, Elizabeth Lowe, 41, 59
Byrd, John, 41, 59

Cabell, William, 142
California School for the Deaf and Blind (Berkeley), 255, 266–267
California Writers' Club, 267
Case, Theano Wattles, 70, 118, 187, 278, 311n46
Cayleff, Susan, 122
Channing, William Henry, 94
Chevaillier, Josephine, 201
Cincinnati Sisters, 11, 26, 27, 31, 287n46
Clayton, Adaline McGraw, 145
Clayton, Powell, 138, 141, 154, 167, 305n27
  background and reputation, 143
  defense of Pine Bluff, 142
  opinion of Eaton Morse, 146, 305n29
Cleaveland, Agnes Morley, *No Life for a Lady*, 267
Clinton Domestic Seminary, 12, 14
Collins, Mrs., 199
colonization movement, 17, 21–23. *See also* American Colonization Society
Colorado gold rush, 108–110
Colorow, Chief, 219–220
communitarianism, 37–38
Confederate Veterans of America, 167
Cowles, Betsy Mix, 48
Cronon, William, 2
Crowder, Minnie Hiatt, 184, 206
Crowder, Paul, 206
Cummings, Byron, 247
Curtis, Patti Morse, 3, 273
Curtis, Samuel, 133, 139
Cushier, Elizabeth, 177, 192, 197, 198, 201

Daniels, Edward, 53
Dansville Water Cure. *See* Our Home on the Hillside

Davidson, John, 141
Day, Sam, 250
DeBlack, Thomas A., 154
Denver, James W., 73
Denver & Rio Grande Railroad
    (D&RG), 217, 218
Desert Wife. See Wetherill, Hilda
    Faunce
dietary reform, 13, 19, 37, 93,
    121. *See also* Grahamite diet;
    vegetarianism
Diggs, Annie, 202, 313n91
Diné. *See* Navajo
Dixon, Chris, 33
Dodge, Thomas H., 250
Dole, William P., 110
domesticity, female, 16, 99
Douglas, Stephen A., 52
Douglass, Frederick, 202
dress reform, 123
dude ranching, 262–266, 281
Dutton, Bertha, 269

Eagleswood School (Perth Amboy, NJ),
    80, 91, 92, 185, 278
Earnest, Ola Mae, 293n16
Eclectic Medical Institute of
    Cincinnati, 113, 121
education for girls, 14–15, 91
Emerson, Ralph Waldo, 94
Emlen, Samuel, 43
Emlen Institute (Mercer County, OH),
    43–45
Etcheson, Nicole, 293n16
Evans, Grace French, 251

family stories, 2–3
Family Tree DNA, 4
Faunce, Christiana Isidore "Issie," 198
Faunce, Eugenia. *See* Wetherill,
    Eugenia Faunce
Faunce, Helen Rose, 236

Faunce, Hilda. *See* Wetherill, Hilda
    Faunce
Faunce, John, 271
Faunce, Laura Rutherford, 236
Faunce, Mary Ann Wattles, 3, 7, 10, 11,
    45, 51, 62, 70, 74, 98, 100, 244,
    254, 273
    in Bleeding Kansas, 100, 118,
        186–187
    in Colorado, 227–228, 231–235, 237,
        258, 260–262
    death of, 266
    domestic responsibilities of, 199
    education of, 118, 185–187, 278
    health of, 203, 228
    marriage of, 197, 198
    medical training in Europe,
        192–194, 311n46
    as nurse, 79, 90, 95, 128–129
    as teacher, 85
    single tax and, 229–230
    temperance and, 229
    woman's suffrage and, 229
Faunce, Mary Ann Wattles, and
    Woman's Medical College of the
    New York Infirmary, 177
    Alumnae Association and, 197
    as faculty, 191, 195–196, 239,
        311n59
    valedictory address (1871), 190–191
Faunce, Sylvanus Carroll, 244, 271
    death of, 267
    disagreement with Eaton Morse,
        233–234
    family background of, 198
    as farmer, 233, 237, 257
    move to Colorado, 227, 231
    Single Tax and, 229, 232
    temperament of, 231
    as textile designer, 203, 228, 234
    Wetherill Ranch and, 262
    woman's suffrage and, 229, 239

Faunce, Theodore Wattles, 198, 235–236, 244
Faunce, Thomas, 1, 2, 272
Faust, Drew Gilpin, 147
Fellman, Michael, 102
5th Kansas Cavalry, 7, 102, 105, 133
  Eaton Morse and Theodore Wattles and, 134–138
  GAR chapter, 167
  occupation and battle of Helena, 139
  occupation of Pine Bluff, 141–153
  reputation for pillaging, 154
Finney, Charles Grandison, 17, 18, 19, 21, 32
Finney, Elizabeth Atkinson, 32
fish farming, 257–260, 265
Fort Defiance, Arizona, 213, 255
Fred Harvey Company, 248
Freeman, Victoria, 5
Frémont, John C., 137
Fröebelianism, 200

Gabriel, Kathyrn, 251
Gage, Matilda Joslyn, 202
Gale, George W., 18
Gardner, A. H., 250
Garretson, J. S., 121
Garrison, George, 137
Garrison, William Lloyd, 21, 35, 137, 277. See also Liberator
Gates, Henry Louis, Jr., Finding Your Roots, 4
Geary, John, 59, 63, 293n26
Geneva Medical College (NY), 189
George, Henry, Progress and Poverty, 230, 316n53
Getz, Carol Ann Wetherill, 3, 186, 265, 268, 269, 271, 273
Getz, Floyd, 263
Gilbert, Amos, 36
Ginzberg, Lori, 89
Glen Haven Water Cure, 123

Goodlander, Charles, 70
Goodman, Paul, 19
Goodwin, Helen, 188
Gould, Jenny, 115, 126, 127–128, 129, 130
Grahamite diet, 93
Grand Army of the Republic, 132
  5th Kansas Cavalry chapter, 160, 167
Grant, Ulysses S., 139
Gray, Susan E., 5
Greeley, Horace, 94
Green, Beriah, 19–20
Grimké, Angelina. See Weld, Angelina Grimké
Grimké, Sarah, 6, 26, 45, 57, 277, 292n4, 296n11
  Eagleswood School and, 80, 90–93
  Letters on the Equality of the Sexes, 84–85
  mentors Sarah Wattles, 82–87, 90–92, 97, 99, 180, 185, 276
  on spiritualism, 113–114
Guernsey, Samuel, 256, 261–262
guerrilla warfare, 72, 102, 139, 147–148

Hairgrove, Mary Ann Kipp, 187, 235, 262–263, 264
Halbwachs, Maurice, 4
Halleck, Henry, 147
Hamilton, Charles, 72–73
Hareven, Tamara, 10
Harpers Ferry raid, 57, 72, 74–75, 77, 79, 95, 137
  Senate investigation of, 58, 68, 73, 74–75, 77, 105, 165
Harrison, Michael, 249–250
Hartman, Mary, 6, 32
Hawkins, Nelson (pseudonym of John Brown), 68
Hayden Geological Survey, 258
Hazlett, Albert, 95

Heilbrun, Carolyn, 27
Herald of Freedom (Lawrence, KS), 56,
 63, 65, 68, 69, 70, 281
 Augustus Wattles as assistant editor,
  56, 65–66
Herald of Progression (Cincinnati, OH),
 38, 43, 121
Hermit Lakes, Colorado, 257–258
Hewitt, Edgar L., 247
Hiatt, Lundy, 132
 family of, 308n7
 medical career of, 180–181,
  205–206
 medical training of, 179–180
Hiatt, Minnie. *See* Crowder, Minnie
 Hiatt
Hiatt, Sarah Grimké Wattles, 7, 51, 79,
 272
 birth and childhood of, 45–48,
  80–81
 Civil War and, 102
 claims land in Kansas, 62, 88, 212
 death of, 208
 Eagleswood School and, 91–96
 education of, 90
 John Brown and, 74, 79, 165–166
 marriage of, 179, 197–198
 medical career of, 179–181, 196
 relationship with Sarah Grimké,
  82–87, 97, 99, 180, 276
 romantic interests, 96–97, 132
 Single Tax and, 99, 183, 207, 230
 as teacher, 70, 85–86, 117, 185
 temperance and, 97–98, 181,
  183–184, 207
 Woman's Relief Corps and,
  167–168, 207
 woman's suffrage and, 181, 183, 229
Hill, Vercy Hathaway, 271
Hinton, Richard, 71, 74–75, 96,
 107–108
Holmes, James H., 69
Holmes, Theophilus, 140

Hooker, Isabella Beecher, 202
Hoskinini, 246
Hoskinini-begay, 246
Howe, Julia Ward, 202
Howells, Harriot, 114, 301n40
Howells, Henry C., 301n40
HrdliĐka, Aleš, 256
Hubbell, Lorenzo, 244, 252
Hunt, Harriot Kezia, 189
 Glances and Glimpses; Or Fifty Years'
  Social, Including Twenty Years'
  Professional Life, 87–88, 185
Hurd, F. Wilson, 123, 124
Hyatt, Thaddeus, 66–67
Hyde, Fred, Jr., 243, 318n11, 319n22
Hyde, Talbot, 243, 250, 318n11,
 319n22
Hyde Exploring Expedition, 243, 246
hydropathy. *See* water cure

International Council of Women, 202

Jackson, Giles, 124, 127
Jackson, Helen Hunt, *Ramona*, 222,
 281
Jackson, James Caleb, 122, 124–125,
 127–128, 129, 278
 Granula and, 123
Jackson, Kate, 123, 124
Jackson, Lucretia, 124
Jackson, William H., 258
Jacobi, Mary Putnam, 7, 177, 190, 198
Jacobs, Margaret, 211
Jameson, Elizabeth "Betsy," 8, 9
Jayhawkers, 102, 103, 104, 105, 119
Jennison, Charles, 104, 105
Jensen, Joan, 5
Johnson, Hamilton P., 105
Johnston, Philip, 249–250
Jones, Baker, 24

Kagi, John Henry, 74
"Kansas Brigade," 117

Kansas Emigrant Aid Society. *See*
National Kansas Committee
Kansas Legion, 56
Kansas-Nebraska Act (1854), 49, 52,
66, 70, 106, 212
Kansas State Historical Society, 51,
164, 274
Kansas Territory
constitutional convention, Big
Springs (1855), 55–56
constitutional convention, Topeka
(1855), 55–56
elections, 54–55, 56, 66, 69
governors of, 55, 69, 73, 77,
293n26
Lecompton Constitution, 69
Native Americans in, 105–106
Kelley, Florence, 208
Kelley, Mary, 15
Kellogg, John Harvey, 123
Kelsey, Adaline, 194
Kidder, A. V., 256, 262
Kilham, Eleanor, 195
kindergartens, 200
Kipp, Charley, 266
Kipp, Hilda Theano Wetherill, 259,
262, 268, 273
Kipp, Mary Ann. *See* Hairgrove, Mary
Ann Kipp
Klah, Hosteen, 248
Knoblach, Frieda, 265

La Farge, Oliver, 250
Lane, James, 65
Lane Rebels, 24, 26, 31
Lane Seminary (Cincinnati, OH), 20,
21, 94
Lane debates, 21–23
See also Lane Rebels
Lasser, Carol, 16
Lawrence, Amos, 54
Lawrence, Kansas, raid on (1863),
102–103

Lawrence, Kansas, Sack of (1856), 63,
65, 66, 94
Lecompton Constitution, 69
Lerner, Gerda, 8, 84
Liberator, 21, 30, 35
Liber College (Jay County, IN), 40
Lieber, Francis, 148
Lily, 86–87, 185
Limerick, Patricia Nelson, 264
Lincoln, Abraham, 100, 137, 148, 219
Lind University, 180
Lister, Joseph, 194
Little Pilgrim, 87
Lowe, David P., 40–41, 49, 59–61, 117,
308n7
Lowe, Eli, 117, 308n7
Lowe, Elizabeth. *See* Byrd, Elizabeth
Lowe
Lowe, Jonathan, 14, 40, 48
Lowe, Julia Ann. *See* Weber, Julia Ann
Lowe
Lowe, Perkins, 40
Lowe, Susannah (stepmother of Susan
Lowe Wattles), 40
Lowe, Susanna Perley (mother of
Susan Lowe Wattles), 14
Lowe, Tilney Hiatt, 117, 308n7
Lukens, Mary, 26

manual training schools, 18–21, 27,
41–42
Marais des Cygnes Massacre, 72, 73,
76, 96
Mark's Mill, battle of, 157
Marmaduke, John, 142, 157
Marrett, Cora, 196
Marshall, Helen, 198
Mason, Alice, 322n67
Mason, Anna Wetherill, 240, 257–258,
263–264
Mason, Charles "Charlie," 240, 242,
257–258, 260, 263–264
Mason, Debby, 322n67

Mason, Luella, 322n67
Mason, Marion, 322n67
Mason, Olive, 322n67
Massachusetts Single-Tax League, 230
Mathews, Phebe, 11, 26, 27, 31
Matthews, John, 110–111
Mattison, Emeline Bishop, 11, 26, 201
McCulloch, Benjamin, 110–111
McGee, Martha. See Crowder, Minnie
    Hiatt
McNitt, Frank, 213
McNutt, Julia, 195
McNutt, Sarah, 7, 177–178, 195–196,
    201
Medary, Samuel, 77
medical training in nineteenth-
    century United States, 120–121,
    179–180
Meeker, Nathan, 220
Meeker Massacre, 220
memory keepers, 4–5
Mine Creek, Battle of, 128
Moneka Literary Society, 135
Moneka Woman's Rights Association,
    88, 135, 302n52
Montgomery, James, 72, 74, 76, 96,
    102, 104, 105, 187
    attempted rescue of John Brown
    and, 164–165
Montgomery, Jennie, 187
Morantz-Sanchez, Regina, 197
More, Ellen, 178, 196, 197
Morgan, Elizabeth "Lizzie," 188
Morgan, Eugenia, 188, 196, 230
Morgan, Frank, 214, 217
Morgan, John, 188
Morgan, Shubel (pseudonym of John
    Brown), 96. See also Shubel
    Morgan's Company
Morley, Ray, 267
Morrison, Emma, 114
Morse, Eleanor, 160, 185, 273
    tuberculosis and, 233–234, 317n65

Morse, Emma Wattles, 3, 7, 70, 74,
    184–185, 226
    birth of, 45
    Civil War in Kansas and, 102, 103,
    116
    courtship of, 135
    correspondence with soldiers,
    139–140, 142
    death of, 273
    family stories and, 11, 51, 63
    health of, 117–118, 122
    marriage of, 159–160
    migration to Kansas, 62
    Our Home water cure and, 123–128
    "Sketch of the Life and Work of
    Augustus Wattles," 166
    teaching, 85, 117
    temperance and, 98, 229
    women's rights and, 88, 229
Morse, John Otis, 273–274
Morse, Orlando, 160
Morse, Orlin Eaton (O. E.), 7, 128, 213,
    226, 273
    aftermath of Battle of Poison Spring
    and, 157–158
    "An Attempted Rescue of John
    Brown from Charlestown, VA.,
    Jail," 164–165
    Civil War and, 101, 104, 133
    defense of Pine Bluff and, 142
    disagreement with Carroll Faunce,
    233–234, 257
    enlists in 5th Kansas Cavalry, 105,
    135
    5th Kansas Cavalry Association of
    GAR and, 167
    marriage of, 159–160, 213
    migration to Kansas, 135
    opinion of Colonel Clayton,
    143–145
    provost marshal of Pine Bluff,
    146–153
    women's rights and, 88

Morse, Orlin Raymond, 273–274
Morse, Sara "Sadie" Trego, 272
Morse, Stanley, 273
Morse, Stuart Tellson, 273–274
Morse, Theodore Wattles, 273–274
Morse, Wilton Lowe, 213, 226–227, 233, 273
Moss, John, 214
Mott, James, 34
Mott, Lucretia, 34, 42, 113

National Dress Reform Association, 123
National Kansas Committee, 53, 66–67
Native Americans, 70, 280–281
  Civil War and, 110–111
  Colorado gold rush and, 109–110
  relocation to Kansas of, 105–107
  See also Navajo; Utes
Navajo (Diné), 242
  culture, preservation of, 245
  Fort Defiance agency, 213–214
  Hilda Faunce Wetherill and, 251–255
  Louisa Wetherill and, 246–248
  Marietta Wetherill and, 248–251
  Navajo Tribal Council, 250
  Reservation, 244–245
  weaving and wool trade of, 214
Newcomb, Frances "Franc" Johnson, 248, 251
New England Emigrant Aid Society (NEEAS), 54, 56, 64
New York Infirmary, 177, 189, 228
New York State Woman's Suffrage Association, 202
Nichols, Clarina I. H., 88–89
Nordenskiöld, Gustaf, 242, 256

Oberlin College, 19, 132, 278
  Wattles girls attend, 186–187
Oertel, Kristen Tegtmeier, 106

Officer, Lora, 259–260
Ohio Anti-Slavery Society (OASS), 31, 39
  Granville meeting, 30
  Putnam meeting, 29–30
Oneida County, New York, 11, 14, 17–19, 276
Oneida Institute, 17–19, 41
Oppey, L. C., 266
Osawatomie, Battle of, 63, 90
Ouray, Chief, 219–220
Our Home on the Hillside (Dansville, NY), 123–128, 129, 149, 159

Panic of 1893, 228–229
Parrott, Tiburcio, 214
Pepper, George, 256
Perry, Adele, 212
Phelps, Eliza B., 198, 200
Philanthropist, 31
Phillips, Wendell, 89
Pierce, Franklin, 293n26
Pierson, Michael, 16
Pine Bluff, Battle of, 142
Poison Spring, Battle of, 157
Pottawatomie Massacre, 63, 68, 75, 163
Potts, Anna Longshore, 201
Prairie Home community (OH), 37–38, 289n79
Price, Sterling, 102, 128, 157
Price, William Redwood, 213
Prudden, T. Mitchell, 256, 261–262
Ptolemy, Alex, 216
Purvis, Robert, 202

Quantrill, William C., 102–103

Rakestraw, Emily. See Robinson, Emily Rakestraw
Ransom, Thomas, 147
Raritan Bay Union, 92, 95, 301n40
Redpath, James, 71
Red River Expedition, 157

Reed, Faith Morley, 267
Reeder, Andrew, 55
Remington, Frederick, 264
Ripley, David, 38, 83, 92, 95, 160, 278, 296n11, 311n46
Ripley, Mary Ann Wattles, 18, 83, 92, 95, 311n46
Robertson, Stacey M., 16
Robinson, Charles, 56
Robinson, Emily Rakestraw, 31
Robinson, Marius, 24, 31, 129
Roosevelt, Quentin, 261, 263
Roosevelt, Theodore, 261, 264
"rosewater policy," 146, 148
Ryder, E. B., 192–193

Sanborn, Franklin B. (F. B.), 68
San Juan Ranch, 259
Scharff, Virginia, 27
School of American Archaeology (Santa Fe, NM), 247
Seaman, Henry C., 104
Second Great Awakening, 13, 17
separate spheres doctrine, 6, 15–16, 32, 34–35
Sarah Grimké and, 83–84
settler colonialism, 7, 211–212, 225, 237–238, 254, 281
Shawnee Methodist Missionary Station, 106
Shelby, Jo, 157
Sherman, William T., 139
Shubel Morgan's Company, 73–74, 96
silver, monetization of, 229, 237
single tax, 99, 183, 207, 229–230, 232
Slenker, Elmina Drake, 223
Society for Universal Inquiry and Reform, 36, 37
spiritualism, 13, 19, 112–115
Spring, Marcus, 79, 92
Spring, Rebecca, 79, 92, 95–97
Stanton, Elizabeth Cady, 31, 87, 94, 113, 131, 185, 202, 275, 276

Stanton, Henry B., 29, 31, 94
Stearns, John H., 302n52
Steele, Frederick, 141, 157
Stephens, Ruth, 151–152
Stevens, Aaron, 95
Stone, Elizabeth, 13
Stone, Lucy, 27, 33, 87, 202
Stratton, Harris, 232

Tabernash, 220
Tappan, Arthur, 20, 21, 55, 287n46
Tappan, Lewis, 21, 30, 55
temperance, 37, 97–99, 132, 183–184, 202, 207, 230–231, 229
Thayer, Eli, 54
Thomas, Peleg, 18
Thomson, Samuel, 121
Thomsonianism, 121
Thoreau, Henry David, 94
Tidd, Charles P., 95–96
Tompkins, Justus, 258
Townsley, James, 163
Turner, Nat, 21
23andMe, 4

ultraists, 19, 33, 35, 55, 112, 136, 288n70
Una, 86–87, 185
Underground Railroad, 43, 59, 76
Utes, 109, 241
history of, 219
utopian communities, 19, 37–38, 92, 186

Vassar College, 188
vegetarianism, 47, 93, 123
Villard, Fanny Garrison, 277
voluntary associations, female, 16, 98, 182–183

Wakarusa War, 62
Wakefield, W. H., 231
Walker, Robert J., 69

Ward, Emma F., 198
Washington, Lewis, 95
water cure, 122
Water-Cure Journal, 122, 123
Wattles, Ann Otis, 18
Wattles, Augustus, 6, 11–12, 80–81, 85,
  93, 104, 189, 272, 289n83
  AASS agent, 30, 39, 82, 83
  attempted rescue of John Brown,
    164–165
  Bleeding Kansas and, 55–56,
    63–68
  colonizationist movement and,
    19–20
  Colorado gold rush and, 108–110
  death of, 131
  disapproval of Charles P. Tidd,
    96–97
  Emlen Institute and, 43–45
  family background of, 17–18
  health of, 111–112, 114, 129
  Herald of Freedom and, 65–66, 107,
    281
  John Brown and, 51, 58, 68, 72–77,
    79, 90, 162
  Lane debates and, 22–23
  marriage of, 31–32
  medical training of, 45, 121
  Mercer County colony and, 39–43
  migration to Kansas, 51–54,
    292nn4–5
  Native Americans and, 105–111, 212
  Ohio Anti-Slavery Society and,
    29–31
  Oneida Institute and, 17–20
  opinion of son's military service,
    135–136
  organizes schools for Cincinnati
    blacks, 23–26, 28, 36
  as reformer, 13–14, 19, 32–34, 49,
    129
  residence in New York during Civil
    War, 115, 126–128, 160

on sex reform, 223
spiritualism and, 112–115, 126, 129
testimony in congressional
  investigation of Harpers Ferry,
  58, 68, 73, 74–75, 77, 105, 165
on violence, 56–57, 293n16
water cure and, 122, 127
on women's rights, 35, 83–84
Wattles, Daniel, 18
Wattles, Eliza, 18
Wattles, Erastus, 18, 289n83
Wattles, Esther Whinery, 6, 13, 70, 88,
  92, 118, 132, 181, 279
  attends International Council of
    Women, 202
  Civil War in Kansas and, 102,
    129–130
  family background of, 37
  marriage to and life with John
    Wattles, 36–39
  move to Oberlin, 187–188
  property of, 302n48
Wattles, Harmonia. *See* Woodford,
  Harmonia "Monie" Wattles
Wattles, Howard Hammond, 235–236,
  317n75
Wattles, John Otis, 6, 13, 20, 45, 49,
  58, 88, 189, 278
  character of, 35
  death of, 36, 115, 129, 132
  dietary reform and, 47, 121
  family background of, 17–18
  Herald of Progression and, 38, 42–43,
    121
  on marriage, 37
  observations of Kansas, 39, 70–71,
    106–107
  sex reform and, 223
  spiritualism and, 113, 129
  utopian communities and, 36–38,
    92
Wattles, Lucretia Celestia "Cettie," 70,
  118, 187, 278, 311n46

Wattles, Mary Ann (daughter of Augustus). See Faunce, Mary Ann Wattles

Wattles, Mary Ann (sister of Augustus). See Ripley, Mary Ann Wattles

Wattles, Melvina "Mell" Hammond, 222, 227, 236, 272
marriage of, 223
sex reform and, 223–225

Wattles, Ruth Jocelyn, 188, 235–236, 252, 272, 317n75

Wattles, Sarah Grimké. See Hiatt, Sarah Grimké Wattles

Wattles, Sarah Thomas, 18, 83, 92

Wattles, Susan Elvira Lowe, 6, 10, 11–12, 19, 84, 98, 272
attends International Council of Women, 202–203
Bleeding Kansas and, 56–57, 61–63, 76
Cincinnati Sisters and, 26–28, 30–31
Civil War in Kansas and, 101–102, 115–119, 129–130
death of, 207
family background, 14
healing practices of, 47–48
marriage of, 31–34
Mercer County colony and, 39–42
opinion of son's military service, 137–138
as parent, 45–49, 80–81
property value of, 302n48
as reformer, 13–14, 32–33
remembers John Brown, 165
residence in New York City, 200–203
sex reform and, 222–225
support for career of Mary Ann Wattles Faunce, 179, 188, 200, 239, 278
as teacher, 14, 27–28, 41, 48, 70, 85, 187

Underground Railroad and, 290n99
women's rights and, 35, 88–89

Wattles, Theano. See Case, Theano Wattles

Wattles, Theodore Weld, 7, 62, 70, 206, 236, 272, 278, 316n39
birth of, 45
cavalry missions and, 153–156
defense of Pine Bluff, 142
enlists in 5th Kansas Cavalry, 101, 105, 133, 135
at Fort Defiance, 213–214
friendship with Wetherill family, 240–241
homesteads in Mancos Valley, 216
marriage of, 223
Native Americans and, 219–222
occupation and battle of Helena and, 139–140
opinion of Eaton Morse, 135
as rancher, 232
as settler colonialist, 212–213, 221–222, 225–226, 237
sex reform and, 222–225
woman's suffrage and, 222, 229

Wattles, William, 18, 113

Way, James, 117

Weber, Julia Ann Lowe, 40, 59

Weer, William, 105

Weld, Angelina Grimké, 26, 31, 33, 34–35, 82, 83, 113, 275, 277
Appeal to the Christian Women of the Southern States, 82
Eagleswood School and, 80, 92, 186

Weld, Cornelia, 93

Weld, Theodore Dwight, 6, 11–12, 26, 29, 30, 45, 82, 83, 121
Eagleswood School and, 80, 92–93, 186
health of, 129
at Lane Seminary, 19–21, 23
marriage of, 31, 34–35
at Oneida Institute, 19–20

Wellesley College, 188
Wetherill, Anna. *See* Mason, Anna Wetherill
Wetherill, Benjamin (John's son), 268
Wetherill, Benjamin Alfred "Al," 240–243, 252
Wetherill, Benjamin Kite (B. K.), 240–241, 318n2
Wetherill, Carol Ann. *See* Getz, Carol Ann Wetherill
Wetherill, Carroll Clayton, 260, 262–263, 268
Wetherill, Clayton, 235–236, 240, 243–244
  death of, 261
  fish hatchery business and, 239, 258–260
  as outfitter, 239, 243, 256, 260, 261
  Richard Wetherill's death and, 261
Wetherill, Eugenia Faunce, 1, 2, 3, 7, 10, 234, 235, 244, 273
  birth of, 198, 200
  childhood of, 239
  death of, 268
  fish hatchery business and, 258, 260
  marriage of, 236, 243–244, 256–257
  trips with Clayton Wetherill, 261
  Wetherill Ranch and, 236, 262–263, 266
Wetherill, Gilbert Faunce, 258, 259
Wetherill, Helen, 243, 269
Wetherill, Hilda Faunce, 1, 2, 7, 271, 273, 278, 321n46
  birth of, 198
  Black Mountain Trading Post and, 245, 251–252, 254, 320n26
  California School for the Deaf and Blind and, 255, 266–267
  California Writers' Club and, 267
  childhood of, 239
  death of, 269
  Desert Wife and, 252–255

  divorce of, 256
  feud with Carroll Faunce, 234–235, 244
  marriage of, 236
  retirement of, 267–268
  Wetherill family reunion and, 269
Wetherill, Hilda Theano (Eugenia's daughter). *See* Kipp, Hilda Theano Wetherill
Wetherill, Ina Wills, 268
Wetherill, John, 236, 240, 242, 252, 256, 268
  Richard Wetherill's death and, 261
  trading posts and, 246
Wetherill, Louisa Wade, 7, 245, 251, 268, 319–320n25
  family of, 246
  opinion of Marietta Wetherill, 250
  relations with Navajo, 246–248
Wetherill, Marian Tompkins, 240–241, 264, 318n2
Wetherill, Marietta Palmer, 7, 245, 256, 264
  "Death of a Medicine Man," 249–250
  family of, 248–249
  financial difficulties of, 320n26
  personality of, 248–249
Wetherill, Mattie Pauline Young, 243
Wetherill, Milton, 243, 269
Wetherill, Richard, 240, 242–243, 248–250, 256
  death of, 261, 320n26
Wetherill, Winslow "Win," 235–236, 240, 268–269, 321n46
  courtship and marriage with Hilda Faunce, 243–244
  first marriage of, 243
  as trading post operator, 239, 243, 245, 251–253, 255
Wetherill Ranch, 10, 262–263, 266, 268, 273
Wheelwright, Mary Cabot, 248

White, Victoria, 177–178
Willard, Frances, 99, 183, 202
Willetts, Samuel, 194
Wills, Frank, 266
Wilson's Creek, Battle of, 143
Wister, Owen, 264
Wolfe, Patrick, 211
Wolfkiller, 247
Woman's Christian Temperance Union
    (WCTU), 99, 183–184, 202, 207,
    231
    Union Signal, 230
Woman's Journal, 181, 230, 241
Woman's Medical College of
    Pennsylvania, 189
Woman's Medical College of the New
    York Infirmary, 121, 177, 188–
    190, 194–195
    Alumnae Association of, 197
    Samuel Willetts and, 194–195

Woman's Relief Corps, 132, 167–168,
    207
woman's suffrage, 13, 99, 132, 202, 277
Women's Medical Association of New
    York City, 197
women's rights movement, 6, 19,
    26–27, 32, 45, 87–89, 131, 132,
    202
Women's Tribune, 202
Woodford, Harmonia "Monie"
    Wattles, 70, 118, 187, 278, 311n46
Wright, Lucy, 11, 26
Wright, Mabel C., 251
Wright, Martha Coffin, 113
Wright, Pauline Kellogg, 87

Yellow Singer (Sam Chief), 246, 248